Freedom's Battle

✳

VOLUME II:
THE WAR IN THE AIR
1939–1945

Freedom's Battle

A series of three volumes

The War in the Air
1939–1945

*An anthology of personal experience
selected and edited by Gavin Lyall*

'For Freedom's battle once begun,
Bequeathed by bleeding Sire to Son,
Though baffled oft is ever won.'
LORD BYRON, *The Giaour*

ARROW BOOKS

ARROW BOOKS LTD
3 Fitzroy Square, London W1

AN IMPRINT OF THE HUTCHINSON GROUP

London Melbourne Sydney Auckland
Wellington Johannesburg Cape Town
and agencies throughout the world

✳

First published by
Hutchinson & Co (*Publishers*) Ltd 1968
Arrow edition April 1971
Second impression September 1971

*Made and printed in Great Britain
by The Anchor Press Ltd,
Tiptree, Essex*
ISBN 0 09 004470 3

Contents

Illustrations

Acknowledgements

The author and publisher thank the relevant copyright holders for permission to quote from:

Guy Gibson, *Enemy Coast Ahead,* Pan 1957; Air Ministry, *Bomber Command,* HMSO 1941; Tom Moulson, *The Flying Sword,* Macdonald; Paul Riley, *Fighter Pilot,* Hutchinson 1955; P. R. Reid, *Winged Diplomat,* Chatto and Windus 1962; Noel Monks, Fighter Squadron, Angus and Robertson, Sydney 1941; Peter Wykeham, *Fighter Command,* Putnam; J. E. Johnson, *Wing Leader,* Chatto and Windus; Ian Gleed, *Arise to Conquer,* Gollancz 1942; *Winged Words,* Heinemann 1941; Al Deere, *Nine Lives,* Hodder and Stoughton; Richard Hillary, *The Last Enemy,* Macmillan; John Gillespie MacGee, *High Flight*; D. M. Crook, *Spitfire Pilot,* Faber and Faber; Larry Forrester, *Fly for your Life,* Frederick Muller 1956; John Pudney, *For Johnny*; William L. Shirer, *Berlin Diary,* Hamish Hamilton; Hector Bolitho, *A Penguin in the Eyrie,* Hutchinson 1955; Adolf Galland, *The First and the Last,* Methuen; Winston Churchill, *The Second World War,* Cassell; Graham Wallace, *Biggin Hill,* Putnam; Sholto Douglas, *Years of Command,* Collins; C. F. Rawnsley and Robert Wright, *Night Fighter,* Collins 1957; Alan Moorehead, *Desert Trilogy,* Hamish Hamilton; *Atlantic Bridge,* HMSO 1945; Edward Lanchbery, *Against the Sun,* Cassell; Roderick Chisholm, *Cover of Darkness,* Chatto and Windus; J. R. D. Braham, *Scramble,* Frederick Muller 1961; John Beede, *They Hosed Them Out,* Australasian Book Society, Sydney 1965; Constance Babington Smith, *Evidence in Camera,* Chatto and Windus; Sir John Slessor, *The Central Blue,* Cassell; Roderic Owen, *The Desert Air Force,* Hutchinson; Sir Bernard Fergusson, *The Black Watch and the King's Enemies,* Collins 1950; Arthur G.

Donahue, *Last Flight from Singapore*, Macmillan 1944; John Masters, *The Road past Mandalay*, Michael Joseph; Sir Philip Joubert, *Birds and Fishes*, *The Fated Sky*, *Fun and Games* and *The Forgotten Ones*, Hutchinson; Ralph Barker, *The Ship Busters*, Chatto and Windus 1957; Flying Officer 'X' (H. E. Bates), *The Greatest People in the World*, Jonathan Cape 1942; Herbert Corby, *Missing*; George W. Stoughton, *They Flew Through Sand*, Jarrolds Ltd. 1942; Kenneth Hemingway, *Wings Over Burma*, Qualits Press (London) 1944; I.M.S.H.I., *A Fighter Pilot's Letters to his Mother*, W. H. Allen 1943; Pierre Clostermann, *Flames in the Sky* and *The Big Show*, Chatto and Windus; J. E. Johnson, *Full Circle*, Chatto and Windus; Donald Bennett, *Pathfinder*, Muller; Sir Gordon Taylor, *The Sky Beyond*, Penguin; J. A. Crosby Warren, *The Flight Testing of Production Aircraft*, Pitman 1943; Michael Foot, *S.O.E. in France*, HMSO; Ralph Barker, *The Thousand Plan*, Chatto and Windus; Group Captain Dudley Saward, *The Bomber's Eye*, Cassell 1959; Sir Arthur Harris, *Bomber Offensive*, Collins 1947; Ralph Barker, *Down in the Drink*, Chatto and Windus; C. H. Ward-Jackson, *The Airman's Song Book*, Sylvan Press, London, 1945; Ivan Southall, *They Shall Not Pass Unseen*, Angus and Robertson 1956; Mike Lithgow, *Vapour Trails*, Hamilton & Co. (Stafford) Ltd. 1957; Gavin Ewart, *When a Bean Goes In*; Paul Brickhill, *The Dam Busters*, Evans Bros. 1951; Martha Gelhorn, *The Face of War*, Rupert Hart-Davies 1959; Sir Basil Embry, *Mission Completed*, Landsborough Publications Ltd.; A. H. Wheeler, *That Nothing Failed Them*, G. T. Foulis & Co. 1963; Henry Treece, *Lincolnshire Bomber Station*; Wilhelm Johnen, *Duel under the Stars*, Kimber Pocket Edition 1958; Geoff Taylor, *Piece of Cake*, Peter Davies 1956; W/Cdr. Barry Sutton, *Jungle Pilot*, Macmillan 1946, *Wings of the Phoenix*, HMSO 1949; Alison King, *Golden Wings*, C. Arthur Pearson Ltd. 1956; Paul Brickhill, *Escape or Die*, Evans Bros. 1952; RAAF Directorate of Public Relations, *R.A.A.F. Saga*, Australian War Memorial, Canberra; David Irving, *The Destruction of Dresden*, Kimber; S/Ldr. R. Raymond and S/Ldr. David Langdon, *Slipstream*, Eyre and Spottiswoode 1946.

Glossary

AI (Airborne Interception): radar used in fighter fighters.

ASV (Air to Surface Vessel): radar carried by Coastal Command for, in particular, detecting surfaced U-boats.

Beehive: radio jargon for formations of bombers and close-escort fighters used on 'Circus' operations (see below).

Circus: heavily-escorted day-bomber formations sent out mainly to create fighter battles over occupied Europe.

Gee: early form of bomber-navigation radar, dependent on ground station transmitting pulses which are picked up in the aircraft.

H2S: the first self-contained airborne navigational radar; no ground stations needed.

Oboe: radio beam navigation system. Two ground stations transmit tight beams which intersect at the target. So accurate that bombers could bomb 'blind' on it, but limited in range to about 350 miles.

Rhubarb: low-level fighter sweeps.

Serrate: radar receiver used for detecting German night-fighter radar emissions.

Window: metal foil strips cut to the same length as the wavelengths of German ground radar transmitters. When dropped from bombers it could either swamp the radar screens, or (used more selectively) create a false impression of a major raid arriving—or even of a seaborne convoy.

IFF (Identification Friend or Foe): a transmitter which gave an aircraft a distinctive shape or 'blip' on a radar screen, enabling it to be distinguished from enemy 'blips'. Also known in radio jargon as 'Canary'—e.g. 'Make your Canary sing' meaning 'Press your IFF button'.

Lichtenstein or Li: Luftwaffe code for their AI equipment.

Freya: Luftwaffe code for their ground radar.

Naxos: Luftwaffe code for their version of 'Serrate'.
'Finger-four' formation: standard fighter combat formation; four aircraft in roughly the same relative positions as the fingertips of a spread hand.
OTU: Operation Training Unit, the last stage before joining a squadron.
ETA: Estimated Time of Arrival.
SASO: Senior Air Staff Officer.
ASI: Airspeed Indicator.
U/S: unserviceable. An abbreviation that led to some misunderstandings with Americans.

Editor's Preface

This is intended simply to be an anthology of writings from, and about, the British and Commonwealth Air Forces in the 1939–45 war. It is not a history. However, I found that I had to give it an historical framework, both by arranging the items chronologically (as far as possible) and by explaining some of the background of the campaigns and the technical developments. If I have intruded too much, or explained the obvious too often, then I apologise—but not quite whole-heartedly. The war was a long time ago, and I hope this collection will find some readers among those who are too young to have any ingrained memory of its pattern.

During the war, the RAF was dependent on technological developments to a rather great extent than either other service. A pilot who wrote poetry about his Spitfire's fleetness might, a few weeks later, be putting down in cold and bitter technical terms the exact improvements needed to make the aircraft worth taking off at all. This concern with technology penetrated even into the Air Force's songs. Indeed, air historians might find these songs fruitful sources of contemporary opinion concerning certain aircraft. Take one version of 'I ain't a-gonna grieve My Lord no more' which goes:

> You'll never get to Heaven in a Deffy Two
> You ought to see that glycol spew.

So we now know that the Defiant II used, at one time at least, to lose its coolant and suffer engine over-heating—which is something the official histories don't always tell you. However, the point I was working around to is that a number of items in this collection don't concern combat. Several are simply about wartime flying and the development of aircraft in a hurry. On occasions during the war, pilots watched their tails not just to see if an enemy was behind them, but to make sure the tail was still on the aeroplane. I hope this anthology shows that expanding the frontiers just of flying required as much courage and skill as fighting the air war that made that expansion necessary. And, moreover, was as typical of the RAF's work.

Still, it was only a minority of those serving in the RAF who actually flew. For obvious reasons, the majority of this collection concerns that minority. So I would like to make a completely whole-hearted apology to the ground crews whose skilled but dull and monotonous work made any and every aerial victory possible, but which tends to make dull and monotonous reading (one type of fighter engine needed to be run up every twenty minutes throughout a freezing night at one stage in the war; otherwise the oil would freeze. To trudge out and do that required a different sort of courage from that of the pilot himself, sleeping throughout, but it was certainly courage.)

Another point arises from this: with such a relatively—small number actually experiencing aerial warfare, it proved impossible to take all first-hand accounts. In too many famous actions, particularly towards the beginning of the war, hardly anybody survived to tell the personal story. And in any case, you cannot fit a war correspondent into a Spitfire. I am rather fond of Douglas Bader's foreword to 'Johnnie' Johnson's book (which I have quoted extensively) *Wing Leader*. It starts: 'Dear Johnnie —I did not know that you could read and write!' Luckily for us, Johnson was not only the RAF's highest-scoring fighter pilot, but could write, and write very well. But not every flying man was so versatile. So I have cast a wide net, taking in accounts by post-war historians and biographers, official publications and reports, even the views of some enemy pilots. I know that anybody familiar with the field will probably discover that I have missed out his favourite piece; I can only plead that, in the end, any anthology has to be a personal selection. This is mine.

Finally, a word about the verse. I have included the handful of poems that seem to belong; they are sadly few. I have used rather more contemporary songs; these, I be-

14

lieve, capture the true flavour of the times, and I hope that nobody who is not familiar with those times will be too offended to find that the RAF took, in song, a somewhat wry view of itself, its colleagues and its equipment. There can be no definitive version of these songs; for those who once sang them and think I have misquoted them, I only hope my version will remind them of the true and authorised words that their squadron knew. My bowdlerisations were inevitable but, I think, pretty transparent.

GAVIN LYALL

1939

For the RAF—as for the Army and Navy—the war really started on 1st September with Hitler's invasion of Poland. Guy Gibson, already a professional bomber pilot and later leader of the Dam-Busters, tells the story of

THE FIRST OF THE FLAPS

The next two days moved very quickly with tremendous activity on all sides. Complete bedlam reigned all over bomber stations in the north and ours was typical. There were tractors driving round the perimeter roads in the sweltering heat, some with long bomb trailers bouncing behind; others pulling our Hampdens along cinder tracks far into the country to dispersal points fairly safe from enemy bombs. All round the airfield sand-banked gun emplacements were being put up by aerodrome defence squads, but there were not many guns. Gas officers were running round placing yellow detectors in the right places. These detectors were of two kinds and always amused me. The yellow ones were supposed to turn red in the presence of gas, but they failed to do so on many an occasion. Then there was another which resembled a piece of cheese hanging on a hook. What these were meant to do I never found out, but the cheese was always disappearing—perhaps the birds in the district liked the stuff!

All the station transport was spread out over the whole area of the camp, so it was nothing out of the ordinary for the co to find a petrol bowzer in his back garden. No one was allowed to leave the camp.

Deep down in the ground below station headquarters lived the denizens of the operations room. This was strictly out of bounds to everyone. At the door, a great half-inch steel structure, sat a couple of airmen armed with rifles. Many an identity card was examined here, and the two lads had the time of their lives turning away such ogres as the station warrant officer. Inside, in the gloom of the blue lights, moved WAAFS and clerks, preparing maps in many shapes, cutting them, clipping them, rolling them, folding them. There were maps of Holland, maps of France, the Siegfried Line; there was even a map of Berlin.

In another corner two officers were sorting out target maps. I noticed as I passed by that there was a photograph of Wilhelmshaven clipped to each. In the middle, surrounded by a huge desk, was the Station Commander, looking very harassed. He had cause to be for in front of him was a great pile of files marked 'War Plan: phase 1, phase 2', etc. All these were directives to be used only in time of war, or in case of mobilisation. His round face was a puzzle, frowning at all this extraordinary activity. The frown would develop into a very black look now and then, especially when some WAAF giggled at something whispered to her by the pimply young airman who spent most of his time standing on a ladder pushing pins into a map on the wall.

In the hangars there was the ringing of metal against metal as cowlings were being beaten out and dents knocked in. There was that empty noise which all hangars have, drowned occasionally by the raucous voice of some fitter singing his weary love-song. And then the Flight-Sergeant, or 'Chiefy', would come rushing in and the song would stop.

Taking things all round there was, as the saying is, a tremendous flap going on.

Not so the air crews. We were sitting or lying on the grass in front of the Squadron Mess most of the day. The sun was beating down and most of us had taken off our flying kit, which was lying strewn around untidily and scattered in all directions. We were officially 'standing by'. For what, we did not know, but we thought it was sure to be a bombing raid somewhere, sometime. Conversation was carefree—of girls, of parties, but strictly limited about the war. We had all heard that our ambassador in Berlin had presented Hitler with an ultimatum asking for the withdrawal of German troops from Poland. There was still some hope. I was holding forth to my crew that we had been recalled from leave too early and that it was a damn shame because Hitler would never bomb Great Britain until after the Nuremberg Rally on 13th September.

As no one had been allowed to leave the camp, there had been some pretty heavy drinking going on at nights. As usual on these occasions, the squadrons concerned—our own and 49th, our deadly rivals in the camp—had had a pretty good beat up, and all the boys were quite content to sleep off their hang-overs. At such a time as this I can only remember kaleidoscopic scenes: the CO roaring someone up for not having his parachute handy; anxious faces crowding round the radio for their hourly news bulletins, snatching hurried meals, then back to the hangar in an overcrowded truck. One poor chap fell off when the back dropped and broke his leg—he was our first war casualty. Those gramophone records, the heat. Extra large headlines in the newspapers every day, including a memorable 'No war this year'. My old batman, Crosby, coming in to wake me every morning at four o'clock saying in his doleful bass voice: 'Here's your cup of tea, sir. The news is much worse today, sir. Shall I run you a bath, sir?'

A world about to go mad. For us a funny feeling that the next day we might not be in this world.

Wing Commander GUY GIBSON VC DSO DFC

*

The next day was 3rd September.

The message arrived. It was from the British Ambassador to the German Reich and its purport was that there was no message. Hitler had not replied to the ultimatum of the British Government. While they were talking of this, the Secretary of the Cabinet entered. 'Gentlemen,' he said, 'we are at war with Germany. The Prime Minister directs that the "War Telegram" be despatched immediately.' The hour was a few minutes after eleven. In the streets outside men and women watched the barrage balloons rise to operational height. At 11.15, the Prime Minister began to speak to this country and to the world. While he was still at the microphone the War Telegram went out to all those in authority appointed to receive it. Relayed through Group Headquarters, it reached the Commander of the Royal Air Force Station at Wyton. Upon the aerodrome, waiting to take off, was a Blenheim of Bomber Command. Three men were standing by—the pilot, the observer who was a naval officer, and an air gunner. They had been waiting since the 1st September, the day on which the Germans launched their attack on Poland. A minute after noon, about half an hour after the War Telegram had been received, the Blenheim was airborne. Some two hours later its crew were busy photographing units of the German Fleet, then on its way out of Wilhelmshaven. The Blenheim was flying at 24,000 feet. At that height in the conditions of weather then prevailing the wireless set froze, so that it was not until 4.50 in the afternoon, when the aircraft returned, that Bomber Command and the Admiralty became aware of the position of the war's first target. That evening an entry appeared in the log-book of the squadron: 'Duty successful. 75 photos taken of German Fleet. The first RAF aircraft to cross the German frontier.'

On the next day as the result of a second reconnaissance the German cruiser *Leipzig* was discovered near the entrance to Wilhelmshaven, four destroyers in the Jade Bay and two warships at Brunsbüttel at the western end of the Kiel Canal. Twenty-nine Blenheims and Wellingtons took off in the afternoon to attack these units of the German Fleet. The weather was very bad. There was heavy rain and low cloud over all that part of the coasts of Germany. Though many of our aircraft went astray, one reached Brunsbüttel and bombed a warship with no observed result.

Five Blenheims reached the Schillig Roads. They were carrying 500-lb bombs, fused for a delay of eleven seconds. Up the Roads they flew in open formation some 500 feet above the sea. Two of them in the rear lost touch, but the other three held on and presently sighted, between rain squalls, a German battleship, the *Von Scheer*. She was to port of them. No. 2 of the squadron, flying to starboard and abreast of his leader, pulled up over him, turning very sharply. This manœuvre put him in a position to attack first. He did so, but his first bomb missed the ship by ten yards and his second failed to leave the aircraft.

Meanwhile his leader was coming in to the attack. To deliver it he descended almost to the surface of the water. A tender alongside the stern of the warship provided momentary cover. The leader skimmed over this and pulled up just high enough to clear the mast of the *Von Scheer*. His observer saw men leaning against the rails of the ship and a line of washing hanging out to dry. Then the bombs fell and pieces from the catapult gear, used to launch the ship's aircraft, flew into the air. The third Blenheim attacked a second later, but its crew were uncertain whether they had scored hits. The attack was a complete surprise. One moment the German crew were taking their ease on deck, the next they were doubling to their action stations as the British bombers climbed up and away into the thick air, bullets flashing past their wings 'like small blue electric sparks'.

These Blenheims were followed by five more, who attacked from a very low level. Only one returned. The exact fate of the others is not known, but months later a German, talking of this raid to a friend in a compartment of a train crossing Northern Italy, remarked upon the reckless gallantry of their crews. It appeared that the crew of at least one Blenheim attacked the enemy so closely that the blast of their bombs when they exploded on the warships destroyed their aircraft. Our total losses were two Wellingtons and five Blenheims.

AIR MINISTRY

This, and a few other equally costly raids, showed that the RAF bombers could not operate economically over Germany in daylight (Gibson himself had flown in the Wilhelmshaven raid, but his section of Hampdens turned back when lost in bad weather rather too near the neutral Dutch coast).

*

For Fighter Command the first 'scramble' came a few minutes after the war started. An unexpected French aircraft

heading for Croydon triggered air-raid sirens across half
the country, Similar 'flaps' happened over the next few
days, the biggest and best-known on 6th September. Many
accounts of this exist, written from many angles; since none
seemed to have covered the whole battle, I have taken the
liberty of writing myself

THE BATTLE OF BARKING CREEK

It started when an East coast radar station reported an
unidentified 'plot' over the North Sea. A section of
fighters was scrambled to investigate. The plot got bigger.
A whole squadron was sent up. The plot got bigger still—
apparently waves of aircraft were sweeping in towards the
Essex coast. More squadrons were scrambled. Plenty of
people believed Hitler would start the war with a display
of aerial frightfulness. This looked like Der Tag.

By chance, the King happened to be visiting the Bentley
Priory headquarters of Fighter Command at the time. He
found an impressive display of coloured plaques building
up on the Ops Room map—and a distracted host in the
Commander-in-Chief, Dowding.

The Battle raged for about an hour, with the air full of
fighter leaders' pleas for further course to steer; it stretched
as far as Kent, where two Hurricanes were shot down—by,
it turned out, Spitfires. Then, as the fighters' fuel ran low
and the squadrons returned to land, the radar plot
dwindled, faded out, died. No bombs seemed to have
fallen; no enemy aircraft had been sighted. A hasty investigation started.

The answer was embarrasingly simple. The fixed radar
aerials of that time, like any directional radio transmitter,
threw out their beams simultaneously in opposite directions (i.e. North *and* South, East *and* West, as the case
might be) and picked up the return signals indiscrimin-
ately. This meant that the radar screen could show two
formations apparently wingtip-to-wingtip when they were
actually sixty miles apart: one thirty miles in front, one
thirty miles behind the aerial. To avoid the obvious dangers in this, the inland side of each aerial was electronic-
ally screened off to make the radar 'blind' inland (thus the

RAF had to rely on visual sightings from the Royal Observer Corps and their own fighters once the enemy had crossed the coast).

And of course the electronic screening had chosen this moment to fail—unnoticed. Every buildup of 'enemy' aircraft over the sea had in fact been the buildup of British fighters inland; every plot in truth a counterplot. Given the nervous tension of the time, and the RAF's unfamiliarity with German aircraft, it was lucky that an hour of literally chasing each other's tails produced only two casualties.

Yet in its own way, the Battle of Barking Creek was a famous victory. A loophole in the defensive system had been discovered—and was promptly plugged—without the enemy having slipped through it. Just suppose the Battle had never happened; suppose the fault had waited, say, exactly a year to reveal itself?—until 6th September 1940.

*

The Auxiliary squadrons—pilots who had trained at weekends and summer camps—were immediately called to full operational status. Among them was 601 County of London squadron, reputedly comprised almost entirely of millionaires. Their squadron historian describes how they faced the rigours of war at Biggin Hill:

FILL HER UP!

Biggin was more businesslike than the year before—the camouflage had been rectified, communications improved, security tightened up and the aircraft made capable of shooting. Since, however, the Blenheims had no armour plating, Whitney Straight ordered some armoured seats on his own account from the Wilkinson Sword Company and had them installed in the machines. Some armour plating which he obtained privately from Bristols, which proved on trials to be too heavy, had to be taken out again.

Many officers were using motor-cycles for petrol economy, and when it was learned that petrol rationing would take effect within a few days the squadron came nearer to panic than it had ever been. Thynne called a hurried meeting of the 'soviet' at which it was decided to stockpile fuel. First they had to get some. Willie Rhodes-Moorehouse was appointed petrol officer, relieved of all other duties, and told not to come back without results. The next morning he was back at the aerodrome.

'Well,' said Thynne. 'How much have you got?'

'Almost enough to last the war.'

'What you done?'

'I've bought a garage.'

The owner of the filling station had been glad to sell. The road it was in, which ran through the camp, had been closed a few days before, and Rhodes-Moorehouse had drawn a cheque on the spot. But the tanks were only half full and his estimate sounded a little optimistic, so the 'soviet' convened again to discuss this problem. A light dawned slowly in Loel Guinness's eye.

'I'm not sure,' he said hesitantly, 'but I think I'm a director of Shell.'

'What do you mean, you think you are?' snapped Thynne. 'Telephone your secretary and find out!'

Guinness's secretary confirmed that he was on the board of a Shell subsidiary, and within days the tanks of the garage were brimfull, a matter of hours before the enforcement of rationing.

TOM MOULSON

*

Meanwhile, the first RAF squadrons—mainly Hurricanes, Fairey Battles, Blenheims and Army Co-operation Lysanders—were being prepared for despatch to France in support of the BEF. Appropriately, the first to go was 1 Squadron from its traditional home at Tangmere.

At about nine-thirty on the morning of Friday, 8th September, I was getting a few minutes' sleep in my room when my batman came in and said: 'Colonel Richey to see you, sir,' and in walked my father. I was very glad to see him, and we sat and talked of nothing in particular. At ten-thirty my batman dashed in again to say: 'No 1 Squadron called to Readiness, sir!' I kissed my father goodbye and hurried down to the airfield with the other pilots, and we were soon grouped beside our aircraft on the far side of it. As they were started up one by one, Leak Crusoe took a photograph of us. We tore the Squadron badges off our overalls (by order), and I gave mine to a fitter to give to my father, who was leaning over the fence watching us. We jumped into our cockpits, and as I taxied out I waved him goodbye. I think we knew each other's thoughts. There was no time, or inclination, for more.

We took off in sections of three, joining up, after a brief individual 'beat-up', into flights of six in sections-astern, and then going into aircraft-line-astern. Down to Beachy Head then, and with a last look at the cliffs of England we turned out across the sea. As we did so, over the radio from Tangmere came a farewell from our old friends and rivals: 'Good-bye and good luck from 43 Squadron!'

There was not a cloud in the sky, scarcely a breath of wind on the sea, and the heat in the cockpits was almost unbearable, for we wore all our gear—full uniform, overalls, web-equipment, revolver, respirator slung, and 'Mae West' life-jacket. Only the almost complete absence of shipping in the Channel brought home to us that there was a war on somewhere. Then, in about thirty minutes, Dieppe appeared through the heat-haze and we turned down the coast towards Le Havre.

Our airfield at Le Havre lay north-west of the town on the edge of the cliffs, which were some 400 feet high. It was large and new, with an unfinished hangar on one side, and among some trees on another was a long low building that turned out to be a convent which had been commandeered for us to live in. The Squadron closed in, broke up into flights of six, then sections of three, and after saluting the town came in to land individually. We taxied in and found our troops ready to welcome us: No 1 Squadron had arrived in France, the first of the British fighter squadrons to do so.

Wing Commander PAUL RICHEY DFC

It is interesting to note that five days had elapsed from the start of the war to the landing of the first RAF fighters in France. After D-Day, it took less than three days. Perhaps there are fewer administrative problems to capturing an airfield from an enemy than there are to borrowing one from an ally.

*

But soon the Western Front settled down into its own quiet routine. Paul Richey continues the story of

THE PHONEY WAR

Shortly after arrival here I had my first combat, but not quite in the way I had expected. I was sent up alone one afternoon to patrol the airfield at 20,000 feet on the off-chance of intercepting a machine of doubtful nationality we had noticed floating about at a great height recently. On directions given by radio by Pete Matthews, who was sitting in an aircraft on the ground, I flew west for ten minutes after a suspected enemy aircraft. The sun was low and I was flying into it, and I could see little and found nothing. On my way back, I was diving at about 10,000 feet when I saw what I took to be six Hurricanes about five miles away on my starboard side flying in the same direction. I went over and had a look at them. Here I made the mistake of approaching at the same level, thinking they were friendly.

I soon saw the fighters were not Hurricanes. I thought they couldn't be Messerschmitts this far over France. While I was still studying them, the No 2 aircraft saw me, waggled his wings beside his leader, and dived down below me and towards me. He pulled up, and as he did so I saw the tricolour on his tail and that he was a French Morane fighter. I then saw him open fire, taking a full-deflection shot on me as he climbed. Then another Morane also attacked me.

I had by this time turned steeply left towards the first Frenchman and passed over him. I then dived in a turn to the right, did an Immelmann to the left which took me above a small cloud, stood on my tail, stall-turned and dived in a vertical left-hand spiral at full throttle. One Morane got on my tail, but I reckoned he was out of effective range, and knowing the Hurricane to be less manœuvrable but faster than the Morane, I straightened out at some 200 feet above ground and kept a straight course at full throttle. I shook off both the Frenchmen and then found I was lost. I had taken off in a hurry and had no maps, and after circling until it was nearly dusk and I had only 20 gallons of petrol left, I returned to a town I had seen, chose a field on top of a hill (for dryness), flew low over it and examined the surface, did two practice approaches with wheels and flaps down, and eventually landed on it up a gentle slope beside some trees and towards a farmhouse.

The town turned out to be Joinville. Soon some French officers took charge of me and we went down and had an excellent dinner in their mess. They were very considerate and treated me like a prince. I learned that one of the French fighters had also forced-landed through lack of petrol and had nosed over and broken his prop. He had rung the police up in great excitement and told them to find the 'German aircraft' that had landed in the district. When told it was British his first comment was 'Merde!', which after all was natural enough.

Wing Commander PAUL RICHEY DFC

More bitter comments were made when the Moranes met Messerschmitts, considerably faster than a Hurricane.

*

And back at base, there was always the laundry problem.

During the 'Phoney war' we had endless conferences, often attended by French officers. We were stationed in the Amiens, St Pol and Arras area, and we were preparing to go forward into Belgium if the Germans attacked. Although most of my time was taken up in staff work and improving the fitness and training of our flying crews, I had to attend to a number of administrative matters as well. One morning, when visiting No. 13 Squadron, I asked

27

Squadron Leader 'Fatty' Gray, the squadron commander, about arrangements for the washing and mending of socks and for laundry in general for his men. He remained silent. So did his adjutant. And I thought I detected 'Fatty' blushing, which was a most unusual occurrence.

'Well, sir,' he said when I pressed him, 'it's rather delicate.'

'What do you mean, "delicate"? It's a simple question.'

'The answer, sir, is the local brothel.'

'The local brothel!'

'You see, sir, within our area there are two such places allotted to us. I was asked to go and inspect them. Three of us went one morning and we saw "Madame" and the girls all busy washing and mending and that gave us the idea. We discussed matters with "Madame" on the spot and made a satisfactory arrangement. Our men are not much good at mending socks and pants, and we're extremely satisfied with the work done.'

'Well, Fatty,' I said, 'these arrangements, I'm sorry to say, must be discontinued. At the moment we've no war on, and consequently we're pestered by visiting delegations from the UK, all poking their noses in to see how "the boys" are doing—Members of Parliament, ecclesiastical authorities, representatives of women's associations and so on. Can you imagine the fuss they'd raise if they knew the RAF used a brothel for a laundry?'

'All we need tell them,' urged Fatty, 'is that the washing is done privately by some local French laundry and nobody will be any the wiser. The men are happy, and I suggest you forget all about it.'

I did.

Air Commodore 'FREDDIE' WEST VC and P. R. REID

*

Even the phoney war had its hard centre. In December, Flying Officer Richard Martin and two companions attacked twelve Messerschmitts. Martin's Hurricane stopped a cannon shell in its oil system, which resulted in

28

THE PRISONER OF LUXEMBURG

The Terrible Child had got himself into a pretty tough spot. There he was 20,000 feet above the earth, sitting helpless in a slimy mess of oil, while his aircraft hurtled among twelve enemy machines at 350 miles an hour. It did not occur to him to slide back the hood of the cockpit and bale out. His aircraft was still serviceable. That meant he must stick it. So he carried on for a few more minutes, which at that speed was as good as half an hour in the last war.

Smoke was belching from the cockpit now, and Martin was choking. He tried to slide the hood back to get some air, but it had jammed. Then a shell from a Messerschmitt tore a hole in the side of the cockpit, only a few inches from the pilot's head. It proved a godsend. The Terrible Child, just about to pass out for want of air—his oxygen outfit had long since ceased to function—put his mouth to the jagged hole torn by the shell, spat out a mouthful of oil and smoke, and drank in some stratosphere. Then he put the Hurricane's nose down. He had to keep breathing through the shell-hole. He was definitely out of action now, so he started to look round for a place to land. He enlarged the shell-hole and used it to see through, as his windscreen was thick with oil.

Espying a nice patch of even ground in what he thought was France, he put his ship down. Getting out of his plane, he walked a few yards away from it, and started scraping off the oil and filling his lungs with air. Then he saw half a dozen men running towards him in what he took to be Gilbert and Sullivan uniforms. Dazed as he was, he realised he was not in France. So he streaked towards his battered Hurricane, and was climbing into the cockpit when they caught him.

The Duchy of Luxemburg had captured its first prisoner of war.

Young Martin was treated like a king. First he was given a bath and his dirty uniform was dry-cleaned. Then while waiting for it to be returned to him he was asked to give his parole that he would not try to escape. He gave it, grudgingly, but at the time it seemed the only thing to do.

Overnight, Flying-Officer Martin, RAF, became a world figure. As 'the Prisoner of Luxemburg' he was front-paged everywhere from London to Melbourne, from Rio to Chicago.

In the tiny Duchy itself the Terrible Child was given full freedom of movement. He could wander about the town at will, but this became so embarrassing that he begged to be given a suit of civvies. Every time he went out in his RAF uniform traffic stopped. He got writer's cramp signing autographs. Then one day he received some English newspapers and read stories about Cobber Kain and his old squadron. They were doing great things.

From that moment his internment got under the little fellow's skin. He sat down and wrote a most heart-rending letter to his CO, Red Knox. He 'tore a bigger strip' off himself than any that had been detached by the CO. If only he could be back with his squadron, fighting the Nazis, he would be happy, he said. Would Squadron-Leader Knox have him back in the squadron after he had made such an ass of himself, getting interned like that? he asked.

He concluded with: 'And now I'm going to the Mayor to take back my parole. I'm going to get out of this dump or go crazy. I hope to be seeing you all soon. Merry Christmas.'

And that is just what the Terrible Child did. He went to the Mayor and said he was awfully sorry and all that, but he simply could not stand the strain of the hospitality he had received. He must rejoin his squadron and get back to work, so if His Worship did not mind, he was taking back his parole and was going to escape just as soon as he could.

The Mayor merely laughed. He had taken a fatherly interest in this little flying man, and liked having him for a prisoner. So did the whole Duchy.

But Luxemburg's prisoner meant business.

At the very moment 73 Squadron were sitting down to their Christmas dinner at Rouvres young Martin was walking into a thick blanket of fog that had come down over the Duchy. Taking advantage of the fact that everyone was having a good time, he walked off into the fog, right into France.

NOEL MONKS

1940

The year began as quietly as the old year had ended.
British night bombers sprinkled German cities with leaflets—some aggressive but frustrated bomb-aimers not
bothering to untie the parcels first. Fighter Command
watched its grass fields dry out and noted the first daffo-
dils in its war diaries. On 8th April the Prime Minister,
Neville Chamberlain, declared: 'Hitler has missed the bus.'
The next day, Hitler caught the bus for Denmark and Norway.

Five days later British troops landed in Northern Norway. But already all the airfields, in the south, were in
Luftwaffe hands.

BACK EVERY FRIDAY

It was apparent that no hope existed for any military success unless some fighter support could be provided: on the
other hand there seemed nowhere to base it. An RAF
Intelligence officer who landed at Aandalanes on the 17th
borrowed a Tiger Moth from the Norwegians and reconnoitred the surrounding countryside. All he could find
that gave any chance was the frozen Lake Lesjeskog,
thirty-two miles to the south-east. Its surface was covered
by three feet of snow, but Squadron Leader Whitney
Straight, who was the first man on the spot, organised a
force of two hundred civilians and cleared it.

In England, No 263 Squadron from Filton was chosen
to go to Norway, though at first no one could say how
or where. They were chosen because their Gladiator bi-
planes could land and take off in a comparatively short
distance. The aircraft carriers *Glorious* and *Ark Royal* had
been recalled from the Mediterranean, and on the 23rd

263 Squadron was embarked in *Glorious* and sailed for Norway. The previous day an RAF advance party had arrived at Aandalanes, and the servicing equipment followed twenty-four hours later. Only two lorries were available to shift everything to the lake, and only the most vital items could be moved. But by the afternoon of the 24th Wing Commander Keens, in charge of the advance party, signalled Air Ministry that 263 could land on the lake, and this message was transmitted to the *Glorious*.

It was a desperate situation from which to begin air operations. One hundred and eighty miles out to sea, *Glorious* was ploughing through a snowstorm. On the flight-deck the Gladiators were already icing up. None of the pilots had ever taken off from a carrier and they had four maps between them, no radio facilities, and their destination was not even an aerodrome. Squadron Leader J. W. Donaldson, the CO, arranged for a Naval Skua to lead his squadron in, since it could carry a navigator. The carrier turned into wind and the Skua left the deck, and then the Gladiators took off in rapid succession, until eighteen of them had vanished into the mist and low cloud.

All arrived safely at Lake Lesjeskog and landed on an ice strip some eight hundred yards long by seventy-five wide. The centre of the lake only was used, as the ice was already starting to melt round the edges. There were no refuellers or starter batteries. Petrol was brought to the lake in four-gallon tins carried on sledges. There was no warning radar, and the Luftwaffe had been watching every move in the creation of the base. No 263 Squadron had been put on the chopping block, but their spirits were high and their only fear was that their antiquated aircraft might not be able to catch up with the enemy. They turned in that night with orders to patrol Dombaas at three o'clock next morning.

In the semi-Arctic twilight of the next day their first serious troubles began. The Gladiators were frozen up; engines would not start; controls were rigid with ice; landing wheels stuck to the surface of the lake. But by five o'clock two aircraft got off and patrolled Dombaas, where their appearance cheered the soldiers in the way that the actual sight of our own aircraft was always to cheer them.

Seeing aeroplanes, however ineffective, they were comforted. Air action unseen, however effective, left them cold. While this first part was airborne, the German reconnaissance aircraft were already brooding over the lake, while frantic attempts went on to start the remaining Gladiators. At last the Luftwaffe began leisurely bombing and machine-gunning the grounded fighters, and should certainly have eliminated the whole base in the first thirty minutes. Somehow two more Gladiators got into the air and drove off the bombers, while a Naval light AA detachment gallantly fired their Oerlikon guns from the lake's edge.

This day, 25th April, was an agony at Lake Lesjeskog. As soon as the few Gladiators flying landed, they were set upon by the German aircraft overhead, while the lake began to break up under the bombing. It is almost past crediting that, in this hopeless situation, 263 managed to fly thirty sorties during the day, and shot down five enemy aircraft. By noon ten of their fighters were destroyed on the lake, and by the end of the day only five were left serviceable. But no pilots were lost, for no aircraft had been shot down in air fighting. In the evening, Squadron Leader Donaldson took his surviving Gladiators to a small clearing at Setnesmoen, slightly to the south, and set them down on a strip four hundred yards long by eighty yards wide. By superhuman efforts some of the ground equipment was forced through to join them, and on the 26th the five flew patrols and reconnaissances once more. Their oxygen was exhausted and they could not reach the heights which the prudent Luftwaffe now maintained.

At the end of the day they were reduced to one Gladiator and no fuel. The gallant efforts of the Naval aircraft from *Glorious* and *Ark Royal* to preserve Namsos and Aandalanes had been equally fruitless, and without air support the whole campaign in Central Norway began to collapse. No 263 were safely evacuated in a merchant ship, arriving at Scapa Flow on the 1st of May. Their smashed aircraft and wrecked equipment still lie in Norway as a sad monument to a gallant but utterly hopeless attempt at air defence of an area, and as a proof that the weapon itself is only a component in the air defence system.

In the meantime, the operations against the far more

isolated Narvik showed some possibility of success. An Anglo-French force was ashore nearby, and were building up for an assault on the town. As our forces withdrew from the Trondheim area Wing Commander R. L. R. Atcherley arrived at the British HQ near Narvik to arrange the air support for the next move. The Luftwaffe were now operating from Trondheim, and bombing had already begun. Atcherley, whose dynamism attained almost frightening proportions, borrowed a Walrus amphibian from the Navy, sought for and found two possible sites at Bardufoss and Skaanland, enrolled civilian volunteers by the hundred, and blasted a series of landing-grounds out of the snow, ice and rocks. The work went on for twenty hours a day under conditions of appalling difficulty. Mindful of the lessons of Lake Lesjeskog, Atcherly and his engineers built taxiways and protection pens, camouflaged positions for aircraft, and air raid shelters for ground crew. Melting snow flooded the works and was repelled again, and when the transport lorries proved inadequate two hundred mules were drafted to help out. In three weeks the landing grounds were ready.

Back at Fighter Command yet another Air Component HQ had been assembled at Uxbridge, and sailed for Norway on 7th May. Four days after Hitler's main European offensive opened, the carrier *Furious* left for the Narvik area, carrying on board the undaunted crews of 263 Squadron, now furnished with a fresh batch of Gladiators, and 46 Squadron with Hurricanes, commanded by Squadron Leader K. B. Cross. Early on 21st May the first flight of 263 took off from the flight-deck, in villainous weather, and the guiding Swordfish led it straight into a mountainside. The Naval aircraft and two of the Gladiators crashed, but the rest managed to turn back and find the carrier, and what is more to make their first landing on a flight-deck. Next day they got safely to Bardufoss and immediately began operations.

The 46 Squadron Hurricanes were still aboard *Furious,* which had withdrawn farther out into the North Sea. Their destined base of Skaanland was flooded by the thaw, and until they arrived the assault on Narvik was not to begin. *Furious* returned to Scapa Flow and transferred 46 Squadron to *Glorious*. In the meantime, the Germans were pushing north from Trondheim. On the 26th *Glorious* was back in Norwegian waters and 46 flew off, but after the first three aircraft had nosed over in the soft ground at Skaanland the rest were diverted to Bardufoss and operated from there.

Both squadrons now began working together. Yet again they were without radar, and had little or no warning of enemy raids. Moreover they were some fifty miles north of the bases and anchorages of the expeditionary force, while the Germans were coming up from the south. Thus they had to fly the wasteful system of standing patrols until another tiny strip was prepared at Bodo, south of Narvik. Three Gladiators under Flight Lieutenant Caesar Hull put into this little gluepot, refuelled from tins, took off and shot down two German aircraft over the heads of the Allied troops. Next morning Me 110s and Stukas descended on the landing-ground and began systematically destroying everything in sight. Hull got off the ground minus his flying helmet and shot up a number of Ju 87s before his aircraft was so badly damaged that he crashed attempting to land.

On 28th May the Allies finally took Narvik. But events in France and the Low Countries had now made a farce of the whole operation, and there was nothing left but to withdraw. The soldiers themselves, with their usual grim humour, were now maintaining that the initials B.E.F. stood for 'Back Every Friday'. 263 and 46 flew patrol after patrol to guard Narvik and the fleet of evacuation. It was arranged that the RAF should maintain this defence until all had left but the demolition engineers, when the Gladiators were to land on to *Glorious*, and the Hurricanes, which had never landed on a carrier and supposedly could not, were to be destroyed on their landing-ground. 263 duly took off from Bardufoss for the last time and landed their Gladiators safely on *Glorious*. Squadron Leader Cross, knowing that Fighter Command was desperate for Hurricanes, begged for permission to try to fly his aircraft on, and this was granted.

Air Marshal PETER WYKEHAM KCB DSO OBE DFC AFC

*

There were no arrester hooks on their fighters, so they strapped bags of sand into the rear of the fuselages to hold their tails down when they hit the deck. Jameson would have the first crack at it with three aircraft. If successful, he would send a signal to his squadron commander, who would follow with the remaining seven.

Jamie's small formation, led by a slow Swordfish from the *Glorious,* was soon lost to sight. Hours passed and there was no news. They were either safely on the carrier or in the drink. Cross and the remaining pilots took off, with another Swordfish leading, and flew a long way out to sea before they found the *Glorious.* Fighter pilots, with their single-engined aircraft, do not relish lengthy flights over the sea. But on this occasion their spirits rose as they left Norway behind. They were going home and taking their Hurricanes with them. All the fighters got down on the *Glorious* and were soon stowed away in the hangar below.

Cross soon made a tour of the *Glorious* and visited the chart room, where he found they were about two hundred miles from the Norwegian coast. The chief dangers in these waters, he was told, was from submarines, but no sub. could harm them at their present speed of seventeen knots. On their previous crossing to Norway the carrier's own Swordfish had patrolled ahead and on the flanks of the *Glorious.* Now, on the return journey, there were no such flights, but one Swordfish armed with anti-submarine bombs was at readiness on the flight-deck. (The official report on the loss of the *Glorious* stated that the carrier was an old ship whose endurance was limited; had she possessed sufficient fuel she would have accompanied a larger group of ships on the return journey. Five torpedo-spotting reconnaissance aircraft were aboard, but no re-connaissance patrols were flown on the day she went down.)

When 'action stations' was sounded, Cross made his way to the quarter-deck and saw that all eyes were focused on two distant plumes of smoke. Almost immediately three large columns of water, some twenty yards from the *Glorious,* announced the arrival of the first salvo of shells from either the *Scharnhorst* or the *Gneisenau.* Cross thought: I'm going to see a full-scale naval action. Must

36

watch it very closely. Most useful when I get to staff college!

He walked to the flight-deck and another salvo hit the carrier on the starboard side, destroying the very stairs from which he had just stepped. A single round fell a few yards ahead of him. Fortunately it didn't explode, but merely left a large hole with a raised lip through which came a wisp of smoke. Soon the German cruisers seemed to be hitting the *Glorious* with about two salvoes out of every three they fired. The noise when the shells struck home was quite different from anything Cross had heard before. It was like the noise of tearing calico, but magnified a thousand times. Someone came up to him and said: 'That last salvo set fire to your Hurricanes below. But don't worry. We'll soon have it out.'

The *Glorious* was burning and listing. The discipline was magnificent. Cross saw frantic efforts by officers and men of the Fleet Air Arm to raise their Swordfish to the flight-deck and get them armed with torpedoes. These efforts were of no avail, and about half an hour after the attack began the ship's intercommunication failed. Then the 'abandon ship' order was passed from man to man, and someone said that the bridge had received a direct hit and the captain was dead. The abandon ship order was cancelled, but soon the original command was heard again. The *Glorious* was still moving and there was a trail of rafts, wreckage and bodies in the wake of the ship.

Cross said to a young lieutenant: 'What's the best way to get on a raft?'

'Wait till they drop a Carley float, sir. Then jump after it bloody quickly or else you'll have a long swim!'

The squadron leader jumped overboard and swam to a Carley float which had just been dropped. Already three or four sailors were on the float and soon afterwards he saw a strong swimmer knifing through the sea with an immaculate Pacific crawl. Jamie slid on to the float but immediately plunged in again and returned with a half-drowned sailor. Finally there were about thirty-seven men aboard the raft.

The *Glorious* seemed to come to a stop about a mile from their float and one of their escort destroyers appeared to be stationary a good deal farther off towards the German cruisers. Cross and Jameson did not see the *Glorious* sink, for they were sitting with their backs to her. One moment she was there, and then the sea was empty except for the rafts and a thousand pieces of wreckage. The German cruisers came quite close to the rafts, and Cross took his squadron records from inside his Irvine jacket and threw them into the sea. But the enemy ships turned away and left.

On the third day they were picked up by a small Norwegian ship, but by then only seven of them were still alive.

Group Captain J. E. JOHNSON DSO DFC

'Jamie'—Pat Jameson—also survived to become one of Fighter Command's first wing leaders eighteen months later.

*

A month and a day after moving against Norway, the German army struck through Holland and Belgium against France. Paul Richey takes up the story in the early hours of 10th May.

THE BALLOON GOES UP

I finally woke to find the guard entering my room.

'Wanted on the 'drome immediately, sir!' he announced.

I cursed and rolled out. I looked at my watch: three-thirty. It was already light. I dressed and dashed along to the Mairie. Johnny Walker and one or two others were waiting.

'What's up?' I asked.

' "B" Flight have taken off,' Johnny answered.

'Blast!' I said. 'I've only been in bed about two hours!'

Soon we were hanging all over the lorry that took us up on these occasions. Johnny rang up Operations from the tent on the airfield. He came out laughing. 'Colledge' (the operations officer at Wing) 'is in a hell of a stew!' he said. 'Plots all over the board!'

At five the telephone rang. 'Patrol Metz Angels 20'

38

(20,000 feet). We took off and soon were in formation and climbing east. There was thick haze up to 5,000 feet, and although visibility above it was very good, the ground was practically invisible. The low sun made things worse, of course. The only features of the landscape one could pick out at all from our altitude were a few lakes and rivers, so finding our patrol-line was not easy.

We could see no aircraft in the sky at all, and had been droning up and down for some forty minutes, feeling very fed-up and hoping 'B' Flight wouldn't have all the luck, when over the radio came, very faintly and from another aircraft: 'Enemy aircraft going east from Ibor!' (Rouvres). 'Enemy aircraft going east from Ibor! Hurry up for Christ's sake and get the buggers!' We all woke up with a jerk and closed in on Johnny, who swung away west.

Soon we saw something—a speck against the haze, miles away and to the right, lower than we were and flying on a course parallel with our own but in the opposite direction. We opened up to full throttle, black smoke pouring from our exhausts, and turned across the aircraft's path. He was still some way off when he saw us and dived north. We gave chase, still not quite certain of his identity. 'Line astern—Line astern—Go!' came Johnny's quiet voice over the radio. Then, as we got nearer and to one side: 'Yes—I think so—yes—yes—yes—that's him! No 1 Attack —No 1 Attack—Go!'

Johnny was No 1, Hilly Brown No 2, and I No 3. We watched Johnny go down, his little Hurricane looking graceful but deadly, on to the still-diving Hun—a Dornier 215, the new version of the 17. We watched him open fire, but when his incendiaries were finished couldn't see him firing. We watched him gradually close the range to about a hundred yards, then break away to the left and go down in a steep glide. Looks as though he's hit! Hilly got on to the Hun next, and then it was my turn. We were now only about 1,000 feet above the ground, and the warm air was condensing on our cold windscreens and forming ice on the inside; we had been scrubbing at them on the way down to clear them. I got in some good long bursts at close range, but things were made tricky by this ice, and also by the fact that the Hun was now right 'on the deck', flying along valleys full of factory chimneys and skimming over thickly-wooded hills. I made room for someone else, and we attacked singly like this for another three minutes or so. The Hun did some magnificent flying and put up a jolly good show; it seemed almost a pity to smack him down. I had seen no fire from his rear gun—probably Johnny or Hilly had killed the gunner.

Eventually the Dornier slowed up so much that we had to zig-zag in order not to overshoot him. There were only three of us left by now—Hilly, Sergeant Soper and myself —and we hauled off and watched him. Obviously he was going to crash or forced-land. We saw him make a slow half-circuit round a large field and then go in to crash-land. He hit a ridge, bounced in the air, came down again and slithered along the ground, knocking off panels and bits of engine-cowling, and eventually came to rest.

Wing Commander PAUL RICHEY DFC

*

That afternoon we sat and waited. Everything seemed very quiet. Along the road more and more army straggled, the sun beating piteously down on their sweating forms. We lay in our shirt-sleeves, sunbathing and chatting quietly, watching the road and wondering what the hell was happening. Now and then a section or flight of planes took off, and returned having seen nothing.

Tea-time came along. We were just arguing whose turn it was to go first, when one of the crews shouted that there was a plane in flames. There it was over Lille, very high. As we looked it came plummeting down, trailing a dirty black streak behind; at about 20,000 feet there was a puff of white as a parachute opened. A cloud of dust rose from the ground where the plane had hit; high above we could see the tiny white canopy bringing its pilot slowly down to safety. 'Theirs or ours?' Whoever it was, he was going to have a long ride down, and would eventually land fairly near us, as there was a gentle wind blowing our way.

I rushed off to tea with my section, 'Watty' and Banks. Tea tasted good. The batmen had fantastic rumours that the Jerries had broken through south of us. They told us

40

that the village behind the mess was practically deserted. Back to dispersal to relieve the others for tea. When we arrived there about forty minutes after we had left the parachutist was still about 5,000 feet, and looked as if he would land slap in the middle of Lille. Opps had phoned us and said that it was one of ours—a 504 bloke who had been shot down by a 109.

We still sat around and waited. Things weren't so comfortable now, as most of our comforts were piled high on the lorries, waiting for the move to Heaven knows where. At about six the phone rang. The Squadron was to move to Merville immediately. Hell and damnation! We hoped that our batmen had packed our kit OK. 'Well, here goes, boys. Cheerio, "Chiefy"; we'll see you at Merville.' It wasn't too big a move, as Merville was only 40 miles behind Lille. It took as a bare fifteen minutes to fly there.

We arrived over the aerodrome in company with another Squadron. The ground seemed covered with aircraft already. Where we were meant to go nobody seemed to know. We taxied round the drome trying to find somewhere to put our planes. At last we found a corner—not too far away from a café, we noted. Several of the boys knew Merville well, as they had been stationed there earlier in the war.

There we were, with no men to start us up, even. We got the starter handles out and arranged to start each other up. We had left one of our 'Hurryboxes' back at Lillemark. It was 'Watty's' old 'G', which had had its control wires and main longerons shot away that morning; the tail was just about falling off. We hoped to send a crew back to fix it up; we never saw 'G' again.

Dusk began to fall just as our lorries arrived. Thank God they had arrived, anyway. Where we, or they, were going to sleep that night nobody knew. The Doc arrived in his car, so 'Watty' and I went into the village to find some billets for the men, and for ourselves. 'Doc' Curry was damned good at French, which helped a lot. After a lot of arguing we eventually found the key of the school-house, so commandeered that. Everywhere else was crammed full of refugees; we managed to oust some of these from part of the little cinema, and put the rest of the men there. Now

41

where the hell were we going? That seemed a different matter.

Actually I had already found myself a bed, in one of the houses next to the drome—a huge double bed. All I was worrying about now was my tummy, which felt very empty. A crowd of us wandered along to the café at the cross-roads; it was full of soldiers and local inhabitants. After a spot of arguing we managed to get them to produce big plates of bacon and eggs; this went down damned well with plenty of beer. We had found several old friends at Merville, who were in the other Squadrons there. Eventually I wandered down the road with young Banks, with whom I had offered to share my room.

He was a young boy who was looking very tired. He had come out three days before, having ferried a new Hurricane over to us. God knows where our luggage was; we didn't bother about that. After asking the lady of the house to wake us at four-thirty, we retired to our room with a couple of candles, stripped and leapt into bed naked. When the candles were blown out I lay in bed and thought. Oh hell! I suddenly remembered that I hadn't told anyone where we were sleeping. I hope she wakes us. My thoughts wandered. In two minutes I was asleep.

Wing Commander IAN GLEED DFC

*

Luftwaffe strength at that time was some 3,500 warplanes.
Almost immediately, a critical target for the Allies became the bridges across the Albert Canal near Maastricht. Belgian and French bombers attacked without result. Then it became the turn of the RAF's Blenheims and Battles.

THE BRIDGES

I suppose as a sergeant observer I ought to be able to give a good picture of that raid—and afterwards. But I doubt whether words could describe what really happened.

As you probably know, the two bridges at Maastricht should have been blown up on the night of 11th May, but for some unknown reason they were left standing. It was absolutely necessary that the bridges should be destroyed, for they were the only route open to the enemy, and I am quite certain that their eventual destruction by the RAF did much to slow down the German advance.

Our squadron leader asked for volunteers, and there is no need for me to tell you that not a single one of us hesitated. I wasn't there at the actual time, but when I arrived my pilot told me he had put my name down. I am glad he did.

We had been up since three in the morning, and as we had a pretty strenuous time ahead of us my pilot decided on a few hours' sleep—but not before we had studied our maps and plotted out our route.

Maastricht was about 100 miles away from our aerodrome, but from the preparations we made for the journey you might have thought we were off on a journey across miles of uncharted land. We are thorough about all our routes, of course, but the vital importance of this raid made us even more careful. It was absolutely essential that we should not waste any time in finding the bridges and it was absolutely essential that they should be destroyed.

Five aircraft set out on the task. One flight of three were detailed to destroy the larger bridge and the other two bombers—in one of which I was the observer—had the smaller bridge to deal with.

We were given a fighter escort of three aircraft which cheered us up, but, unfortunately, we were not to have their company for long. When we were about twenty miles from our target thirty Messerschmitts tried to intercept us, but we continued on our course while the three fighters waded into the attack. The odds were ten to one against us, but even so several of those Messerschmitts were brought down. And so we arrived near Maastricht. All the company we had was more enemy fighters and heavier anti-aircraft fire.

The Messerschmitts attacked us from the rear. The first I knew about it was when our rear gunner shouted: 'Enemy fighters on our tail. Look out, Taffy.' Our pilot turned and took evasive action whilst the gunner shot one of them down. That seemed to frighten the others, for they soon sheered off. The barrage was terrific, the worst I have ever struck, and as we neared our target we saw the flight of three bombers, now returning home, caught in the thick of the enemy's fire. Later on all three were lost.

The big bridge looked badly knocked about and was sagging in the middle. It had been hit by the bombs dropped by the three bombers ahead of us. When we delivered our attack we were about 6,000 feet up. We dived to 2,000 feet—one aircraft close behind the other—and dropped our load. On looking down we saw that our bridge now matched the other. It sagged in the middle, and its iron girders were sticking out all over the place. Immediately after we had dropped our bombs we turned for home, but the barrage was there waiting for us. It was even worse than before, and it was not long before our aircraft began to show signs of heavy damage. Soon the rear gunner shouted: 'They have got our tanks,' and as it looked as if the machine would soon be on fire the pilot gave orders to abandon aircraft.

The rear gunner jumped first. We saw nothing of him after that, though we believe he is in hospital somewhere. Then I jumped. The pilot remained with his aircraft and managed to bring it down safely. When I jumped we were near Liège. On the way down, I saw I was going straight for the Meuse, so I pulled my rigging cord on one side, altered my direction to make sure of falling somewhere in the town. But as I came near the ground I saw a reception committee waiting for me. Hundreds of people were dashing from one street to another and all were pointing at me. As I got nearer I realised that the mob was angry: they were shouting and waving their fists. I then began to wonder whether the river wouldn't be safer after all, but by that time it was too late to change my mind.

I landed in a small cottage back-garden. Before I had time to disentangle myself from my gear the crowd rushed into the next-door garden and dragged me over the fence shouting 'Salle Boche', which means 'Dirty German', and other insulting remarks. I shouted back: 'Je suis Anglais,' 'I am English,' but either they didn't believe me or didn't understand my French.

Soon they had dragged me into the street where there were hundreds of people waiting. Men and women held my arms and an angry old man got ready to shoot me. Again I shouted: 'Anglais,' 'Anglais,' and I am glad to say somebody must have thought it just possible that I was telling the truth.

ANON

(BBC broadcast)

One bridge was finally destroyed—by a Battle which crashed headlong into it. Nobody had appreciated the speed with which mobile light flak units were disposed around such crucial targets. One pilot who survived by baling out at very low level found himself not merely captured but soundly ticked off by a German officer for having acted so suicidally. He didn't feel inclined to argue.

*

'Never reinforce failure' is one of the oldest, most funda-mental, military maxims. But how do you recognise failure before it has turned into utter defeat? And what if it is an ally appealing for reinforcement? Can you cut your friends along with your losses? This was the prob-lem facing the War Cabinet with the increasing French demands for more British fighters to be pitched into the Battle of France. On 16th May the C-in-C of Fighter Com-mand sat down and wrote a letter that may, just may, have changed history.

Sir,

I have the honour to refer to the very serious calls which have recently been made upon the Home Defence Fighter Units in an attempt to stem the German invasion on the Continent.

2. I hope and believe that our Armies may yet be victori-ous in France and Belgium, but we have to face the possi-bility that they may be defeated.

3. In this case I presume that there is no-one who will deny that England should fight on, even though the re-mainder of the Continent of Europe is dominated by the Germans.

4. For this purpose it is necessary to retain some mini-

mum fighter strength in this country and I must request that the Air Council will inform me what they consider this minimum strength to be, in order that I may make my dispositions accordingly.

5. I would remind the Air Council that the last estimate which they made as to the force necessary to defend this country was 52 Squadrons, and my strength has now been reduced to the equivalent of 36 Squadrons.

6. Once a decision has been reached as to the limit on which the Air Council and the Cabinet are prepared to stake the existence of the country, it should be made clear to the Allied Commanders on the Continent that not a single aeroplane from Fighter Command beyond the limit will be sent across the Channel, no matter how desperate the situation may become.

7. It will, of course, be remembered that the estimate of 52 Squadrons was based on the assumption that the attack would come from the eastwards except in so far as the defences might be outflanked in flight. We have now to face the possibility that attacks may come from Spain or even from the North coast of France. The result is that our line is very much extended at the same time as our resources are reduced.

8. I must point out that within the last few days the equivalent of 10 Squadrons have been sent to France, that the Hurricane Squadrons remaining in this country are seriously depleted, and that the more squadrons which are sent to France the higher will be the wastage and the more insistent the demand for reinforcements.

9. I must therefore request that as a matter of paramount urgency the Air Ministry will consider and decide what level of strength is to be left to the Fighter Command for the defence of this country, and will assure me that when this level has been reached, not one fighter will be sent across the Channel however urgent and insistent the appeals for help may be.

10. I believe that, if an adequate fighter force is kept in this country, if the fleet remains in being, and if Home Forces are suitably organised to resist invasion, we should be able to carry on the war single-handed for some time, if not indefinitely. But, if the Home Defence Force is

drained away in desperate attempts to remedy the situation in France, defeat in France will involve the final, complete and irremediable defeat of this country.

I have the honour to be,

Sir,

Your obedient Servant

Air Chief Marshal

THE LORD DOWDING OF BENTLEY PRIORY GCB GCVO

No more Hurricanes went to France. Few of those already there returned.

*

As British troops pulled back into Dunkirk and Calais, evacuation became essential—and seemingly impossible. Then the panzers halted, the Luftwaffe took a pace forward, and Goering promised to finish the BEF from the air. To protect the troops, Fighter Command set up standing patrols of British-based squadrons behind Dunkirk. So, for the first time, Spitfire met Messerschmitt in

A PRIVATE DUNKIRK

While breakfasting with 'Wonky' I was called to the telephone to speak to 'Prof' Leatheart, the flight commander.

'Al,' he said, 'Will you collect Johnny Allen and get down here right away for immediate take-off. The Station Commander has suggested to Group that we fly the Master [a two-seater training-type aircraft] over to Calais/Marck to pick up the CO of 74 Squadron. The AOC has agreed and we have been given the job; I'll fly the Master and you and Johnny can act as escort in a couple of Spitfires. I understand that there is a lot of enemy activity over there now and I think we stand more chance of getting away with it if just the three of us go. We can nip across at sea level and should avoid being spotted by Hun fighters as the airfield is right on the coast.'

The trip to dispersal in my old barouche was made in record time. The plan was for the Master to land at Calais/Marck, pick up the squadron commander, if he was still on the airfield, and take off again immediately without stopping the engine. Johnny and I were to remain orbitting the airfield to protect the Master whilst landing and taking off. It sounded a piece of cake. The trip out was uneventful and the Master landed without incident. There was broken cloud over the area which meant there was a likelihood of being surprised from above. I decided therefore to send Johnny above cloud, at about 8,000 feet, while I remained below circling the airfield. I watched the Master taxi towards a small hangar, and was wondering if his passenger was about, when an excited yell from the usually placid Johnny pierced my ear-drums.

'Al, they're here. Huns! About a dozen just below me and making towards the airfield. I'm going in to have a go at them.'

'OK, Johnny, for God's sake keep me informed. I must remain in sight of the airfield to try and warn "Prof", and stop him taking off.'

To warn the Master was not going to be easy. It carried no R/T and at best I could dive down towards where it stood on the airfield and waggle my wings hoping that 'Prof' would interpret this as a danger signal. With these thoughts in mind I wheeled my Spitfire around only to see the Master taxi-ing out for take-off. At the very moment I turned, a Messerschmitt 109 came hurtling through the clouds straight for the defenceless Master which by now was just becoming airborne. By the grace of God the Hun flew right across my line of flight and I was able to give him a quick burst of fire which I knew had little hope of hitting him but which, I hoped, would divert his attention from the Master. It did, but not before a stream of tracer spouted from his guns and disappeared, it seemed, into the fuselage of the trainer. By this time my throttle was fully open and with the stick hard back to turn inside the Me 109 I was in range to fire. Just as I did so I heard Johnny screaming on the R/T:

'Red One—I'm surrounded, can you help me?'

'Try and hang on, Johnny, till I kill this bastard in front of me, and I'll be right up.'

In a last desperate attempt to avoid my fire, the Hun pilot straightened from his turn and pulled vertically upwards, thus writing his own death warrant; he presented me with a perfect no-deflection shot from dead below and I made no mistake. Smoke began to pour from his engine as the aircraft, now at the top of its climb, heeled slowly over in an uncontrolled stall and plunged vertically into the water's edge from about 3,000 feet. Immediately I broke back towards the airfield thankful to observe the Master parked safely by the perimeter fence apparently unharmed. Now to help Johnny.

'Hello, Red Two, how goes it?' I called over the R/T. 'I'm coming up now.'

Zooming up through the cloud I found myself crossing the path of two Me 109s which were diving inland. They must have seen me at the same moment because immediately the leader went into a steep turn. Again I found no difficulty in keeping inside the turn and was soon in range to fire. A long burst at the number two caused bits to fly off his aircraft which rolled on to its back and careered earthwards. Whether or not he was *hors de combat* I couldn't be sure but the leader was still there and must be dealt with. Reversing his turn very skilfully he too dived towards the ground. Momentarily I lost distance, but I had got in range again before he flattened out above the tree tops and headed homewards. A quick burst caused him to whip into another turn and from this point onwards he did everything possible to shake me off. After a second burst I ran out of ammunition but determined to stay behind him for as long as possible, if for no other reason than the fact that I didn't know quite how to break off the engagement. I had the feeling that he must know I was out of ammunition and was just waiting for me to turn for home. Fortunately for me his next manœuvre was to straighten out and determinedly head eastwards at which I pulled hard back on the stick and looped through the broken cloud before rolling out and diving full throttle towards the coast.

I now called Johnny on the R/T and was relieved to hear his cheerful but somewhat breathless voice answer.

'I'm just crossing out North of Calais but am rather worried about my aircraft. I can't see any holes but felt hits and she doesn't seem to be flying quite right. I'll make for the North Foreland at my present height of 8,000 feet. See if you can join up.'

We managed to join up in mid-Channel and sure enough his aircraft had been holed. However, it didn't seem too bad and on my advice he decided to continue back to Hornchurch rather than land forward at Manston. He accomplished a safe landing to the accompaniment of a victory roll from me.

Excited pilots and ground crew clustered around us on the ground and our stories had to be recounted in detail. Johnny's only comment was that he hoped next time he encountered the Huns there would be fewer of them and he would not be alone; after all, odds of 20 to 1 and 12 to 1 in consecutive engagements were too much for one's nerves.

Shortly afterwards 'Prof' arrived in the Master with his passenger, both none the worse for wear. From the safety of a ditch, into which he had dived on scrambling out of his aircraft, he had observed the air battle and was able to give his account of the affray. His story is best related by quoting verbatim from the official intelligence report he later made:

'. . . The moment I left the ground I saw from the activities of Red One that something was amiss. Almost at once a Me 109 appeared ahead of me and commenced firing. I pulled around in a tight turn observing as I did so the Messerschmitt shoot past me. I literally banged the aircraft on to the ground and evacuated the cockpit with all possible speed, diving into the safety of a ditch which ran along the airfield perimeter. Just as I did so I saw a Me 109 come hurtling out of the clouds to crash with a tremendous explosion a few hundred yards away. Almost simultaneously another Me 109 exploded as it hit the sea to my left.

'From the comparative safety of the ditch my passenger and I caught momentary glimpses of the dog-fight as first Me 109 and then Spitfire came hurtling through the cloud banks only to scream upwards again. It was all over in a matter of about ten minutes but not before we observed a third enemy aircraft crash in flames. We waited about ten minutes after the fight ended, and when it seemed safe made a hasty take-off and a rather frightened trip back to England and safety.'

Group Captain ALAN DEERE DSO OBE DFC

A few days later Deere himself was shot down by a bomber over Dunkirk; he reached Britain, by boat, the same day. It was only the start of an exciting few weeks, in which he collided with a Messerschmitt 109, was shot down by another Spitfire and finally had a wing blown off by a bomb during a scramble. Sent on rest to teach new pilots combat tactics, he baled out from another mid-air collision.

*

'What did you do in the war, Daddy?
 How did you help us to win?'
'Takeoffs and landings and stalls, laddie,
 And how to get out of a spin.'

*

Despite the heavy aircraft losses, the true shortage in Fighter Command that summer was to be in experienced pilots. It took time—a year at least—to train a pilot from scratch; a year of war had not yet passed. But there were a few—mainly from the RAFVR and the University Air Squadrons—who had flown in peacetime. Their training was hurried on. Among them were two who became, for different reasons, among the most famous of RAF fighter pilots.

The industrial smoke from the north had increased and when I trundled the Master across the grass I noticed, with some dismay, that the visibility had worsened since our previous flight. I had a strong urge to turn back and simply say that the conditions were too bad for my limited night experience, but the winking green light from the end of the runway urged me on. Full of apprehensions, I tore down the uneven surface of the flare path. A bump or two and we were airborne. Wheels up. Throttle back to climbing revs. Concentrate on the instruments. 500 feet and all's

51

well so far. A slow, climbing turn to port through 180 degrees and level out at 1,000 feet. Throttle back again, this time to cruising revs. Trim the Master to fly with the least pressures from feet and hands. All set. The flare path is about 1,000 yards distant on the port side. Or is it? I peered from the cockpit, but all I could see were the eerie opaque reflections from the red and green wing-tip lights on the swirling cloud. This was my third trip at night in a Master, and my second solo experience, and to make matters worse I suddenly hit some turbulent air. The Master didn't feel right, and in a moment of panic I had the most vivid sensation that she was plunging earthwards in a steep twisting dive and automatically I began to take corrective action. But the instruments revealed that she was flying straight and level with a slight tendency to climb. Concentrate on the instruments! I concentrate to such an extent that my grip on the stick is like a vice and my feet are braced against the rudder pedals as if they were steel struts. Relax! Sing or swear or shout! But relax, and with only the slightest pressures from feet and hands climb through the cloud for safety. And time to think.

At 3,000 feet we lurched out into a clear sky. There was no moon, but the stars seemed bright and friendly after the cold, treacherous belly of the cloud. Soon I could make out a vague but real horizon and obtained some relief from the strain of the unaccustomed instrument work. Remote in a world bounded by cloud and stars, I found time to determine the next step, and reasoned judgment gradually replaced the near panic of a few moments ago. I had no radio to guide me back to the airfield, which was now shrouded in cloud down to about 600 feet. The local countryside was hilly; the foothills of the Welsh mountains were but a few miles away and to the east the Pennine Chain reared its formidable bulk. I had sufficient petrol for about half an hour, and in this time I had to be on the ground in one piece, either with the Master or in my parachute. I was careful to fly for five minutes on one course and then to turn on to its exact reciprocal for a similar period. In this manner I wouldn't drift from the vicinity of the airfield, which I must try and find. I would make my let-down to the west, for this course would take me away from the hills to the flat Lancashire coast. I would descend to 500 feet, try to pick up my position, and if this proved to be impossible I would climb and bale out. Now that I had a definite course of action I felt considerably better and I tightened the harness straps, checked my parachute webbing, and began the descent.

The stars vanished as the Master slipped into the top of the cloud and once more we were imprisoned in a hostile world of clammy, swirling vapour. Now we are descending at 500 feet a minute. Rather gentle but still fast enough to make a nasty hole in a hillside! Nonsense! Concentrate on the job. Still in the 'clag' at 1,000 feet. Once more tremors of fear wrestle with logic and training. 800 feet! At 600 the cloud thins and I see a glimmer of light from some remote farmhouse. Now, a square search for the airfield. Two minutes on each of the four legs and then if I haven't found it back through the clouds for the jump. Two minutes to the south—no luck. Two minutes to the west and not a sign of activity. Then to the north and I see a wavering pencil of light playing to and fro on the base of the cloud. I speed towards it and as I circle over the thin beam I see the lights of the flare path below. I have to repress a wild instinct to smack the Master on to the flare path there and then. Deliberately I carry out a wide, slow circuit and flash out the identification letter of my aircraft. My signal is acknowledged from the ground. I put her down and taxi in to our dispersal, feeling quietly elated at having reached the ground without breaking either myself or the Master.

Group Captain J. E. JOHNSON DSO DFC

*

We learned many things then new, though perhaps no longer true, so swiftly do fighter tactics change. We learned for the first time the German habit of using their fighter escorts in stepped-up layers all around their bombers, their admitted excellence in carrying out some prearranged manœuvre, and their confusion and ineffectiveness once this was in any way disturbed.

We learned of the advantage of height and of attacking

53

from out of the sun; of the Germans' willingness to fight with the height and odds in their favour and their disinclination to mix it on less favourable terms; of the vulnerability of the Messerschmitt 109 when attacked from the rear and its almost standardised method of evasion when so attacked—a half roll, followed by a vertical dive right down to the ground. As the Messerschmitt pilots had to sit on their petrol tanks, it is perhaps hard to blame them.

We learned of the necessity to work as a Squadron and to understand thoroughly every command of the Squadron Leader whether given by mouth or gesture.

We learned that we should never follow a plane down after hitting it, for it weakened the effectiveness of the Squadron; and further was likely to result in an attack from the rear. This point was driven home by the example of five planes over Dunkirk, all of which followed each other down. Only the top machine survived.

If we were so outnumbered that we were forced to break formation, we should attempt to keep in pairs, and never for more than two seconds fly on a straight course. In that moment we might forget all we had ever learned about Rate-1 turns and keeping a watchful eye on the turn-and-bank indicator. We should straighten up only when about to attack, closing in to 200 yards, holding the machine steady in the turbulent slipstream of the other plane, and letting go with all eight guns in short snap bursts of from two to four seconds.

We learned of the German mass psychology applied even to their planes, of how they were so constructed that the crews were always bunched together, thus gaining confidence and a false sense of security.

We learned the importance of getting to know our ground crews and to appreciate their part in a successful day's fighting, to make a careful check-up before taking off, but not to be hypercritical, for the crews would detect and resent any lack of confidence at once.

And we learned, finally, to fly the Spitfire.

I faced the prospect with some trepidation. Here for the first time was a machine in which there was no chance of making a dual circuit as a preliminary. I must solo right off, and in the fastest machine in the world.

One of the Squadron took me up for a couple of trips in a Miles Master, the British trainer most similar to a Spitfire in characteristics.

I was put through half an hour's instrument flying under the hood in a Harvard, and then I was ready. At least I hoped I was ready, Kilmartin, a slight dark-haired Irishman in charge of our Flight, said: 'Get your parachute and climb in. I'll just show you the cockpit before you go off.'

He sauntered over to the machine, and I found myself memorising every detail of his appearance with the clearness of a condemned man on his way to the scaffold—the chin sunk into the folds of a polo sweater, the leather pads on the elbows, and the string-darned hole in the seat of the pants. He caught my look of anxiety and grinned.

'Don't worry; you'll be surprised how easy she is to handle.'

I hoped so.

The Spitfires stood in two lines outside 'A' Flight Pilot's room. The dull grey-brown of the camouflage could not conceal the clear-cut beauty, the wicked simplicity of their lines. I hooked up my parachute and climbed awkwardly into the low cockpit. I noticed how small was my field of vision. Kilmartin swung himself on to a wing and started to run through the instruments. I was conscious of his voice, but heard nothing of what he said. I was to fly a Spitfire. It was what I had most wanted through all the long dreary months of training. If I could fly a Spitfire, it would be worth it. Well, I was about to achieve my ambition and felt nothing. I was numb, neither exhilarated nor scared. I noticed the white enamel undercarriage handle. 'Like a lavatory plug,' I thought.

'What did you say?'

Kilmartin was looking at me and I realised I had spoken aloud. I pulled myself together.

'Have you got all that?' he asked.

'Yes, sir.'

'Well, off you go then. About four circuits and bumps. Good luck!'

He climbed down.

I taxied slowly across the field, remembering suddenly what I had been told: that the Spitfire's prop was long and that it was therefore inadvisable to push the stick too far forward when taking off; that the Spitfire was not a Lysander and that any hard application of the brake when landing would result in a somersault and immediate transfer to a 'Battle' Squadron. Because of the Battle's lack of power and small armament this was regarded by everyone as the ultimate disgrace.

I ran quickly through my cockpit drill, swung the nose into wind, and took off. I had been flying automatically for several minutes before it dawned on me that I was actually in the air, undercarriage retracted and half-way round the circuit without incident. I turned into wind and hauled up on my seat, at the same time pushing back the hood. I came in low, cut the engine just over the boundary hedge, and floated down on all three points. I took off again. Three more times I came round for a perfect landing. It was too easy. I waited across wind for a minute and watched with satisfaction several machines bounce badly as they came in. Then I taxied rapidly back to the hangars and climbed out nonchalantly. Noel, who had not yet soloed, met me.

'How was it?' he said.

I made a circle of approval with my thumb and forefinger.

'Money for old rope,' I said.

I didn't make another good landing for a week.

Flight Lieutenant RICHARD HILLARY

*

HIGH FLIGHT

Oh, I have slipped the surly bonds of Earth,
And danced the skies on laughter-silvered wings:
Sunward I've climbed and joined the tumbling mirth
Of sun-split clouds—and done a hundred things
You have not dreamed of—wheeled and soared and swung
High in the sunlit silence. Hov'ring there,

I've chased the shouting wind along and flung
My eager craft through footless halls of air.
Up, up the long delirious, burning blue
I've topped the wind-swept heights with easy grace,
Where never lark, or even eagle flew;
And while with silent lifting mind I've trod
The high untrespassed sanctity of Space,
Put out my hand, and touched the face of God.

JOHN GILLESPIE MACGEE

*

The storm broke slowly. For a month, the Luftwaffe hit at Channel and East Coast shipping, inadvertently giving the radar stations, ground controllers and the squadrons themselves valuable practice. Then, on the 12th August came the first big

SCRAMBLE!

On the morning after our arrival I walked over with Peter Howes and Broody. Howes was at Hornchurch with another Squadron and worried because he had as yet shot nothing down. Every evening when we came into the Mess he would ask us how many we had got and then go over miserably to his room. His Squadron had had a number of losses and was due for relief. If ever a man needed it, it was Howes. Broody, on the other hand, was in a high state of excitement, his sharp eager face grinning from ear to ear. He left Howes at his Dispersal Hut and walked over to where our machines were being warmed up. The voice of the controller came unhurried over the loud speaker, telling us to take off, and in a few seconds we were running for our machines. I climbed into the cockpit of my plane and felt an empty sensation of suspense in the pit of my stomach. For one second time seemed to stand still and I stared blankly in front of me. I knew that that morning I was to kill for the first time. That I might be killed or in any way injured did not occur to me. Later, when we were losing pilots regularly, I did consider it in an abstract way when on the ground; but once in the air, never. I knew it could not happen to me. I suppose every pilot knows that, knows it cannot happen to him; even when he is taking off for the last time, when he will not return, he knows that he cannot be killed. I wondered idly what he was like, this man I would kill. Was he young, was he fat, would he die with the Fuehrer's name on his lips, or would he die alone, in that last moment conscious of himself as a man? I would never know. Then I was being strapped in, my mind automatically checking the controls, and we were off.

We ran them at 18,000 feet, twenty yellow-nosed Messerschmitt 109s, about five hundred feet above us. Our Squadron strength was eight, and as they came down on us we went into line astern and turned head on to them. Brian Carberry, who was leading the Section, dropped the nose of his machine, and I could almost feel the leading Nazi pilot push forward on his stick to bring his guns to bear. At the same moment Brian hauled hard back on his control stick and led us over them in a steep climbing turn to the left. In two vital seconds they lost their advantage. I saw Brian let go a burst of fire at the leading plane, saw the pilot put his machine into a half roll, and knew that he was mine. Automatically, I kicked the rudder to the left to get him at right angles, turned the gun button to 'Fire', and let go in a four-second burst with full deflection. He came right through my sights and I saw the tracer from all eight guns thud home. For a second he seemed to hang motionless; then a jet of red flame shot upward and he spun to the ground.

For the next few minutes I was too busy looking after myself to think of anything, but when, after a short while, they turned and made off over the Channel, and we were ordered to our base, my mind began to work again.

It had happened.

My first emotion was one of satisfaction, satisfaction at a job adequately done, at the final logical conclusion of months of specialised training. And then I had a feeling of the essential rightness of it all. He was dead and I was alive; it could so easily have been the other way round; and that would somehow have been right too. I realised in that moment just how lucky a fighter pilot is. He has none of the personalised emotions of the soldier, handed a rifle and bayonet and told to charge. He does not even have to share the dangerous emotions of the bomber pilot who night after night must experience that childhood longing for smashing things. The fighter pilot's emotions are those of the duellist—cool, precise, impersonal. He is privileged to kill well. For if one must either kill or be killed, as now one must, it should, I feel, be done with dignity. Death should be given the setting it deserves; it should never be a pettiness; and for the fighter pilot it never can be.

From this flight Broody Benson did not return.

Flight Lieutenant RICHARD HILLARY

*

It is an odd thing when you are being fired at by a rear gunner that the stream of bullets seems to leave the machine very slowly and in a great outward curve. You chuckle to yourself, 'Ha, the fool's missing me by miles!' Then, suddenly, the bullets accelerate madly and curl in towards you again and flick just past your head. You thereupon bend your head a little lower, mutter 'My God,' or some other suitable expression, and try to kill the rear gunner before he makes any more nuisance of himself.

Flight-Lieutenant D. M. CROOK DFC

*

One of the greatest fighters and leaders of the time was the South African 'Sailor' Malan; then a squadron leader, later a group captain. His 'rules for air-fighting' were later posted on many squadron notice boards.

MALAN'S TEN COMMANDMENTS

Ten of my rules for air fighting

1. Wait until you see the white of his eyes. Fire short bursts of one to two seconds, and only when your sights are definitely 'on.'
2. Whilst shooting think of nothing else. Brace the whole

of the body, have both hands on the stick, concentrate on your ring sight.

3. Always keep a sharp look-out. 'Keep your finger out.'
4. Height gives you the initiative.
5. Always turn and face the attack.
6. Make your decisions promptly. It is better to act quickly, even though your tactics are not of the best.
7. Never fly straight and level for more than thirty seconds in the combat area.
8. When diving to attack, always leave a proportion of your formation above to act as top guard.
9. INITIATIVE, AGGRESSION, AIR DISCIPLINE, and TEAM WORK are words that MEAN something in air fighting.
10. Go in quickly—Punch hard—Get out!

*

STANFORD TUCK'S TWO BATHS

When the first 'flap' came through, Tuck was having a bath. Hearing the 'scramble' bell pealing, ground crews shouting and engines firing, he leapt out of the water and struggled into his clothes without bothering to reach for a towel. But by the time he reached dispersal Kingcome had already taken-off with seven others.

Titch Havercroft, Bobbie Holland and Sergeant Peter Eyles—one of the replacements who'd joined them after Dunkirk—were taxi-ing out, also having arrived late at their aircraft. He caught up with them as they climbed, formed them in loose echelon and then received a course from ground control which he realised with a glow of excitement would take them straight across England to the Sussex coast.

He wriggled about in his seat, uncomfortable because his clothes were sticking to his damp body. There was no sign of Kingcome and the others, but though he cursed at missing them, his lateness proved a blessing. For the main body of the squadron returned without having sighted an enemy machine, while the smaller section, stooging around off Portsmouth looking for their colleagues, caught three Ju 88s speeding out from the land.

The raiders had dropped their dirt and were going all out for home, a few feet over the smooth water. Tuck wheeled and sliced down after them.

'Holland and Eyles were a little slow in turning, but Titch stayed right up with me. The 88s were in a fairly wide line-abreast, and honestly you couldn't see anything between them and their own shadows on the surface. I managed to get up behind the port one and hit him hard. He started to lose speed immediately and streamed black oil and muck. I gave him another bash. He went splat! into the water, and as I flashed over him I could see him ploughing along like a bloody great speedboat in the middle of a tremendous cloud of white spray.

'All this time Titch was banging away at the starboard one. I tried to get on to the leader, but by now we'd lost the extra speed from our dive, and it was all we could do to keep up. The Ju 88 was a wonderfully fast kite, especially when it had unloaded and the pilot was homeward-bound with a Spit up his backside. . . .

'I was at long range—I think about 900 yards—but I was managing to lob a bit on to him. This was one of the many times I cursed because I didn't have cannon. I was hitting him all right, but nothing was happening. We got well out over the Channel, and I remembered to take a quick check on fuel—we'd been bending our throttles on the end of the "emergency" slots for minutes on end now. My gauge was reading a bit low, so I lined up very carefully and gave him a last, long burst. This time a few bits flew off him. Then I called up Titch and we broke off the attack. Titch left his Hun streaming a thick trail of oil.

'Heading back for the land we saw Holland and Eyles, very low on the water, circling the wreckage of the one I'd shot down. The crew of three were huddled in their rubber dinghy, looking up at the Spits, obviously very worried. I think the poor sods were afraid we'd strafe them.

'I climbed to fifteen hundred, called up base and let them get a good fix on the position so that the Air Sea Rescue boys could come out and collect. Then all four of us went down and once around the dinghy, making V-signs and rude versions of the Nazi salute.

'Brian Kingcome was furious when we got back. His crowd hadn't seen a thing. I told him if only he'd take a bath more often he'd be more successful in life.'

*

A few days later, Tuck met another Junkers 88; this time head-on.

He had the sudden unsettling conviction that this one was different from all the others. This one was more dangerous. It wasn't going to stop firing at him, it wasn't going to break off no matter how much lead he pumped into it.

This one could be death.

All this was happening, all these thoughts and feelings were crowding on him, in the space of a mere two or three seconds. But everything was so clear, so sharply focused. The moment seemed to stand still, in order to impress its every detail on his mind.

The silhouette grew and grew until it seemed to fill the world. He clenched his teeth and kept firing to the last instant—and to the instant beyond the last. To the instant when he knew they were going to crash, that each had called the other's bluff, that they could not avoid the final terrible union.

Then it was a purely animal reflex that took command, yanked the stick over and lashed out at the rudder. Somehow the Spitfire turned away and scraped over the bomber's starboard wing. There could have been only a matter of inches to spare, a particle of time too tiny to measure. Yet in that fleeting trice, as he banked and climbed, showing his belly to his foe, several shells smashed into the throat of the cowling and stopped up the Spitfire's breath. The elaborate systems of pipes and pumps and valves and containers which held the coolant and the oil, and perhaps the oil sump too, were blent and kneaded into a shapeless, clogging mass that sent almost every instrument on the panel spinning and made the Merlin scream in agony.

'With what speed I had left I managed to pull up to

around fifteen hundred feet. I was only about sixteen miles out, but I felt sure I'd never get back to the coast.

'I can't understand why that engine didn't pack up completely, there and then. Somehow it kept grinding away. I was very surprised, and deeply grateful for every second it gave me.

'As I coddled her round towards home I glimpsed the 88 skimming the waves away to port, streaming a lot of muck. In fact, he was leaving an oily trail on the water behind him. I had the consolation of thinking the chances were that he wouldn't make it either.

'I trimmed up and the controls seemed quite all right. The windscreen was black with oil. Temperatures were up round the clocks and pressures had dropped to practically zero. But she kept on flying after a fashion. Every turn of the prop was an unexpected windfall—that engine should have seized up, solid, long before this.

'I knew it couldn't last, of course, and I decided I'd have to bale out into the Channel. It wasn't a very pleasant prospect. Ever since my pre-war air collision I'd had a definite prejudice against parachutes. But the only alternative was to try to "ditch" her, and a Spit was notoriously allergic to landing on water—the air scoop usually caught a wave and then she would plunge straight to the bottom, or else the tail would smack the water and bounce back up hard and send you over in a somersault. Baling-out seemed the lesser of two evils, so I opened my hood, undid my straps and disconnected everything except my R/T lead.

'It got pretty hot about now. The cockpit was full of glycol fumes and the stink of burning rubber and white-hot metal, and I vomited a lot. I began to worry about her blowing-up. But there were no flames yet, and somehow she kept dragging herself on through the sky, so I stayed put and kept blessing the Rolls-Royce engineers who'd produced an engine with stamina like this. And in no time at all I was passing over Beachy Head.

'I began to think after all I might make one of the airfields. The very next moment, a deep, dull roar like a blowlamp started down under my feet and up she went in flame and smoke.

'As I snatched the R/T lead away and heaved myself up to go over the side there was a bang and a hiss and a gout of hot, black oil hit me full in the face. Luckily I had my goggles down, but I got some in my mouth and nose and it knocked me right back into the seat, spluttering and gasping. It took me a little while to spit the stuff out and wipe the worst of it off my goggles, and by that time I was down to well under a thousand. If I didn't get out but quick, my 'chute wouldn't open in time.

'It wasn't the recommended method of abandoning aircraft—I just grabbed one side with both hands, hauled myself up and over, and pitched out, head first. As soon as I knew my feet were clear I pulled the ripcord. It seemed to open almost immediately. The oil had formed a film over my goggles again and I couldn't see a thing. I pushed the goggles up, then it got in my eyes. I was still rubbing them when I hit the ground.'

It was an awkward fall and he wrenched a leg and was severely winded. He was in a field just outside the boundaries of Plovers, the lovely, old-world estate of Lord Cornwallis at Horsmonden, Kent, and several people had witnessed his spectacular arrival. The blazing Spitfire crashed a few hundred yards away in open country. An estate waggon took him to the house, where His Lordship had already prepared a bed and called his personal physician. But Tuck, once he'd stopped vomiting, insisted on getting up to telephone his base—and once on his feet, wouldn't lie down again. He had a bath, leaving a thick coat of oil on His Lordship's tub, then despite the doctor's protests, borrowed a stick and hobbled downstairs in time to join the family for tea.

But after that, very suddenly, exhaustion took him. They helped him back upstairs and he slept deeply for three hours. When he awoke his leg felt better and his host's son, Fiennes Cornwallis, was waiting to drive him to Biggin Hill, where a spare Spitfire would be available.

'Drop in for a bath any time, m'boy,' said His Lordship.

Wing Commander STANFORD TUCK DSO DFC
and LARRY FORRESTER

Tuck got his own squadron within a few weeks, became one of the first wing leaders the next year, and was shot down and taken prisoner in January 1942. He escaped in 1945, got through the Russo-German lines, and returned via Moscow and Odessa.

*

The gratitude of every home in our island, in our Empire and, indeed, throughout the world, except in the abodes of the guilty, goes out to the British airmen, who, undaunted by odds, unweary in their constant challenge and mortal danger, are turning the tide of the world war by their prowess and their devotion. Never in the field of human conflict was so much owed by so many to so few.

WINSTON S. CHURCHILL 20th August 1940

*

FOR JOHNNY

Do not despair
For Johnny-head-in-air;
He sleeps as sound
As Johnny underground.

Fetch out no shroud
For Johnny-in-the-cloud
And keep your tears
For him in after years.

Better by far
For Johnny-the-bright-star,
To keep your head,
And see his children fed.

JOHN PUDNEY

*

DEFINITIONS OF ENEMY CASUALTIES

Destroyed

(a) Aircraft must be seen on the ground or in the air destroyed by a member of the crew or formation, or confirmed from other course, e.g. ships at sea, local authorities, etc.

(b) Aircraft must be seen to descend with flames issuing. It is not sufficient if only smoke is seen.

(c) Aircraft must be seen to break up in the air.

Probables

(a) When the pilot of a single-engined aircraft is seen to bale out.

(b) The aircraft must be seen to break off the combat in circumstances which lead our pilot to believe it will be a loss.

Damaged

Aircraft must be seen to be considerably damaged as the result of attack, e.g. under-carriage dropped, engine stopped, aircraft parts shot away, or volumes of smoke issuing.

AIR MINISTRY

*

Meanwhile, at night, Bomber Command was hitting back at the most immediate targets: the invasion barges, gathered from the Rhine and Holland, lined up in the French Channel ports, and the Luftwaffe airfields themselves. But perhaps the most significant raid of all came on 25th August. An American radio correspondent describes

THE FIRST BOMBS ON BERLIN

We had our first big air-raid of the war last night. The sirens sounded at 12.20 am and the all-clear came at 3.23 am. For the first time British bombers came directly over the city, and they dropped bombs. The concentration of anti-aircraft fire was the greatest I've ever witnessed. It provided a magnificent, a terrible sight. And it was strangely ineffective. Not a plane was brought down; not one was even picked up by the searchlights, which flashed back and forth frantically across the skies throughout the night.

The Berliners are stunned. They did not think it could happen. When this war began, Goering assured them it couldn't. He boasted that no enemy planes could ever break through the outer and inner rings of the capital's anti-aircraft defence. The Berliners are a naive and simple people. They believed him. Their disillusionment today therefore is all the greater. You have to see their faces to measure it. Goering made matters worse by informing the population only three days ago that they need not go to their cellars when the sirens sounded, but only when they heard the flak going off near by. The implication was that it would never go off. That made people sure that the British bombers, though they might penetrate to the suburbs, would never be able to get over the city proper. And then last night the guns all over the city suddenly began pounding and you could hear the British motors humming directly overhead, and from all reports there was a pell-mell, frightened rush to the cellars by the five million people who live in this town.

I was at the Rundfunk writing my broadcast when the sirens sounded, and almost immediately the bark of the flak began. Oddly enough, a few minutes before, I had had an argument with the censor from the Propaganda Ministry as to whether it was possible to bomb Berlin. London had just been bombed. It was natural, I said, that the British should try to retaliate. He laughed. It was impossible, he said. There were too many anti-aircraft guns around Berlin.

I found it hard to concentrate on my script. The gun-fire near the Rundfunk was particularly heavy and the window of my room rattled each time a battery fired or a bomb exploded. To add to the confusion, the air-wardens, in their fire-fighting overalls, kept racing through the building ordering everyone to the shelters. The wardens at the German radio are mostly porters and office boys and it was soon evident that they were making the most of their temporary authority. Most of the Germans on duty, however, appeared to lose little time in getting to the cellar.

I was scheduled to speak at 1 am. As I've explained before in these notes, to get to the studio to broadcast we have to leave the building where we write our scripts and have them censored, and dash some two hundred yards through a blacked-out vacant lot to the sheds where the microphones are. As I stepped out of the building at five minutes to one, the light guns protecting the radio station began to fire away wildly. At this moment I heard a softer but much more ominous sound. It was like hail falling on a tin roof. You could hear it dropping through the trees and on the roofs of the sheds. It was shrapnel from the anti-aircraft guns. For the first time in my life I wished I had a steel helmet. There had always been something repellent to me about a German helmet, something symbolic of brute Germanic force. At the front I had refused to put one on. Now I rather thought I could overcome my prejudice.

WILLIAM L. SHIRER

The raid itself seems to have killed nobody. But it, and another three nights later which did cause casualties, are often credited with turning the Luftwaffe attack away from the fighter airfields and against London. Although the airfields, which were mainly grass, were almost impossible to knock out, their telephone communications (which alone could link the fighters and their controllers with the radar information) were being steadily eroded. One airfield— Manston—had already been abandoned, and Fighter Command was within a few days of a planned withdrawal to bases north of London, beyond range of fighter-escorted day attacks. London suffered, but the fighter stations began rebuilding their strength.

*

Fighter Command was an international force. Not only Commonwealth pilots but those from Czechoslovakia, Poland and, later, France, Belgium, Norway and Holland flew in RAF squadrons. Considering the long pilot-train-

*ing period, it was often easier to take a man who was a
guaranteed competent pilot and teach him English (most
airmen knew some English anyway) than take an Englishman and chance his turning out a good pilot. And there
were the American, who already spoke a form of English:*

THE YANKS ARE COMING

One evening, about mid-July, I was working late at my
desk when Group Captain Sir Louis Greig came in and
said, 'I want you to write a speech for the Secretary of
State, announcing the formation of the Eagle Squadron.'
So I went upstairs and faced the curious task of being a
ghost for Sir Archibald Sinclair. I asked first for some
of his own prose, so that I could absorb his vocabulary
and style, then I sat at my desk and reduced an exciting
story to a few hundred words.

Some months before, Mr Charles Sweeny, an American
now deep-rooted in England, offered to form a Home
Guard unit of Americans in London. The authorities
agreed, so he wrote quickly to his father in New York and
asked for fifty tommy guns, which were landed at Liver-
pool a few weeks later. Guards instructors were detailed
from Wellington Barracks to train the Americans, who
were attached to London Area Headquarters. They were
the first United States forces to arm themselves for defence, in England.

Then Charles Sweeny had another brave idea: he imagined and inspired what became the Eagle Squadron—the
first unit of American pilots to fly in battle against the
enemy. He wrote to his uncle, and namesake, a West Point
graduate and a romantic soldier who had fought in
Mexico, Venezuela, the Honduras, Poland and Morocco,
and who was rich enough to make gestures. He is one of
those fearless, restless men who like the smell of war,
wherever it is. And he was the man to travel about America
and startle young pilots of fortune with the thought of
fighting, and fulfilling his nephew's dream. He agreed to
gather the squadron together and began his journey.

Charles Sweeny the younger had already described his
idea to the Air Ministry and was asked to call. He was

69

shown into Sir Archibald Sinclair's office where he expected an amiable conversation across the desk. But another door was opened and he was urged into the presence of the entire Air Council. He has since told me: 'I sat down and I simply could not think. I had no ideas, or words; I was so intimidated by all those Marshals and Air Marshals, I just could not speak.'

Sir Sholto Douglas whispered the first words of encouragement; he said, 'We won't bite your head off.' Charles Sweeny plucked up his courage and told his story.

The political implications and the publicity value of the formation of a squadron of United States combatant pilots, in Britain, were obviously vast and delicate. But everyone acted quickly, and, a few days later, Sir Louis Greig telephoned Charles Sweeny and said, 'I have the first three of your boys; come and see them.'

The 'three' had hurried across the Atlantic, early in the war, to fight for France—to fight anywhere, so long as they were allowed to fly, and destroy Germans. The fall of France drove them to the coast; then they escaped to England, offered themselves to the RAF, and became the nucleus of the Eagles.

In the meantime, Colonel Sweeny had travelled through America, gathering pilots on the way: parachute jumpers, crop dusters from the cotton fields of Georgia and stunt fliers from Hollywood. When the volunteers numbered sixty, Colonel Sweeny flew with them across the Atlantic and delivered them to the RAF.

I wrote the speech for the Secretary of State and, for some days after, I spent my spare hours with the Eagle pilots, enjoying the sound of their American accents in the offices of the Air Ministry. It was a change, and a promise of what was to come, to hear a rich Californian voice say, 'Oh, that Spitfire; it's the sweetest little ship I've ever flown,' and to hear Colonel Sweeny say, when he was asked what he thought of his new war, 'Well, it's the only one we've got, so I guess we've got to think it is a good one.'

HECTOR BOLITHO

*

And meanwhile, back at the Luftwaffe ranch-house, Goering met the leading German fighter ace, Adolf Galland, to discuss the future of the Battle.

ACHTUNG, SCHPITFEURE!

To my mind, he went about it the wrong way. He had nothing but reproaches for the fighter force, and he expressed his dissatisfaction in the harshest terms. The theme of fighter protection was chewed over again and again. Goering clearly represented the point of view of the bombers and demanded close and rigid protection. The bomber, he said, was more important than record bag figures. I tried to point out that the Me 109 was superior in the attack and not so suitable for purely defensive purposes as the Spitfire, which, although a little slower, was much more manœuvrable. He rejected my objection. We received many more harsh words. Finally, as his time ran short, he grew more amiable and asked what were the requirements for our squadrons. Molders asked for a series of Me 109s with more powerful engines. The request was granted. 'And you?' Goering turned to me. I did not hesitate long. 'I should like an outfit of Spitfires for my group.'

ADOLF GALLAND

That remark became legendary throughout the Luftwaffe. Galland didn't get his Spitfires, and admits he demanded them mainly to jolt Goering into a realisation that, for once, the Luftwaffe was in real danger of defeat.

*

ALERT WARNING NO. 1: INVASION IMMINENT, AND PROBABLE WITHIN THE NEXT TWELVE HOURS.—Issued by the War Cabinet, 7th September.

At Coltishall we found that Alert No 1, 'invasion imminent and probable within twelve hours', had been declared by the responsible authorities and the defences were to be brought to the highest state of readiness. The scene in the Mess could only be described as one of some confusion.

Elderly officers, mobilised for the duration, darted about in various directions. Our own CO was not to be seen, and we tried to get a coherent explanation of the situation. We soon heard half a dozen different versions, the most popular of which was that the invasion was under way and some enemy landings were expected on the east coast. Perhaps the CO and the flight commanders were already at our dispersal, and I left the ante-room to make a telephone call from the hall. As I hastened along the corridor I almost collided with a squadron leader who stumped towards me with an awkward gait. His vital eyes gave me a swift scrutiny, at my pilot's brevet and the one thin ring of a pilot officer.

'I say, old boy, what's all the flap about?' he exclaimed, legs apart and putting a match to his pipe.

'I don't really know, sir,' I replied. 'But there are reports of enemy landings.'

The squadron leader pushed open the swing doors and stalked into the noisy, confused atmosphere of the ante-room. Fascinated, I followed in close line-astern, because I thought I knew who this was. He took in the scene and then demanded in a loud voice, and in choice, fruity language, what all the panic was about. Half a dozen voices started to explain, and eventually he had some idea of the form. As he listened, his eyes swept round the room, lingered for a moment on us pilots and established a private bond of fellowship between us.

There was a moment's silence whilst he digested the news.

'So the bastards are coming. Bloody good show! Think of all those juicy targets on those nice flat beaches. What shooting!' And he made a rude sound with his lips which was meant to resemble a ripple of machine-gun fire.

The effect was immediate and extraordinary. Officers went about their various tasks and the complicated machinery of the airfield began to function smoothly again. Later we were told that the reports of the enemy landings were false and that we could revert to our normal readiness states. But the incident left me with a profound impression of the qualities of leadership displayed in a moment of tension by the assertive squadron leader. It was my

first encounter with the already legendary Douglas Bader
Group Captain J. E. JOHNSON DSO DFC

*

So there were no targets on the beaches.

The last opportunity to make invasion feasible came just a week later. The wartime Prime Minister records the date that has become

BATTLE OF BRITAIN DAY

We must take 15th September as the culminating date. On this day the Luftwaffe, after two heavy attacks on the 14th, made its greatest concentrated effort in a resumed daylight attack on London.

It was one of the decisive battles of the war, and, like the Battle of Waterloo, it was on a Sunday. I was at Chequers. I had already on several occasions visited the headquarters of No 11 Fighter Group in order to witness the conduct of an air battle, when not much had happened. However, the weather on this day seemed suitable to the enemy, and accordingly I drove over to Uxbridge and arrived at the Group Headquarters. No 11 Group comprised no fewer than twenty-five squadrons covering the whole of Essex, Kent, Sussex, and Hampshire, and all the approaches across them to London. Air Vice-Marshal Park had for six months commanded this group, on which our fate largely depended. From the beginning of Dunkirk all the daylight actions in the South of England had already been conducted by him, and all his arrangements and apparatus had been brought to the highest perfection. My wife and I were taken down to the bombproof Operations Room, fifty feet below ground. All the ascendancy of the Hurricanes and Spitfires would have been fruitless but for this system of underground control centres and telephone cables, which had been devised and built before the war by the Air Ministry under Dowding's advice and impulse. Lasting credit is due to all concerned. In the South of England there were at this time No 11 Group HQ and six subordinate Fighter Station Centres. All these were, as has been described, under heavy stress. The Supreme Command was exercised from the Fighter Headquarters at Stanmore, but the actual handling of the direction of the squadrons was wisely left to No 11 Group, which controlled the units through its Fighter Stations located in each county.

The Group Operations Room was like a small theatre, about sixty feet across, and with two storeys. We took our seats in the Dress Circle. Below us was the large-scale maptable, around which perhaps twenty highly-trained young men and women, with their telephone assistants, were assembled. Opposite to us, covering the entire wall, where the theatre curtain would be, was a gigantic blackboard divided into six columns with electric bulbs, for the six fighter stations, each of their squadrons having a sub-column of its own, and also divided by lateral lines. Thus the lowest row of bulbs showed as they were lighted the squadrons which were 'Standing By' at two minutes' notice, the next row those at 'Readiness', five minutes, then at 'Available', twenty minutes, then those which had taken off, the next row those which had reported having seen the enemy, the next—with red lights—those which were in action, and the top row those which were returning home. On the left-hand side, in a kind of glass stage-box, were the four or five officers whose duty it was to weigh and measure the information received from our Observer Corps, which at this time numbered upwards of fifty thousand men, women, and youths. Radar was still in its infancy, but it gave warning of raids approaching our coast, and the observers, with field-glasses and portable telephones, were our main source of information about raiders flying overland. Thousands of messages were therefore received during an action. Several roomfuls of experienced people in other parts of the underground headquarters sifted them with great rapidity, and transmitted the results from minute to minute directly to the plotters seated around the table on the floor and to the officer supervising from the glass stage-box.

On the right hand was another glass stage-box containing Army officers who reported the action of our anti-aircraft batteries, of which at this time in the Command there were two hundred. At night it was of vital importance to stop these batteries firing over certain areas in which our fighters would be closing with the enemy. I was not unacquainted with the general outlines of this system, having had it explained to me a year before the war by Dowding when I visited him at Stanmore. It had been shaped and refined in constant action, and all was now fused together into a most elaborate instrument of war, the like of which existed nowhere in the world.

'I don't know,' said Park, as we went down, 'whether anything will happen today. At present all is quiet.' However, after a quarter of an hour the raid-plotters began to move about. An atack of '40 plus' was reported to be coming from the German stations in the Dieppe area. The bulbs along the bottom of the wall display-panel began to glow as various squadrons came to 'Stand By'. Then in quick succession '20 plus', '40 plus' signals were received, and in another ten minutes it was evident that a serious battle impended. On both sides the air began to fill.

One after another signals came in, '40 plus', '60 plus'; there was even an '80-plus'. On the floor-table below us the movement of all the waves of attack was marked by pushing discs forward from minute to minute along different lines of approach, while on the blackboard facing us the rising lights showed our fighter squadrons getting into the air, till there were only four or five left 'At Readiness'. These air battles, on which so much depended, lasted little more than an hour from the first encounter. The enemy had ample strength to send out new waves of attack, and our squadrons, having gone all out to gain the upper air, would have to refuel after seventy or eighty minutes, or land to rearm after a five-minute engagement. If at this moment of refuelling or rearming the enemy were able to arrive with fresh unchallenged squadrons some of our fighters could be destroyed on the ground. It was therefore one of our principal objects to direct our squadrons so as not to have too many on the ground refuelling or rearming simultaneously during daylight.

Presently the red bulbs showed that the majority of our squadrons were engaged. A subdued hum arose from the floor, where the busy plotters pushed their discs to and fro in accordance with the swiftly-changing situation. Air

Vice-Marshal Park gave general directions for the disposition of his fighter force, which were translated into detailed orders to each Fighter Station by a youngish officer in the centre of the Dress Circle, at whose side I sat. Some years after I asked his name. He was Lord Willoughby de Broke. (I met him next in 1947, when the Jockey Club, of which he was a Steward, invited me to see the Derby. He was surprised that I remembered the occasion.) He now gave the orders for the individual squadrons to ascend and patrol as the result of the final information which appeared on the map-table. The Air Marshal himself walked up and down behind watching with vigilant eye every move in the game, supervising his junior executive hand, and only occasionally intervening with some decisive order, usually to reinforce a threatened area. In a little while all our squadrons were fighting, and some had already begun to return for fuel. All were in the air. The lower line of bulbs was out. There was not one squadron left in reserve. At this moment Park spoke to Dowding at Stanmore, asking for three squadrons from No 12 Group to be put at his disposal in case of another major attack while his squadrons were rearming and refuelling. This was done. They were specially needed to cover London and our fighter aerodromes, because No 11 Group had already shot their bolt.

The young officer, to whom this seemed a matter of routine, continued to give his orders, in accordance with the general directions of his Group Commander, in a calm, low monotone, and the three reinforcing squadrons were soon absorbed. I became conscious of the anxiety of the Commander, who now stood still behind his subordinate's chair. Hitherto I had watched in silence. I now asked: 'What other reserves have we?' 'There are none,' said Air Vice-Marshal Park. In an account which he wrote about it afterwards he said that at this I 'looked grave'. Well I might. What losses should we not suffer if our refuelling planes were caught on the ground by further raids of '40 plus' or '50 plus'! The odds were great; our margins small; the stakes infinite.

Another five minutes passed, and most of our squadrons had now descended to refuel. In many cases our resources could not give them overhead protection. Then it appeared that the enemy were going home. The shifting of the discs on the table below showed a continuous eastward movement of German bombers and fighters. No new attack appeared. In another ten minutes the action was ended. We climbed again the stairways which led to the surface, and almost as we emerged the 'All Clear' sounded.

WINSTON S. CHURCHILL

Park could hardly have known that Churchill had asked almost the same question of the French General Gamelin, four months earlier in the Battle of France: 'Ou est la masse de manœuvre?' Gamelin had also replied: 'Aucune.' But this time, the enemy had no masse de manœuvre, either. It was lying on the bottom of the Channel and among the hop-fields of Kent.

*

After the 15th, the daylight battle ebbed. With worsening weather, the prospect of invasion receded (in fact Hitler announced indefinite postponement on the 17th) Exhausted squadrons were rotated to quieter posts in the north; depleted squadrons crept back towards ful strength. Commanders changed (Dowding was retired and Park removed from 11 Group).

One new squadron commander at Biggin Hill addressed his squadron thus:

'I have been CO of this squadron exactly a month and have several comments to pass on to you all. My NCOs are slack and slipshod. They have allowed the men to get lazy and out of hand. The Station Warrant Officer has complained to me that they are blatantly arrogant and so conceited that they refused to take orders from anyone but their own officers. This will stop immediately, or I will be forced to take drastic action.

'I have studied my officers' behaviour with concern and frankly I think it stinks. You are the most conceited and insubordinate lot I have ever had the misfortune to come up against.

'Admittedly you have worked hard and got a damn good score in the air—in fact a better score than any other squadron in Fighter Command—but your casualties have been appalling. These losses I attribute to the fact that your discipline is slack; you never by any chance get some sleep; you drink like fishes, and you've got a damn sight too good an opinion of yourselves.

'Now, your billets. It appears that you have turned the living quarters which were alloted to you to provide a certain amount of security and rest into a night club. It also appears that you ask your various lady friends down to spend week-ends with you whenever you please.

'This will cease. All women will be out of the house by 2300 hours sharp.

'Your clothes—I can scarcely call them uniform. I will not tolerate check shirts, old school ties, or suède shoes. While you are on duty you will wear the regulation dress. Neither will I tolerate pink pyjamas under your tunics.

'You all seem to possess high-powered automobiles. None of these appear to be taxed and insured, but I hear from the Adjutant that you have an understanding with the local police. Well, that may be, but how do you explain where you get your petrol from? Your cars reek of 100-octane, and I can assure you you're not fooling the Station Commander.

'Finally, I want to see an immediate all-round improvement. At the moment I think you're a lot of skunks!'

Squadron Leader JOHN KENT
quoted by GRAHAM WALLACE

*

Night bombing by the Luftwaffe had been increasing ever since mid-August, when it had been realised that not all its bombers could be used by day, there being not enough fighters to escort them. With the invasion shelved and the nights lengthening, more and more bomber crews were retrained for night raiding. So began the long bombardment which the British public, with its usual contempt for foreign languages, misnamed the 'Blitz'.

Against this attack, Fighter Command was virtually helpless. Lacking not only airborne and inland-looking ground radar but even the right aircraft themselves, it tried with what it had: Blenheims (which were slower than some of the bombers they were chasing), Defiants and the ubiquitous Hurricane.

BY EYE ALONE

There was no horizon owing to the atmosphere, and in my very inexperienced state where night flying was concerned, I was continually 'crossing my controls' and finding myself at all sorts of angles. This necessitated constant reference to instruments and therefore relaxed vigilance.

Soon, however, Operations warned me of five enemy aircraft approaching my patrol line and almost immediately an intersection of twelve searchlights appeared in the south. I moved to a position roughly 500 yards behind, and a few hundred feet below the apex of the intersection, and followed almost in to the lights. The guns of Bristol opened fire, and though the shell bursts around were somewhat disturbing, I was too busy concentrating on seeing the Hun who was obviously somewhere ahead.

I eventually passed out of the light zone. The beams swung back after fresh targets and I was forced to return to my patrol line. This was not difficult as there were now at least six intersections, some containing up to twenty lights.

I was climbing up towards the apex of the nearest one to have another try when I spotted a bomber intersected in a web of lights right over the heart of the city.

Turning on all the taps I dived flat out at an indicated airspeed of 290 mph in an attempt to close the range. The distance began to close, but too slowly. The Ju 88, as I now recognised it, was diving also and was already south of Bristol. My altimeter was reading 6,000 feet and I knew the balloons must be uncomfortably close.

With the range at least 400 yards the Hun opened fire. He was shooting well, his tracers sailing by quite near to me. I was frightened that I should be unable to close any more, and fired a short burst to see the effect.

One of the anti-aircraft shells which had been much in evidence chose that instant to go off under my tail and threw me off aim. The blast sent me skidding around the sky before I managed to get the sights back on to the enemy and let fly burst after burst.

It is difficult to put into words the picture I shall always have in mind of that moment. The dark outline of the hood frame: the glimmer of the instruments and the glowing red bead of the gunsight on the windscreen: and outside nothing but a confused jumble of brilliant beams of searchlights. In the centre, the aeroplane, light grey in the glare with little white flashes appearing all over it, and apparently connected to my aircraft by red and white curving lines. The spurts of flame from the gun muzzles in the wings and the momentary impression that there was neither earth nor sky. Everything except that 88 and myself seemed to have been obliterated by the glare of the searchlights in which we were both suspended.

Diving still more steeply I managed to get in a burst from some 200 yards' range but ammunition ran out in the middle of it. I was sure, however, that one of his engines had been hit. He promptly half-rolled slowly on to his back. Not wishing to go downstairs inverted at night at that altitude, I watched him fall away vertically out of the last of the searchlights. I avoided these beams myself and looked over the side hoping to see an explosion, but nothing happened.

When I came to check my position I found I was approaching Avonmouth from the sea at 3,000 feet. Our chase had taken us right through the balloon barrage.

Wing Commander ROLAND BEAMONT DSO OBE DFC
quoted by EDWARD LANCHBERY

The Hurricane was better at night than the higher-performance Spitfire, because of its more stable wide-track undercarriage and its better cockpit vision. 'Sailor' Malan (commanding a Spitfire squadron) managed to 'borrow' a Hurricane and shot down two night raiders. Another Hurricane pilot, R. P. Stevens of 151 Squadron, actually scored fourteen victories before being killed. His wife and family had died in the night blitz; when he landed one night with German blood on his wing, he refused to have it cleaned off.

*
80

But if 'Cat's-eye' fighters could not do the whole job, there was no shortage of ideas about what could.

*

TAKE CAT IN NIGHT-FIGHTER, AIM GUNS WHERE CAT IS LOOKING
—Suggestion sent to Fighter Command, late 1940.

*

It was one of the ideas thought up by Lindemann for night air defence that was to give Fighter Command a particularly acute headache. Almost rammed down our throats because of Churchill's very strong wish—the wretched thing could almost be described as having been, for a time, his favourite project—it was a scheme rejoicing in the unenterprising code name of 'Mutton', or the Long Aerial Mine. This fanciful idea called for the sowing from an aircraft of aerial mines suspended from parachutes at the end of two thousand feet of piano wire.

This particular piece of gadgetry was supposed to enable the aircraft to drop a curtain of these mines in the path of the incoming bombers, and we were even driven to having a squadron specially equipped for this work. It was in operation in the West Country for a year, and the sceptics saw the prospect of the countryside being festooned with miles of wire and parachutes and unexploded bombs. The whole scheme was far too impractical and difficult to operate, if only because the defending aircraft had to be placed in exactly the right position to fly at right angles directly in front of the oncoming enemy bombers. That in itself was asking for far more than could then be achieved by the controllers on the ground.

We were compelled to go on with this ridiculous scheme long after it was proved to be a complete waste of time and effort, and even after a normal radar-equipped night fighter squadron flying from the same airfield had proved that its simpler methods of operation were infinitely more effective. Lindemann was too sceptical for too long about the value of airborne radar in fighters, while we at Fighter Command were sure that it would turn the trick. But it took that whole year of frustrating experiments before I was finally able to convince the Prime Minister that the idea of 'Mutton' was worthless and he agreed to abandon it.

Another of the bright schemes thought up for us was the free balloon barrage. This one originated in some fertile brain in the Royal Navy, and it called for the use of a whole lot of balloons with mines attached to the end of considerable lengths of wire. They were to be released from the ground in the path of the oncoming enemy bombers. It was much the same as 'Mutton' in its idea, but the great snag here, apart from the impracticability of the device, was a meteorological one. We were entirely dependent on the wind conditions being such that they would allow the balloons to rise in an effective way in the faces of the enemy bombers. But we had to try it out, and over a period of months we released the barrage on several nights without any apparent success, and eventually that also was abandoned.

A more promising idea upon which there was spent a great deal of money and time and effort was an extension of the use of airborne radar. Known as Turbinlite it called for the combined use of radar and an airborne searchlight. This special type of high-powered light was fitted into the nose of the Havoc, a twin-engined American light bomber which was built by the Douglas people in California and which we had adapted for use as a night fighter. The Havoc became a radar-equipped aircraft, and it was accompanied by a Hurrican flying in formation with it.

The object aimed at with Turbinlite was to place the two aircraft behind the enemy raider. The Havoc would detect it with its radar and illuminate it with its searchlight in such a way that the Hurricane could then close in for the kill. But the weight of all its equipment and the obstruction in its nose slowed up the Havoc too much when it came to chasing the enemy bombers. There were also technical difficulties which were hard to overcome, and although quite a number of Turbinlite Flights were formed, in operation they were surpassed in effectiveness by the straight-forward radar-equipped night fighter.

Throughout that winter of the Blitz and on into the spring of 1941, we who were concerned with the defence of the United Kingdom were groping in the dark in more senses than one, as well as in more ways than were ever suspected. There were times when I could not help feeling that we were trying out altogether too many schemes, and that we were getting to the state where we were rather casting around in desperation. It would have made life a little easier if I had known that the answer was not so very far off.

Marshal of The Royal Air Force
LORD DOUGLAS OF KIRTLESIDE GCB MC DFC
with ROBERT WRIGHT

(Sholto Douglas had just become C-in-C Fighter Command)

*

The answer was the Beaufighter, the first reliable Airborne Interception radar—and operators.

There she stood, sturdy, powerful, fearsome, surrounded by an enthusiastic crowd. Most of us admired from the outside as only those with influence or possessed of extreme cunning got inside. Pilots, engineers, fitters, riggers, armourers and signals mechanics were in attendance, and they probed and tinkered and adjusted until they had brought her to a state of good-tempered serviceability. Then they all tiptoed quietly away for, like all young monsters in unfamiliar hands, she showed promise of being temperamental. Even Mick Wheadon, the Flight Sergeant in charge, was said to have been seen walking away backwards from the Presence.

For the gunners, however, there was a shattering disappointment. Where the turret should have been there was nothing but a plain, moulded dome of perspex. Here was our dream fighter. But where were the four free guns in the turret in the back that could fire forwards and upwards into the belly of an enemy bomber? There was not even a single free gun with which we could foster our delusion of usefulness.

Eventually I managed to elbow my way through the crowd and get to the aircraft. Just aft of the perspex dome a panel in the bottom of the fuselage hinged downwards leaving open the back entrance. I ducked down, set my feet on the steps cut in the panel, and climbed in.

Right in front of me there was a very serviceable swivel-seat, set high up under the dome, with back-rest and safety harness, and scooped out to take the one-man dinghy. That was a good start.

I squeezed past the seat, swivelling it around, and found Sandifer, one of the oldest gunners from the point of service in the Squadron, red in the face, sitting on the cat-walk that led forward. Stan Hawke, another of the senior gunners, was standing behind him, bent down under the curving roof, with a stop-watch in his hand.

'Where's that turret we've heard so much about?' I demanded.

Sandi was breathing hard. 'We've had that,' he grunted. 'The only gunnery we're likely to get will be this job.' He pointed at a row of 20 mm ammunition drums set in racks above his head on either side of the cat-walk.

'From now on we're just powder monkeys,' Stan said. 'We're having a go to see how long it takes to reload.'

Sandi chuckled. 'Wait until Tommy catches sight of this lot!' he commented. He patted something set in the floor.

It was dim in the tunnel-like fuselage, but as my eyes became accustomed to the half-light I saw them, two on each side of the cat-walk: four, solid great cannon, firmly set in place just below floor level! Their massive breeches gleamed with an evil beauty.

'Four twenties!' Sandi gloated. 'They ought to do a bit of no good . . . if we ever catch anybody!'

In spite of my disappointment over the turret my gunner's heart warmed at the sight. My face must have shown it, because when I looked up Stan was smiling.

'How's the reloading going?' I asked.

Sandi was nursing one of the drums. 'These thing weigh sixty pounds each,' he said. 'God knows what it's going to be like hauling them out of the racks and fitting them on the cannon with all your kit on, oxygen tubes and phone cords and all . . . and in the dark.'

'And with the pilot going into a tight turn just as you get it off the rack,' Stan added. 'That'll make it weigh a darn sight more.'

'Probably go straight through the floor,' Sandi said, 'if it doesn't chop off your fingers against the breech.'

I went back aft and wriggled into the seat under the dome and swung around to look out over the tail. There was a fine, unobstructed view all around above the horizon, and with a little squirming one could even see into that old Blenheim danger spot below and behind.

The radar equipment appeared to be a new version of what we had had in the Blenheim, with the Box suspended from the low roof just behind the dome. One could look into its rubber visor or keep a visual watch over the tail with only a slight movement of the head.

I looked around inside, and found that there were catches to release the whole dome in case of ditching or a belly landing. The bottom hatch, through which I had entered, was opened automatically by the slip-stream at the turn of a lever. There were an altimeter and an airspeed indicator; and—bless my frozen feet!—there was a hot-air duct discharging into the lap from the starboard side.

Squeezing past the others, I went forward along the catwalk, stooping under the low roof, through a pair of armour-plate doors, and into the pilot's compartment.

His seat was in the centre. The windscreen was one large sheet of bullet-resisting glass sloping back fairly close to the face. There would be no more mad craning and peering trying to see out, with the glow from the instruments reflecting back from a half a dozen small panes. And perspex panels gave a clear view to both sides and up through the roof.

Getting out in an emergency, I found, would be a bit of a gymnastic feat for the pilot. There were parallel bars set high, one on each side, by means of which the pilot, having collapsed the back of his seat by pulling a lever, could swing himself up and back and down on to a forward escape hatch, hinged like the one at the back. When shut, this hatch formed the floor of a small well between the pilot's seat and the armour-plate doors, with enough

85

room for a passenger to stand and look out forward over the head of the pilot.

I pulled the hatch open, dropped down on to the ground, and walked around to the front of the aircraft. She was good, whichever way you looked at it, sturdy and aggressive, although perhaps a bit heavy. But the two gigantic Hercules engines with which she was powered, air cooled and close cowled, with their huge propellers, sweeping through a wide arc, could surely lift anything. From the tip of that forked aerial at the nose to her shapely rudder she was a beauty. I knew that somehow, as gunner, powder-monkey, operator, or stowaway, it did not matter which, I just had to fly in her.

C. F. RAWNSLEY and ROBERT WRIGHT

*

We're leaving Khartoum by the light of the moon
We're flying by night and by day.
We're out in the heat and we've nothing to eat
'Cos we've thrown all our rations away.

*

In Africa, the desert war had opened; basically a holding operation in the north while the Italians were deprived of their recent conquests south of Egypt. A famous Australian writer, then war correspondent for the Daily Express, described

TARGET KASSALA

Matthews and I had put in for a flight on a bombing raid and to our surprise it was granted. Such requests had always been turned down in France and England.

We flew down from Khartoum to RAF headquarters, north of Kassala at Erkowit—an intolerable journey of four and a half hours in a rattling Valencia. Erkowit, about three thousand feet up in the Red Sea Hills, had a rest-house to which the overheated white people of the Sudan used to go to relax and cool off a little. It recalls Mexico or the Texan desert. Cactus with long upward-reaching fingers grows out of the grey rocks. Lizards scuttle in the shadows. Donkeys cart you around the barren hilltops. There was nothing to see, nothing to do, but the Governor-General of the Sudan and members of his staff had built themselves houses round about, and it was enough just to be cool. Now the rest-house was crowded with wives and children unable to make the usual summer-leave trip to England. Each night the RAF officers used to come to the rest-house from their two steaming landing-fields on the plain below. There would be music and dancing and mild flirtation and drinking. From every direction on the dark cool terrace in the evening would come the voices of the guests shouting 'Walad', which was the signal for a soft-footed native waiter to come up and take orders for the bar. Every day the British bombers would whirl up from the desert and fly off to Eritrea and Abyssinia. Old and few as the machines were, they were having it pretty much their own way against the Italian air force. And now today a squadron of Blenheims had come down from the Western Desert to lay on a few days of really intensive bombardment in order to distract the Fascists from an important convoy of ships which was due to sail up the Red Sea to Suez. Tired after the flight from Khartoum, Matthews and I went to bed in tents pitched beside the house. We had to be up at five-thirty the next morning since we were promised a flight in one of the raids which were to bomb Kassala throughout the following day.

There can, I think, be no exact analysis of fear or any complete assessment of courage. This raid as I know now was of little importance and less danger. But it was my first, and I went to bed that night with a little constriction in my throat, a faster, uncomfortable beating inside my chest. This was danger, I thought, asked for and accepted and one might be dead tomorrow. Or wounded or crashed somewhere beyond that jebel without water. One of the pilots had shown me a little card they all carried written in Amharic and English. It said something about the bearer being a British officer and asking that he be given food and water and taken to the nearest settlement. 'Since the bastards can't read,' the pilot had said lightly, 'I guess some of the tribesmen will slice you up in the usual way and start asking questions afterwards.' He hadn't seemed worried about it. And, strangely, neither did I. I was just afraid of being hit at all while in the air. I started examining this, searching round and round in my head for a way of dealing with myself, and I felt angry with myself and ashamed. This was the hard moment. In the morning it was not nearly so difficult.

An RAF truck fetched us in the yellow early light, and down at the nearest landing-field we bundled into the unaccustomed heaviness of flying kit and parachutes. Already the machines, some ten of them, had been 'bombed-up' and now their engines were turning over in a scurry of desert dust. The wing commander was very precise. He had photographs of Kassala showing clearly the two jebels where the air currents were sometimes difficult; the straggling native village a mass of grass huts; the River Gash, now in yellow flood; the rectangular compound of the railway yards which was our target. Inside the compound were neat lines of concrete tukals built in the shape of the other conical huts. These had been erected by the railway company to shelter native railway workers. Now it was believed that they housed Italian troops and native levies and our object was to bomb them out. Machine and possibly AA guns were noted at either end of the compound. We were to dive-bomb down to about three or four hundred feet. The aircraft would go out in flights of three.

I sweated in the hot flying kit as I walked over the far side of the field smoking a last cigarette with the flying officer who was leading our flight. I will give this man a fictitious name, Watson. He was perhaps twenty-two or twenty-three. He was six foot, unusually slim and boyish with dark hair and a serious shy face, and he had been very gay last night at the rest-house. Someone had said to him, 'I hear you are going to do something pretty intrepid tomorrow.' 'Yes,' he had said, 'pretty intrepid.' They had got the word out of some newspaper report and it was a joke among them to use it. I do not think that they ever felt brave. They felt tired or exhilarated or worried or hungry and occasionally afraid. But never brave. Certainly never intrepid. Most of them were completely unanalytical. They were restless and nervous when they were grounded for a day. They volunteered for every flight and of necessity some each day had to be left behind. They lived sharp vivid lives. Their response to almost everything—women, flying, drinking, working—was immediate, positive and direct. They ate and slept well. There was little subtlely and still less artistry about what they did and said and thought. They had no time for leisure, no opportunity for introspection. They made friends easily. And never again after the speed and excitement of this war would they lead the lives they were once designed to lead. They were no material for peace.

So then Watson and Matthews, the other pilots and I climbed into three separate Blenheims and squeezed down among the instruments. We carried no observer, so there was a spare seat for both Matthews and me with a good view. Matthews was in the left-hand machine, Watson in the centre, and myself in the right being piloted by a laconic young Canadian who handed me a stick of chewing-gum —a welcome thing at that moment. I wanted now only to get into the air. But one of the other machines heaved and stopped in its take-off. A tyre was punctured, and endlessly, it seemed, we waited for the wheel to be changed. Then quite suddenly we were off—Watson first, us next, then the third machine; and soon all three were coasting evenly over the dried-up land in an immaculate Vee. There was a flight of an hour and a half to the target—ninety minutes of pondering what it would be like. I hated that ride. It was slightly bumpy, and the other machines, so close that one felt their wings would touch, kept rising and sinking out of sight. I watched the other rear gunners, spinning their glassed-in turrets in search of enemy aircraft I traced the path of the Gash River and the thin ribbon of railway that led us to Kassala. I tried to work out the meaning of the dials before me. But it was no good. There was nothing to do, nothing to arrest the mind and lift it away from its dread and senseless apprehension.

In despair I fingered my wrist-watch again and again, believing it must have stopped. Then, unexpectedly, my Canadian bumped me on the arm and pointed ahead. There was Kassala breaking through the ground mist.

There the jebels, there the town, there the railway yards. And in a few seconds we were going down to bomb. It wasn't necessary to wait any more. With huge overwhelming relief I leaned over for a fuller view. As I moved, the three aircraft dipped in a long easy dive and, inexplicably, I was suddenly lifted with a wave of heady excitement, more sensuous than release from pain, faster than the sating of appetite, much fuller than intoxication. I felt keyed to this thing as a skier balancing for his jump or a surfer taking the first full rush of a breaker. There was no drawing back nor any desire for anything but to rush on, the faster the better. Now the roar of the power-dive drowned even these sensations, and with the exhilaration of one long high-pitched schoolboy's yell we held the concrete huts in the bomb sights and let them have the first salvo. I saw nothing, heard no sound of explosion, as the machine with a great sickening lurch came out of the dive and all the earth—jebels, township, clouds and desert—spun round and sideways through the glass of the cockpit. Then, craning backward, I glimpsed for a second the bomb smoke billowing up from the centre of the compound. It all looked so marvellously easy then—not a human being in sight on the brown earth below; all those ten thousand men huddled in fear of us in the ground. A burst of tracer shells skidded past the slanting windows of the cockpit. So they were firing from the ground then, and it meant nothing. Nothing now could interrupt the attack. Already Watson was shaping for his second run and closer in this time. We followed him into the dive, skidding first left then right at over three hundred mph to throw off the aim of the gunners below. Then the straightening at last for the final swoop dead on the target. This time I heard the machine-gun spouting from the leading edge of our machine, felt the lift as the load of bombs was released and heard again the rear gunner blasting from his turret as the aircraft nosed upward into the sky again. Watson was away ahead on a long sweep round the jebels and into Eritrea trying to pick up transport on the roads leading back to Asmara and we followed him hotly. But everything back along the yellow grey country was quiet. Over the border even the villagers were pressed to the ground in terror of

90

the raid. We turned at length, all three of us, for the last attack, flying back over a forest to the west of the town. Coming now at this new angle we found new points to bomb, and faintly Watson's salvo sounded through our motors as we came down for the last time. Looking across as he dived, I saw where his starboard wing was ripped in two places and the fuselage was peeling back under the force of the wind. Then again the earth was turning and pitching as we came out of it and I felt sick. Sick, and nursing a roaring headache. Like that I was borne up and out of it into the pure air beyond the ground-fire, beyond harm's way. I experienced pleasure then, calmer but deeper than my earlier excitement. To have had that dread, to have lost it in excitement at the crisis, and now to have come sailing back safely into this clean open sky—that was much and more than one could ever have foreseen. In a lazy pleasurable daze I sat back through the journey home. I could have laughed at anything then. It was all very intrepid. As we came down toward the home field three more aircraft setting out for Kassala passed us in the air. Three more were warming up on the ground. We made an easy landing. My Canadian slid back the transparent roof. I stepped out along the wing, caught my foot in a piece of splintered fuselage and fell flat on my face on the ground.

ALAN MOOREHEAD

*

As the year dragged to an end, the RAF was desperately short of aircraft—but nobody as much as Coastal Command, which was using some unarmed single-engined training machines for sub-spotting. The most immediate source of such aircraft was America. Roosevelt's Lend-Lease programme had started—if Britain could get the aircraft across the Atlantic. A radio operator recalls the first flight from Newfoundland to Northern Ireland.

BRIDGE OF AIR

'For the first hour there seemed to be planes all around us, and which one was the leader was the question. Ralph turned over to Dana and with the torch began to check

over the ship and found oil leaking badly from the starboard tank. I passed a message to the leader, Captain Bennett, that our oil tank had ruptured but we were watching
closely and would keep him advised. Our Skipper, being
in some doubt as to whether to go on or not, held back.
Finally he decided the oil flow was diminishing; and, decid-
ing to go on, we found ourselves quite alone. Then my
radio blew up by shorting in the Antenna switch box and
giving us all a good scare. Ralph hollered to me "Shut the
—— thing off," but I had beat him to the gun. With that
load of gas it isn't pleasant to have fire skipping around the
cockpit, and the corona from that transmitter was really
something.

'When the Skipper decided to go on, we climbed up to
16,000 feet, which afterwards proved a smart move as we
gained on the rest right from there. At 0014 GMT Captain
Bennett figured his position at Lat. 50.58N, Long, 48.38W.

'I will always appreciate Adams' friendly advice to forget the radio for a while, as we were pretty high and it was
no use tiring myself out. What with the excitement of
the take-off and leaking oil tank, I was glad to sit back
and relax and I think I actually enjoyed myself. When I
look back now I can't feel that I was actually relaxing, but
at the time it felt good just to sit there and try not to think
of anything. If Ralph and Dana were doing the same thing,
we all snapped out of it at 0207 when our bomb bay tank
ran dry and both motors started cutting out, I was not expecting it, and even if Ralph and Dana were, the way they
went for that hand pump and gas valve made me think
they didn't like it any better than I did. I don't think anything ever sounded so good to me as hearing those big
Wrights hit their stride again and settle down to a steady
drone. From then on the Skipper didn't need to watch any
gauges. I could tell him every minute how much gas was
left in whatever tank he was on. He got quite a kick out of
this and I took some kidding afterwards, Dana calling me
the "human gas gauge".

'At 0203, while I was trying to take a bearing on Captain
Bennett, the indicator on the radio compass broke and I
really felt up the creek without a paddle. No transmitter
or compass and out over the Atlantic Ocean. I didn't have

the heart to tell Ralph the compass was on the bum, but from then on I couldn't sit there and do nothing, so asked permission to go to work on the transmitter.

'At 0225 GMT we were at 18,000 feet and we must have looked funny sitting there with a rubber tube stuck in our mouths. I sometimes get scared when I think of how we started out that first trip with one little tank of oygen and nothing but a rubber tube to suck it through. Ralph did the regulating and knew what he was doing, as none of us suffered any ill effects, although at one time I felt my stomach would cave in and Ralph got down in the nose and had trouble getting up. I didn't know until afterwards why he turned the oxygen full on for a few seconds.

'At 0340 I felt very pleased to be able to tell the skipper we had a transmitter again and I think it was a load off his mind although he said nothing.

'At 0440 Captain Bennett reported at Long. 24.50W., and we knew we were doing well too. Gentry was a treasure, the way he fooled around as though we were just on a pleasant jaunt and didn't have a care in the world. The one thing I won't ever forget is the look we had together at the moon, which was full, through the Astro hatch. It was a beautiful and awe-inspiring sight and made us realise what a very small part of the world one really is.

'At 0500 the Captain spotted what appeared to be a light off our starboard bow, and Columbus himself could not have looked more longingly at North America than we did at that light. We were sure it was one of the other planes, and when it proved to be a star, we couldn't help but feel a bit let down. The Skipper had been losing altitude, and when he couldn't get contact at 2,000 feet, he pulled back up to 6,000 and stayed there. We were in rain cloud off and on: after the cold of 18,000 feet, we were forced to take off our heavy clothing as it was quite warm. Even cutting off the heat didn't seemed to cool the plane off, and for a time I was in my shirt sleeves.

'All was quiet on the air, as we were keeping W/T silence east of 20 west. Control was trying to pass Met. traffic but no one could read him through the rain static. Once W/T silence was broken, it became a wild scramble. The Skipper casually mentioned that he could use a bearing but, after listening to the static, realised it was hopeless.

'At 0800 we started to descend, and at 5,000 feet came contact. Dana was down in the nose, and I don't know who was the most surprised when he casually stuck his head up and said, "Say, Captain, there's land down there." It was a big moment.'

AIR MINISTRY

1941

The country had become air-minded. I suppose it had been air-minded before, in a way; aerial attack had been the bogey of the nineteen-thirties—but as a sudden, unheralded pounce from the clouds, hitting every target with every bomb and flooding every street with poison gas. Now we realised that many bombs missed; they dug just five-foot holes in the road. Five feet isn't impressive. Going out in the morning to look for craters, we used to pass occasional incendiary bombs—something like an overlarge mortar shell—stifled at birth by an ARP Warden who had dumped a sandbag on top of it.

The nameless fear now had names: Heinkel, Dornier, Junkers. Our own side had names, too: Hurricane and, particularly, Spitfire. It was difficult for the older generation; I remember one mother waving cheerfully at what she claimed was a 'Spitfire'. I, with the lofty knowledge of an eight-year-old, dashed into my own house and brought out a magazine photograph of exactly the same twin-engined twin-finned aircraft: a Whitley bomber. She'd probably have waved at a Heinkel 111 with the same conviction. But maybe it was the conviction that really mattered.

At night it was different, of course. I don't remember the throb-throb-throb of unsynchronised motors that the Luftwaffe allegedly specialised in (and ten years later, when I trained on twin-engined aircraft in the RAF, I wondered why German pilots were supposed to have preferred that nerve-racking throb to the steady drone that was so easily achieved. Maybe they were trying to keep themselves awake?). But at night all cats were grey and all aircraft enemy. We could see the red glow of fires outlining the horizon; hear the thud of bombs a mile away; occasionally see, through an opened door, the lime-yellow light of an incendiary burning itself out in the street.

Then, one night, we heard the rattle of machine-gun fire. Ah! The Spitfires were at work again. Some Heinkel/Dornier/Junkers would never see the Fatherland again. It never occured to us that although bombers could miss—I mean theirs, not ours—it was odd that Spitfires couldn't. Although we couldn't see the enemy, the Spitfires could.

A day or two later, we heard that a local barrage balloon had been shot down that night.

COLIN DRINKWATER

The writer can be forgiven for thinking 'Spitfire'; the Beaufighter was still an Official Secret. Indeed, it was only just getting into the night war. Training AI operators took time, and the shortage of aircraft spun out the time; almost every serviceable Beaufighter was needed operationally almost every night. At the turn of the year there were less than two dozen fully operational Beaufighter crews. Nor was the enemy the only enemy.

*

Suddenly I heard an excited voice outside: 'Mr Hunter has crashed.' I went outside: 'Where, where?' 'Not sure, sir,' and 'They say he was coming in to land,' and I thought: 'That will be all right. He has probably undershot and landed short, breaking the undercarriage.' It had happened before, that sort of thing.

I was joined by Stanley Skinner, and I gave him the news; he also was not unduly worried. It never entered our heads that Alastair could have met with a serious accident; he was a very capable pilot and he had done hundreds of hours at night. We waited, Stanley and I, telephoning now and again to the operations-room to ask for news; but they had none and none seemed forthcoming. It was only known that there had been a crash somewhere off the aerodrome in the down-wind direction, which was on the opposite side to our dispersal area.

We decided to go over and see for ourselves. I think the idea we both had was that we might be able to cheer the crew up if they had been hurt; but the thought that they had been hurt had hardly entered my head. We trudged across the aerodrome to the beginning of the flare path, and there we talked to the control officer. It was he who had seen the crash and reported it. 'Oh no. It was some distance away. I saw the lights go down. It seemed as if he was turning.' So it was not just a landing accident. Still, there had been no fire. Perhaps the motors had cut and he had had to make a wheels-up landing.

We walked on in the direction he had shown us, still thinking that all must be well, yet hoping and hoping that all was in fact well. We went on outside the aerodrome boundary; we plodded on across heavy ploughed land. The mud stuck to my flying-boots and, still in my voluminous flying-clothes, I began to sweat with the exertion. We talked about the crash as we trudged, and we discussed how it could have happened. The idea was fixed in my mind that the crew was safe, and I almost expected to meet them walking in; I believed firmly that the miracle which sometimes happened had happened once more. I was able to ignore the fact that a Beaufighter would hit the ground at the speed of an express train.

We saw lights ahead and we went towards them. We passed a large shape, and I saw that it was a petrol tank. It was well ahead of the rest of the machine where the lights were. I knew what this meant and my heart sank. This was no ordinary forced landing; this was a serious crash. We approached the lights, and we saw that some lorries, probably the fire-tender and the ambulance, were there playing their headlights on the scene. We drew nearer and saw a semi-circle of men facing the wreck with their backs to us. As I came close I saw between two of those people, in the glare of the headlights, a mass of wreckage, and across and over it there sprawled helplessly a leg in a flying-boot. This glimpse told me the whole story, and I drew back into the darkness, murmuring mechanically to one of the men in the semi-circle who, I suppose, had helped to pull them out: 'Are they dead?' I knew what the answer was going to be. He said: 'Yes. Both dead.' I walked away into the darkness by myself, feeling a bit dizzy and trying to say a prayer.

Air Commodore RODERIC CHISHOLM CBE DSO DFC

*

A key factor in night fighting was the ground radar which led fighters towards a victim until they were within their own—very short—airborne radar range. Rotatable aerials solved the inland-looking problems of the older fixed variety. How do you rotate an aerial? Simple: you just press a button.

THE BINDERS

The chief controller of the GCI station in our sector was Squadron Leader John Lawrence Brown, a big, fleshy man with a roving eye and a rich, fruity voice, and that genial, well fed look that one usually associates with gentlemen farmers. But although Brownie—as he became known to all night fighters—liked the comforts of life he did not allow them to interfere with the job in which he was completely absorbed. Being a pilot himself he could discuss our problems knowledgeably and he was able to make constructive suggestions. One of the first was that we should visit his GCI and see for ourselves how he was trying to run his shop.

Small parties were made up on our nights off duty, and several of us at a time drove down to a remote field near the coast where 'Starlight'—the code name of our GCI—had been set up. It was not at all easy to find, and when we did get there it was not a very impressive sight. There were a few wooden huts, with some lorries scattered about, a caravan draped in a tarpaulin, and a strange contraption which looked more like a huge, flattened bird cage than an aerial array slowly revolving on its base.

We were escorted to the caravan, and we felt our way in the darkness up the steps. Inside we found Brownie seated before the control panel which looked something like a desk, and grouped around him were several airmen and airwomen, all muffled up against the cold, and all concentrating on their various tasks. A second glance around revealed that there were apparently more airwomen than airmen, and that they were an unusually attractive lot of girls, good looking and alert.

'Just like a Sultan in his harem,' Tommy whispered in my ear.

But under Brownie's guidance we soon forgot all about the beauty chorus, and we listened with the closest attention as he explained things to us. His enthusiasm was infectious, and he went carefully over everything. It was reassuring to know that our guidance from the ground was to be in the hands of such a man.

In the centre of the control desk at which Brownie sat there was a very large cathode ray tube on the face of which there had been painted the neighbouring coastline of our sector. On this tube—called the Plan Positioner Indicator, or, for short, the PPI—all aircraft coming within range of the station produced small blips which automatically marked their position on the map. The airmen and airwomen hovering around were giving readings in brisk monosyllables to others at the far end of the caravan. These, in turn, were plotting the tracks of the aircraft, juggling nimbly with navigation computers, and working out courses and speeds. Others were sitting in front of another cathode ray tube working out the height of the aircraft. The whole team was working smoothly and quietly and with an impressive absence of fuss and confusion.

In the midst of it all sat Brownie, microphone in hand, quite the genial host. Now and again he could break off from his explanations to us about what was going on to ask one of his team for a height or speed, or to pass a vector over the radio-telephone to the fighter on patrol.

We were able to see a practice interception between two of our own squadron's aircraft, and under Brownie's seemingly casual directions we watched as he brought together the two blips on the cathode ray tube. As they merged he excused himself to give the matter his undivided attention. And then from the loudspeaker in the corner the voice of the pilot of the fighter announced:

'O.K., Starlight. Contact. Thank you.'

There was a smile of the proud showman on his face as Brownie turned back to us and went on with his explanations. He showed us how friend could be distinguished from foe on the PPI, something that originated in the little mystery box we had in our aircraft which we knew as IFF.

And there were the limitations with which they were faced. Low-flying aircraft were very hard to track, and

99

high ground and other obstacles had a masking effect in a way similar to the swamping of our own AI picture from the ground returns. By the time Brownie had finished we were only too ready to overlook the occasional blunders which had been vexing us, and even to forgive being placed in front of the target instead of behind it, as had already happened more than once.

In order to maintain a complete coverage of the sky the aerial outside had to keep sweeping around in a full circle. But by pressing a simple bell-push Brownie could quickly stop or reverse the sweep and direct the aerial to any particular part of the sky on which he wanted to concentrate.

'It's quite simple,' he explained. 'The bell just signals the Binders to pedal the other way.'

He led us out of the caravan and across towards the aerial. And there in a shack underneath it we saw the Binders, anonymous and humble heroes. They were two airmen sitting on a contraption something like a tandem bicycle pedalling away to nowhere as they drove around the heavy structure of wire mesh above them. For them there was nothing but the sheer drudgery of pedalling: they could not even see the blips of the aircraft they were to help to pick up and destroy.

C. F. RAWNSLEY and ROBERT WRIGHT

*

Put on to north-bound raid 13,000 feet. Final vector 360° and buster.

Told to flash but no contact received. Starlight then told me to alter course to 350° and height 11,000 feet. While going from 13,000 to 11,000 feet a blip was picked at max. range ahead. On operator's instructions I closed in and obtained a visual at 2,500 feet range (checked on A.I. set) and about 30° up.

Identified E/A as He 111 which was flying just beneath cloud layer and occasionally going through wisps which allowed me to get within 80 yards of E/A and about 20-30 ft. beneath before opening fire.

Immediately there was a big white flash in the fuselage

centre section and black pieces flew off the fuselage. E/A went into a vertical dive to the right and about half a minute later the sky all around me was lit up by an enormous orange flash and glow. Bits of E/A were seen to be burning on the ground.

I estimated my position to be about Shaftesbury but called Harlequin and asked for a fix so that my exact position could be checked.

One He 111 destroyed.

Rounds fired 64.

from a combat report by

Squadron Leader JOHN CUNNINGHAM DSO DFC

A few explanations: 'buster' meant 'full speed', E/A was Enemy Aircraft, Starlight and Harlequin were ground control stations, and the unnamed 'operator' was Sergeant C. F. Rawnsley, author of the preceding account.

Cunningham went on to become the leading RAF night-fighter pilot of the war, bedogged by the alliterative nickname 'Cats-eyes'. This was the result of a 'cover story' released to the newspapers, attributing Cunningham's successes to his night vision, this in turn being attributed to the amount of Vitamin C he absorbed by eating (for a widely-quoted instance) raw carrots. In fact the story concealed Rawnsley and his A.I. set. The story has lasted better than the secret.

*

Gradually the night-fighters took command:

On the night of 13th March 1941, the unexpected happened. I destroyed two enemy aircraft. This was luck unbounded, and these were experiences which I knew could never be equalled. For the rest of that night it was impossible to sleep; there was nothing else I could talk about for days after; there was nothing else I could think about for weeks after.

With these victories—and even one of them would have sufficed—a great deal had suddenly become worth while, and this was success such as I had never dreamt of; it was sweet and very intoxicating. I saw my name in the papers, and the Squadron, so long in obscurity, coming into the limelight; for these were its sixth and seventh confirmed successes. It became suddenly 'a famous night-fighter squadron'. The public was let into the secret: it was equipped with Beaufighters and there were veiled allusions to a secret weapon. There was a lot of glamour and excitement attached to being a night-fighter pilot; we felt a good deal beyond ourselves.

On that night there was an almost full moon and the weather was very fine. We had been flying for more than an hour when we were put on to a bomber that was going back empty. We were overtaking fairly well, and by the time we passed over Bournemouth were about a mile behind. We closed in a bit more and Ripley, my observer, got a close radar contact over to the left. I turned a little to the left, and I could hardly believe my eyes, for there was another aircraft about a hundred yards away and on the same level. It was black and its fish-like fuselage glistened dully in the moonlight; it was unmistakably a Heinkel.

Converging rapidly, I turned to come behind and dropped below with an automatism that surprised me; my machine seemed to be on rails, so easily did it slide into position. I was afraid I would be seen in that light—and the Beaufighter would have been a sitter—but interceptions were not expected then, and the enemy gunners were not keeping a good look-out. I was able to creep up unmolested until I was within a hundred yards and forty-five degrees below. The machine looked enormous; the wings seemed to blot out the sky above me; now, a squat silhouette, it had lost its recognisable form. I saw the four rows of exhausts, each with six stubs, and now and again one of them would belch out a bigger flame than usual.

The moment had come to shoot; it was now or never. Holding my breath I eased the stick back a little and the Heinkel came down the windscreen and into the sight. It went too far and I found myself aiming above. Stick forward a bit and the sight came on it again. How ham-fisted this was! I pressed the firing-button. There was a terrific shaking and banging, and to my surprise I saw flashes appearing, as it seemed, miraculously on the shape in front of me. Pieces broke away and came back at me. I kept on firing, and it turned away to the right slowly, apparently helplessly and obviously badly damaged. My ammunition finished I drew away farther to the right. I had overshot, and I could see the Heinkel over my left shoulder still flying all right. Nothing happened, perhaps nothing was going to happen, and suddenly I thought that it was going to get away. I had had a chance, a sitter, and I had not hit hard enough. It seemed that I had succeeded in the almost impossible feat of firing two hundred 20-millimetre shells at this aircraft at point-blank range without destroying it. It had been like the crazy kitchen side-show at a fair, impossible not to hit something; but here, so I began to think, I had hit nothing vital.

And then I saw a lick of flame coming from the starboard engine. It grew rapidly, and enveloped the whole engine and soon most of the wing. The machine turned east and started to go down slowly; it looked by now like a ball of flame. We followed it down from 11,000 feet until, minutes later, it hit the sea, where it continued to burn.

It was said that the crew baled out, but none was picked up. I did not think of them any more than they probably had thought of the people they had been bombing. This kind of warfare, though in some ways cold-blooded murder, was as impersonal as it was mechanical. This was a big-game hunt, and thought was focused on personal achievement. In the aftermath it was satisfactory to know that the enemy bomber force had been reduced by one, but immediately it was the elation of personal success with neither regrets nor outraged scruples that monopolised my thoughts.

We had one or two more chases which came to nothing and, having been on patrol for three and a half hours, we went back to land. The aircraft was refuelled and re-armed, and within thirty minutes we were again at 'readiness'. It was about midnight, and although activity usually stopped by midnight, there were on that night still a few enemy bombers going back from the Midlands. We were ordered off.

A chase started soon after take-off; it went on, and I began to despair, for I knew that these bombers without their loads would be going back quickly. After nearly fifteen minutes I was told to turn back north and come home. We were then at about 10,000 feet over the sea, and there was a lane of reflected moonlight on the water stretching south to a small bank of cloud. As I started to turn left towards the north I saw far below a sight which I could hardly believe—the navigation lights of an aircraft flying south. I called up and asked if there were any friendly aircraft about, and the answer came 'No', so I made to follow the lights I had seen. Enemy aircraft had been seen before now flying home brazenly with all lights on; this perhaps was another of them.

I watched the lights intently and started to lose height, trying not to overshoot them. Then they went out and I followed blindly. The thin layer of cloud I had seen to the south intervened, and I reckoned that if the aircraft was skimming along the top, I would have a good chance of seeing it—it was tempting, day or night, to skim along just above the cloud—but I saw nothing. We were now at 5,000 feet and we went down to 4,000 where we were below cloud. As we came out into clear air, Ripley got a contact ahead and close. I started to search and soon, in that light, I saw an aircraft about 2,000 feet away and dead ahead.

I closed in quickly and, recognising it as a Heinkel, dropped below and crept up to sure firing range. Coming up I opened fire from about a hundred and fifty yards. There were flashes on the fuselage and the starboard engine, which lost a cowling and started to emit smoke and sparks. I drew away to await developments, thinking that it would be forced down at once, but instead it started to climb, making for the cloud layer not far above. Hurriedly I opened fire again, but the rear gunner, recovered by now, opened fire and red streaks came past which made me wince and break away to the left.

I followed, climbing well above so that I might see it against the cloud below. Soon I saw that about a mile ahead there was clear air, the cloud ending abruptly. This Heinkel was hard hit and its chances of getting back were, I reckoned, nil; and then I saw ahead—how far I could not judge, but it was perhaps not more than a few miles—

a vivid explosion on the sea. We went to the spot and circled, but there was nothing to be seen. I called up to report the combat and find my position, and I was surprised that we were only a few miles south of the Isle of Wight.

We went home to bed, tired after five hours' very active flying and blissfully contented. After this successful but wakeful night, I discovered that I had become, according to the more exaggerated Press accounts, a minor 'ace'.

Air Commodore RODERICK CHISHOLM CBE DSO DFC

In January, night fighters shot down three enemy aircraft; in May, they got 96.

*

If there was trouble with aircraft identification even by day, it was trebly difficult at night. Still,

SUCH THINGS HAPPEN

Ross and I were fired on by a Wellington bomber. It was a bright moonlight night and GCI had vectored us on to a 'bogey' which indicated that they were uncertain of its identity. When we got AI contact we closed cautiously. I saw the aircraft at the same time as it saw us. The night was so light and clear we had no trouble in identifying it as friendly. But I got a little too close for the liking of the bomber crew and we were greeted by a well-directed burst of fire from the tail gunner. I heard an unpleasant rattling sound as bullets bored into my aircraft. I broke away violently to the starboard, asking Ross if he was O.K. He said yes, and as nothing appeared to be seriously wrong with us we continued with our patrol. I could still faintly see the Wellington turning away towards the north and below, on the coast near Dover, there was a mass of small fires probably caused by incendiary bombs. I called control, advised them that we had intercepted a Wellington and that we had been fired on. They told us they thought the aircraft was hostile as it had dropped bombs and asked us to go and investigate again. Soon we regained contact and again as I closed, much more cautiously this time, we confirmed it was a Wellington. I called GCI and said, 'It is definitely friendly.' But still they weren't convinced because of its apparent hostile action. So I decided to shadow it as long as possible to see where it was headed. Perhaps the Germans were using a captured Wellington to fool us, but this was doubtful. It crossed the Thames estuary heading due north and after a while started to descend. It was clearly going to land at an airfield in Norfolk. Again I broke away and headed for home after advising the GCI.

Our ground crew told us there were six bullet-holes in the fuselage between Ross's position and my cockpit. One bullet had lodged in Ross's detachable chest parachute which he had put in the rack close to his seat. Our friendly bomber was certainly a most unsociable chap. We asked the 'spy' to try to track down the offending friend and next day the story came out. The Wellington had taken off from Marham, Norfolk, for a bombing raid on Boulogne. The crew had lost themselves and mistaken Dover for their target. Luckily their bombs landed in fields and only set fire to haystacks. They did, however, claim to have been attacked by a Ju 88 and to have shot him down. I felt like sending them a congratulatory message, but realised that this would be rubbing it in too much since they must already be far from popular at their own base.

Wing Commander J. R. D. BRAHAM DSO DFC AFC CD

*

Near the coast the radio voice warned me of the presence of another aircraft, saying ominously: 'You are being followed by another aircraft. Orbit once.' Without any further clue as to the identity of my shadower, I construed that it was the needle in the haystack which, in my optimism, I almost expected to find. I turned the switch that cut off all contact with the outside world so as to have uninterrupted conversation with my observer. We started to search and soon got a contact. After a few changes of course, we were going west and were closing in comfortably. Then I saw a small indistinct shape, barely a silhouette, about 2,000 feet away; for there was a half moon.

We had found to our cost that the enemy were, by then, keeping a good look-out in moonlight; they had been able to get away several times, diving as the fighter closed in or opening fire unexpectedly early. I wanted no mistake this time, and with my eyes glued to this almost shapeless patch of darkness I came in fast, all set to fire as soon as I was satisfied that it was what I expected it to be, hostile. The shape became more distinct; it had all the squatness of the Heinkels I had seen before; there was no doubt in my mind: it was a Heinkel. My approach was not seen, and I was able to close well in before opening fire. I gave a burst and I saw hits on the starboard wing. With another there was a big flash on the port engine; the port wheel came down. It was still flying, but probably, damaged as it was, it would not get home. We had only to follow, reload the guns and finish it off, if it had not already fallen into the sea. The experimental graticule pattern in the gun-sight which I was using had done nothing to improve my shooting; it had perhaps made it worse.

I was overtaking all the time, and I overshot, pulling away to the right. The damaged machine turned left towards the sea and across the moon. As the moon caught it I saw something that I would not accept; that tail was familiar. Was it familiar? A thought came to my mind, and I smothered it. It was not possible; it was unthinkable. There was no question that this was not an enemy aircraft; I had been told it was hostile. But had I? One had to make up one's mind in moonlight quickly and from a long way off; otherwise the chance would be lost. And once one's mind was made up there was no drawing back; the rear gunner might shoot first, and his aim would be deliberate. Perhaps it was not a Heinkel; it might be a Junkers 88; I had never seen one of them at night. But there was the shape of that tail, and back came the awful doubt.

All this flashed through my mind, and then I called up, as was the normal procedure, to report that I had had a combat. The answer to my excited message was calm and there were no congratulations. The voice said: 'That was probably a friendly aircraft. Follow it and report its position. How badly damaged is it?' I felt as if I had taken an ice-cold plunge. The bottom fell out of my world. I knew now why the tail of that aircraft had looked familiar. The two men inside it were on my side and I had probably killed them; probably they were from my squadron. John Cunningham and Edward Crew were flying; it might be either of them.

'Why the hell didn't you tell me that it was a "friendly" which was following me?'

'We could not get in touch with you.' Of course they could not get in touch with me when it was too late. Why could they not have warned me at once, when they told me I was being followed? What I had done scarcely bore contemplation.

We followed the crippled aircraft, with one wheel hanging grotesquely down, for four or five minutes as it turned slowly from south to east and then towards north. And then, against a darker part of the sky, I lost sight of it. That this aircraft was still flying did not mean that the pilot was still alive; damaged aircraft can fly on with no one in control for some time. But there was a little hope. Then on the radio I heard:

'One engine is still working. They hope to make their base.' That meant that the pilot was still alive.

'Follow close and report your position if you can.'

'I have lost sight of him and I do not know my position.'

'The crew is going to bale out. Is it over the sea or land?'

'I do not know.'

I was instructed to return to base; there was nothing I could do now. The sight, some minutes later, of a fire on the ground suggested that the machine had crashed on land, and that the crew, had it been possible to bale out, was safe. I reported what I had seen and went home, my mind a seething, unhappy turmoil. I had done a terrible thing. Was it possible, I wondered, that the crew was safe and sound? It would have been a miracle if neither member had been touched.

It seemed to take an age to fly the eighty miles to base. I landed, taxied in, got out and stumbled towards the 'readiness' room. I pushed the door open and went in, blinking and dazzled by the lights. Someone—I forget who it was —was lying on a bed; he was the only chap left there. He said sleepily: 'Hullo.' I said: 'I've shot down a Beau,' and he said: 'God! I'm sorry. Bloody bad luck.' That, I felt was decent of him. I would not have been surprised had he said something like 'I never want to speak to you again.' A stupid idea, but that is how I felt.

Air Commodore RODERICK CHISHOLM CBE DSO DFC

The Beaufighter crew survived. They turned out—perhaps inevitably, in that small, select company—to be friends of Chisholm's.

*

I didn't want to join the Air Force;
I didn't want my bollocks shot away.
I'd rather hang around
Piccadilly Underground,
Living on the earnings of a high-born lady . . .

*

. . . WILL REPORT BY 0001 HOURS . . .

Night travelling in England was a nerve-racking experience. All stations were blacked out and, except for a shaded light over the nameboard, there was no indication of where you were. At some stations, a voice speaking the dialect of whatever area you happened to be in called the name but, as we were unable to understand these blurred and unintelligible announcements, they might as well have been calling in Chinese or Czech. If no one in the carriage knew the locality, it entailed someone getting out and racing along to see just where you were. As the train stopped only a minute or so, this could be hard on the nerves, particularly if the scout came panting back to announce: 'This is it!' As our train stopped at every station it was 11 p.m. when we finally arrived.

We were met by an English flight-sergeant and the usual RAF blitzwagon and driven to the air force station. It was so dark that we were unable to see what kind of place it was. A supper was waiting and after this was consumed we were conducted to an igloo hut with a promise that accommodation would be sorted out in the morning.

One very obvious feature of the place was the almost continuous roar of plane engines. Like lions roaring, the stillness of the night would be shattered by the sudden starting up of a motor, closely followed by a second one. These would run in unison on a gradually increasing note, fall away, and start again, then sometimes splutter to a stop. We soon found that this was a diapason that was to become a part of our lives, sometimes muted, sometimes ear-shattering, day and night.

We were so tired, that despite the lack of luxury we slept like logs. In the early grey of the morning we woke to the din of returning planes. Mac querulously complained, 'Can't they show some consideration and cut out some of the bloody racket?'

That morning we were paraded first before the adjutant, a dapper, middle-aged squadron leader who welcomed us to the squadron and informed us that it had a long and illustrious history having been formed during the First World War and he felt sure we would worthily uphold its traditions. He further stated that the aircraft we were to fly in were Wellingtons and that on the previous night the squadron had been on a strike into Germany. Preliminary checks had shown it to be a successful one.

He then handed us over to the gunnery officer, a thin-faced flight lieutenant with a DFC. He didn't prove as matey as the adjutant and informed us, in no uncertain terms, what was expected of us and even made an inspection in which he made several biting criticisms as to our general military appearance. Blondie growled, 'I don't think I'm going to like this bastard.'

Our quarters were Nissen huts. Smithy, Hally, Blondie, Smiler and myself found quarters in one. At lunchtime some of the crews that had been on the previous night's operations appeared. They looked a tousle-haired, taciturn group, eating their meal in silence, although now and then one would make a remark regarding the night's operation.

'Glum lot of bastards,' said Hally.

It was not till later we realised the reason for the silence

110

—four planes had failed to return and two dozen faces had disappeared from the mess.

After lunch, five of us cadged a ride and went out to hangars to look at the planes in which we were to fly. They appeared to be solid kites in comparison to the ones in which we had previously flown—two-engined black-fuselaged monsters that squatted in their bays like huge black crows. The Wellington was an unusual bomber; its fuselage, instead of being steel, was made of ribbed, latticed wood covered with fabric. Its crew comprised six men: pilot, co-pilot, navigator, wireless operator, front and rear gunners.

We palled up with some of the ground crew who were working on one of the planes in the hangar and they let us look it over, first warning us to be careful not to step off the catwalk leading down to the rear turret as one mis-step would mean a foot through the cloth covering and this was a chargeable offence.

Next morning we were allocated to crews. Kiwi and I were told we were flying with a Flight-Sergeant Snowden. The rest of the boys went into various crews. Blondie and Hally, like ourselves, were lucky enough to be together, but the rest were placed singly. We were amused to find there was some competition to obtain our services, this being due to the idea that because we came from Australia, the land of great open spaces, we must all be crack shots. One WAG informed Hally and Blondie that they would make tophole gunners with all the practice they had had shooting wallabies and kangaroos. We thought he was being facetious but found that this was a generally accept-ted idea.

After lunch in the mess, a tall, fair-haired pilot came up, introduced himself as Walter Snowden, and said, 'I believe you're in my crew.' He had a clipped, incisive speech, his handshake was firm and I liked him from the start. I called Kiwi over and after introductions he said, 'You'd better come and meet the rest of the crew.' He led us to a group of three airmen and said, 'This is Williams our dicky pilot, Stan Jones our WAG, and Bill Ninnes our navigator.'

Williams was a Welshman with a big toothed grin, Jones a little sharp-faced Cockney, and Ninnes, a tall, thin bloke,

111

almost as dark as our skipper was fair. He spoke the same good English. We afterwards found the skipper was a solicitor and Ninnes was doing an engineering course at Oxford. He and the skipper had been close friends in civvy life and were inseparable companions on the squadron. There was an awkward air of reserve between the six of us, mainly because we didn't seem to be able to find a common subject of interest. Jones broke the ice a little by suggesting a trip out to see our kite, S for Sugar.

We then learnt each aeroplane on a squadron had a particular letter of the alphabet which coincided with some well-known word, i.e., A for Apple, F for Freddie, C for Charlie, S for Sugar, etc. Jones explained the crew had done only one operation and that was a pamphlet run over France. This was a way of breaking crews in before sending them on the hazardous German trips. Generally they were uneventful ops in which, apart from some flak, nothing much happened. However, on this journey a surprise burst had severely wounded the rear gunner who was still in hospital. The front gunner had broken a leg the previous week in a game of football, hence the two replacements.

S for Sugar was a comparatively new machine, her paper run into France having been her first trip. 'Not that they last too bloody long,' said Jones. 'There isn't one kite on the squadron with more than twenty ops up.'

'Why don't they do more than twenty ops?' Kiwi enquired in all innocence.

'They get the "chop",' our companion said grimly.

JOHN BEEDE

*

Who'll fly a Wimpey, who'll fly a Wimpey,
Who'll fly a Wimpey over Germany?
I, said the Pilot, I, said the Pilot,
I'll fly a Hercules Mark Three.

I'll set the course, sir, I'll set the course, sir,
I'll set the course on my little csc.
And if you keep to the course that I have set, sir,
Then we will fly over Germany.

I'll shoot 'em down, sir, I'll shoot 'em down, sir,
I'll shoot 'em down if they don't shoot at me.
Then we'll go to the Ops Room and shoot a horrid line, sir,
And then we'll all get the DFC.

I'll press the tit, sir, I'll press the tit, sir,
I'll press the tit at the first flak we see.
'Cos I don't like the flak, sir, I don't like the flak, sir,
I want nothing but plenty of height for me.

How is the Met, sir, how is the Met, sir.
How is the Met?—it looks very dud to me.
Let's scrub it out, sir, let's scrub it out, sir,
'Cos I've got a date fixed with my popsie.

*

*Bomber Command was going through a difficult time.
Facing the same basic night-navigation problems as the
Luftwaffe, it had fewer and slower aircraft and at least
twice the distance to fly to reach Germany as German
bombers, based in France, flew to British targets. Not
every crew or commander, counting the losses, was prepared to believe*

THE CAMERA NEVER LIES

When the statistics for three whole months had been com-
piled, a summary of them was sent to Bomber Command.
It showed that out of the 151 flashlight photographs that
had been attempted in three months by the bombers of
Nos 3 and 5 Groups, not more than 21 showed the target
area. And in one case a crew had estimated its position
as within fifty miles of a certain pinpoint when in fact it
was a hundred miles further east.

To Pat and Bernard, these facts and figures were heart-
rending, chiefly because they seemed to show that Bomber
Command was concerned with the wrong issue. The reason
the photographs were being taken was to help with damage assessment, but their value was much higher in bringing
to light errors of navigation. The crews were being asked to

do the absolutely impossible; to navigate accurately from almost double the heights they had been trained at; heights to which they were forced up by anti-aircraft fire, and from which a momentary glimpse of a river winding far below might just as well be the Meuse as the Rhine.

The urgency of the need to improve matters would not be realised unless the whole painful situation were brought to light; but it was hardly to be expected that everyone would take this objective view. During the spring of 1941, as the stark facts began to be known throughout Bomber Command, various people reacted in various ways. The intelligence officers who were the first to see the bombers' night photographs had to decide whether to draw attention to failures of navigation, and it was not an easy decision. Some of the crews who were told of their errors frankly disbelieved the photographs; while others took them very seriously and got worried and depressed.

Perhaps it is hardly surprising that night photography was not very popular with the crews. Although some of the men were only too pleased to be able to check their results with a view to doing better next time, others felt strongly that they had quite enough to do, and enough risks to take, without learning a lot of extra drill (not to mention carting about a whacking great cylinder which might explode at the wrong moment), and filling in a lot of extra forms, and having to fly straight and level when they ought to be weaving. And what was it all in aid of? You might just as well have a malicious snooper on board, to tell tales to the intelligence officers if everything hadn't gone right.

At higher levels also there were some who could not bring themselves to face the facts, and others who faced them and were deeply disturbed. At one Group headquarters, the intelligence officers found it was best not to say anything about the photographs which did not show the target area; and at another an officer who passed to his chief an interpretation showing that an attack had missed its mark found it later on his desk with scrawled across it in red: 'I do not accept this report.' But such a reaction seems less unreasonable if it is regarded in the light of a long-standing attitude towards photography within Bomber Command. Photographs were considered as a useful adjunct to bombing, but not a vital necessity. The camera was regarded somewhat as a motorist regards his mileage gauge. It's nice to know how far you've been, and sometimes very useful too. But you certainly do not expect your mileage gauge to turn round and accuse you of having lost your way almost every time you've been out. When the photographs began to do precisely this, it was very natural that many of those whose work it affected jumped to the comforting conclusion that something must have been wrong with the camera or the photographs or the man who wrote the report.

CONSTANCE BABINGTON SMITH

Even ignoring radar/radio navigation aids that provided the real solution, it is not always remembered how the sheer increase in speed has made air navigation easier. An unexpected 20-mph sidewind would blow an 180-mph Wellington 66 miles off course over the 600-mile trip to Berlin. A jet bomber at 600 mph would be only 20 miles off.

*

But even before radar aids, there were still

BRIGHT IDEAS MARK II

It was soon after taking over 5 Group that I first came in contact with the operational research scientists, with whom I was later to enjoy a close and fruitful connexion when I was Commander-in-Chief of Coastal Command. I often look back with some amusement upon my first encounter with a representative of that excellent body of men, Mr G. A. Roberts, with whom I have had the pleasure of working in different fields since he first came up to my headquarters at Grantham in 1941. I had become impressed with the extent to which the terrific belt of searchlights and flak stretching from the Zuider Zee southwards weighed upon the unquenchable spirits of my crews. It really was a beastly thing to get through, and the impression had taken firm hold in the group that a few beer bottles tossed overboard had a disturbing effect on the accuracy of the searchlights. The boys had convinced themselves that the major villains of the piece were a number of 'master' searchlights, radar-controlled and with a sinister blue tinge, which were always the first to pick them up and upon which scores of other lights then concentrated; and nothing would persuade them that an empty bottle had not some effect in 'foxing' the master light. A few empty bottles had therefore become part of the battle equipment of the rear gunner in his cold and lonely turret. I found it extremely hard to believe that there was really anything in this, but told Roberts on no account to pour scorn on the idea—even if there was nothing whatever in it, the boys thought there was, and it gave them a warm feeling.

Robert attended several interrogations of crews returning from Germany and played up well, showing no incredulity at the stories of the way the master lights had faltered and fallen away in the face of the faithful beer bottle. This rather Heath-Robinson counter-measure no doubt was relegated to obscurity by the later development of 'window', but to the end of my time in 5 Group the beer bottle remained a highly-regarded piece of operational equipment.

Marshal of the RAF SIR JOHN SLESSOR GCB DSO MC

Some cranks, and a few wise men, send in suggestions for winning the war. One correspondent has gone so far as to propose that we drop bombs down the throat of Vesuvius' and thus 'explode Southern Italy'. The same idea has come from educated people, in South Africa, Australia and America. The thought is painful to those of us who dream of returning some day to the enchanting coast that runs south from Naples.

Pilots who find their tasks monotonous might like the plan of another correspondent who asks for a 'fleet of fighter planes, thirty strong' which would pretend to 'run away from the enemy'. While pretending, they would 'squirt out from the rear of each aircraft a fine spray of chloroform or the strongest narcotic possible.' The trusting German pilots 'would fly into this strata and so lose control of their machines.'

116

There is another plan, to drop 'enormous quantities of sticky stuff, like treacle, in front of advancing German troops'. If this failed to stop them, 'coils of barbed wire could then be dropped, to trip and entangle them'. Another patriot suggests that 'you can buy a kind of open-work dishcloth with a wide mesh for washing greasy dishes'. These could be 'scattered among the enemy formations to entangle their airscrews'. A less gentleman-like suggestion is that 'long projecting knives of razor-sharpness' should be fitted to the undercarriages of obsolete and unemployed planes: thus equipped, 'they could chase the enemy airman who baled out and fly over him in such a way that the knives would cut the parachute cord, thus causing the Hun to drop to the earth with a bump'.

A correspondent from Durban proposes that 'millions of snakes' should be shipped from South Africa and released from our aircraft 'on dark nights only', over German towns. He also suggest that 'millions of cabbage leaves' should be steeped 'in a deadly poison' and dropped among the livestock in the German and Italian fields. The same man from Durban wrote, 'The war will finish 2.30 p.m. 4th May 1945, with Britain on top.'

HECTOR BOLITHO

Perhaps the Durban correspondent knew a thing or two after all.

And meantime, Bomber Command went on with what aircraft, aids and men it already had.

*

LACK OF MORAL FIBRE

If possible, with the passing of time, Mac had become more doleful. He seemed to hold me responsible for the fact that he was on the squadron and would come to my bed and bleat out his fears. He was a coward, he declared. It was impossible, he said, for anyone to complete a tour.

In the afternoon, Mac sat on my bed. His voice was querulous, his jaws quivered, there were bags under this eyes and he looked more like a melancholy bloodhound than ever. 'This bloody racket,' he declared, 'is just plain suicide. 'I'm going to the MO to tell him I'm not going to fly again. They can classify me as LMF if they bloody well like but, in five years' time, I'll be alive sunbaking at Bondi while the rest of this outfit's bones are bleaching somewhere in Europe. What's an LMF anyway? Did you know two weeks ago? If you told someone in Australia you had got an LMF they'd congratulate you. They'd think it was a bloody decoration. Everyone is packing them, only they're too bloody frightened to say so.'

Consciously or subconsciously we felt his piking would cast a reflection on the rest of the Australians in the squadron. So I did nothing to help him.

Talking to Hally I said, 'I know I pack them while I'm out in the blackness and I feel that, although you talk tough, you do too.'

He was completely frank. 'My bloody oath I do, but I'd sooner be dead than let anyone know.'

'Supposing,' I continued, 'a man packs them 1,000 times, perhaps 10,000 times more than we do. If you were in his shoes, how would you face up to it?'

'I'm buggered if I know—but if I was as bad as that I'd get off ops.'

'That's the way I think Mac is.'

'Then, tell the silly bastard to give it away,' he said, 'but don't worry me about him. I've enough troubles of my own.'

I thought, 'Mac'll raise the subject again and I'll not only advise him, I'll take him up to the MO.'

We were both on the battle order that night. We sat together in silence going out in the bus. As we got out I gave him a reassuring pat and said, 'We'll talk about it tomorrow.' I couldn't see his expression in the glow of the little blue light but he gave a sepulchral laugh and said, 'Perhaps there mightn't be any tomorrows for either of us.'

It was a hell of an op. The weather was lousy and Jerry turned it on from the time we crossed the coast and kept it up all the way to the target and back. It was seven hours of hell and suspense.

As we came back over our coast Kiwi said, 'What a

bloody night! I'm completely fugged. Will I be glad to get into bed.'

Somehow I couldn't get Mac out of my mind. This, I thought, will be the end. He'll give it away after this.

Hally was already in when we arrived back. He said, 'What a bloody op. I was beginning to wonder if you'd made it.'

We searched around to see who was missing. He said, 'I can't see Mac.' We stayed long after the time limit for the plane and crew to arrive. The bus waited until the occupants and driver grew impatient. After sundry tootings and irritable queries, someone said, 'Let the silly bastards walk.' The driver called, 'Are you blokes coming?' Hally said, 'No.'

As we walked back a new day was breaking. The mists were rising from the flat, grey countryside and a cold breeze from the east blew in our faces. I didn't sleep for a while, wondering and worrying how the reluctant gunner had met his end, three miles up in the blackness of the night. Fatigue finally took over and I fell into an uneasy slumber.

JOHN BEEDE

Oh, a little bit of Heaven fell from out the sky one day;
It landed in the ocean, oh, so *very* far away.
And when the Air Force saw it, it looked so effing bare,
They said 'That's what we're looking for, we'll put the
squadron there.'

DESERT SONG

In Middle East a typical RAF Other Rank had enjoyed a variety of experience quite unlike anything that might have come his way previously. He was with a body of men who had little but their work to occupy their minds, who were divorced from all the normal amenities of life, and who had somehow to make the best of it. He was in surroundings which lacked any of the usual landmarks, where often for miles in every direction there were no houses, no trees, no hills and no roads. He was on a ration scale which allowed for liberal quantities of bully-beef and tea, but which made few concessions to the degree of latitude. He was rarely given enough water; sometimes the ration was only half a gallon a day per head for all purposes, including cooking and washing, and even this meagre dole could not always be guaranteed. He was not only away from home, but, except for the postal services, completely cut off from his family circle. And there were no women.

Service in other overseas commands could embody many of these disadvantages, but seldom all of them at once. An airman had to become more and more mobile as retreat and advance swayed him to and fro across the Desert; and that meant a sacrifice of even the few personal belongings which had served to remind him that there was, somewhere at least, another kind of existence.

By the end of February 1941 the airman would have seen enough of the Desert to last him all his life. He would probably have arrived in Alexandria, and might have stayed a few days in a transit camp outside the port. He would have seen very little of the town apart from the NAAFI, a few shops and the esplanade, whose concrete sea walls suggested some eastern Blackpool.

A photograph of himself, in strange clothes and unfamiliar surroundings, must of course be sent home. There were plenty of people to remind him of this as of everything else. The eagerness of the street hawkers melted away excuses; those who managed to fend off the boot-blacks fell prey to the trinket-sellers.

Posting, perhaps to a fresh unit, often provided fresh surprises. With men in such short supply, squadrons fought to get anyone they could, and the personnel officers, notoriously incorruptible, were hard put to it to maintain their reputation. But anyone who thought that last-minute changes and unfamiliar conditions were but passing phases was due for a succession of further setbacks. Loaded on to the back of a three-ton truck, he would soon be on the road out to El Daba, his view of the fig plantations obscured by a cloud of sand, which, faithful as a shadow, would follow him closely all the way. Seasick after the road journey, he would arrive at Daba like a man stepping out of a boat after a stormy Channel crossing. There, with a mug of sweet, hot, NAAFI tea, he would try to forget the road, winding away into the distance like a tarmac snake, undulating over the surface of the Desert.

He would see Mersa Matruh, and would become familiar with the 'Ship Inn'; and perhaps there would be time for a bathe in the clear blue water of the lagoon. Then he would take the road to Sidi Barrani, where uplands parody green fields, and herds of goats nibble near the side of the road. And so onwards through the solitude of Halfaya Pass, where 'the carved brown edge of Libya stood up from the dismal levels like a coast, as Doughty had once seen the coast of Harra riding high upon the plain'.

He would be introduced to his new aerodrome, a patch of Desert flatter than usual, cleared of stones, where tents and caravans spread out in imitation of a country fair.

Christmas at Sidi Haneish found a chronicler who gives a faithful picture of one of the brighter periods. His account is quoted at length.

'Sidi Haneish lay at the top of an escarpment, and was exposed to every wind that blew. From this drome "Imshi" Mason, "Nobby" Clark and "Judy" Garland made daily sorties against the Italians. Taking off at dawn, the formations of Hurricans roared away, leaving a trail of black exhaust fumes in the cold winter air. The ground crews eagerly awaited their return, and there were smiles of satisfaction on the faces of those crews who recognised their returning pilots doing a victory roll over the 'drome, thus notifying the squadron of their success. Not a day passed but the jubilant pilots gave vent to their satisfaction at besting the Axis by shooting up the 'drome and doing victory rolls. To this 'drome many pilots limped home with the fuselage of their kites riddled with bullet holes, but they gave far more than they ever received.

'A great amount of captured war material found its way from the forward areas to the 'drome. Motor-cycles, staff cars, transport of every description, including push-bikes, were soon in evidence. Flight-Sergeants would go their rounds in Italian staff cars, whilst the Commanding Officer, "Paddy" Dun, could be seen calling at the Orderly Room riding a brand new motor-bike. Soon all ranks, from the lowest erk upwards, had obtained some sort of enemy transport to propel them over the bumpy desert scrub that

121

surrounded the 'drome. Ground crews, who walked from kite to kite doing their various jobs, were looked upon as having their fingers in. Foraging parties returned with rifles, ammunition, Breda guns, and all the paraphernalia of war that the fleeing Italians had left behind.'

RODERIC OWEN

The 'loot' had come from General Wavell's successful attack along the North African coast. But then, on 6th April, the German army and Luftwaffe entered the Greek-Italian war—which had been going for some months and which the Greeks looked like winning. Trying to reinforce the Greeks, Wavell had to cancel his African assault and split his forces yet again. For the RAF it was a familiar story: a handful of outdated aircraft tossed hastily into the path of the Luftwaffe storm. It was a short war.

LAST FLIGHT FROM MENIDI

'Evacuation started on Tuesday 22nd April 1941 from Menidi. The 23rd dawned with Fred Archer, Corporal Dickenson, Porky Blyth, a small Flight-Sergeant Fitter (I can't remember his name) and myself left as a sort of Demolition party. The Jerries completed the job for us and left only a very-much-shot-up short-nose Blenheim, port cowling missing, oil leaking out, and some cockpit instruments missing. As well as a very flat tyre it was full of holes. Also the cockpit hood would not slide shut.

'As time went on in between Me 109 raids we seriously considered trying to get this kite into the air. During a lull in the proceedings a pilot appeared who had previously been shot down and said that if we could service the Blenheim up to a point, he would get it and us into the air.

'One thing I remember very clearly is a great hoarding carrying a poster of "Vote for General Metaxas" slap bang in the line of take-off and it presented a problem. Late in the afternoon we all scrambled into the Blenheim, now capable of flight. Porky Blyth was in the turret, Fred Archer in the bomb-well, and Corporal Dickenson somewhere in the nether regions. Myself, in the nose complete with instructions as to the course and colours of the day (which I made a complete balls of).

122

'We ran up the engines that grunted and groaned, the wing flapped and we charged at the image of the General on the hoarding. I swear to this day that we passed through his left ear-hole (if you remember he died shortly afterwards). We took off during a raid on the port of Athens but they were too busy to bother with us.

'We wallowed along at sea level partly from choice and partly from circumstances, and as the shipping was pretty active I fired the colours of the day at a destroyer and was greeted by a very fine burst of naval ack-ack and some unprintable abuse from the pilot (I had got the colours mixed up).

'We steered by visual map-reading, by spotting the islands en route and by the sun (the compass was U/S), and finally we located Crete with a very much overheated engine owing no doubt to the oil leak.

'After cruising around for a little time we spotted Heraklion strip and prepared to come in (downwind, I think) only to see a perishing clot in a steam-roller systematically rolling the surface. When he saw us he nipped away smartly, leaving us and the roller to fight it out.

'We got down after a fashion, churned off the runway and came to an ungraceful stop in the grass and shrubs at the end of the runway.

'After getting out gingerly we dashed off into the rocks as some flipping Huns decided to have a look more closely at the strip.

'The pilot and I some time later set fire to the A/C as it was U/S and the Jerry was now very obviously in charge of the situation.

'One thing I always think about: not one of us had the faintest idea whether we had enough petrol for the trip. It wasn't even checked as far as I know.'

LAC L. ROBINSON quoted by SIR PHILIP JOUBERT

*

Crete, already dominated by the Luftwaffe, now based little more than 100 miles away, was invaded by air and sea on 19th May.

At the beginning of the battle there were still three aircraft left serviceable on the airfield. There is some doubt as to whether they were three Gladiators, or two Gladiators and a Hurricane; but there is complete agreement that so long as they lasted they did wonders. One South African sergeant took the air alone against ten Messerschmitts, and broke up their formation; he landed all right, but that was his machine's last sortie. The people of Heraklion tell of the Hurricane pilot, that when at last he was shot down he descended safely by parachute, and then gave it in token of gratitude to one of the churches, from which it was afterwards removed by the Germans.

There was apparently some doubt at Air Headquarters in the Middle East of the conditions obtaining. Long after the place was invested and under small arms fire at short range, aircraft landed on three separate occasions expecting to be refuelled and rearmed. It would then fall to some unlucky Jock to make the hazardous trip across the open to the aircraft to tell the pilot what was the real situation. On one occasion the refuelling of a Hurricane was actually achieved under the friendly lee of an 'I' tank, but the tail assembly was so shot about in the process that it could not take off. Jim Donaldson made a spectacular dash on a motor-cycle across the bullet-swept aerodrome to warn a Hurricane, and this was the only aircraft that, having landed, succeeded in getting away again. It was luckier than Donaldson: he crashed into a bomb crater on the way back, and spent the next few weeks in hospital.

BERNARD FERGUSSON

In the battle for the airfield the RAF groundcrews, left behind to refuel and re-arm visiting fighters, borrowed small arms and fought as infantry. Crete was lost, but the German airborne forces were cut up so badly that they were not available for the Russian campaign. Indeed, they never did another major assault.

*

Over Britain, the German bombers—still uncertain that the RAF had airborne radar—tried to cut their losses by choosing the worst weather for attack. This only gave greater opportunity to the third force involved: gravity, dubbed by some crews 'Sir Isaac' after its discoverer, Isaac Newton.

THE KNIGHT HE COMETH

Some weeks later, on the 23rd of May, the Germans looked at their weather reports and decided to have another try. It was as dank and as horrible a day as it was possible for the English spring to produce, with weeping clouds dragging right down over the hills and layered above right up to twenty thousand feet.

At four o'clock in the afternoon we scraped off after them into the drizzle and set course for Swanage. The earth was gone in a flash, and we were alone in the centre of a ball of white emptiness. Only the needles of the instruments of the blind-flying panel could tell us what was happening: air speed, height, rate of climb, altitude, direction. Without them we were anywhere and nowhere, and we had to believe them or perish. We were still, floating motionless in a void, going neither up nor down, until we looked at the instruments.

Calling Starlight, John received an answer in the reassuring voice of Keith Geddes, who was now on a rest from operational flying and acting as a controller at the GCI. Keith gave us a lead to a quick and easy stern chase, and very soon John had a Heinkel in sight a thousand yards ahead. And almost immediately it was obvious to us that the crew of that aircraft were not going to be caught napping.

The Heinkel banked steeply over to the left and came running back at us, the gunners firing broadsides as they flashed past only a hundred yards away on the beam. John had the Beaufighter already staggering around after them, the force of the turn pressing me down outrageously into my seat. But this German pilot knew what he was about, and he had already faded into the mist before we were around. I pushed my head down into the visor, but my eyes had been so dazzled by the glare outside that nearly a minute passed before I could make out anything on the

125

face of the cathode ray tubes; and by that time there was nothing worth seeing.

'More help, please,' John appealed to Starlight.

It was acutely embarrassing to hear my failure broadcast in such a way, but Starlight were still coping with things, and they had our customer tracked to the north of us, near Shaftesbury. They passed to us more vectors, and another chase followed. Our luck was in, and again John caught sight of the Heinkel. I tried resolutely to keep my head down on the AI set, but sitting in a ring-side seat with champions in the lists and not watching what was happening was more than I could endure. And the pilot of that Heinkel was a champion. Then suddenly I remembered the sun-glasses I always carried for daylight practices. The pull of gravity was viciously building up again as I groped in my pockets, but finally I got the glasses on. I looked out just in time to see the Heinkel flash past, heeling over at a staggering angle, with the gunners still blazing away, wasting their ammunition. John was holding his fire, saving his ammunition until he could be sure of getting in a lethal shot.

I twisted quickly back on to the set, and this time the blip showed up clearly as soon as I whipped off the glasses. The other aircraft had straightened up, apparently thinking he had thrown us off. I wondered what his feelings were and if he was beginning to despair when we reappeared behind him a few minutes later. He certainly showed no signs of any panic for he immediately repeated his sound tactics of turning in to our attack.

But this time John was already turning inside him, determined not to be thrown off. The turns steepened until the Heinkel appeared to be almost upside down over our heads. The effects of the 'G' were becoming intolerable as the duel developed into a grim winding match, a term John always used to describe two aircraft trying to out-turn each other. My eyeballs were dragging at their sockets, and my neck muscles were aching with the sheer effort it took to try and hold up my head. Over the inter-come I could hear John's breathing becoming laboured as he relentlessly lugged those tons of metal around the sky.

Finding that he could not out-turn us, the German began to twist and dive. I kept losing sight of him under the wing, and then he would reappear on the opposite track, flashing past at seemingly impossible angles. It was a contest between masters of flying, but the pace was becoming too hot to last. I began to wonder which of the two would be the first to crack, and whether it would be machine or man.

But a third champion had slipped by now into the lists. That sinister Black Knight Sir Isaac was standing quietly waiting for one of his human adversaries to over-reach himself so that he, too, could join in and make it a three-cornered contest. And the way things were going he would not have long to wait.

The whole fuselage of the Beaufighter was shaking and the engines were howling as the airspeed steadily climbed. The needles of the altimeter raced backwards around the dial as we ran out of feet; and the blind-flying panel had long since gone crazy. The artificial horizon had given up trying and was sulking in one corner. Things were happening altogether too fast.

'Hm . . . this isn't good enough,' John said very quietly, talking half to himself. He went through a little soliloquy as he calmly and deliberately sorted out the outrageous story that the instruments were trying to tell him. 'Now . . . let me see . . . left bank . . . that's better . . .'

The Beaufighter lurched over drunkenly, and peculiar things happened to its trim. The floor re-established itself in a position that was totally different from where I had supposed it should be. But now things began to quieten down, and as we swung back on to what must have been an even keel I had a clear picture of the Heinkel as it flashed past in full plain view, heading straight downwards.

'If I'd only brought my camera,' I commented.

'A fine time to start worrying about cameras!' John snapped with justifiable asperity.

It needed only a quick glance at the AI set for me to see how horribly close we were to the ground, and I did not need to look at the altimeter to see what it was showing. We were over high ground rising in places to nine hundred

127

feet. As I watched the blip from the other aircraft it raced swiftly up the shortened trace and was swallowed in those menacing ground returns.

'More help, please, 'John appealed again.

But Starlight could not give us any further help as the blip from the customer had faded from their tube.

I was feeling quite exhausted as I searched for our homing beacon on the AI set and guided John back to Middle Wallop. He felt his way down through the cloud and finally broke out into the welcome reality of a dripping landscape, thankful for the relief after two and a half hours of argument with the staring—and often angrily glaring—dials of his instrument panels.

And then we were told that our adversary had also seen the blessed earth again, although it could only have been for a brief, horrifying moment. The German was still diving almost vertically in a last desperate bid for escape when he broke cloud a few hundred feet above that unexpectedly high ground of the sodden slopes of Cranbourne Chase. He must have failed by only a few feet to pull out in time; and close to the lonely crossroads of Alvediston there was found the wreckage of the Heinkel with what was left of that spirited pilot and his crew.

Our Intelligence people discovered that the pilot—Hauptmann Langar—was the Commanding Officer of the proving, or development, unit of the famous K. Gr. 100. Since John had not fired a single shot, it had indeed been a match between champions. John later confirmed that his air speed indicator was reading three hundred and forty miles an hour when he broke off, a speed that was decidedly high for the Beaufighter and under those conditions.

C. F. RAWNSLEY and ROBERT WRIGHT

*

K. Gr. 100 was the crack Luftwaffe 'Pathfinder' group charged with going in first to mark the target with incendiaries. To get there, its aircraft flew along radio beams. To combat them, the RAF used not only night fighters, but 'radio counter-measures', otherwise

What, in simple terms, is a radio beam? The answer to this question needs to be known if this, the opening round of the radio war, is to be understood. A radio beam is analogous to two parallel and slightly over-lapping searchlight beams. A man walking across the path of these two beams would be illuminated by one, then by both and then by the second. If the searchlights were transmitting not light but radio waves, and if the man had a radio receiver tuned to them, he would hear one, then both and then the second, as he moved across their path. Suppose that the first was turned on for a short period and turned off for a long period, while the other was on during that same long period and off for the short period—that the transmissions were in fact of interlocking dots and dashes—then the observer crossing the paths would hear first dots, next a constant note and finally dashes; and by contriving always to hear a constant note he would be following the path of what is known as a radio beam. Properly directed, this beam could provide a pre-determined track to a target.

RCM began by using radio-therapy apparatus taken from hospitals, not, as was the common belief, on account of the help it might give the bombers, but because it was the only apparatus available which could in any way interfere with the beams. It was re-installed in certain key targets, and was turned on when the beams were laid on them. Ground listening stations were opened to watch constantly for the beams, and their detection became the signal for the despatch of aircraft fitted with the necessary radio receivers to find and fly down them, thus detecting the enemy's target intentions early.

Special gear for transmitting dots or dashes on the beam frequencies was designed, manufactured and installed at strategic positions. It could produce spurious constant notes in a nearby beam, and the bomber pilot, hearing a constant note composed of enemy dots and our dashes, or vice-versa, would wrongly believe himself to be on the beam. Known to the public as bending the beam, this counter-measure was sometimes highly successful, and it led to a general discrediting of bombing on these beams.

To make beam flying more unpopular, it 'leaked' out that our fighters had been equipped with beam receivers and were flying down the beams. Reacting to this, the enemy pilots would tend to fly in dots or dashes, just out of the constant-note path, and so were more easily led up the garden path on a bogus beam.

Other enemy navigational aids were likewise attacked. Radio beacons were listened for and their signals automatically re-transmitted at high power. Thus two signals, one probably from France and the other from England, would be heard by the enemy radio operators as one signal from somewhere in between (for the time interval between reception of the two signals would be so short as to pass unnoticed); and so beacons, too, were brought into some disrepute.

The reaction to all this was the adoption of pathfinder tactics by the enemy, a special force going ahead with incendiaries to find the target by one or other highly specialised method, and to start fires as guides for the following forces. As one counter-measure, while efforts were made to extinguish these fires quickly, a realistic decoy fire would be lit some distance from the threatened city. There could be no relaxing. As soon as one navigation or bombing system had been countered, one or more others, probably more complex and harder to interfere with, would be introduced—and they too had to be identified, nailed down and rendered useless to the enemy.

Besides spoiling bombing accuracy, these early countermeasures sometimes led to the complete undoing of a crew. The Junkers 88 I saw on an unfinished airfield in Somerset in the autumn of 1941 had been flown by such a crew. The machine had landed that morning, the pilot believing he was somewhere in France. It was said that the crew were arguing hotly as they tumbled, cold and cramped, out of the kennel-sized Ju 88 cockpit to discover their mistake. During one of our motor journeys I learnt from the AOC that this bomber, one of the last over the country, had been given the undivided attention of the radio countermeasure organisation. It was plotted coming south, and was then seen to wander off, as it received false beacon bearings. Then our beacon transmissions were turned off, and, receiving true bearings, it turned south again. It was given more of this treatment with variations, and was soon hopelessly lost. One can imagine what was going on in that small cockpit. Which bearing was right? Were any right? What did the navigator think? What did the pilot think? Perhaps they had gone too far. Better go back north a bit. Try again; and perhaps this time the beacon bearings were true for a short time, but not for long. All the time the aircraft was being plotted by our Observer Corps; all the time the annoyance and mutual distrust in that cramped cockpit must have been growing. And so this tragi-comedy went on to its finale, when in a misty dawn the pilot, insisting that the Severn was the English Channel, landed at the first airfield he saw.

Air Commodore RODERICK CHISHOLM CBE DSO DFC

*

A service highly dependent on technology, the RAF knew only too well Murphy's First Law: if it can go wrong, it sooner or later will. The Second Law states: if it can be put on upside down, it sooner or later will be. They also knew the executors of such laws. An American in the RAF recalls

THE GREMLINS

If you ask a student pilot about Gremlins, he'll probably tell you of the ones who hide in training planes during flight. When the student is coming in to land, they all run out to the end of one wing and, just when he's about to touch down for a perfect landing, give a great heave upwards, tipping his machine over so that the opposite wing hits the ground. Or the ones who cause crack-ups by moving trees or telephone poles in front of you when you're gliding in to land, or push other air-planes into your way when you're taxi-ing on the ground. Or the tribe known as the 'Ground Wallopers', who are responsible when a student bounces on landing; they shove your control stick forward or backward just as you're touching down, caus-

131

ing you either to hit the ground too hard or else to zoom up too high and pancake.

Another gang of them have an ingenious and destructive prank, which they sometimes work even on experienced pilots. Two of them stand by in your cockpit, out of sight, while you're flying, and when you move the lever to lower your wheels in preparation for landing, one of them sneaks up and throws the lever back into neutral so that your wheels stay up, retraced. Then the other one, hiding behind your instrument panel, re-wires the position indicator for your wheels, so that it shows 'WHEELS DOWN' when in reality they're still up, and you glide in for a perfect crack-up, landing your plane on its belly.

After the dust clears away, while the crash truck is approaching and you're still sitting in your cockpit, gazing stupidly at your bent or broken propeller and wings, the two little fellows jump up on your wind-shield, stick their tongues out at you in a final gesture of insolence, and vanish, leaving you to figure out how you're going to explain it all to the CO. At least, that's how some pilots claim it happens.

There's no end to the kinds of tricks they'll pull if they have it in for you. They hide behind your compass and hold magnets by it, causing the compass to point the wrong way, and you get lost. They steal your maps, hide in your radio set, and bang on it with hammers so you can't hear any messages. They sneak into your gas-tank and drink up your gasoline, steal the bullets from your machine-guns and put in corks, paint Messerschmitts on top of your cockpit hood to scare the life out of you, and so on, until they've driven you half crazy.

Flight-Lieutenant ARTHUR DONAHUE DFC

*

Information on the results of bomber attacks was, as shown earlier, hard to come by. One exception came in Syria which Wavell (forced to split his forces yet again) had been ordered to capture from the pro-German Vichy French government. The French resisted and bombed the British columns, day after day.

They came again at midday, and at dusk. The next morning they returned at dawn, only four of them now. At midday we again heard the sound of aircraft engines. In a flash everyone was at his post, and ready. Two twin-engined planes appeared from the west and came in with single front guns firing. This was nothing, and the return fire of twenty Bren guns lashed up at them. They roared low overhead, bullets ripping into their bellies, and dropped about twenty small bombs in our B Company area, damaging no one. They swung round and came in again. More bombs, more machine-gun fire from the nose. As one of them wheeled, a few hundred yards out over the desert, I distinctly saw the RAF roundels on its side. It leaped to my mind, and to Willy's at the same time, that from their shape they could only be Blenheims, a British light bomber.

'Cease fire!' the colonel yelled.

The nearest man to me was a machine-gunner who had got a Vickers gun loosened on its tripod so that it would make an effective anti-aircraft weapon. The Blenheim came in, our machine-gunner took a good lead and pressed the buttons, while the aircraft's fire ripped somewhere over our heads.

'Cease fire!' I bellowed at the machine-gunner. 'Ours, ours!'

'Why's he firing at us, then?' the gunner asked politely, swinging round and sending a hundred rounds up the Blenheim's arse.

A little later two battered Blenheims landed at Mosul and reported a successful raid on the French at Tel Abiad, some sixty miles to the north of Raqqa. By then the radio waves were boiling with furious signals from Willy. Next day we heard that the officer responsible for the error had been removed from command of his flight. Willy looked sick with worry. He didn't want the chap to suffer for an honest mistake. Dashed brave attack they'd put in, really.

I made two mental notes to add to the many I was accumulating through the campaign: (One) A loaded warplane is like a pregnant woman. When its time comes, it is under a compulsion to drop its burden, however unsuitable the circumstances. (Two) Airmen, though splendid at finding their way to Gosnau-Feldkirchen in night, fog, and rain, cannot tell Raqqa from New York in broad daylight. Some soldiers were inclined to believe that no airman's brain functions at all under 3,000 feet, but I thought this was an oversimplification.

JOHN MASTERS

*

As the weather cleared, Fighter Command started to reach out across the Channel with its Spitfires. Partly to keep the Germans off balance and under observation—invasion was once more a distinct possibility—partly to show the flag to the occupied countries. An ex-fighter-pilot sets the scene:

A KNIGHT IN DULL ARMOUR

First, if it's anything but high summer, dress up warm. The temperature above 30,000 feet falls to minus 60 fahrenheit and they haven't got around to heating fighter cockpits yet. Thick underwear, long socks, heavy sweater under your uniform. Fleece-lined leather flying boots (you can keep your maps tucked in the top of them; easiest place to reach, in flight. Put your revolver in the other boot, if you've bothered to bring it. It'll jerk out when your parachute opens anyway).

Now your flying overalls: nobody wears the heavy Sidcot suit now, so it's just a lightweight job to keep oil off your uniform. Then the Mae West—your life-saving jacket. A bright yellow waistcoat with a thick kapok-filled collar to keep your head above water and a number of knobs and whistle pockets in front (if you believe that blowing a whistle whilst floating in the English Channel will help). Tied with tapes in front and up from between your legs.

Flying helmet: leather, with earphones built in over each ear, an oxygen mask with microphone that fits over nose, cheeks and chin and always smells of old rubber. Goggles, too. Surprisingly good vision, but not all pilots wear them; some use them just with tinted lenses and pull them down when looking into the sun. Still, they may save your eyes if the instrument panel starts blowing burning petrol back in your face. It's up to you.

You don't leave your parachute in the cockpit unless it's a fine day and you're expecting a 'scramble'. You'll never need a 'chute, of course. Still, it's nice to know it won't screw up because it's been packed too long (which causes static electricity) or damp or had oil dripped on it. Put it on before you climb in. Straps around waist, over shoulders, up between legs. And pull them *tight*. Unless you want to break your back when it opens. You'll walk out to the aircraft bent over like a ruptured chimpanzee, but the ground crew will give you a tactful nudge with their shoulders to help you climb onto the wing.

Your seat is just a shallow metal pan designed to fit the parachute pack. You sit on your 'chute. They used to have a sorbo rubber cushion between it and you, but replaced it with a one-man-dinghy pack. Not as comfortable, but possibly more useful. What feels like a lump of sharp metal under your backside is the CO_2 bottle for inflating the dinghy in a hurry.

Strap yourself in. Straps over the shoulder, and up across the thighs. Tight. Tighter still. If you find yourself on your back you don't want to be rolling around the cockpit like a pea in a drum. Plug in your R/T lead and your oxygen tube—something like an elephant's trunk dangling from your mask.

The cockpit—let's say it's a Spitfire—fits you like a glove. It just about touches your shoulders on either side. The perspex canopy almost touches your head above. You can move your booted feet a few inches in either direction; you can stretch your arms right forward or down, but need to bend your elbows if you pull them back or up. No matter; you can control a fighter with just a few inches' movement of hands and feet.

You can still turn your head. You can turn it like a roulette wheel if you think a non-friend might be behind you. But you should have remembered to wear a silk scarf—or stocking—to stop 'fighter pilot's neck'. Tie it tight and tuck it in. It might strangle you if it catches when you try to bale out.

135

And your gloves—you didn't forget those? Silk first, then fleece-lined, for winter. Wash-leather for summer. Don't expect them to keep your hands warm. But at least they'll save a bit of blood when you grab around the cockpit for the flaps and undercart levers.

You feel like Henry the Fifth in armour and Joan of Arc tied to the stake at the same time? That's about right. You can move your hands, feet and head the few inches that are required; your Spitfire will do the rest. You are the most powerful, the fastest, the most manœuvrable fighting man in the world.

J.G.M.

*

The operations were mainly 'Rhubarbs'—low-level fighter sweeps, mostly disliked by the pilots—or 'Circuses'—heavily escorted bomber attacks intended to provoke the Luftwaffe fighters into aerial combats. Now on the offensive, it was easier for the RAF to assemble large formations: three, four or six squadrons. This was the day of the Wing Leader. Such leaders painted their initials on their aircraft and chose call-signs based on those initials. Such as

DOGSBODY

High summer at Tangmere. I shall never forget those stirring days, when it seemed that the sky was always blue and and the rays of the fierce sun hid the glinting Messerschmitts; or when there was a high layer of thin cirrus cloud (although this filtered the sun and lessened the glare, it was dangerous to climb through it, for your grey-green Spitfire stood out against the white backcloth); when the grass was burnt to a light brown colour and discoloured with dark oil-stains where we parked out Spitfires, and when the waters of the Channel looked utterly serene and inviting as we raced out of France at ground-level, hot and sweating in that tiny greenhouse of a cockpit.

High summer, and the air is heavy with the scent of white clover as we lounge in our deck-chairs watching a small tractor cut down the long clover and grass on our airfield. In some places it is almost a foot high, but it is not dangerous and we know that if we are skilful enough to stall our Spitfires just when the tips of the grass caress the wheels then we shall pull off a perfect landing.

It is Sunday, and although it is not yet time for lunch we have already escorted some Stirlings to bomb an inland target. For some obscure reason the Luftwaffe seem to oppose our week-end penetrations with more than their usual ferocity, and now we are waiting for the second call which will surely come on this perfect day.

For once our chatter is not confined to Messerschmitts and guns and tactics. Yesterday afternoon Nip and I borrowed the Padre's car, a small family saloon, and drove to Brighton for dinner. Before the return journey we collected two pilots from 145 Squadron, and in the small hours, wedged together, began the journey back to Tangmere. Nip was driving, the rest of us asleep, and along the front and Hove he had a vague recollection of some confusion and shouting and a half-hearted barrier stretched across part of the road. He pressed on and thought little of the incident, but soon after the engine ran unevenly and became very hot. Somehow we coaxed the car home. Next morning a close inspection revealed a sinister hole just below the rear window. Shocked, we traced the path of the bullet, for it turned out that a sentry at Hove had challenged us and, not receiving a suitable reply, had opened fire. The bullet had passed between the two pilots on the back seat, had continued between Nip and met at shoulder height, drilled a neat hole through the dashboard, grazed the cylinder head and ploughed out through the radiator. Small wonder that the little car had barely struggled back to Tangmere! The Padre is more concerned with our lucky escape than the damage to his car, but Billy Burton is incensed that his pilots should have to run a gauntlet of fire at Hove. He is busy penning a letter to the military, but we keep out of his way, for we think that he is opening his attack from a very insecure base.

There is a fine haze and the soft bulk of the South Downs is barely discernible. We can just see the spire of Chichester cathedral, but above the haze the visibility is excellent and you can see Lille from fifty miles.

Lille! It lies seventy miles inland from Le Touquet and marks the absolute limit of our daylight penetrations over France. We often escort bombers to Lille, for it is a vital communications centre and contains important heavy industries. Not unnaturally the Luftwaffe are very sensitive about it. Their ground-control organisation has time to assess our intentions and bring up fighter reinforcements, and the run-up to the target is always strongly contested. We can be sure of a stiff fight when Lille is the target for the bombers.

The ops phone rings and the airman who answers it calls out to the co; Billy Burton listens and replaces the receiver.

'That was the wing commander. Take-off at 13.25 with 610 and 145. We shall be target-support wing to the bombers. It's Lille again.'

Suddenly the dispersal hut is full of chatter and activity. We shall be the last Spitfires in the target area, for our job is to see that the beehive leaves the area without interference. The sun will be almost directly overhead, and the Messerschmitts will be there, lurking and waiting in its strong glare. We shall fight today.

Highly coloured ribbons are pinned across the large map on the wall to represent the tracks of the beehive and the six supporting fighter wings, so that the map looks like one of the those bold diagrams of London's Underground system. The two flight sergeants talk with their respective flight commanders about the serviceability of our Spitfires, and our names and the letters of our aircraft are chalked up on a blackboard which shows three sections of finger-fours.

It is fascinating to watch the reactions of the various pilots. They fall into two broad categories; those who are going out to shoot and those who secretly and desperately know they will be shot at, the hunters and the hunted. The majority of the pilots, once they have seen their names on the board, walk out to their Spitfires for a pre-flight check and for a word or two with their ground crews. They tie on their mae-wests, check their maps, study the weather forecast and have a last-minute chat with their leaders or wingmen. These are the hunters.

The hunted, that very small minority (although every squadron usually possessed at least one), turned to their escape kits and made quite sure that they were wearing the tunic with the silk maps sewn into a secret hiding-place; that they had at least one oilskin-covered packet of French francs, and two if possible; that they had a compass and a revolver and sometimes specially made clothes to assist their activities once they were shot down. When they went through these agonised preparations they reminded me of aged countrywomen meticulously checking their shopping-lists before catching the bus for the market town.

A car pulls up outside and our leader stumps into the dispersal hut, breezy and full of confidence. 'They'll be about today, Billy. We'll run into them over the target, if not before. Our job is to see the Stirlings get clear and cover any stragglers. Stick together. Who's flying in my section?'

'Smith, Cocky and Johnnie, sir,' answers Billy Burton.

'Good,' Bader grins at us. 'Hang on and get back into the abreast formation when I straighten out. O.K.?'

'O.K., sir,' we chorus together.

The wing commander makes phone calls to Stan Turner and Ken Holden. Brief orders followed by a time check. Ten minutes before we start engines, and we slip unobtrusively to our Spitfires, busy with our own private thoughts. I think of other Sunday afternoons not so very long ago when I was at school and walked the gentle slopes of Charnwood Forest clad in a stiff black suit. Our housemaster's greatest ambition was to catch us seniors red-handed smoking an illicit cigarette. And I think of my own father's deep-rooted objections to any forms of strenuous activity on the Sabbath during the holidays at Melton Mowbray.

My ground crew have been with the squadron since it was formed and have seen its changing fortunes and many pilots come and go. They know that for me these last few moments on the ground are full of tension, and as they strap me in the cockpit they maintain an even pressure of chatter. Vaguely I hear that the engine is perfect, the guns oiled and checked and the faulty radio set changed and tested since the last flight. The usual cockpit smell, that strange mixture of dope, fine mineral oil, and high-grade fuel, assails the nostrils and is somehow vaguely comforting. I tighten my helmet strap, swing the rudder with my feet on the pedals, watch the movement of the ailerons when I waggle the stick and look at the instruments without seeing them, for my mind is racing on to Lille and the 109s.

Ken starts his engine on the other side of the field and the twelve Spitfires from 610 trundle awkwardly over the grass. Bader's propeller begins to turn, I nod to the ground crew and the engine coughs once or twice and I catch her with a flick of the throttle and she booms into a powerful bass until I cut her back to a fast tick-over. We taxi out to the take-off position, always swinging our high noses so that we can see the aircraft ahead. The solid rubber tail-wheels bump and jolt on the unyielding ground and we bounce up and down with our own backbones acting as shock absorbers.

We line our twelve Spitfires diagonally across one corner of the meadow. We wait until Ken's Squadron is more than half-way across the airfield and then Bader nods his head and we open out throttles together and the deep-throated roar of the engines thunders through the leather helmets and slams against our ear-drums. Airborne, and the usual automatic drill. We take up a tight formation and I drop my seat a couple of notches and trim the Spitfire so that it flies with the least pressure from hands and feet.

One slow, easy turn on to the course which sends us climbing parallel to the coast. Ken drops his squadron neatly into position about half a mile away and Stan flanks us on the other side. Wood-hall calls from the ops room to his wing leader to check radio contact:

'Dogsbody?'

'O.K., O.K.'

And that's all.

We slant into the clean sky. No movement in the cockpit except the slight trembling of the stick as though it is alive and not merely the focal point of a superb mechanical machine. Gone are the ugly tremors of apprehensions which plagued us just before the take-off. Although we are sealed in our tiny cockpits and separated from each other, the static from our radios pours through the earphones of our tightly fitting helmets and fills our ears with reassuring crackles. When the leader speaks, his voice is warm and vital, and we know full well that once in the air like this we are bound together by a deeper intimacy than we can ever feel on the ground. Invisible threads of trust and comradeship hold us together and the mantle of Bader's leadership will sustain and protect us throughout the fight ahead. The Tangmere Wing is together.

We climb across Beachy Head, and over Pevensey Bay we swing to the starboard to cross the Channel and head towards the French coast. Some pilot has accidentally knocked on his radio transmitter and croons quietly to himself. He sounds happy and must be a Canadian, for he sings of 'The Chandler's Wife' and the 'North Atlantic Squadron'. He realises his error and we hear the sudden click of his transmitter, and again the only sound is the muted song of the engine.

Now Bader rocks his wings and we level out from the climb and slide out of our tight formation. We take up our finger-four positions with ourselves at 25,000 feet and Ken and Stan stacked up behind us. It is time to switch the gun button from 'safe' to 'fire' and turn on the reflector sight, for we might want them both in a hurry.

'O.K., Ken?' from Bader.

'O.K., Dogsbody.'

'Stan?' from Bader again.

'You bet.'

The yellow sands of the coast are now plainly visible, and behind is a barren waste of sandhills and scrub. Well hidden in these sandhills are the highly trained gunners who serve the 88 mm batteries. We breast the flak over Le Touquet. The black, evil flowers foul the sky and more than the usual amount of ironmongery is hurled up at us. Here and there are red marker bursts intended to reveal our position to the Messerschmitts. We twist and pirouette to climb above the bed of flak, and from his relatively safe position, high above, Stan sees our plight and utters a rude comment in the high-pitched voice he reserves for such occasions. The tension eases.

On across the Pas de Calais and over the battlefields of a

half-forgotten war against the same foe. From the Tangmere ops room Woodhall breaks the silence:

'Dogsbody, from Beetle. The beehive is on time and is engaged.'

'O.K.'

'Fifty-plus about twenty miles ahead of you,' from Woodhall.

'Understood,' replies Bader.

'Thirty-plus climbing up from the south and another bunch behind them. Keep a sharp look-out,' advises the group captain.

'O.K., Woodie. That's enough,' answers the wing leader, and we twist our necks to search the boundless horizons.

'Looks like a pincer movement to me,' comments some wag. I suspect it is Roy Marple's voice, and again the tension slackens as we grin behind our oxygen masks. Woodhall speaks into his microphone with his last item of information.

'Dogsbody. The rear support wing is just leaving the English coast.' (This means we can count on some help should we have to fight our way out.) 'Course for Dover —310 degrees.' (This was a last-minute reminder of the course to steer for home.) Woodhall fades out, for he has done his utmost to paint a broad picture of the air situation. Now it is up to our leader.

'Dogsbody from blue one. Beehive at twelve o'clock below. About seven miles.'

'O.K. I see them,' and the wing leader eases his force to starboard and a better up-sun position.

The high-flying Messerschmitts have seen our wing and stab at Stan's top-cover squadron with savage attacks from either flank.

'Break port, Ken.' (From a pilot of 610.)

'Keep turning.'

'Tell me when to stop turning.'

'Keep turning. There's four behind!'

'Get in, red section.'

'We're stuck into some 109s behind you, Douglas.' (This quietly from Stan.)

'O.K., Stan.'

'Baling out.'

'Try and make it, Mac. Not far to the coast.' (This urgently from a squadron commander.)

'No use. Temperature's off the clock. She'll burn any time. Look after my dog.'

'Keep turning, yellow section.'

So far the fight has remained well above us. We catch fleeting glimpses of high vapour trails and ducking, twisting fighters. Two thirds of the wing are behind us holding off the 109s and we force on to the target area to carry out our assigned task. We can never reform into a wing again, and the pilots of 145 and 610 will make their way home in twos and fours. We head towards the distant beehive, well aware that there is now no covering force of Spitfires above us.

The Stirlings have dropped their heavy load of bombs and begin their return journey. We curve slowly over the outskirts of Lille to make sure the beehive is not harried from the rear. I look down at a pall of debris and black smoke rising from the target five miles below, and absurdly my memory flashes back to contrast the scene with those other schoolboy Sunday afternoons.

'Dogsbody from Smith. 109s above. Six o'clock. About twenty-five or thirty.'

'Well done. Watch 'em and tell me when to break.'

I can see them. High in the sun, and their presence only betrayed by the reflected sparkle from highly polished windscreens and cockpit covers.

'They're coming down, Dogsbody. Break left.' And round to port we go, with Smith sliding below Bader and Cocky and me above so that we cover each other in this steep turn. We curve round and catch a glimpse of four baffled 109s climbing back to join their companions, for they can't stay with us in a turn. The keen eyes of Smith saved us from a nasty smack that time.

'Keep turning, Dogsbody. More coming down,' from Cocky.

'O.K. We might get a squirt this time,' rejoins Bader. What a man, I think, what a man!

The turn tightens and in my extreme position on the starboard side I'm driving my Spitfire through a greater radius of curve than the others and falling behind. I kick

143

on hard bottom rudder and skid inwards, down and behind the leader. More 109s hurtle down from above and a section of four angle in from the starboard flank. I look round for other Spitfires but there are none in sight. The four of us are alone over Lille.

'Keep turning. Keep turning.' (From Bader.) 'They can't stay with us.' And we keep turning, hot and frightened and a long way from home. We can't keep turning all bloody day, I think bitterly.

Cocky has not re-formed after one of our violent breaks. I take his place next to Bader and the three of us watch the Messerschmitts, time their drives and call the break into their attacks. The odds are heavily against us.

We turn across the sun and I am on the inside. The blinding light seems only two feet above Bader's cockpit and if I drop further below or he gains a little more height, I shall lose him. Already his Spitfire has lost its colour and is only a sharp, black silhouette, and now it has disappeared completely, swallowed up by the sun's fierce light. I come out of the turn and am stunned to find myself alone in the Lille sky.

The Messerschmitts come in close for the kill. At this range their camouflage looks dirty and oil-stained, and one brute has a startling black-and-white spinner. In a hot sweat of fear I keep turning and turning, and the fear is mingled with an abject humiliation that these bastards should single me out and chop me at their leisure. The radio is silent, or probably I don't hear it in the stress of trying to stay alive. I can't turn all day. Le Touquet is seventy hostile miles away; far better to fight back and take one with me.

Four Messerschmitts roar down from six o'clock. I see them in time and curve the shuddering, protesting Spitfire to meet them, for she is on the brink of a high-speed stall. They are so certain of my destruction that they are flying badly and I fasten on to tail-end Charlie and give him a long burst of fire. He is at the maximum range, and although my shooting has no apparent effect some of my despair and fear on this fateful afternoon seems to evaporate at the faint sound of the chattering machine guns. But

144

perhaps my attack has its just reward, for Smith's voice comes loud and clear over the radio.

'One Spit behind, Dogsbody. A thousand yards. Looks like he's in trouble.'

Then I see them. Two aircraft with the lovely curving wings that can only belong to Spitfires. I take a long breath and in a deliberately calm voice:

'It's me, Dogsbody—Johnnie.'

'O.K., Johnnie. We'll orbit here for you. Drop in on my starboard. We'll get a couple of these ——'

There is no longer any question of not getting home now that I am with Bader again. He will bring us safely back to Tangmere and I know he is enjoying this, for he sounds full of confidence over the radio. A dozen Messerschmitts still shadow our small formation. They are well up-sun and waiting to strike. Smith and I fly with our necks twisted right round, like the resting mallard ducks one sees in the London parks, and all our concentration focused on the glinting shoal of 109s.

'Two coming down from five o'clock, Dogsbody. Break right,' from me. And this time mine is the smallest turn so that I am the first to meet the attack. A 109 is very close and climbing away to port. Here is a chance. Time for a quick shot and no danger of losing the other two Spitfires if I don't get involved in a long tail chase. I line up my Spitfire behind the 109, clench the spade-grip handle of the stick with both hands and send short bursts into his belly at less than a hundred yards. The 109 bursts apart and the explosion looks exactly the same as a near burst of heavy flak, a vicious flower with a poisonous glowing centre and black swirling edges.

I re-form and the Messerschmitts come in again, and this time Bader calls the break. It is well judged and the wing leader fastens on to the last 109 and I cover his Spitfire as it appears to stand on its tail with wisps of smoke plummeting from the gun ports. The enemy aircraft starts to pour white smoke from its belly and thick black smoke from the engine. They merge together and look like a long, dirty banner against the faded blue of some high circus cloud.

'Bloody good shooting, sir.'

145

'We'll get some more.'

Woodhall—it seems an eternity since we last heard him—calls up to say that the rear support wing is over Abbeville. Unbelievably the Messerschmitts which have tailed us so long vanish and we are alone in the high spaces.

We pick up the English coast near Dover and turn to port for Sussex and Tangmere. We circle our airfield and land without any fuss or aerobatics, for we never know until we are on the ground whether or not a stray bullet has partially severed a control cable.

Woodhall meets us and listens to his wing leader's account of the fight. Bader has a tremendous ability to remember all the details and gives a graphic résumé of the show. The group captain listens carefully and says that he knew we were having a hard time because of the numerous plots of enemy formations on his operations table and our continuous radio chatter. So he had asked 11 Group to get the rear support wing over France earlier than planned, to lend a hand. Perhaps the shadowing Messerschmitts which sheered off so suddenly had seen the approach of this Spitfire wing.

Bader phones Ken and Stan while the solemn Gibbs pleads with us to sit down and write out our combat reports.

'Please do it now. It will only take two minutes.'

'Not likely, Gibbs. We want some tea and a shower and...'

'You write them and we'll sign them,' suggests a pilot.

Cocky walks in. He came back on the deck after losing us over Lille and landed at Hawkinge short of petrol.

'Dinner and a bottle at Bosham tonight, Johnnie?'

'Right,' I answer at once.

'Count me in too,' says Nip.

The group captain is trying to make himself heard above the din.

'You chaps must watch your language. It's frightful. And the Waafs seem to be getting quite used to it. They don't bat an eyelid any more. But I'm sure you don't know how bad it sounds. I had it logged this afternoon.' And he waves a piece of paper in his hand.

Someone begins to read out from the record. We roar

146

with laughter, slap each other on the back and collapse weakly into chairs, but this reaction is not all due to the slip of paper. Woodhall watches us and walks to the door hoping that we don't see the grin which is creasing his leathery countenance.

We clamber into our meagre transports, one small van per flight, and drive to Shopwhyke. We sit on the lawn and drink tea served by Waafs. These young girls wear overalls of flowered print and look far more attractive and feminine than in their usual masculine garb of collar and tie. One of our officers is a well-known concert pianist and he plays a movement from a Beethoven concerto, and the lovely melody fills the stately house and overflows into the garden. The sweat from the combats of but an hour ago is barely dry on our young bodies.

Group Captain J. E. JOHNSON DSO DFC

*

FIGHTER

Bright metal bird, you skyproud Icarus,
Slide on your insolent and cloudborne wings,
They wave, those European peasants,
and wait, not for the sound your engine sings . . .

They wait a sound when all you've said
Is done, the leaden soldiers tread.

T. B. HUTTON

*

Oddly enough, the claim of 'outstanding interest' that this article makes for itself was true—if not before publication (in Punch) *then at least shortly afterwards. Many an RAF mess actually developed discussions on these lines—once they'd been provoked into thinking about*

FLIES

In the RAF Mess, Prangmere, a self-appointed committee went into session on Sunday night to discuss a topic of

147

outstanding interest to the whole of the Royal Air Force. The question before the meeting was, in short, just how does a fly land on the ceiling.

Pilot-Officer Prune, opening the proceedings, said he was of the opinion the fly cruised along at the correct height below the ceiling and then did a half-loop, landing upwards at the top of the loop.

Squadron-Leader Undercart said that was all very well, but how did the fly judge his distance, so as to avoid nose-diving into the ceiling a quarter way through the loop? Presumably he wasn't fitted with an altimeter that worked inversely from the ceiling downwards instead of from the ground up. He personally took a poor view of Prune's theory.

Pilot-Officer Stall said he didn't get that half-loop idea either, though for exactly the opposite reason. Surely, as soon as the fly lost flying speed sufficiently to effect a good three-pointer ceiling landing, he would stall in an upside-down position, go into an inverted nosedive, and have to pull out of it by completing the loop and, so to speak, going round again. The same thing would probably happen several times before he hit it off at last, which would mean that the majority of flies—especially the inexperienced ones who had only just joined the squadron from their OTU—would be making a series of vertical circuits before getting a 'bump', a thing he had never seen yet—and please God never would! He here stopped for lack of breath.

Flight-Lieutenant Lyne-Shute said let them fight it out between themselves: he personally was ordering a beer.

Pilot-Officer Nosedyve said that any sort of landing made at the top of a loop meant that the fly landed facing in the opposite way to his direction of flight, which must be very confusing to the ceiling-staff, though very useful if the fly found he was overshooting on coming in.

Flying-Officer Flaps said he too thought the loop theory was just sheer bull. The normal act of landing was really stalling, and you couldn't stall upwards! It'd be much the same sort of thing as having your aircraft drop up to stratosphere just as you were going to touch down—like that, see! What he thought the fly really did was to come in close up

148

—like that!—do a half slow-roll—like that!—and there he was, going gently along still in the direction of flight—like THAT! Sorry!

Flight-Lieutenant Lyne-Shute said that if Flying-Officer Flaps had been in the RFC in 1915 he'd have learnt to keep his hands under control: now he'd have to order more beer.

Pilot-Officer Rudder said perhaps the tougher fighter flies, with many hours' operational flying behind them, had some wizard landing dodge of their own—especially with those sticky feet, which had the most powerful brakes beat to a frazzle. He suggested that they might zoom right up to the ceiling, suddenly put a leg up and come up, all standing.

Pilot-Officer Nosedyve said the strain on the fly's undercarriage if he did that must be terrific: it would certainly be against fly flying regulations.

Flight-Lieutenant Lyne-Shute said the very idea made him feel faint and he was ordering some beer.

Squadron-Leader Undercart said a fly didn't have one undercarriage only: he had six.

Pilot-Officer Stall said, surely eight.

Squadron-Leader Undercart said, nuts, six.

Flying-Officer Talespin said it was common knowledge that the house-fly, or Musca domestica, possessed . . . His speech was interrupted by the attempts of Pilot-Officer Stall and Squadron-Leader Undercart each trying to try to bring down a fly and prove the other wrong. No victory, however, could be confirmed, though several combats took place, in one of which Squadron-Leader Undercart claimed a 'probable', the fly attacked being last seen, he stated, heading for home with black smoke coming from its port wing.

Flight-Lieutenant Lyne-Shute said that if they'd quite finished upsetting his beer, he'd order some . . .

Flying-Officer Talespin, interrupting, said how about the fly turning on its back and flying upside down when nearing the ceiling level, if they saw what he meant.

Flying-Officer Flaps said something rude about upside down, Flying-Officer Talespin, what he meant, and flies in general.

149

Flying-Officer Talespin disagreed. . . .

Wing-Commander Blower said, now, boys, chuck it and, anyway, if one wanted to get the real gen on the fly-landing business they ought to get up close to the landing ground and watch.

There was then another lull in the discussion, while Squadron-Leader Undercart, two Flying-Officers and three Pilot-Officers formed a pyramid to enable Pilot-Officer Prune at the top to examine the flying ground situation and report. Wing-Commander Blower turned on the cornice lights to give the flies a proper flare path, and said they should be warned that an electric-light-pendant barrage was flying in the centre of the ceiling. He was still looking round for a torch as an angle-of-glide indicator when Squadron-Leader Undercart, who was the base of the pyramid, suddenly got tired. The object of the exercise was thus not achieved.

Flight-Lieutenant Lyne-Shute asked heatedly which of them it was that had upset his beer this time: now he'd have to order some more.

Group-Captain Boost, taking part in the discussion for the first time, said no one was ordering more beer, it was late enough at it was: if they felt so keen about the thing, let them write to the Brains Trust: meanwhile Lyne-Shute was to take off for his quarters at once, to be followed by the others at three seconds' intervals, or else . . .

Thereupon the meeting broke up and the Mess emptied in half a minute.

The flies continued to alight on the ceiling in their own inscrutable fashion.

ANTHONY ARMSTRONG (Squadron-Leader A. A. WILLIS)

(Operational research since the war, based on a firmer footing than S/Ldr Undercart, has shown that, for the first time in his life, P/O Prune was actually right: high-speed cameras reveal that flies do land off half-loops. However, P/O Rudder was right also: flies touch down on their front legs, swinging their back four up into position immediately afterwards. So S/Ldr Undercart was right about the six-leg undercarriage, too.)

*

We may recall that, nearly a year earlier, the German fighter ace Werner Molders has been promised a new version of the Messerschmitt 109. It now came: the '109F', and soon proved it could outclass the Spitfire II in speed and climb. The Chief of Fighter Command went to see what the Minister of Aircraft Production was doing about it.

IN SINGLE COMBAT

We who were 'bloody Air Marshals', as Lord Beaverbrook used to refer to us, all had, from time to time, our differences and disagreements with him, and the occasion upon which I was subjected to my particular fracas with him came over that letter that I had written to the Air Ministry about the performance of our fighters. A few days after sending it off I was asked to go and see Lord Beaverbrook in his office at the Ministry of Aircraft Production. I had no idea what it was that he wanted to see me about, and when I was ushered into Beaverbrook's office I found him sitting in such a way that he seemed to be crouching behind his enormous desk. There were no papers whatsoever upon it, but there was a row of telephones of various colours in front of him, and to one side there was a battery of push-buttons, also in different colours.

'Good morning, sir,' I said as I entered the office.

My civil salutation met with nothing more than a glowering silence. Whipping open the top right-hand drawer of his desk, Beaverbrook pulled out some sheets of paper, which he slapped down on the desk in front of me. 'Did you write that?' he growled.

When I looked at the papers I saw that they were a copy of the letter that I had sent to the Air Ministry. 'Yes,' I said. 'I wrote it.'

That was all that was needed to touch off the explosion. The little man started to roar and shout and wave his fists in the air, and for several minutes he set about roundly abusing me, Fighter Command, and everything to do with us. At first there was nothing that I could do but listen; but after a while I began to feel my own temperature rising. There were echoes in my mind, and this outburst sounded to me too much like the political brow-beating of the military about which I had heard so much but of which this was my first experience.

It takes a great deal to make me lose my temper and control of myself to the point where I make any physical demonstration; but the way in which Beaverbrook was going for me was stretching things, I began to feel, altogether too far. All said and done, I reminded myself, I was the Commander-in-Chief of Fighter Command, and a high-ranking officer in the Royal Air Force; but in the face of what, as the completely informed and responsible commander, I had stated in an official letter about a fact which we all knew was perfectly correct I was being subjected to a humiliating display of bad temper.

But I knew that I was right, and there came into my mind one simple question. Why the hell should I take this outburst lying down? With that I promptly lost my temper. I went what felt like being red in the face, and I started thumping Beaverbrook's desk with my fist and shouting back at him. It was all quite stupid. But there we were, a Cabinet Minister and a Commander-in-Chief, each trying to shout down the other.

All of a sudden, and to my astonishment and even bewilderment, Beaverbrook threw himself back in his chair and lifted his head, and the shouts of anger gave way to an outburst of the extraordinary but infectious cackle of laughter which was characteristic of him. I was completely taken aback by this abrupt change, and thrown right off my stride. And then the little man started to play a fandango on the panel of multi-coloured push-buttons at the side of his desk, which smartly brought into the office on the run a whole lot of rather frightened-looking civil servants.

'Here is the Chief of Fighter Command,' Beaverbrook announced. 'He says that his fighters are not good enough. His boys are being shot down.' He pointed to one poor wretch and demanded: 'What are you doing about it?'

The unfortunate underling singled out for this interrogation started to make some stuttered explanation for which he promptly had his head bitten off. There were more stammered explanations all round, and no doubt many of them were perfectly valid ones; but Beaverbrook would have none of them. Angrily he told them all to go away and to improve without further delay the performance of the Spitfire, and with that the company shuffled out.

'I think you'll find it will be all right now,' Beaverbrook said, and he smiled in the broad, cheerful way for which he was so well known.

Marshal of the Royal Air Force
LORD DOUGLAS OF KIRTLESIDE GCB MC DFC
with ROBERT WRIGHT

*

But one of the victims of the 109F was the famous legless wing-leader, Douglas Bader, otherwise 'Dogsbody'.

One day the Commander of the 1st Wing came, full of enthusiasm, to tell me of the kind of 'eagle' we had caught. 'You must come and meet him,' he said. Bader's ribs were more or less healed, and I sent my large staff car, a Horch which I rarely used myself, to the hospital of St Omer. An officer, a sergeant-major and the driver fetched Bader in style. Some of our commanders and several other officers had tea with their British guest at the Group Staff Headquarters, and he was obviously surprised and impressed by the lavishness of the reception. Only after some time did he overcome the distrust he could not hide in spite of his charming and winning manners.

Bader was on his guard against giving the slightest hint of any military information, and in any case we were strictly forbidden to interrogate prisoners: this was left entirely to specialists at the interrogation centres. Nevertheless, I had given instructions that nothing should be said which could even resemble a question. He did not even admit how many enemy planes he had to his credit.

'Oh, not many,' he said. He did not know how many had been recognised, and confirmations were still outstanding. 'Well, you must know approximately how many,' I urged him. 'No,' he replied, avoiding the issue defensively. 'Compared with Molders and your bag, they are so few that it's hardly worth talking about them.' Actually he had some twenty to his credit. Perhaps it really was only modesty that he did not want to talk about it with us.

Bader loosened up during the course of this free-and-easy conversation, so I proposed a little tour of our installations, which he accepted with pleasure and obvious interest. The leg which had been salvaged from the wreckage squeaked and rattled like a small armoured car. Bader asked me if we could not drop a message over England to tell his boys and his wife that he was well and to get him his spare legs, a better uniform than his battle-dress, tobacco, and a new pipe to replace the broken one he had stuck together with adhesive tape. His wife would know what to do. The spare legs were on the left in the wardrobe. I offered him some tobacco and one of my pipes, but he refused. Naturally, it was outside my province to give him a definite promise to fulfil this request, which was certainly of considerable originality, but I promised I would do my best.

The masterly way in which our airfield was camouflaged attracted his attention as an expert, and a long conversation about technical details followed, during which he praised the better points of the Messerschmitt while we praised the Spitfire. Would I allow him to sit in the cockpit of my plane? 'Why not!' Everything had to be explained to him in the smallest detail. I enjoyed the interest and understanding this great pilot showed. He would have fitted splendidly into our 'Club'.

Bader bent down to me from the cockpit of my plane, in which he was sitting, and said, 'Will you do me a great favour?' 'With pleasure, if it is my power,' I answered. 'At least once in my life I would like to fly a Messerschmitt. Let me do just one circle over the airfield.' He said it with a smile and looked me straight in the eyes. I nearly weakened, but replied: 'If I grant your wish, I'm afraid you'll escape and I should be forced to chase after you. Now we have met, we don't want to shoot at each other again, do we?' He laughed and we changed the subject. After a hearty goodbye, he went back to the hospital.

ADOLF GALLAND

*

The good weather also helped the Atlantic Bridge—now formalised as RAF Ferry Command (later Transport Command). But Atlantic weather was never dependable even in summer.

EVERYTHING BUT SEA-SICKNESS

The first crossing from Bermuda was a memorable flight by Captain Fleming and Captain Meikle as co-pilot, radio operators Hodgson and Eyre, all Canadians, and Flight-engineers Latimer and Clark, who belonged to the Fleet Air Arm. They were six hours out, flying at 18,500 feet, when their troubles started. Their automatic pilot suddenly jammed, the starboard aileron went full down, and the machine fell into a spiral dive. Immediately the ailerons began to flutter because of the steep angle at which they were meeting the flow of air.

'I was sitting at the radio table when the plane very suddenly went completely out of control,' said one of the radio operators. 'The night was pitch black, so it was hard to tell what was happening, but we started some sort of spiral dive for the sea. On orders from Fleming I sent out an SOS, but just at that time our aerials gave way and wound themselves about the ship. This state of things lasted for several minutes as we had been flying at 20,000 feet. Our altimeter at one time showed 1,000 feet.' The pilots fought the spin. The crew jettisoned smoke flares, spare parts, tool kits, the £40 outfit just bought by one of the engineers. They recovered control when the Catalina was only a few hundred feet from the water. 'And sure enough,' continued the radio operator, 'when daylight came we were flying along with both ailerons completely torn away.' There was no lateral control. To remain airborne without lateral control, the pilot had to fly straight ahead, as use of the rudder without ailerons would be liable to put the machine into a fatal flat spin.

Although they were only six hours from their departure base, and hours and hours of Atlantic waste lay between them and Britain, Captain Fleming ordered no further SOS. From the trailing aerial, which was quickly fixed up, they

155

simply signalled 'Both ailerons gone'; and flew on. The signal was received, but no one believed it. It seemed impossible that a Catalina weighing some fifteen tons could be handled under such conditions.

Fleming and Meikle sat side by side, using all their strength to keep the machine in the air. They dared not remove their hands from the controls to look at a map. They were flying due south. Fleming had memorised the course, and bit by bit they managed very gently to turn back on to it. Hour after hour they flew on with great fortitude and physical endurance. After weathering a storm they succeeded in coming down on the water at Milford Haven. They had been flying for twenty-eight hours, fifty minutes.

The sea was rough, and in spite of all that they had endured they could not face seasickness. So they actually took off again and flew skimming over the surface to within three miles nearer the moorings.

AIR MINISTRY

*

Most of the Transatlantic aircraft were still allotted to Coastal Command, recently given top priority by a War Cabinet directive anticipating a major U-boat campaign. Part of the story behind the directive is told by an air-photo interpretess:

A YARD OF U-BOATS

Next day he sought out Peter Riddell. 'I think you ought to see our figures for U-boat production,' he said with a secretive little smile. 'The totals are just ready.' Riddell went over the figures with him, and then sprang to his feet exclaiming, 'I must get Denning at once.'

On the following afternoon, Captain John Godwin, RN, who was responsible for the study of German ship-building at the Admiralty, was sent down to 'Paduoc House'.

'I'd like you to tell me how you have made your deductions,' he said to Brachi. 'How can you possibly tell from photographs what launchings to expect six months ahead?'

Brachi's dark little eyes twinkled. 'I'll show you, sir. I've got some stereo pairs ready. Here first of all at the Blohm and Voss yard is a keel that's just been laid down for a 500-tonner.'

Godwin had never used a stereoscope before, and at first all he could see was a confusing double image. Brachi checked the position of the prints. 'Now try again, sir.' He pointed to the U-boat keel with a pencil. 'Oh yes, I've got it now,' said Godwin. 'Yes, I can see the keel. Let's have some more.'

Brachi put another pair of photographs in position. 'This is the same keel when the sections of the midships portion of the hull were just going to be put into position. There's the crane. And now here's another yard, Deschimag at Bremen,' he went on, 'and these photographs were taken a month after a new keel was laid down. The midships part of the hull has been finished, and the camouflage "cradle" is being put up over it.'

'I see,' said Godwin. 'Yes, I do see.'

'Now here, sir,' Brachi continued, 'is a later cover of the same submarine, and the "cradle" has been extended fore and aft. That's because the hull has been extended to its full length, so they've had to lengthen the "cradle" to screen it. The Germans are so methodical about their camouflage that once you get to know their methods you can tell quite a lot from the camouflage itself.' Brachi produced yet another pair of photographs and set them in place. 'And now this is a cover taken six months after the laying of the keel, and you see what's happening.'

'They've taken away some of the camouflage,' said Godwin.

'Yes, they've had to remove some of the "cradle' so as to finish work on the conning tower,' Brachi explained. 'And the day before yesterday these photographs came in. As you see the whole "cradle" has been removed, so that means she'll be launched any moment now.'

By the end of the afternoon Godwin was more than convinced: he was carried away. But he hardly dared to think what the photographic evidence was going to mean in terms of Allied shipping losses. As he got up to go he took a last look at Brachi's calculations.

'There's no doubt then. If we allow for the yards that haven't been covered, we can definitely expect a doubled production of U-boats four months from now. Ten this month, and at least twenty in July. My God!'

Back at the Admiralty, Godwin prepared an urgent new appreciation of the U-boat production programme, based almost entirely on Brachi's figures. It was at once submitted to Admiral Godfrey, the Director of Naval Intelligence. Next day Sir Dudley Pound raised the matter at a meeting of the Chiefs of Staff, and from there the new production estimate went on to the Prime Minister. It was very shortly after this, on 6th March 1941, that the 'Battle of the Atlantic' directive was written.

CONSTANCE BABINGTON SMITH

*

But even with its new Hudsons and Catalinas, the Command was still some way from mastering the U-boat.

From the work at Birmingham and Wembley came the 10 cm radar. Strictly speaking it was 9.1 cm but 10 cm is easier to remember. This was the device which, accompanied by the Leigh searchlight, hit the U-boats for six, forced them to surface by day, exposed them to the attack of Coastal's daylight patrols and of the escort groups, and finally caused Admiral Doenitz to cry halt to his operations. His losses were too heavy to be borne. But it was not centimetric radar, or the Leigh light alone that produced a temporary victory over the U-boat. Years before a young naval officer whose name is lost in the mists of time had thought of the depth-charge as a proper method of attack against submarines. In the early months of the Hitler War it became perfectly obvious that the delay-action bomb, whether of 100 lb or 250 lb weight, was perfectly useless against the U-boat. It had no hitting power and it always exploded at the wrong moment, if indeed it exploded at all. Happily for Coastal there was on the Ordnance Board an air commodore, Huskinson by name. 'Husky' had been blinded by a bomb burst during the night blitz of 1940–1. Within days he was back at work, his mind as active as ever though he has never regained his sight. Regularly he attended Coastal conferences on armament, and in co-operation with his naval colleagues he produced the lethal weapon—the Torpex-filled depth-charge with a shallow 'pistol'. Months before the Command had been provided with the ordinary naval depth-charge filled with Amatol and set to explode at fifty feet or more. This setting had been worked out to correspond with the accepted idea of the tactics of submarines when in danger from an Asdic attack by surface vessels. But if an aircraft was to make an attack on a surfaced submarine the depth-charges would have to be dropped by eye, when the enemy was only a few feet below the surface. So the deep setting was valueless. The need for the shallow exploding device was great, and in addition it was felt by Coastal that, in view of the probable inaccuracies of an air-drop, the weapon should be as powerful as possible. 'Husky' and his friends produced his part of the answer to the previous failures. 'The probable inaccuracies!' Yes indeed, they were very probable. It is not easy without any aiming device to drop an object accurately on a target when one is moving at 250 mph. First, an analysis had to be made of these errors. In the tail of our anti-submarine aircraft cameras were fitted to take pictures of the drop of the depth-charges as they straddled the target U-boat. From these pictures the Operational Research Section made an analysis of the factors governing the accuracy of drop. From this analysis emerged the low-level bomb-sight which was to play hell with the enemy.

Air Chief Marshal
SIR PHILIP JOUBERT, KCB CMG DSO

*

Having effected two major improvements—the new tactics of seeking out and attacking the U-boat rather than waiting for him to come to the convoy, and the better usage of ASV—the Command began to reap rewards. Within a few weeks sinkings near our coasts were greatly reduced, and little by little the U-boats were pushed farther and farther out into the Atlantic.

This success, however, only aggravated a need that had

been urgent for some time—that of very long-range aircraft to accompany the convoys when they were far out in mid-Atlantic, and to search out the U-boats on their more remote patrol lines. But at every point the requirements of Bomber Command and the priority that was given to its needs thwarted our desires and intentions.

By a fortunate chance for us Bomber Command decided that Liberators, American heavy four-engined aircraft, were unsuitable for night bombing because of the very visible flame from their exhaust pipes, which was a great help to the enemy night-fighters. Coastal Command therefore obtained the reversion of a small order for these aircraft which, when fitted out to our requirements, were a godsend to us and a menace to the U-boats. But it was not until late in 1942 that a reasonable number of Liberators reached the Command, and by then much mischief had been done to our shipping.

It was during the late summer of 1941 that Hudson aircraft of No 269 Squadron, based on Iceland, made history by first damaging and then obtaining the surrender of a U-boat in the open sea. The U-boat hoisted the white flag some hours before dark and the question was whether the Navy could arrive in time to put a boarding-party in charge before darkness would enable the U-boat to slip away from the relays of aircraft that were circling round it and threatening to destroy it if it made an attempt to escape. I was in my Operations Room at the time, reading signal after signal from my aircraft, and biting my nails with fury at the thought of the enemy escaping. The approaching trawler seemed to be crawling, and it appeared almost inevitable that it would arrive too late to accept the enemy's surrender. Finally I gave the order that the U-boat was to be sunk at last light. Within half an hour the signal was received that the trawler had boarded the U-boat and taken her in tow. My relief was tremendous, but I observed that according to the position reports we had received, the trawler must have taken wings for the last fifty miles—so fast had she moved.

Another engagement with a U-boat which took place south of Iceland had an unusual sequel. A Catalina aircraft spotted a submarine and attacked. One of the 'stick' of

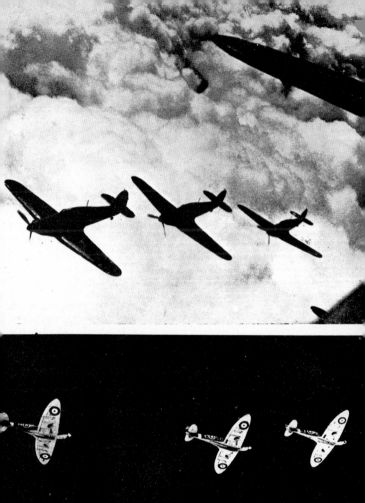

Hurricanes and Spitfires, victors in the Battle of Britain, flying in the then-standard, but outmoded, line-astern battle formation

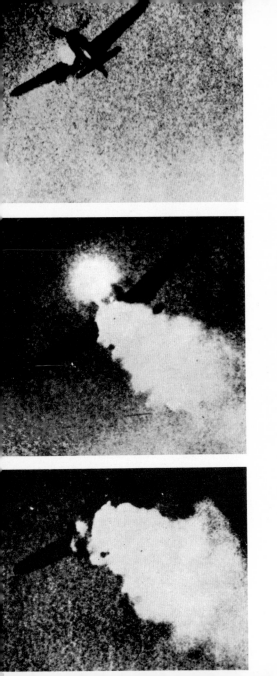

The sting in the nose of the Beaufighter: the double arrowhead is the aerial of the earliest airborne radar. Just below it, canvas patches cover the muzzles of the 20mm cannon

A Messerschmitt 109 caught by the guns – and camera – of a Spitfire over Southern England, summer 1940

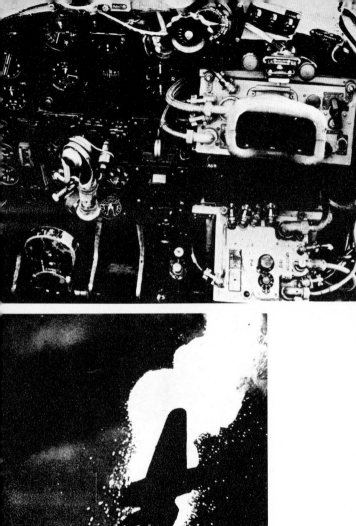

The Mosquito night-fighter cockpit. On the right is the rubber-framed eyepiece for the radar screen. Pilot and operator sat shoulder-to-shoulder

A Heinkel III dies at night, cascading burning petrol . . .

. . . and a Mosquito which ran into such a fire-cloud. Night ranges were often down to 100 yards – and the Mosquito was a wooden aircraft

The 'heavy bomber' of 1940, the Wellington, and the 'heavy' bombs: 500-pounders

Weight increase: the heaviest bomb of the war, a ten-ton 'Grand Slam' at the moment of release from a modified Lancaster (the bomb-bay doors have been removed) of 617 'Dam-busting' Squadron in March 1945

Crete, 1941: a paratroop-dropping Junkers 52 goes down burning over Maleme airfield

The 'stolen Stuka' – a Junkers 87 in Italian markings – being examined by a mechanic after it had reached the British lines

Fighter boy: 'Johnnie' Johnson, top-scoring RAF fighter pilot, in a Spitfire cockpit

depth-charges hit the vessel and lodged in the deck gratings, the other three exploding harmless at a distance. Apparently the captain of the U-boat decided not to dive until he had got rid of the unwelcome object lodged under his deck, and sent a rating to remove it. This bright lad, instead of getting the armourer to remove the fuse and make the charge harmless, dropped it over the side, where, since it was a depth-charge, it blew up and sank the U-boat. Some of the crew who lived to tell the story were picked up by a Naval vessel in which was travelling the First Lord of the Admiralty, Mr Alexander.

Air Chief Marshal
SIR PHILIP JOUBERT KCB CMG DSO

*

One type of aircraft Coastal Command did have in some numbers was the Beaufort bomber/torpedo-bomber (the Beaufighter was a much-modified deritative of this). These were used against German shipping—in particular the commerce-raiders which were now based along the 2,000-mile coastline from northern Norway to the Bay of Biscay. In Brest was the Gneisenau.

FROM FIFTY FEET

Braithwaite was on detachment at St Eval with nine of the squadron aircraft and crews. These were the only aircraft within striking distance of Brest. Three of the crews were already out on a strike when the request for an attack on the *Gneisenau* came through. Braithwaite decided to send the remaining six aircraft off for a dawn attack next day. Three aircraft would go in first and bomb the torpedo nets, and the other three would follow up with torpedoes. The aircraft carrying the bombs would fly at 500 feet, which would give them virtually no better chance of escaping. They would, however, get the advantage of whatever degree of surprise the operation could achieve. But they would stir the harbour up for those that were to follow.

The crews carrying the torpedoes were to take off first so as to be sure of being stationed outside the harbour when the bombing aircraft went in. The signal for torpedo attack would be the explosion of the bombs.

The crews chosen to carry the torpedoes were Hyde, Campbell and a sergeant-pilot named Camp. Hyde was the most experienced pilot on the squadron; he had been awarded the DFC only nine days previously. Campbell was on his twentieth operational trip. Camp had been on the squadron for some months and had shown great keenness.

The operation began badly. Heavy rain swamped the airfield at St Eval. Two of the aircraft carrying bombs got bogged. In revving up their engines to pull out they only succeeded in embedding themselves more firmly. The plan of attack, such as it was, was thus upset from the start. Hyde, Campbell and Camp got off safely with their torpedoes, but of the rest only Menary was able to take off. There were no standby aircraft available.

Under normal conditions the four aircraft might have been recalled. But there was Churchill's directive. The Battle of the Atlantic was at its height and this might prove to be one of the decisive actions of the war. By tomorrow the *Gneisenau* would be back in dry dock; or both ships might be out in the Atlantic again, ready to rendezvous with the *Bismarck*. Conscious as they were of the slender hope that the four aircraft represented, the men responsible for despatching them, from the AOC-in-C downwards, knew that the RAF had been called upon and that, no matter what the odds, it could not be found wanting in the will to try.

The four aircraft took off at various times between 0430 and 0515. But the weather that had waterlogged the airfield now upset the navigation. Menary, the only man carrying bombs, lost his way completely and eventually dropped his bombs at a ship in convoy near the Ile de Batz. It was broad daylight and he was many miles from Brest. Camp also got a long way off course and did not arrive at Brest until 0700. He approached the harbour from the south-west as briefed, crossing the Ile de Longue at 800 feet. It had been daylight for over half an hour and he knew he had missed the rendezvous, but he was still prepared to go in. The weather was atrocious, thick with early-morning haze and mist, but Camp felt that if he could somehow

162

locate the docks the weather might help him to make his approach unseen. He came right down to sea-level, and almost before he realised it he found he was flying between the two arms of land encircling the outer harbour. But the outline was evanescent and he could not get a definite pin-point. Suddenly his aircraft was boxed in by flak as he came under heavy fire from the flak-ships and shore batteries. He had little idea of his precise direction and it was point-less to go on. He pulled up in a climbing turn to the east and almost immediately found himself in cloud.

Camp was unaware that every gun in the harbour had been alerted half an hour earlier by the arrival of Camp-bell and Hyde.

These two pilots had reached Brest independently soon after dawn. Both had loitered outside the harbour, wait-ing for the bomb explosions. Neither knew that two of the bomb-carrying aircraft had failed to take off, nor did they know that the third had lost its way. Campbell, a few min-utes ahead of Hyde, began a wide circuit, watching for some sign of the other aircraft. The light was seeping in under the horizon, like a chink in a curtain. It was going to be virtually a daylight attack, and that would surely mul-tiply the already mammoth odds tenfold. Campbell had seen no explosions, but perhaps he was the last to arrive. He had better go straight in.

As Campbell set his compass to steer for the inner har-bour, as yet invisible in the mist ahead, Hyde was making his landfall. Suddenly Hyde saw an aircraft flash by be-neath him. He just had time to pick out an 'X' on the fuse-lage, the aircraft letter. He called his navigator.

'Who's in "X"?'

'Campbell.'

'It looks as though he's going in. Has anyone seen any-thing? Any explosions, I mean?'

'Not a thing.'

'He's going in all right. I can't think why.' Hyde con-tinued to circle outside the harbour, waiting for Camp-bell to come out. He had been a long time on 22 Squadron, longer than anyone. Throughout he had been that rarity, a pilot who coupled dash with steadiness and a strict regard for orders. There had been no explosions, so there could have been no bombs. The orders were to wait for the explosions. No sense in throwing away his life, his aircraft, the lives of his crew, for the sake of putting a torpedo into a torpedo net. They could always come back again later.

Meanwhile, Campbell had brough his aircraft down to 300 feet and was aiming for the right-hand end of the mole. In the outer harbour the cloud base was low and he streaked along beneath it, intermittently in cloud. Ahead of him out of the mist he picked out the flak-ships. There was the mole, a thin line on the water. If the *Gneisenau* was still anchored to the same buoy, he was perfectly placed for a stern attack.

The failure of the plan to rupture the torpedo nets, added to the fact that it was to be a lone daylight attack, meant that the original odds had multiplied themselves into something like a million to one.

Campbell began his dive down towards the east end of the mole. He could see the flak-ships clearly now. Beyond the mole, a massive shadow was resolving itself into the stern of the *Gneisenau*. He swung away to starboard and then back to port, making an angle of forty-five degrees with the *Gneisenau*. He flattened out his dive, 50 feet above the water. The flak-ships were upon him. He raced between them at mast height, unchallenged, squinting down the barrels of their guns. The mole was only 200 yards away. He looked steadfastly ahead, every nerve alert, steadied the aircraft, and aimed the nose deliberately. When the mole disappeared under the windscreen, he released the torpedo.

Aircraft and torpedo crossed the mole independently, the nose of the torpedo tilted downwards towards the water. The defences of Brest were taken by surprise. Still the Beaufort was unchallenged by anti-aircraft fire.

Th *Gneisenau* towered above them like a mammoth warehouse. There was no sign of any torpedo net. Campbell began to pull away to port to clear the hills behind the harbour, making for the sanctuary of cloud. In perhaps another fifteen seconds they would be safe.

But the peaceful harbour of Brest had been aroused from its lethargy. The Beaufort now had to fly through the fiercest, heaviest, most concentrated barrage that any single aircraft had ever faced or would ever face again. Nothing could live in such a wall of steel.

This was the blinding, withering fire which they had awaited and which they knew must come. Their last sight was of the flashing guns of the *Gneisenau,* lighting the hills behind the harbour, the hills over which they had watched the last dawn they would ever see.

The Beaufort, out of control, crashed into the harbour. What happened in those last moments will never be known. Stabbed by a hundred points of steel, the Beaufort kept flying when almost any other type of aircraft must have been brought down. Campbell himself may have been killed some seconds before the crash came. Scott, the navigator, a contemporary of Al Morris, Loveitt's navigator, may have tried to drag Campbell off the stick and take over. When they lifted the aircraft out of the harbour, it was said by the French Resistance that they found a blond Canadian in the pilot's seat. Campbell and his gallant crew took the secrets of those last despairing seconds with them.

RALPH BARKER

The Gneisenau *was indeed hit; it took nine months to repair. A year after the attack, when intelligence sources had pieced together the full story, Campbell was awarded a posthumous VC.*

*

'We shall bomb Germany by day as well as night in ever-increasing measure, casting upon them month by month a heavier discharge of bombs, and making the German people taste and gulp each month a sharper dose of the miseries they have showered upon mankind.'

WINSTON S. CHURCHILL 22nd June 1941

*

On the night of 7th July, a Wellington bomber was returning to the English coast, having dropped bombs on Münster. One of the crew was Sergeant James Allen Ward of the 75th (New Zealand) Squadron. He was already an old hand at bombing the enemy: in his own words, he had done 'two Kiels, one Düsseldorf, one Cologne, one Brest, one Münser and a Mannerhiem'.

The Wellington was passing over the Zuider Zee at 13,000 feet when a Messerschmitt 110 rose out of the darkness beneath and hit the bomber with cannon shell and incendiary bullets which set the starboard engine on fire. The flames were fed by petrol from a split pipe and it seemed that they might spread over the entire wing. As the bomber flew on and the fire increased, the crew broke a hole in the fuselage so that they might turn the extinguishers on to the flames. In desperation, they even used the coffee from their flasks. But the fire was too strong and it continued to spread.

Jimmy Ward then volunteered to climb out, along the wing, and smother the flames with an engine cover: he said he would go without his parachute, to reduce the wind resistance, but his companions induced him to take it. A rope was tied to him as he climbed out of the fuselage: but this precaution was also a danger—had he been blown off the wing. He broke footholds into the fabric, with his boots, then he descended, three feet, on to the wing. He said, afterwards: 'It was just a matter of getting something to hang on to. It was like being in a terrific gale, only much worse than any gale I've ever known. As I got along the wing I was behind the airscrew, so I was in the slipstream as well. Once or twice I thought I was going.'

He hung on to the wing and smothered the flames in the fabric with the canvas engine cover: then he tried to push the canvas into the hole and on to the leaking pipe. Each time he withdrew his hand, the cover was blown away. In the end it was dragged out of his hands by the violence of the wind and lost in the night, but the flames had been subdued. Jimmy Ward began his cautious return, along the wing and into the aircraft. He said: 'Getting back was worse than going out; by this time I was pretty well all in. The hardest of the lot was getting my right leg in. In the end the navigator reached out and pulled it in.'

In the official report that came to the Air Ministry I read, 'The flight home had been made possible by the gallant action of Sergeant Ward in extinguishing the fire on the wing in circumstances of the greatest difficulty and at the risk of his life.'

A few days later I read that Jimmy Ward had been given the Victoria Cross.

HECTOR BOLITHO

*

IT'S NEVER IN THE PAPERS

Every morning when I came downstairs I sat in the mess and looked for it in the papers. 'Last night our bombers . . ' I would read. 'Yesterday evening at dusk a strong formation . . .' But what I really looked for was never there.

I used to consider the case of Dibden. Dibden was 25. He was a pilot with 33 operational trips and a DFC to his name. He flew Stirlings and looked more than anything else like a dark, very handsome little Eskimo. You felt that it was a pure accident that he was flying a bomber instead of doing a roll in a kayak or having a snooze in an igloo.

Dibden was a good type, and a very good pilot indeed. But there were some who would not fly with him. Navigators, changed from their own crew, would suddenly develop violent toothache or trouble with their ears. Dibden was rather proud of the way he could land a Stirling in fair imitation of a golf-ball.

Once, on circuit and bumps, Dibden began to come in for landing with his air-speed down to ninety. He pulled her off again and did a sickly turn over the telegraph posts on the railway line and came back to land on the established golf-ball principle, hastily. 'It was quite a moment,' Dibden said.

There was nothing about that in the papers. Nor, of course, was there anything about the way he had all his operational hours carefully added up. His 33 trips amounted to 150 hours.

Very soon, with another 50 hours, Dibden would be a veteran; an old man of 25 who had watched others do their three and five and perhaps 15 trips and not return. Dibden always returned; like a ball thrown at a wall he came back, and the harder you threw him the faster he returned.

Once or twice a week, when not on ops, Dibden got a

little whistled, but the papers, of course, did not mention this either. You came into the mess late at night, tired, perhaps, after a spell of duty, to find Dibden bouncing from chair to chair, table to piano, like a smiling cherubic little Eskimo chasing an invisible bear.

At intervals he stopped being the Eskimo and became the bear, rushing up to other people, especially newcomers, to embrace them. 'Bad type, bad type!' he would say. 'Seize him, knock him down. Bad type!' We were all bad types when Dibden was whistled, but the papers, of course, did not mention this either. We are very good types really.

After these adventures others came down to breakfast with faces looking the colour of the sheepskin on their flying-boots; they looked at the mess of kidneys and bacon and said, 'My God, I've had it,' and crawled away.

But not Dibden. He bounced in very late, more cherubic than ever, charmed the first overworked waitress into bringing him crisp rashers, potatoes, kidneys, fresh toast, and coffee, looked at the clock and said something about five minutes to make the hangars, and then began to eat as if he had returned from a hunting expedition. 'Pretty whistled last night, boys,' he would say. 'Rather off my feed.'

He spent most of the rest of his life being brassed off. 'Good morning, Dibden,' you would say. 'How goes it?'

'Pretty much brassed off, old boy.'

'Oh, what's wrong?'

'Just brassed off, that's all. Just brassed off.'

This phrase, which, of course was never in the papers either, covered all the troubles of Dibden's life. It covered all his troubles with his kite, his crew, his ops, his leave, his food, his popsie.

He was brassed off when ops were on because of the increasing monotony of trying to prang the same target; he was brassed off when ops were scrubbed because there was no target at all. He was brassed off because there was fog on the 'drome or because his popsie could not keep her date.

But however brassed off he was he succeeded in looking always the same: cherubic, grinning, bouncing, handsome, too irresponsible and altogether too like a schoolboy to be engaged in the serious business of flying an expensive bomber.

One afternoon Dibden was out over the coast of Holland on a daylight. It was his thirty-third trip: the veteran adding another four or five hours to his flying time. Down below, off the coast, he saw what he took to be an enemy tanker and he went down to have a look-see.

The tanker opened up at him with a fury of flak that surprised him, holing his port wing. I do not know what his emotions were, but I imagine that he was simply, and as always, just brassed off. He went in and attacked the tanker with all he had, bombing first and then diving to machine-gun the deck.

The tanker hit back very hard, clipping a piece out of the starboard flap, but the more the tanker hit the more Dibden bounced back, like the ball thrown hard against the wall. His rear-gunner was very badly wounded, but Dibden still went in, firing with all he had left until the flak from the tanker ceased.

The next day there was in fact something about this in the papers. It did not sound very epic. 'Yesterday afternoon one of our bombers attacked a tanker off the Dutch coast. After the engagement the tanker was seen to be burning.'

It did not say anything about the holes in Dibden's wings or the way the outer port engine had cracked coming home. It did not in fact really say anything at all about that brief, bloody, and very bitter affair in which Dibden had bounced back repeatedly like an angry ball, or about the long journey home.

It did not say anything about Dibden landing on three engines with damaged flaps and a dying rear-gunner, or about a very tired, very brassed-off Dibden coming in very late, with an unexpected hour on his flying time, to boiled beef and tea.

Nor did it say anything about what happened that night. A little after midnight I came into the mess and there, under the bright lights of the ante-room, Dibden was doing some acrobatics. It was a very nice little party. At one end of the room two leather settees were placed endwise against each other, and then against them, endwise again, two chairs.

169

As I came in, Dibden, more cherubic, more smiling, more like a handsome Eskimo than ever, took a drink of light ale and then did a running somersault over the long line of furniture, landing with a wild whoop on his feet. His eyes were shining wildly. After him one or two other pilots tried it, but none of them was really good, and the only one who was good landed on his head. Then Dibden tried it again and the fat, smiling ball of his body went over as easily as a bird.

Perhaps there was no connection between the schoolboy Dibden joyfully throwing a somersault and the veteran Dibden angrily pranging a tanker. But as I saw Dibden hurling his fat little body into the air I felt suddenly that I understood all about his 33 trips, his golf-ball landings, his affairs with the tanker, and the long, hard journey home. I understood why he flew, and why he flew as he did, and I understood the man he was.

But there was nothing about that, of course, in the papers.

Flying Officer 'X' (H. E. BATES)

*

MISSING

They told me when they cut the ready wheat,
    The hares are suddenly homeless and afraid,
And aimlessly circle the stubble with scared feet,
    Finding no place in sunlight or shade.

It's morning, and the Hampdens have returned.
    The crews are home, have stretched and laughed and
gone,
Whence the planes came and the Chance-light burned
    The sun has ridden the sky and made the dawn.

—He walks distraught, circling the landing-ground,
    Waiting the last one home that won't come back,
And like those hares, he wanders round and round,
    Lost and desolate on the close-cropped track.
HERBERT CORBY

*

And in the Western Desert, they were learning

HOW TO STEAL A STUKA

The plain facts are as follows. On 14th September 1941, the discovery of a number of crashed Ju 87s to the south of Sofafi hinted that a whole enemy squadron had been obliged, by petrol shortage, to force-land in our territory. News was received at an RAF base that some Junkers were probably intact. It was desirable to have them flown out of the danger zone.

The information on the subject was both scanty and unreliable. A battle was in progress, and communications were disjointed.

Two RAF officers—Wing Commander Bowman, DFC with Bar, and Squadron Leader Rozier, DSO—got permission to go forward for a general reconnaissance, and if possible they were to fly back in the captured aircraft.

Taking with them one of the Italian prisoners who had offered help in finding serviceable aircraft, they set off. By midday their aeroplane had reached Thalata, where one Ju 87 was found. It had crashed, still loaded with bombs, and turned on its back. Continuing the search, they flew to Hamra, twenty-five miles away. But it was soon evident that the enemy were also interested in the missing Junkers, for seven Macchis flew over at low altitude. Little was discovered at Hamra, but after consultation it was decided to contact a South African Amoured Car unit operating ten miles to the north. The prisoner of war was left with a guard by the aircraft, and the journey was continued by truck. At the prospect of being left in a zone where there was an element of risk, the prisoner was visibly unhappy. He whimpered that the last thing he wanted was to be rescued by his compatriots.

Again the search was unfruitful and the two RAF officers returned to their aircraft with the intention of penetrating even further into enemy territory. They made a landing near Maddalena, an old fort on the Libyan frontier wire. The situation was tricky, and the flyers were not surprised to find more enemy aircraft overhead. But apparently they were unobserved.

By that time dusk was approaching and they were no nearer finding their intact Junkers. One thing was obvious, their own aircraft, rather than assisting in the search, was making them vulnerable to enemy attack. They decided to send it back with the Italian prisoner on board; a decision which raised the latter's spirits. That night the two RAF officers were guests of a famous Hussar regiment.

And so ended the first day of the search.

Dawn broke and an early start was made to follow a definite plan of action. The Hussars had refitted the expedition with rations and water for three days. They had loaned two trucks, an officer and some men; with this equipment the flyers again started out to scour the desert. They were careful to watch out for enemy ground forces as well as aeroplanes, knowing that they were well within the enemy patrolling area.

A cloud of dust on the horizon heralded something. A halt was called and as the moving vehicle gradually came into sight, suspense relaxed. It was a British patrol and they brought good news. The occupants of the truck knew where there was an intact German dive-bomber. But they advised caution. Not five minutes before they had been shot-up and bullet-ridden by four G.50s. The enemy were also seeking their lost Junkers.

Off with a dash, and in due course the German aircraft was reached. It was standing on a stretch of firm sand and by its side, with a certain air of possession, reclined a very young British officer. He was delighted to hand over his charge and intimated that although this was the only intact Junkers he had seen, he suspected that others were in the neighbourhood. There had been an increase of enemy air activity, and he told how he had seen a large Italian aircraft escorted by two fighters make a landing the previous evening, then take off again. He had found the bodies of two Italian airmen. They were slashed and had bled from knife wounds apparently inflicted in a fight for a water-bottle.

Surveying their prize, the RAF officers were faced with three problems. How to remove the bombs from the aircraft? How did the taps work? (all instruments were labelled in German). Were there any bobby traps?

One at a time these questions were examined and answered. The most anxious moment of all was when the Squadron Leader pressed the bomb lever. Even when the first had fallen without blowing them all sky-high, there was no assurance that they would be similarly successful with the others. After two hours' work, however, they decided that the aircraft was airworthy. The officers had brought with them twelve gallons of aviation spirit, and to this they added twenty gallons of ordinary motor car petrol.

It was almost dusk on the second day when, to the echo of a cheer from the soldiers on the ground, the Wing Commander got the engine of the Junkers to purr. Soon they were off. The thrill of stealing a Stuka had begun.

Fifteen minutes of steady cruising in a north-easterly direction, when suddenly, without warning, the engine stopped and the aircraft floated groundwards. It says much for the pilot's skill that he was able to force-land on the rough desert surface with no damage to the aircraft, other than a burst tyre.

It was then almost dark, but when the engine came to life again, after a little tinkering, they decided to make another attempt. Again they were unlucky. The hydraulic gauge burst and the pilot was momentarily blinded with the fluid. The surface of the desert had changed and approaching darkness had increased the difficulties of landing. The aircraft hit the ground with a jolt, rushed forward, then sprang into the air and came to rest at the bottom of a shallow escarpment. With grimaces the flyers climbed out to examine the damage. There was another burst tyre. This, they realised, must be enough for one day.

With a minor shock they realised that in the excitement of getting the aircraft to start, back at Maddalena, they had forgotten their rations, water and maps. Disgruntled, they crawled under the aircraft, wrapped themselves in an Italian parachute, and fell asleep.

Next morning more problems to solve. The flyers were not sure of either their own position or that of the enemy. They had no signal pistol with which they might attract attention. It was impossible to fly the captured aircraft until a new wheel and gauge were procured.

They decided to set off for Sidi Barrani on foot. To

their reckoning it was forty miles away.

There was no doubt about their reluctance to abandon the treasure. It had been tough finding the aircraft. It hurt still more to leave it. Before doing so, they scratched on the ground: 'This Ju 87 is RAF property. Do not touch. W/Cdr Bowman and S/Ldr Rozier left here at dawn 19/9/41 walking north.'

Ten weary, uneventful miles of foot-slogging. Then they met a South African officer, who took them to his camp for breakfast.

Then Rozier had an idea. Why not go back to Thalata and retrieve a hydraulic gauge and spare wheel from the first Junkers which they had found overturned?

So, on the third day, they set off again, this time accompanied by a Tank Corps officer, who had lent them his truck. By this time it appeared that almost every soldier in the forward area was taking a keen interest in the two pilots and their Junkers. The wheel and gauge were wrenched from the upside-down aircraft, and, reinforced by a small RAF unit which had been sent out to help, they bumped off on a truck, determined that this time they would succeed.

The strange sort of thing that can only come about in the Western Desert had happened. They had picked up on the way a naval officer! He was a young, bearded destroyer commander who was on leave, and he was actually spending it in the Western Desert 'having a look around' as he said. He had asked if he could 'join the fun'.

Eventually the party arrived at the Junkers, and an RAF technician soon got to work on the wheel and the defective gauge. The engine revived. The naval officer, to round off his holiday, asked if he could take the gunner's seat. This was agreed to and off they went.

The flight back to the RAF aerodrome was not as peaceful as a stroll in the park. More than once they were heartily fired at by British troops who had not been able to keep up with the rapid sequence of events, and to whom a red-bearded air gunner still spelt 'Nazi'— when he was leaning over the side of a Stuka.

Squadron Leader GEORGE W. HOUGHTON

*

174

WITHOUT PREVIOUS WARNING

(To the Japanese Ambassador, London:)

Foreign Office, 8th December

Sir,

On the evening of 7th December His Majesty's Government in the United Kingdom learned that Japanese forces without previous warning either in the form of a declaration of war or of an ultimatum with a conditional declaration of war had attempted a landing on the coast of Malaya and bombed Singapore and Hong Kong.

In view of these wanton acts of unprovoked aggression committed in flagrant violation of International Law and particularly of Article I of the Third Hague Convention relative to the opening of hostilities, to which both Japan and the United Kingdom are parties, His Majesty's Ambassador at Tokyo has been instructed to inform the Imperial Japanese Government in the name of His Majesty's Government in the United Kingdom that a state of war exists between our two countries.

I have the honour to be, with high consideration

Sir,

Your obedient servant,

WINSTON S. CHURCHILL

1942

It was going to be a long war. A pilot jumping from a burning cockpit thinks only of getting clear, of whether his parachute will open. Only when he reaches the ground safely will he remember that it's a long walk home. Britain was like that: in the last eighteen months nobody had thought too far ahead. Now came the realisation that it was a big war, and due to be a long slogging one.

*

In the Far East, it was the familiar old story: a handful of gallant but inexperienced airmen in outdated aircraft trying to hold off a better-trained, better-equipped and more numerous enemy. Some Hurricanes and pilots, originally intended for the Middle East, had been diverted to Burma and Singapore just in time to be too few, too late.

THE LAST DAYS OF SINGAPORE

We'd hardly had time to get refuelled and rearmed after this flight when we were ordered to scramble again. Another big high-altitude raid was on the way, and we took off in a rush, climbing madly even before we had joined up in formation. Then after a couple of minutes a new order came over the radio from Control.

'Hello, Tiger Leader, Tiger Leader! There are low-flying aircraft attacking our troops in the north-west part of the island. Detach two of your aircraft to deal with them. Over!'

Denny's voice came across at once, acknowledging the order, and then he called to me. 'Hello, Blue One, Blue

One! Will you take your number two and take care of that? Over.'

'O.K.,' I answered. 'Hello, Blue Two. Follow me!' And I led off in a diving turn into the north-west, leaving the others to climb on up after the big raid. My number two's name was Sergeant M——.

Control called again, urging us to hurry, and we opened our engines to full throttles as we swept down under the clouds towards the area given. As we neared it I strained my eyes trying to discern any airplanes there, or anti-aircraft puffs which would indicate their presence, but I could see neither. We arrived and circled that part of the island low down, watching in all directions without seeing anything. Finally I called Control.

'Hello, Rastus, Hello, Rastus! Tiger Blue One calling. We are in the area but we don't see anything about. I'm afraid we're too late. Have you any new instructions for us?'

But I never gave him time to reply, for a couple of seconds later I saw it. We were travelling north just then, toward the section of the Straits where the Johore Causeway crossed into the enemy-occupied city of Johore Bahru, and I caught sight of an airplane in the distance straight ahead, low down over Johore Bahru and travelling north.

I fumbled excitedly for the transmitter switch. 'Tally-ho! Straight ahead for us, Blue Two!' I called, and laid out after it, pushing throttle and propeller pitch controls clear ahead, low down over Johore Bahru and travelling north. which cuts out all governing over the engine's supercharging so that it can put out an emergency power far greater than its normal maximum.

The sound rose to an immense, strained bellowing, and in a few seconds my controls began to stiffen from the increased speed, and the countryside seemed to fairly stream past, close beneath our wings, for we were flying low down over the trees.

Crossing the Straits of Johore we streaked low across the roof-tops of Johore Bahru, chasing our quarry who was now following along the main highway which leads north-west from the city up into Malaya. I remember noticing

177

that the road was packed with military traffic—enemy trucks, buses, cars, etc.

The enemy plane had a good start on us, and at first we hardly seemed to gain on it. We started getting flak—the first Japanese flak I'd seen. There was just an occasional black puff near us at first; then soon a regular hail of it, following us right along. It seemed to make about the same-sized bursts as the British and German 'medium' flak—Bofors and pom-pom guns—with the differences that this stuff seemed to have adjustable fuses so that it was timed to explode near us, and that it had no tracer effect, remaining invisible until it exploded. Ours and the German medium flak doesn't explode unless it actually hits you or reaches the end of its travel, and the shells are all tracers, appearing as red or green balls. We were so intent on overtaking our quarry that we just let them blaze away, without taking any evasive action from the shells.

At last we were gaining noticeably on the other machine, and soon I could discern its shape as that of a single-engined plane with 'fixed' (non-retractable) landing gear hanging down. From pictures I'd seen I took it to be a type of two-seater fighter known as the 'Army 97'. It alternately flew at about five hundred feet for a minute or so and then dived to tree-top height for a way, where we could scarcely see it against the jungle. We stayed at about five hundred feet ourselves. Behind me a couple of hundred yards Sergeant M——'s plane, guarding my tail, appeared as a vicious silhouette against a background of angry anti-aircraft puffs sprinkled pepper-like against the sky.

I think I was perhaps four or five hundred yards behind our quarry, for I remember that I already had my thumb on the firing button ready to press it in a few more seconds, when the beginning occurred of one of those nightmare experiences that last actually but a moment but live for ever after in inescapable memory.

First a bright flash of colour caught my eye. I was staring down fascinated at a green Navy Zero wheeling across below and ahead of me, turning steep left just above the tree-tops, while seemingly without any conscious decision I was twisting over viciously in a diving turn after him. I closed in, still diving, pulling my nose around until my sights lined up with him and a little ahead, leading him. Then I let him have it, the quick, shattering roar from my guns startling me, and my long white tracers reaching out to caress the graceful little green wings ahead of me with their strange red discs painted near each tip. Only for two or three seconds, and then I had to break off to straighten out of my dive before hitting the trees. Just as I was breaking off I heard a bang and felt a jolt, and saw that one of the smaller gun panels was gone from my right wing. I thought it had been shot off; but I forgot about it in what I saw a moment later.

I zoomed up hard, nearly blacking out and just missing the trees. My run-away gun was chattering away on its own irritatingly and spewing its tracers aimlessly out over the jungle. I turned left to get around at any new enemies that might be behind. And there, amid the confusion of anti-aircraft fire bursting all around, I saw Sergeant M——'s Hurricane diving steeply, obviously hit! I was right over him as he struck, in the corner of a little field, at close to three hundred miles an hour, in a terrible ghastly eruption of splintered wings and flying pieces and then steam and dust and smoke that swirled out to obscure the awful sight.

I recall circling cautiously for a moment, dazed and shocked by this and trying to take in the whole situation and see how many new enemies I had. In doing so I apparently lost sight of both the one we'd been chasing and the Navy Zero. There were no new ones to be seen either.

Thinking back on the event, I believe the Navy Zero pilot must have been above us when he saw us chasing the other Jap, so he dived on us from behind, firing and hitting Sergeant M——. Then his speed carried him on down and ahead as he levelled out from his dive, until he was below and in front of me where I first saw him. Sergeant M—— must either have been killed by the bullets or had his controls disabled, and went into the fatal dive that I saw.

A pathetic little wisp of smoke and dust rising above the trees was the last I saw of him, as escorted by the storm of anti-aircraft fire I made my way alone back to Singapore Island.

Control was telling the others about another raid coming in at high altitude, so I headed out over the sea and started climbing. I was late again, though, for I saw the bombers approaching the island when I was far too low. In fact I was able to call up Control and correct him on the position he was giving for them once or twice, while still unable to do anything myself except look up at them and swear. When they were almost over the island they turned away and headed seaward. Later I learned that some of the others chased them and got in a few shots, damaging two or three.

After they had gone away I did a little free-lancing again but nothing more turned up, and finally Control ordered all of us to land. I was down before the rest, and when the others landed and came up to the dispersal hut I had to give them the news of Sergeant M——'s death. I hadn't known him well, but the mute faces and glistening eyes of some of the boys told me how much they thought of him. I wondered if any of them felt it was my fault.

Flight Lieutenant ARTHUR DONAHUE DFC

*

The four of us in our patched-up airplanes now headed out across the Straits of Malacca. When we were eight or ten miles out I noticed that my engine seemed to be working very hard to keep up with the other machines. Then I realised that I hadn't retracted my wheels yet—I'd been so busy looking back and monkeying with my camera that I had forgotten all about them! I raised them hurriedly, feeling embarrassed and hoping the others hadn't noticed, and my airplane speeded up at once so that I was able to ease my engine considerably.

We'd been warned that our airplanes were in very ropy condition, having been patched up and put together so hastily; and I found this was no exaggeration concerning mine. One of my wheels wouldn't lock in its retracted position and kept dropping down. I had to raise it every couple of minutes. The position indicator light for my wheels wasn't working, so at first I could never tell for sure when this wheel was clear up. Then noticing a hole in the bottom of my fuselage right by the place where the wheel came up, I found I could tell by the amount of daylight coming through the hole whether it was clear up or not.

My air-speed indicator registered zero at all times, and the airplane was 'out of trim' so that I had to keep holding the stick to one side to keep it level. However, the engine purred nicely and the oil pressure and radiator temperatures were normal, so I didn't mind the other faults.

Denny also appeared to be having trouble with his landing gear, for one of his wheels kept coming down the same as mine. And Tom, in his Brewster, flew for the first ten or fifteen minutes with both his wheels clear down. His trouble was just that he couldn't find the right gadget to raise them with, not having flown a Brewster before. Brownie seemed to be getting along all right in his Hurricane, although afterwards he said his propeller pitch control wasn't working, so that his engine just ran at any speed it felt like.

Everything went smoothly for the first forty-five minutes, and we were well on our way across the Straits of Malacca. In another fifteen or twenty minutes we should reach the coast of Sumatra, and an hour or so after that would bring us to Palembang.

Then Denny, who was leading us, suddenly began waggling his wings as a sign of distress, and headed downward and left toward an island a few miles in diameter, which we were nearing.

I took over the lead of the remaining three. Denny was obviously planning to force-land on this island, so I followed after him with my three, to see where he landed and whether he made it safely. We circled around above him while he made a couple of passes at a small field in one part of the island; but this seemed to worry him. He came back up alongside me, motioning me to go on, so, regretfully, the three of us headed on southwards.

In a few minutes we struck the coast of Sumatra. We had to follow it southwards now, until we came to the River Musi leading inland to Palembang, all of which had seemed very simple so far. But I had only followed the coast a short distance before I realised that I might soon be in difficulties. The crude map which I had picked up in the dispersal hut for emergency was an absolute menace—it showed only the one river going inland, with hardly any details by which I could identify it, whereas there seemed

181

to be fully a dozen rivers leading in from this section of the coast! Picking the right one was going to be a most delicate matter.

To make matters worse the weather was getting bad, with the ceiling down to a thousand feet and thunderstorms and rain scattered all around, so I didn't have the visibility I needed to discern the course of each river. We didn't have enough gas to allow for errors in navigation; if I picked the wrong one we'd be sunk.

There's something frightening about being unsure of your way in an airplane. You can't stop and debate over your map as to which is the right way before going on. You're going, and fast, whether you've decided which way to go or not, and whether you're headed right or wrong, so your decisions are forced. I had terrible thoughts of our three precious fighter planes lost and crashing in the jungle somewhere, the result of my faulty map-reading.

One after another I passed up these rivers, each one because it didn't seem to check with the one on my map from what I could see of it, until I had gone by several and it seemed I surely must have gone far enough. I began to wonder helplessly if one of those I'd passed up had been the right one, and if so how I'd ever be able to find which it was if I went back now.

Then out of the rain and mist ahead another appeared which seemed to take the right direction in from the coast, curving like the one on my map, so I turned inland on it, praying I wasn't making a mistake. Within a few minutes I saw a couple of steamers on it, so I thought I must be right. And a little farther on we came in sight of Palembang itself. I gave one of my biggest sighs of relief!

Flight Lieutenant ARTHUR DONAHUE DFC

The relief didn't last long. Palembang was invaded a few days later; Donahue escaped, returned to Britain, and died over the Channel later the same year. He had been the first American to fly in combat with the RAF.

*

And in Burma, with the background of the same inadequacy, a young pilot was meeting

182

I became somewhat sleepy. At four I roused myself with more tea. We all started to doze again. Someone lethargically chased a pie dog away and sent it scampering abashed into the scrub and grass behind the dispersal. Looking over the aerodrome one could see the heat rising from the baked ground like the mixing of cordial in water. The Hurricanes stood patiently, their noses pointing skywards like eager game dogs, and periodically an erk would get down from the fuselage and collapse a while in the shade of its wings.

The telephone rang.

It rang gently, nobody paid much attention to it, and Tug actually answered it.

'Scraa-amble . . . Scraa-aamble. . . .'

Jack Gibson and I cannoned into each other as we leapt off the veranda; Stinker Murdoch muttered something like, 'Oh, dear!' in his mild manner, and dropped his half-full mug of tea in the sandy earth; everyone ran like men possessed.

Why it was I, and all the others, had the prescient thought this was A—capital letters—A Raid, I cannot explain. I know we were all especially eager, and I was vilely obscene when one of my straps slipped out of my grasp and entangled itself with the hydraulic pump-lever on the left of the cockpit. It was a troublesome scramble, even if only in my imagination, because I momentarily behaved like a bad-tempered little boy who is apoplectic with his toy-train. The straps were a fuddle, the engine was recalcitrant, and when I did successfully dope it into action, I immediately noticed someone had altered the setting of the rudder-bar. Ugh—urrr!

From all the segments of the aerodrome came the throb of engines, like a challenging, long-drawn 'Bayete', and then the slim-nosed fighters, the sharks' teeth, and the Hurricanes, came eagerly out on to the runways. There was dust and more dust, the rolling beat of pairs of engines as the sections took off, and more dust. I had to abide with as much patience as I could muster by the side of the AVG's runway until they had swept by. Then with a rush and a twitching of rudder and easy puffs of brake, I got down our own runway and opened up. I didn't know who was along-side me until after I had leaned forward to the under-carriage lever and steadied the machine to maximum climb. The CO was ahead, going north as arranged, his fol-lowers a blob of constantly changing outline, and I followed him as fast as I could. I made no attempt to overtake, though, for it would have done my engine no good. Look-ing on either side—after staring around and above care-fully—I found Frank Earnshaw, Warble (Warburton), Owen Reid and, I think, another with me. Instinctively the boys fell into our squadron formation, and I led merely because I had been first off of that group. We curved left, into sun, then headed back over base.

Only as we turned did my R/T function clearly—a not unusual occurrence with the older type of set we had at the time. Ops was nattering away busily. He had a good plot and was happy to be able to put us on the right track.

'. . . Hello, Bandit Blue 1, Loudmouth calling; bogeys are now two miles south-west of base at angels 18: 20 miles south-west of base at angels 18. They are heading for base; they are heading for base.'

A silence, then Ops transmitted unintentionally, for I heard a remark from the Ops room, just as one momentarily cuts into another telephone conversation.

I increased the rate of climb by as much as I dared. We were now at 12,000 feet. Oh, Jesus, this is it, this is it—just time to get above . . .

'Hello, Bandit Blue 1, Loudmouth calling; bogeys now 10 miles south-west of base; 10 miles south-west of base, still heading for base!'

'Oh, Jesus, where the hell!' . . . I bounced up and down on my parachute pad and automatically checked over gun-button, revs, any other knob handy, in the manner of a man fiddling with his tie before he walks to the dentist's chair.

Aaah! I saw them at the same time as Ops, more urgently now, told us, 'Hello, Bandit Blue 1, bogeys now approach-ing base, angels 18; angels 18.'

That is the moment in any pilot's life, when he first sees enemy aircraft in the sky! If he doesn't see them, it's the other kind of moment when, fascinated, he watches cannon-shells rip hell out of his wings! Momentarily I panicked, my mouth became so dry it seemed I had been licking thousands of stamps.

Then my thoughts raced with a hare's swift rhythm: 'Must be calm . . . Jesus, must be calm . . . watch for the fighters . . . must get the bombers . . . hell, they're above us yet . . . must let 'em bomb the drome, can't help it . . . head more east and intercept 'em on the way out . . . Oh Christ, let me get one . . .'

When I picked them out they were flying steadily towards the aerodrome and were just over the town. Behind the bombers, holding their course with the directness of a barge's momentum, was a mass of fighters, weaving and twisting like a swarm.

I settled down, my brain concerned itself automatically with estimation of height and intercepting angles, and as I noticed the earth of the aerodrome seemingly buffet to the lash of bombs I put my nose down and pulled everything, diving shallowly in a tremendous effort to reach them. Peering ahead intently, I saw a slow arc of flame, a comet in ecstatic pirouetting—a Jap fighter—curve down to earth. Battle had commenced!

I got below the level of the bombers, which illusorily fanned out into four sections of four aircraft apiece, but my glance was distracted by a flick of light to my right. A second later I licked my tongue anew and concentrated. What I had seen in that moment of stark apprehension had been a set of shark's teeth, diving as I was diving, but on to the fighters.

For some reason—beginner's luck—the fighters ignored me. I was pulling up and now quite calm. 'Get the bead just a little ahead of the nose . . . steady . . . up to the engines . . .'

I kept my finger on the button and then my mind leaned back and folded arms. 'Yes, they must be firing at me . . . oh, but look, must be my strikes on the wings of that one . . . and the one alongside . . . shift the bead, there we are . . . hmm, getting close . . .'

The silhouettes grew and grew as I overtook them, colours and even structural details became distinct, then I glanced right again to be confronted by the starboard vic

185

of bombers a few yards away, on a level with myself. I saw a gunner swinging . . .

'Holy Jesus!' I kicked over rudder and stick and slapped the Hurricane downwards violently. Fearful of being jumped now, I plummeted to earth until I could level out only by winding back on my tail trim—the stick had frozen ! But that was inexperience, and, of course, self-preservation.

None the less, my first nervousness had gone. I edged away and commenced climbing again, wary of spots in my eyes, grit on the glass screen, as a man stalking a wounded bear. In the way a man's mind will conjure up the most remote subjects under stress, I remembered wondering why the hell there must always be ducks' eggs for breakfast. I was sure I would have been a nerveless ace if I hadn't been eating ducks' eggs. You will notice, too, in my account the question of what damage I'd done hardly occurs . . . strikes on the wings . . . yes. I sprayed the whole vic of four . . . did you see them flame or go down . . . ? Well, no . . .

I climbed up to 20,000 feet without incident, once more pure luck, for the fighters of both sides were now swarming in every direction, slowly following the bombers' trail like the turbulent wake of a large ship.

After going east at that height for a few minutes I quite calmly bethought I had better look behind me. Another fighter was coming along, too, at an easy pace. I banked round to meet it, for it had no fixed undercarriage and I was glad to meet an ally . . . Christ, a radial engine, one of the 01s!

I goggled like a bumpkin at the aircraft, which could not have been chasing me for it went cruising serenely past with no attempt at attack. I caught the glint of the hood glass, the red of the roundel on its wings, then as I half-turned after it, the co's words reminded me 'No dog-fighting!' Obediently, and like a fool, for I might have got in one crack before he turned inside me, I whipped over and dived away.

Being a fool had its compensations, though, for as I looked down at the earth and intervening space I came diving into a cauldron of a dog-fight. In classic words, 'There was I . . .!' One red roundelled fighter flew across my sights and positioned itself perfectly from my point of view. Quite coolly now, my wind working accurately as a predictor, I calculated the deflection, my hand eased the stick back, and then I pressed the gun-button once more.

Most spectacular, when I think of it—roaring down, guns blazing death and destruction! Well, well, well, I think actually about one bullet of mine, perhaps three or four, must in reality have crepitated on his fuselage or wing, for he immediately swung over and dove down. I didn't stay to ascertain whether it was from mortal injury; this time I went slap down to the deck and sheered off. Very wisely, too, for to have lingered in that high-blood-pressured swarm of Japs would certainly have included the riddling of my machine and probably myself. Formating along with the AVG boy back to base, I felt I'd had a good day—I'd damaged three bombers and nicked one fighter. Flying gaily through the buffeting over-heated lower atmosphere, I became immeasurably elated. I let my aircraft down on the runway with the nonchalant, casual, but unerring deftness of experience!

I was out of the cockpit before a mechanic got near and walking rapidly towards the dispersal, from under cover of which the IO came eagerly to question me. There was great excitement, the ground crews lingered near and listened to every spluttered word of my tale of the fight. Apparently it had been seen, up high, and had provided them with a fine spectacle. They had been immensely cheered by the appearance of several flamers in the sky, and I wondered if maybe any of the bombers had eventually become on fire after I had left them.

The IO controlled my gabble and pinned me down to claiming a probable bomber and a damaged fighter. Like all pilots after their first blood-letting, my egotistic impression was that I had been almost the only one in the sky and had personally been responsible for most of the damage.

KENNETH HEMINGWAY

The AVG's were the American Volunteer Group—Chennault's famous 'Flying Tigers' who painted shark mouths (why not tigers?) on their Kittyhawks and had flown for China against the Japanese for many months before

America entered the war. But Burma was evacuated soon afterwards.

*

YOU LEARN LIKE THIS

Telegram OHMS   20.2.1942

IMMEDIATE FROM AIR MINISTRY KINGSWAY REGRET TO INFORM
YOU THAT YOUR SON ACTING SQUADRON LEADER ERNEST
MITCHELSON MASON DFC IS REPORTED MISSING AS THE RESULT
OF AIR OPERATIONS 15TH FEBRUARY 1942 ENQUIRIES ARE BEING
MADE THROUGH INTERNATIONAL RED CROSS GENEVA AND ANY—
FURTHER INFORMATION RECEIVED WILL BE IMMEDIATELY
COMMUNICATED TO YOU LETTER CONFIRMING THIS TELEGRAM
FOLLOWS.

> Air Ministry, London
> 21st February 1942

Madam,

I am commanded by the Air Control to confirm the telegram in which we were notified that your son, Acting Squadron Leader Ernest Mitchelson Mason, DFC, Royal Air Force, is missing as the result of air operations on 15th February 1942.

Your son was flying a Kittyhawk aircraft, was engaged by the enemy, and has failed to return. This does not necessarily mean that he is killed or wounded, and if he is a prisoner of war he should be able to communicate with you in due course. Meanwhile enquiries will be made through the International Red Cross Society and from all possible local sources. As soon as any definite news is received, you will be at once informed.

The Air Council desire me to express their sincere sympathy with you in your present anxiety.

> I am, Madam,
> Your obedient Servant,
> for Air Ministry.

FROM AIR MINISTRY KINGSWAY DEEPLY REGRET TO INFORM
YOU THAT YOUR SON ACTING SQUADRON LEADER ERNEST
MITCHELSON MASON DFC IS NOW REPORTED TO HAVE LOST HIS
LIFE AS A RESULT OF AIR OPERATIONS ON 15TH FEBRUARY 1942
STOP LETTER CONFIRMING THIS TELEGRAM FOLLOWS STOP THE
AIR COUNCIL EXPRESS THEIR PROFOUND SYMPATHY STOP
UNDER SECRETARY OF STATE AIR MINISTRY

> Air Ministry, London
> 27th February 1942

Madam,

I am commanded by the Air Council to inform you that
they have with great regret to confirm the telegram in
which you were notified of the further news that your son,
Acting Squadron Leader Ernest Mitchelson Mason, DFC,
Royal Air Force, lost his life as the result of air operations
on 15th February, 1942.

His body was recovered and buried by Army personnel.

The Air Council desire me to express their profound sympathy with you in your bereavement.

> I am, Madam,
> Your obedient Servant,
> for Air Ministry.

*

*In the spring of the year, Malta came to the critical phase
of its long and, luckily, intermittent siege. With Rommel
apparently en route to Cairo, stretching his supply lines
and demanding reinforcements, Malta had to be subdued.
The island's shortage was always in fighter aircraft—not
pilots. This was a reversal of the Battle of Britain situation.
Malta's repair facilities could hardly cope with damaged
aircraft as Britain's factories could: on the other hand, no
fighter could arrive on the island except in the hands of a
reasonably competent pilot, since the only way to get there
was to fly off a carrier several hundred miles away.*

*Among the new arrivals was a Canadian who was very
quickly to become Malta's top fighter ace:*

189

The *Eagle*, escorted by two destroyers, pressed ahead and left behind the British convoy bound for Malta. It was 5 am, just before sunrise. The carrier's deck was covered with Spitfire Vs equipped with auxiliary tanks.

The pilots gave their planes a final check over. They were Spit V-Cs ('tropical') armed with four 20-mm cannon. They were at least brand-new planes, and at a time when everyone, from Moscow to London, from Australia to Alaska, from Libya to the Caribbean, was screaming for fighters, the pilots felt they had not done too badly to get them.

All the same, they were slightly nervous—not one of them had ever taken off from a carrier. While they strapped themselves in, the fitters finished stowing their meagre possessions in the magazines of the machine-guns and of two of the cannon—the other two cannon were loaded. Over the Tannoy came the naval flight-officer's final instructions: navigation gen, courses, ETA's frequencies, etc.

At 6.05 am the first Spitfire took off. Pointing his yellow flag, the deck officer signalled Beurling to get under way. This was it. Rather tensed, he slowly opened the throttle while keeping the brakes hard on. As soon as the tail lifted and the Spit began to champ at the bit, he let her go. Drawn by its 1,500-hp engine, and with a 30-mph head-wind and the ship's own 20 knots helping, the plane was air-borne almost immediately.

By 6.30 the last Spit had taken off and the *Eagle* immediately turned about. The Algerian coast was only thirty miles away, and there might be enemy submarines lurking around. Already in formation, the thirty-two planes receded in the distance, heading east on their flight to Malta.

The sea was blue, without a wrinkle. To the right was the violet line of the Tunisian coast, down below the white patch formed by the island of Lampedusa, over there to the left at the foot of that thundercloud forming was Sicily, with its fourteen airfields crammed with Messerschmitts.

More and more frequently, as Malta drew nearer, snatches of conversation came over the R/T. Interference from German radio-location also began to jingle in the pilots' ears like an antique telephone bell.

The formation was flying at 24,000 feet and the cold was intense in spite of the sun. Fifteen minutes to go. Malta called:

'Hullo, Condor leader, this is Timber calling. Steer 081 and get a move on. Do not answer. Repeat, do not answer. Out.'

Things must be hotting up, and Woodhall, the controller, getting anxious. He had no doubt seen on his radar screen an enemy raid forming over Sicily. It was probably going to develop into a race, if the Luftwaffe were not to catch them with their pants down as they landed, for the Germans had cathode-ray tubes too.

Malta ahead! A big grey and green oval, perched on white cliffs resting on the sea, and flanked on the north-west by the two small islands of Comino and Gozo.

The formation split up into sections of four, diving separately. Details became discernible—the seething bay of Marsa Xlokh, the deep gash of Valetta harbour, ringed by tiers of flat-roofed houses, the web of hedges and stone walls cutting up the arid fields. Further on, the leprous sore of the main airfield, riddled with bomb craters.

Beurling had pushed back his hood and, while the first sections, with their flaps and undercarts down, were joining the circuit, he had a good look round.

Accustomed to the orderly arrangement of English airfields, he was taken aback at the sight of this stretch of ground, five miles long, with bits of runway everywhere and sinuous tracks disappearing into underground shelters. This extraordinary airfield was really three—Luqa, Safi and Hal Far—connected by two gravel strips, so that in effect a plane could take off or land anywhere, i.e. on whichever the last enemy raid had left intact.

However serious the damage, there was always some serviceable corner left. Enormous heaps of stones were dotted here and there, for filling in the new craters as soon as the raid was over. All round the perimeter, except where it ran along the cliff, there was a series of bays with thick walls, to protect parked planes from splinters. Remains of burnt-out wings and fuselages were scattered about everywhere.

Six Spitfires took off to cover the newcomers' landing.

The field was swarming with men. Beurling did not quite know where to land. In the end he just followed the others down and found himself on a bumpy track at the end of which stood a group of soldiers waving him on. As he came past, two of them grabbed hold of his wing-tips while a third jumped on the wing and caught hold of his shoulder. Through the wind from the propeller this one yelled into his ear that he had better hurry up, Jerry was on the way.

In the end he found himself in a kind of rabbit burrow formed by heaps of petrol cans filled with sand. Before he had time to draw breath he was surrounded by a gesticulating crowd of extraordinary-looking individuals, unshaven and dressed in the relics of the uniforms of all three Services. The fitter who had guided him in switched his engine off. Three muscular types grabbed the tail and swung the plane round so that it faced the airfield again. More men came staggering up with cans of petrol.

Beurling, flabbergasted, was ejected from his seat by a pilot who promptly took his place. Trying to keep out of the way of all these madmen he found himself in a slit trench at the back of the burrow. All his goods and chattels, lovingly stowed away in the wings, were sent flying in every direction.

'Get a move on, get a move on!' Everybody seemed to be shouting the same thing. The armourers came up at the double, screw-drivers between their teeth and festooned with belts of shells and cartridges. The radio-fitter had already clapped on his ear-phones, opened the fuselage panels, changed the crystals in the set and checked the battery terminals. The empty oxygen-bottle was changed for a full one, all ready waiting in a corner.

The pilot was getting impatient and drumming on the fuselage. Beurling, not quite knowing what to do, mechanically lit a cigarette. It was immediately snatched out of his mouth by a type who, before he had time to protest, bawled something at him and rushed back to his job. He might have known better; petrol was being brought up by a chain of soldiers and poured in the open through a large lined funnel.

The auxiliary tank was whisked off the plane.

'Hurry up, for Christ's sake!'

Already in the distance they could hear the Bofors batteries opening up. Bang, bang, bang, bang, bang—the five barks from one charger—bang! bang! bang! bang! bang! The Jerries must have arrived.

The groundcrew worked on frantically. From all over the field came the roar of Merlin engines starting up.

'O.K.? Contact!'

The men sprang off the Spitfire as it too started up, raising a furious wind which picked up Beurling's trampled shirts and underclothes and flung them into the air.

The pilot took the aircraft out of the bay with savage bursts of throttle which made the rudder vibrate. Still flat on one wing was an armourer, hanging on to the leading edge with one hand while he screwed down the last machine-gun panel with the other. Just as the Spit opened up to take off, he let go everything and rolled on to the ground, only just escaping being bashed in by the tailplane.

Beurling was now alone. The crowd of madmen had vanished into thin air. He emerged from his hole and made for the open. He ran into three other pilots from the *Eagle*, just as dazed as himself, who dragged him along in a frantic rush for a shelter. It was high time. The air vibrated with the powerful rumbling roar of a big formation very high up, and the shriller sound of Spitfires attacking. The staccato crackle of the machine-guns stood out above the muffled boom-boom-boom of the 20-mm Hispano cannon.

Look out! He just had time to turn round and see six Messerschmitt 109s, which had sneaked in low over the water, jump Hal Far cliff and streak across the field at 400 mph with all guns blazing.

It was Beurling's first glimpse of a 109. In France, when he was on 22 Squadron, he had met only Focke-Wulf 190s.

One of the 109s passed within ten yards of him, and the deafening roar of his engine mingled with the whine of the 40-mm shells from the AA, firing horizontally and spraying the ground with splinters.

Just at that moment Beurling was sent flying head first into a trench by a push from one of his mates. He raised his head. The Junkers 88s—about fifty of them, escorted by sixty Messerschmitt 109s—were starting their dive. They were peeling off one by one and coming down in a 65-degree dive on the airfield in one unbroken line. The deep tone of the engines had changed to a screaming crescendo. The earth quivered, and sand trickled into the trenches. Bombs ripped down with a noise like an express train. The 88s flattened out at 1,500 feet, their glass-house noses and their elongated nacelles clearly visible.

The bombs exploded with a terrifying crump, great clods of earth flew up, splinters whizzed murderously, mowing down everything in their path. Each explosion sent a shock wave through the earth and each time Beurling felt a thump like a kick in the stomach.

The empty cases of the 20-mm fell like hail, clanging against the empty cans. A Junkers 88, hit, continued its dive and crashed with a tremendous roar between two parked Wellingtons, which immediately burst into flame. Clouds of dust rose, mixed with smoke. The air stank of hot metal, sulphur and cordite. Shell splinters rained down.

A muffled explosion, followed by two others—another Junkers 88 had crashed, the wreck bouncing along in a sheet of flame.

Four parachutes hung above, stupidly silent amidst the infernal din.

A minute's relative calm on the ground while the battle raged 10,000 feet up. Planes circled in pairs, pursuer and pursued; wings glinted in the sun, and all the time the rattle of machine-guns went on. Now and then a plane broke away from the mêlée, trailing white smoke—over there, a Spitfire, and that ball of fire plummeting into the sea was a Messerschmitt 109.

The sky was thick with black clusters of AA bursts—like lumps of coal thrown up by the Bofors batteries.

A new wave of bombers came cascading down. Two Junkers 88s, harried by Spitfires and both with engines on fire, broke from the line and dived towards the sea.

Very high in the sky, well above all the turmoil, five little bright dots could be seen in impeccable formation. They were five Italian Cants. Nobody took any notice of them, but their perfectly grouped stick of bombs fell plumb on the intersection of the two runways on Safi airfield. How those bombs managed to fall through all those whirling planes without smashing a single one was a miracle.

The newly arrived pilots, covered with dust and rubble, shaken by the exploding bombs, huddling down to avoid the hail of stones and splinters, were rocked to their foundations. This really was war!

Ten minutes later it was all over. The Spitfires, fuel running low and ammunition spent, came into the circuit to land. Five Hurricanes from Takali airfield at the other end of the island flew above Luqa to protect the landing and the hurried dispersal of the planes. Beurling went back to his rabbit burrow to look for his belongings and wait for his plane to come back. He failed to find his razor or his toothbrush, which must have been left behind somewhere in the wings.

The planes were now coming in. Two with damaged undercarts had to belly-land, while a third with a good square yard of wing missing did a ground loop and turned a. over t. Just about one plane in three was obviously damaged in one way or another. A promising look-out!

A pilot who came past, exhausted and eyes bloodshot, and humping his parachute, called across: 'No point waiting for your Spit. Norman Lee was flying it and he got the chop. Get weaving, or you'll miss the Mess bus, and it's a five-mile walk!'

PIERRE CLOSTERMANN DSO DFC

*

The Air Officer Commanding Malta, Air Vice-Marshal Lloyd, addressed the newcomer in the billiards room. Life was hard in Malta; there was little food, few amenities, and no respite from bombing. They had been brought to the island with one object—to kill Germans. Fuel and ammunition could be brought to the island only by submarine until the Mediterranean could be made safe for a convoy of ships. Therefore every gallon of petrol, every cannon shell, had to be exploited to the full. Nothing was to be wasted.

While he had been talking the Luftwaffe started their

evening raid, this time directed at the newly arrived fighters. Wave after wave of Stukas and Junkers 88s dived down until it was impossible to count them in the failing light. The newcomers had never seen anything like it. The bombs rained down on the airfield below the windows of the mess; the pilots' attention was distracted and they shifted uneasily. 'Get in close!' shouted the air marshal, above the cacophony of bursting bombs and rattling windows. 'So close that you can't miss! Don't shoot until you see the whites of their eyes! You must kill the Germans or they'll kill you! At this moment they heard the tell-tale whistle of a bomb about to explode close, too close, and, in unison, the pilots dived under the billiard table. The bomb missed the mess and they all came to their feet once more, rather sheepishly. The air marshal was still standing, impassive, and he fixed the company with a cold look. 'You see what I mean,' he said, turned on his heel, and left the room.

Group Captain J. E. JOHNSON DSO DFC

Before that day was out, Beurling had flown in action twice and shot down three confirmed victims. He kept it up: by the end of the year he had 29 victories. He was that rarest of fighters, a natural pilot and a first-class shot; he was never a leader nor tried to be one. Surprisingly, he survived the war—but not his restless character. He died in 1947, crashing an overloaded transport plane on a gun-running flight to Israel.

*

The true value of Malta was as an offensive base; had it boasted nothing but fighters, it would hardly have been worth attacking. But throughout the siege it remained a threat because it maintained not only a submarine base but squadrons of anti-shipping Wellingtons and Beauforts.

One Beaufort crew, shot down into the sea after sinking a merchant ship, achieved one of the wildest escapes of the war. Picked up and captured by a Cant flying boat, Lieutenant E. T. Strever (a South African) and his crew of three were taken to an Italian air-base off Greece; immediately they started considering a

'Tomorrow bad, tonight good,' said the Italians. They realised even more fully what was meant when they were taken to bed. Four of the Italians had given up their two double rooms so that their prisoners should pass a comfortable night.

Strever paired off with Dunsmore, and the two New Zealanders shared the second room. Guards were posted in the passage and outside the windows. They began to feel at last that they were prisoners, and found the realisation disturbingly and surprisingly unpleasant. Their captors' words echoed in their minds. Tomorrow bad.

On the wall of the New Zealanders' room was a map of the Adriatic Sea and the Grecian coast. Brown and Wilkinson turned towards it eagerly. Somewhere on that map was the spot in which they were spending the night. They plotted the approximate position of the Axis convoy, and then looked for land some two hours' flying in a northerly direction.

'We're somewhere here,' said Wilkinson, tapping the map. 'Levkas—or perhaps as far south as Corfu. It's a hundred to one we're somewhere in that area.'

'There's Taranto!' said Brown. 'Should be about an hour and a half's flying.'

Wilkinson did not speak again for some time. When he did eventually break the silence, Brown was nearly asleep.

'I'm going to get out of this mess if I can,' he said.

They were awakened at seven o'clock next morning, and breakfasted well on eggs (the first they'd seen for many weeks), bacon, tomatoes, toast and coffee. While they were at breakfast they were left alone for a few moments. Instantly they began to discuss the possibility of escape.

'I've worked out where we are,' said Wilkinson. 'Either Levkas or Corfu. Taranto can't be more than about 200 miles. If we don't do something quickly we'll be in a POW camp by lunch-time.'

'Not a hope here,' said Dunsmore. 'We've as much chance of eluding them here as a bunch of film stars at a world première. Better wait till we get to Taranto.'

'You know what they say,' said Strever. 'The best chances come immediately after capture. Once they get us to Taranto there'll be no more of this being fêted like transatlantic flyers. Life'll start to get rough then.'

'Has anyone thought of trying to capture the aircraft and fly it to Malta? Malta's about 350 miles, I reckon.'

'I've thought of it, Wilkie,' said Strever. 'I thought of it yesterday. We probably had a better chance then than we'll get today. They're bound to mount a guard on us now. Still, we'll keep our eyes open.'

'Look out,' said Brown. The guards had arrived to escort them to the jetty. They had no further chance to discuss escape.

The whole Italian headquarters staff seemed to have preceded them to the jetty to see them off. Everyone wanted to shake hands with them and take pictures, and as they boarded another Cant floatplane—not the same one as the previous day, and a different crew—a battery of cameras clicked into action. Strever could not help contrasting the carefree atmosphere here with the grim bitterness of life at Malta. Life here was leisurely and luxurious and food and drink plentiful. Life at Malta was hectic and austere. It was hard to believe that their two countries were locked in a desperate battle for survival. Strever tried hard to recapture the bitter enmity of the fighting, but the gaiety of his captors disarmed him. Resenting the feeling of goodwill that abounded, he stepped quickly into the plane.

The Cant crew consisted of pilot, second pilot, engineer, wireless operator/observer, and a corporal acting as escort, armed with a .45 revolver that looked as though it had been rescued from a museum. Strever and his crew entered the plane first, followed by the guard. Then came the Italian crew, in high spirits, each carrying two or more large cases, which they dumped in the fuselage. They were going home on leave. The flight was part and parcel of the party, and the holiday spirit was already abroad.

The Italian pilot introduced himself. 'Captain Gatetama Mastrodrasa, at your service.' He grinned, showing a set of incredibly white, even teeth. 'We go to Italy on leave. I see my bambino'—he rocked an imaginary baby in his arms—'for the first time. For you, it is bad.' He shrugged his shoulders and opened the palms of his hands, then turned on his heel and went forward to his pilot's seat.

Space was restricted in the crew compartment of the Cant and the nine men were in close proximity of each other. Pilot and second pilot sat in the front of the perspex cockpit, with the corporal escort standing behind and between them, facing backwards. Next came the wireless operator, and flight engineer. In the back of the elongated crew compartment Strever and his crew squatted on the floor.

They were airborne at 0940. That meant that they ought to reach Taranto about 1110, barring accidents. They sat quietly and tried to look relaxed and resigned. Nevertheless the corporal's belt and holster fascinated them. How quick would he be on the draw? What firearms might the other members of the crew have ready to hand? And if they could turn the tables on the Italians, what then? Could they effectively subdue the whole crew and at the same time fly an unfamiliar aircraft and navigate it from an unknown point to a tiny island notoriously hard to find, without radio and perhaps without maps?

Well, it might be worth a try.

Staggering along under an overload of men and luggage, unable to climb above 1,000 feet, where the air was sickeningly bumpy and unbearably hot, the Cant made slow and unsteady progress towards the heel of Italy. Four men faced the prospect of years of imprisonment. Four men were going on leave. Poised between the two parties, a kind of neutral umpire, stood the corporal guard.

The corporal sat down behind the pilot. It was a bad day for a non-flyer; a wretched day for a ground type with a queasy stomach. The corporal felt the sweat pouring from his forehead. Yet he felt cold. He longed to set foot on the sure earth again. How long had they said? Ninety minutes? They could hardly be half way yet. He found himself swallowing incessantly. His head ached intolerably and he longed to lie down. Up-currents and down-draughts played battledore and shuttlecock with his stomach. He gritted his teeth fiercely, determined not to be sick. His eyeballs felt like roundshot. His jowls drooped. His energy was spent and he felt an overwhelming apathy. If only the plane would crash or something. Anything to get down on the deck.

Wilkinson sat facing the wireless operator/observer, whose log sheets were strewn on the navigation table between them. Behind the observer sat the corporal, his face a ghastly parchment. Wilkinson looked at his watch. 1025. They must be about half way. They daren't leave it much longer. Perhaps a fighter escort might be sent to meet them. Soon they would be picked up by the Italian coastal radar. It was now or never.

Somehow he had to distract the observer's attention and get his hands firmly planted on the airsick corporal's gun.

The only trick he knew was a schoolboy affair. You pointed suddenly out of the window and while your victim turned his head away you had him momentarily at your mercy. Schoolboys were used to the trick and didn't always buy it. He would have to take a chance with this fellow.

'Look!'

The observer turned his head, and instantly the window clouded into an opaque blackness and then splintered into stars as Wilkinson's fist sank into his jaw. There was no recoil. Wilkinson allowed the impetus of the punch to carry him past the table; then he jumped over the observer's slouched body and snatched the corporal's revolver. His hands closed over it greedily and he tore at it with all his strength. Next moment the pistol was in his hands, and as the corporal fell back into the pilot's lap he handed the pistol to Strever, who had quickly backed him up, leaving Dunsmore and Brown to attend to the observer and flight engineer. The corporal fell between the pilot and the control column, and as he struggled to free himself he fouled the controls and sent the floatplane into a steep dive. Wilkinson, flung forward like a piece of loose cargo, caught the corporal by the scruff of the neck and with a Herculean effort lifted him clear.

By this time Strever was pointing the gun coolly in the pilot's ribs, believing the day had been won, unaware that the second pilot was in the act of turning a Luger on him.

Brown, holding down the stunned observer, saw the Italian second pilot swing triumphantly round with the Luger. Another second and their dreams of capturing the aircraft would be over. The nearest missile to hand was a seat cover. He gathered it and hurled it with one movement, like the throw of a classic coverpoint. The seat cover flew through the air unerringly, striking the Luger and knocking it from the second pilot's grasp. Instantly there was a free-for-all as the two crews struggled for possession of the Luger. Strever kept the pilot covered while Dunsmore hooked the Luger out of the scrum back to Wilkinson. The morale of the Italian crewmen was broken.

But Captain Mastrodrasa was not done with yet. He kept the Cant in a steep dive, determined to foil the Beaufort crew's escape by landing the Cant on the sea.

Strever brandished the revolver before his eyes, and then raised it as though he would smash in the Italian's skull. The horizon came down from above them like a blind as the Cant floatplane slowly levelled out.

Meanwhile Dunsmore and Brown were busy tying up the rest of the crew with a length of mooring hawser. Dunsmore tied them up while Brown seized a monkey-wrench from the took-kit and stood poised above them.

'One move out of you lot and I'll dong you,' he shouted, swinging the wrench. The Italians understood the gesture —and the onomatopoeia. The Italian captain, too, was hustled back to be tied up, but every time Dunsmore thought he had them firmly secured, the Italians shook their heads and wriggled their wrists to show that they could still free themselves. Eventually Dunsmore tied them up with their trouser-belts.

Strever took over the controls and turned the floatplane ninety degrees to port of their previous track in the rough direction of Malta. For one glorious moment they relaxed, breathless and dishevelled, flushed and exultant, revelling in a sense of freedom and power, undisputed masters of the plane in which they had been travelling to Italy two minutes earlier as prisoners of war.

RALPH BARKER

They reached Malta on the last drop of fuel and, despite waving a whitish vest from a cockpit window, were attacked by Spitfires. The Italian pilot took over the controls and made, without further persuasion, a hasty water landing.

A launch towed them in to safety. The Spitfire pilots were up-braided by their squadron commander for poor shooting.

*

We are the heavy bombers, we try to do our bit;
We fly through concentrations of flak and cloud and shit.
And when we drop our cargoes, we do not give a damn;
The eggs may miss the goods yard but they eff up poor
old Hamm.

And when in adverse weather the winds are all to hell,
The navigator's balled-up, the wireless balled as well,
We think of all the popsies we've known in days gone by
And curse the silly effers who taught us how to fly.

They sent us out to Egypt, a very pleasant land
Where miles and miles of sweet eff-all are covered up
with sand.
And when we got to Cairo the girls were heard to say:
'There ain't no hope for us, dears, Thirty-seven's come
to stay.'

And when you get to Hades it's just like SHQ.
With lots of stooges sitting round with eff-all else to do.
They ask you for your flimsies and your pass and target
maps;
You take the ruddy issue and you stuff it down their
traps.

*

In Britain, the buildup of Bomber Command's night force was a slow business. The new four-engined Stirlings (which weren't very successful), Halifaxes and Lancasters were only just coming off the production lines: in February, the Command could muster a daily average of only 44 'heavies'. And when new squadrons of twin-engined aircraft were formed, they were usually snatched away by Coastal Command, whose immediate need was greater.

*The Command made do with what it had got—including a
new but short-lived twin-engined bomber—*

ACHTUNG! MANCHESTER!

Over in the corner was a fellow called Dunlop Mackenzie,
who used to be in 83 Squadron. He had gone to his OTU in
April 1940, where he had been the only chap who dared to
fly the 48-cylinder master-piece, the Hereford, at night.
For reasons of ill-health, however, he hadn't done many
trips. When I told him that I had come to take over the
squadron—

'God! you're a clot' he said, disrespectfully.

'Why?' I said, surprised.

'These Manchesters. They're awful. The actual kite's all
right, but it's the engine. They're fine when they keep turning but they don't often do so. We have had an awful lot
of prangs.'

'I had heard the Manchester had had some teething
troubles, but thought they had all been cured.'

'No, they haven't,' he said. 'If you are hit in one engine
you've had it.'

'But surely they will fly on one engine?'

'Some will, some won't. A fellow called "Kipper-
Herring" from 61 Squadron brought one all the way from
Berlin on one engine and got the DSO for it, but he's an ex-
ception.'

'Have you had a prang in one?' I asked, thinking perhaps
that he had had some troubles which prejudiced his state-
ments.

'Not me, but I've been darn lucky. I have seen enough
of them. Bill Whamond——'

'Who's he?'

'A boy in A Flight. He piled up after a daylight mine-
laying do. He got away O.K., though.'

'I know—the CO told me. Just a belly landing.'

'Maybe, but you should have seen W/Cdr Balston prang
on his return from a daylight raid on Brest.'

'What happened there?'

'Well, he was coming back pretty badly shot up and the
weather was fairly heavy. All the rest of the boys had come

in when he made his approach. It was then we saw that he had his elevators shot off, or most of them. Anyway, he came in, but was slightly high, about one hundred feet over the hedge. He opened his throttles to go round again, but the extra power forced the CG aft, and he began to climb with engines flat out. He went up to about five hundred feet until he was in a nearly vertical position. Apparently he couldn't do anything about it. Then the nose dropped slowly, oh! very slowly, and he went in vertically, dead in the middle of the aerodrome, a few hundred yards from the control tower, where everyone was watching. I believe his wife was there, too.'

'Flames?'

'God! yes, nothing left.'

'Must have been a horrible sight, especially as you could hear him on the R/T.'

'It certainly was. Thing was, he could have baled out, only his rear-gunner was badly wounded.'

As we were talking there came the harsh roar of a Lancaster taking off.

'Now you watch this,' said Dunlop. 'This is a real aeroplane.'

Bob Allen was standing outside, and we watched, all three of us together.

The great tail came up, the engines screamed into full power, but she didn't leave the ground.

'He's going to prang,' said Bob quietly.

'I think you're right,' said I.

There was plenty of time to talk, no need to hurry. Quite slowly, at least it seemed so, the giant bomber rumbled across the aerodrome, at perhaps 120 miles an hour, but she wasn't getting airborne; something was wrong. Then, quite slowly, she struck one wing into the bomb dump and cartwheeled out of sight. A great cloud of dust arose, and seconds later there came a dull thud, as something finally hit something else.

'They've had it,' said Bob unemotionally. We waited for the black smoke, none came. Then we went back into the Mess again.

Wing Commander GUY GIBSON VC DSO DFC

*

The Lancaster—actually a version of the Manchester with four Merlin engines instead of two Vultures—went on to become the Command's most successful bomber. Gibson commanded them soon after.

But the most important addition to the Command was, at the end of February, a new chief: the aggressive Bert 'Bomber' Harris. He describes some of the problems he found on his desk:

With the occupation of France and the Low Countries the Germans were able to build up a formidable system of defence. They set up an early warning system along the coast, as well as on the coast of Denmark, together with a belt of stations for the control of fighters from the ground through Denmark and Holland and down the Western frontier of Germany. Each ground station controlled one fighter within a rather small 'box', and the belt consisted of a whole succession of these boxes touching each other. When the coastal radar stations gave warning, the fighter in each box was ready to intercept any single bomber coming into its box. If a bomber force was scattered, many single aircraft would naturally be entering a large number of boxes at any given time. But if it could be arranged that many bombers passed through one box at the same time, the fighter in that box would only have time to attempt the interception of one of them. A continuous searchlight belt covering the Ruhr made it easier for fighters to intercept the bombers passing through it, and here again it would be better for the bombers to get through this belt in a continuous stream, with the fighters only able to concentrate on one or two of them, rather than to go through it at long intervals and be picked off one by one. The same principle of saturating the defences applied to anti-aircraft guns and to the searchlights operating in conjunction.

A few ground control stations were probably working at the beginning of 1941, but by the end of the year they had become numerous and efficient, and bomber caualties were rising fast. The difficulty was to bring about any real concentration. 'Gee', the first radar aid to navigation, was the real answer, but even before we had the Gee equipment in any quantity it was possible, on a bright, clear night, to plan the route and the attack so thoroughly that the bomber stream became compact. At first even the minute figure, as it seemed later, of 100 aircraft an hour, over the target and along the route, was only an idea, and very seldom achieved; for one thing, captains of aircraft were so used to being told to search for their exact target or aiming point until they found it, that it seemed contradictory to order them to bomb and leave the target area at a particular moment. Along with much else from the past it was necessary to abandon the idea of searching first for the primary target, then for a specified alternative target, and if this could not be found, for a self-evident military objective; military objectives were not apt to be self-evident, but that was the term, usually contracted into 'Semo', that was often and solemnly used. Quick as well as definite identification of the target became of increasing importance towards the end of 1941, and at that time most of the methods we afterwards used were under discussion, the training, for example, of special squadrons to find the target, the use of marker bombs with a distinctive colour to be dropped on the target, at the beginning of the attack, and so forth. Whether or no to begin an attack with fire-raising aircraft was much debated. It had been a widely accepted belief that the right time to drop incendiaries was at the end of an attack, and that at other times incendiaries did not do much harm; there was also, of course, the very real danger that crews trained to bomb fires might go straight for the enemy's dummy fires. At this stage, in fact, the whole theory of bombing tactics was being submitted to agitated revision. Even the principle of concentration had its opponents, on the grounds that, except on really dark nights, this helped the 'cat's eye' night fighter and because it led to congestion at home bases on landing. There were also serious fears that it might lead to collisions and to aircraft dropping their bombs on each other.

The question of the risk from collision was not finally settled until we put 1,000 aircraft over Cologne in an hour and a half.

Marshal of the RAF
SIR ARTHUR HARRIS GCB OBE AFC

The idea of a thousand-bomber raid was simple enough. Execution was something else: Bomber Command was then averaging 416 serviceable aircraft every night. Harris begged, borrowed and scrounged bombers from every corner of the country: squadron reserves, Operational Training Units—even Coastal Command (although they changed their minds and took them back again). Crews were mustered the same way; pupils and staff officers found themselves in unfamiliar cockpits. Finally Harris had his thousand—in fact, 1048. All he needed now was a time and a place for

OPERATION MILLENNIUM

On the Saturday morning of 30th May, the C.-in-C. entered the Operations Room at ten minutes past nine for his planning conference. As usual, he was accompanied by the SASO. There was that characteristic hunch about his shoulders as he walked slowly but deliberately to his desk. After handing his cap to his PA he sat down heavily in his chair and leant back to allow the meteorological synoptic charts to be placed on the desk in front of him. Not a muscle moved and no sign of an expression stirred his face whilst the forecast for the next twenty-four hours was outlined to him by that meticulous and worthy Meteorological Officer, Mr Magnus Spence. I listened carefully to Spence's droning voice and watched with care as his pencil deliberately emphasised each point he made, indicating the hieroglyphics on the chart which symbolised the existing weather conditions and the probable conditions for the period of the coming night, both in England and over enemy territory. As Spence finished his forecast he stood up straight and rather precisely clasped his hands in front of his short, stocky figure.

It was not a forecast which held much promise for good operational conditions: in fact, it rather bordered on the side of being unsuitable. I held my breath, for this was probably the last possible night for the great operation, unless it were undertaken another month hence; tonight was the last on which the moon would be sufficiently full for such a vast experiment to be attempted. If it were impossible on this night, then it would have to be postponed till the end of June. If it were postponed till the end of June, it might never take place at all. I am sure I was not the only one present who held his breath.

The C.-in-C. moved at last. Slowly he pulled an American cigarette carton from his pocket and, flicking the bottom with his thumb, selected the protruding Lucky Strike. He lit the cigarette and then drew from his right breast pocket a short, stocky cigarette holder. Very deliberately he pressed the cigarette into the end of the holder and grasped it firmly between his teeth. He continued to stare at the charts and then slowly his forefinger moved across the continent of Europe and came to rest on a town in Germany. The pressure on his finger bent back the end joint and drove the blood from the top of his finger nail, leaving a half circle of white. He turned to the SASO, his face still expressionless.

'The 1,000 Plan tonight.'

His finger was pressing on Cologne.

Group Captain DUDLEY SAWARD OBE

*

'Cologne,' said the briefing officer at one station, 'is one of the most heavily defended cities in Germany, and one of the most important. In and around Cologne are more than five hundred heavy and light anti-aircraft guns and about a hundred and fifty searchlights, which work in close co-ordination with the gunners. But with this very large force, the belief is that all ground defences will be saturated and overwhelmed. The same should apply to night-fighters. Your track will take you close to several night-fighter stations, but intruder aircraft from Fighter and Army Co-operation Commands and 2 Group will be attacking these stations before and during the raid. Even so, look out for night-fighters. Tail gunners, be careful what you fire at. There will be a large number of friendly aircraft over Cologne. Don't mistake our own twin-engined bombers for Ju 88s.

'The key to the success of this raid is saturation, which itself depends on getting these thousand aircraft over the target in the shortest feasible time-spread. Tonight's attack is to be concentrated into ninety minutes. This means accurate timing, not only for the saturation of defences but to avoid collision. Exact heights are just as important. Follow your briefed timings and course. If you don't, this raid, instead of being the costliest in history for the enemy, could be the costliest in history for us.

'Now I'll come to the collision risk.' Here the crews, already attentive, sat forward apprehensively, eager for reassurance. Ever since the figure of a thousand had been introduced at the start of the briefing, this was the spectre that had haunted them. Mid-air collision was a hideous experience, one which few men had been known to survive.

'The boffins are confident,' went on the briefing officer, 'that the risk is negligible.' There was a murmur of scepticism, which died away as the briefing continued. 'They have assessed the chances'—here the briefing officer paused for a moment, to give full effect to his statement—'at one in a thousand.'

They were being given the bull. That was the instant reaction. A thousand aircraft milling about over a single target at night, beset by searchlights and flak, jinking and weaving, twisting and turning, diving and climbing under fighter attack, jam-packed together along a narrow route, struggling to get back under difficulties into over-crowded circuits and bases—and the long-haired boys at Command had decided that there would be only one collision! At more than one briefing, certainly at Syerston, and certainly at Skellingthorpe, the entire room rocked with derisive laughter.

'Have the boffins worked out,' asked one wag from 50 Squadron at Skellingthorpe, 'which two aircraft it will be?'

There was another gust of laughter, and then the briefing officer, judging his audience correctly, replied in similar vein.

'I have it on the highest authority that it will be a Tiger Moth and an Anson.'

RALPH BARKER

*

THE NEW BOY

First man over the target from Elsham Wolds was Clive
Saxelby. Another pilot, an NCO named Roberts, recently
arrived on the station and unknown to Saxelby and his
crew, had come along as second pilot for the experience,
and Saxelby had stationed him in the astrodome. Their
approach to the target was like a practice run, they were
not picked out by the searchlights and the blaze below was
already the biggest they had ever seen. It was becoming impossible to identify individual aiming-points but they followed the Rhine in and dropped their bombs on the edge of
the existing fires. Then they turned for home.

They had crossed the Dutch/German border and were
approaching Eindhoven when the fighter picked them up.
The first they knew of the attack was a succession of sharp
cracks and a tearing, rending noise in the fuselage, followed by a strangled scream on the intercom. The cockpit had
escaped, but the middle section of the fuselage had been
badly hit and was on fire. The fire quickly contaminated
the oxygen system, half-suffocating the crew. Saxelby
wrenched off his mask but he still couldn't breathe. He
pushed back the cabin window and put his head into the
slipstream, breathing deeply, and as he did so he stared
straight into the silhouette of an Me 110, slanted into a
90-degree bank, turning in again towards him.

'Christ! He's coming in again!'

Saxelby put the nose forward and spiralled but the fighter
followed him down, getting in another accurate burst. The
fire in the midsection had caught hold and the fabric
was peeling and burning. Half of the tail-plane, too, was de-
nuded of fabric, and the trimmers had been shot away. The
hydraulics were hit and the under-carriage and bomb-doors
were drooping, greatly adding to the load on the control
column as the Wellington spiralled. But the worst danger
was the fire.

Pipkin, the navigator, was nearest to the flames. He had
no gloves on, but he attacked them immediately with his
bare hands.

McClean, the wireless operator, clipped on his parachute
and went forward to open the hatch under the cockpit,

expecting an order to bale out. He saw Saxelby struggling with the controls.

'Are you coming, Sax?'

'Not yet—I think I can hold it.'

McClean went back to help Pipkin, and between them they extinguished the fire, ripping off the affected fabric and pushing it out through the holes. The Wellington began to look bare and skeletal amidships, but it still flew. Pipkin went forward and shouted in Saxelby's ear.

'Everything's fine, we're doing well. I know exactly where we are. For God's sake keep her flying.'

But Saxelby was finding the weight of the controls too much for him. The plane was still locked in the spiral and the ground was coming up fast.

'It's no good—I can't hold her.'

Pipkin disappeared, then came back with a rope which he tied round the control column, Saxelby noticed that the skin on Pipkin's hands was shrivelled and burnt. Pipkin lashed the stick back and the Wellington levelled out.

'Good work. But get ready to cut the rope in a hurry if I want to lose height.'

St Pierre, the French-Canadian in the rear turret, had been wounded in the leg. His intercom was cut off, and he crawled forward to see what was happening. He thought he might have missed a bale-out order. Under the astro-dome, leaning against the side of the fuselage, was Roberts, the second pilot, apparently taking it easy. St Pierre gave him a good prod to attract his attention, and like the body in the cupboard Roberts slid in slow-motion to the floor. This eager young pilot who had come along for the experience had been rewarded by the experience of death.

To the rest of the crew Sergeant Roberts was a stranger. He had bought it. The less said about it the better.

Although they were living with the daily expectation of sudden and violent death, and although they shrugged it off with jokes and euphemisms, the men of Bomber Command were not conditioned to the ugliness of reality. St Pierre's reaction was typical. This was something he had to shut his mind to. He didn't want to see any more. He had to dis-sociate himself from it. There was a dead man in the fuse-lage—that was all it meant to him. As he didn't know the man, the incident would be that much easier to forget. Afterwards, over a few pints, he might tell the story of how he pushed the body and of how it slithered to the floor. He might even play it for laughs. Indeed, that was the only way. But right now he was scared, and he had to get away from it. After making sure that the plane was still under control, he turned on his heel and went back to the familiar isolation of his turret.

RALPH BARKER

Losses on Millennium were 44—under 5 per cent.

As important as the material damage to Cologne was the propaganda effect, both in Britain and Germany. Harris, personally shy and aloof, had thrust his 'bomber boys' into the limelight; the British public got, for the first time, an idea of Bomber Command's power. It was an exaggerated idea, but thereafter the War Cabinet was committed to making it come true; Harris had thought of that, too.

*

. . . ALSO ATTACKED TARGETS IN NORTHERN ITALY . . .

I was lying in bed next morning half awake, feeling satisfied that we had in the end done all we could the night before. Suddenly I was jerked into full consciousness. There was an aircraft close and it sounded as if it was coming over the mess. I looked out of the window at a grey wall of drizzle, and cloud at 200 or 300 feet. This was what our forecaster had seen ahead and had mistimed. It looked impossible for a stranger to land at Ford. The machine passed very close, and the noise of its four Merlins gave way momentarily to a swishing sound; it was very low.

The noise faded away. I suspected that he had had a shot at getting in and had given up, but I felt helplessly anxious, because I knew that a returning bomber could not have much petrol left and that a desperate effort to get down—an overwhelming tendency springing from more than a desire to save an aeroplane—could lead to disaster to the north where the Downs would certainly be in cloud. It

212

came over again, and now I felt sure that it must be in difficulties. The noise died away and, as is often the case when one is powerless to help, I thought of other things for a bit, turned over and went to sleep again. I had ample excuse for being late. Had I not flown the night before?

At breakfast there was a stranger, and I sat down next to him and asked where he came from. He mentioned an airfield in Lincolnshire.

'Lancs?' I asked.

'Yes.'

'When did you arrive here?'

'This morning.'

'What was it like?'

'Not so easy. We were on instruments most of the way across France.'

'Did you have any difficulty getting in here? I heard you come over the mess twice.'

'No, not really. We made two bosh shots at it, but got in O.K. the third.'

'Where did you go?'

'Turin.'

'How long did it take?'

'About eight hours.'

'What were the defences like?'

'They've increased. There are two guns now, and they must be manned by Germans because they went on firing after the bombs began to fall.'

Air Commodore RODERICK CHISHOLM CBE DSO DFC

*

One other branch of the RAF flew to the Continent by night: the 'special duty' pilots landing and picking up secret agents. Initially a single flight of aircraft, this later grew to two full squadrons. In this work the single-engined Lysander, something of a flop in its initial Army-co-operation role, came into its own. These are extracts from the 'Notes For Pilots' prepared by the special duty leader.

Loading of aircraft. Three passengers are normally the maximum carried, but four have been carried without incident in the past. As you may well imagine, that means a squash. With either three or four, it is thought impracticable for them to put on parachutes or bale out. If four passengers are carried, one goes on the floor, two on the seat, and one on the shelf. This is not recommended with heavy people.

Luggage. Of course, the heaviest luggage should go under the seat, nearest the centre of gravity. Small, important pieces of luggage, such as sacks of money, should go on the shelf, so that they are not left in the aeroplane by mistake. Mistrust the floor under the shelf, as it is difficult for passengers to find luggage which has slipped down towards the tail.

Emergency kit. If you get stuck in the mud, it is useful to have in the aeroplane some civilian clothes. Do not put these in the passengers' compartment or they may be slung out. A good place is in the starting handle locker. You should also carry a standard escape kit, some purses of French money, a gun or two, and a thermos flask of hot coffee or what you will. A small flask of brandy or whisky is useful if you have to swim for it, but NOT in the air. Empty your pockets of anything of interest to the Hun, but carry with you some small photographs of yourself in civilian clothes. These may be attached to false identity papers. In theory it is wise to wear clothes with no tailor's, laundry or personal marks. Change your linen before flying, as dirty shirts have a bad effect on wounds. The Lysander is a warm aeroplane, and I always wore a pair of shoes rather than flying boots. If you have to walk across the Pyrenees you might as well do it in comfort.

Conclusion. You have a hell of a lot to do to get an operation ready, but there is quite a lot you can do the day before. It never matters if you prepare the op and don't do it. You may go that way some day and somebody else can always use your maps. It is most important to start an op fresh, and a good idea to have a nap or two in the afternoon or evening before you take off. Finally, you get driven to your aeroplane in a smart American car with a beautiful FANY driver, cluttered up from head to toe with equipment and arms and kit of every description, rather like the White Knight, prepared for every emergency.

BEFORE TAKE-OFF

You must make sure that the escorting officer for the agent knows the form. If he does not, you must attend to your agent yourself. Make sure that he knows how much luggage he is carrying and where it is stowed. He must know how to put on and operate parachutes, if carried, and helmets and microphones. He must try the working of the emergency warning lights. He must understand the procedure for turning about on the field. This is, briefly, for Lysanders, that one agent should stay in the aeroplane to hand out his own luggage and receive the luggage of the homecoming agent, before he himself hops out. In the rare case where the agent has night flying experience over the area in question, it may be of use to give him a map of the route. One operation failed when the pilot was very far off track and the agent, a highly experienced Air Force officer, knew perfectly well where he was but could not tell the pilot because the (intercom) was switched off.

CROSSING THE CHANNEL

Once school of thought recommends crossing the Channel low down to approach the enemy coast below the (radar) screen. I am opposed to this, because of the danger of flak from the Royal Navy and from enemy convoys, besides which a heavily laden aeroplane will not climb very quickly to the height at which it is safest to cross the enemy coast....

CROSSING THE ENEMY COAST

It is generally safer to cross the enemy coast as high as possible up to 8,000 feet. This gives you a general view of the lie of the coast and avoids the danger of light flak and machine-gun fire which you might meet lower down. On the other hand, your pinpoint at the coast is of vital importance, for by it you gauge your wind and set your course for the interior along a safe route, so it may be necessary to fly along a much lower route than 8,000 feet to see where you are in bad weather. Don't think that you will be safe off a flak area within four miles. I have been shot at fairly accurately by low angle heavy flak three miles off Dieppe at 2,000 feet, so, until you know where you are, it is not wise to make too close an investigation of the coast-line. In this case you may identify the coast by flying parallel with it some miles out to sea. Notice the course which it follows and any general changes of direction which it takes. By applying these to your map you will generally find that you must be at least on a certain length of coast-line and, at best at a definite point. When you know your postion you may gaily climb above any low cloud there may be and strike into the interior on D(ead) R(eckoning).

TARGET AREA PROCEDURE

On approaching the target area, fish out your target map, refresh your memory of the letters and do your cockpit drill. This involves switching on the fuselage tank, putting the signalling lamp to 'Morse', pushing down your arm rests, putting the mixture control back and generally waking yourself up. Don't be lured away from your navigation by the siren call of stray lights. You should aim to find the field without depending on lights or to find some positive landmark within two miles of the field from which you will see the light. If you don't see the light on ETA, circle and look for it. One operation was ruined because the pilot ran straight over the field twice but did not see the light because the signal was given directly beneath him and he failed to see it because he did not circle. Once you have seen the light, identify the letter positively. If the letter is not correct, or if there is any irregularity in the flare path, or if the field is not the one you expected, you are in NO circumstances to land. There have been cases when the Germans have tried to make a Lysander land, but where the pilot has got away with it by following this very strict rule. In one case where this rule was disobeyed, the pilot came home with thirty bullet holes in his aircraft and one in his neck and only escaped with his life because he landed far from the flare path and took off again at once. Experience has shown that a German ambush on the field will not open fire until the aeroplane attempts to take off, having landed. Their object is to get you alive to get the gen, so don't be tricked into a sense of security if you are not shot at from the field before landing. I repeat, the entire lighting procedure must be correct before you even think of landing.

TAKE-OFF
Generally it is worth while to pull out your boost control override and climb away as speedily as you safely can.

Wing Commander H. S. VERITY DSO DFC

*

Late the previous year, Spitfire pilots had reported meeting a new, very high-performance radial-engined German fighter over Europe. Air Intelligence maintained for a while that it must be the slow, outdated Curtiss Hawk, captured from the French; this might have amused RAF pilots more if the 'Hawk' had not been outpacing, and shooting down, their Spitfires. Finally a camera gun proved their point. Intelligence admitted they were up against the

FOCKE-WULF 190

At 10.30 am, the squadron was airborne again and headed for rendezvous with the rest of the North Weald Wing at Thames Haven, before joining up with the Hornchurch Wing at Hastings for a two-wing fighter sweep of the St Omer area. The North Weald Wing was to fly above the Hornchurch Wing, thus forming a mass formation which would sweep into enemy territory with the object of 'seeking and destroying the enemy' as the order, detailing the operation, put it. My squadron, as the top squadron in the North Weald Wing, was at 27,000 feet.

Shortly after we crossed the French coast on the way in, the Controller reported enemy activity to the raid. Varied reports on the strength of the reaction were passed over the R/T, but there was no sign of enemy fighters until about twenty miles from Le Touquet on the way out. At this point, 'Mitzi' reported a formation of about a dozen FW 190s directly behind, at the same height and closing fast. I picked them up immediately and warned the rest of the squadron to prepare for a 'break'. We had practised a

217

manœuvre to cope with just this sort of contingency: one section would break upwards and in the opposite direction from the other two which would turn into the attacking fighters. It will be remembered I had remarked on the effectiveness of this manœuvre when carried out by a formation of Me 109s which I attacked near Deal in the early days of the Battle of Britain.

'They're getting close, Toby Leader.' A breathless and worried 'Mitzi' urged some action.

'O.K. Blue One, I see them. Wait for the order to break.'

When I judged that the Huns were about the right distance away to suit the manœuvre I intended to carry out, I gave the order:

'Toby squadron, break left.'

On my right, Yellow section broke upwards and away while, with Blue section outside me, I turned hard into the closing enemy fighters. About half-way around the break I looked for Yellow section above and to my left and was startled to see another formation of FW 190s emerging through a thin layer of stratus cloud about two thousand feet above and right on our beam. It was too late to do anything about it; the first formation of FW 190s was head on to my section, which had now almost completed its turn, and there was only time for a split-second burst as the Huns pulled up and above us.

'Watch out, Red Leader, more of them coming down from above and to our right.'

Savagely I hauled my reluctant Spitfire around to meet this new attack and the next moment I was engulfed in enemy fighters—above, below and on both sides, they crowded in on my section. Ahead and above, I caught a glimpse of a FW 190 as it poured cannon shells into the belly of an unsuspecting Spitfire. For a brief second the Spitfire seemed to stop in mid-air, and the next instant it folded inwards and broke in two, the two pieces plummeting earthwards; a terrifying demonstration of the punch of the FW 190s, four cannons and two machine-guns.

I twisted and turned my aircraft in an endeavour to avoid being jumped and at the same time to get myself into a favourable position for attack. Never had I seen the Huns stay and fight it out as these Focke-Wulf pilots were doing.

In Messerschmitt 109s the Hun tactics had always followed the same pattern—a quick pass and away, sound tactics against Spitfires with their superior turning circle. Not so these FW 190 pilots, they were full of confidence.

There was no lack of targets, but precious few Spitfires to take them on. I could see my number two, Sergeant Murphy, still hanging grimly to my tail but it was impossible to tell how many Spitfires were in the area, or how many had survived the unexpected onslaught which had developed from both sides as the squadron turned to meet the threat from the rear. Break followed attack, attack followed break, and all the time the determined Murphy hung to my tail until finally, when I was just about short of ammunition and pumping what was left at a FW 190, I heard him call:

'Break right, Red One; I'll get him.'

As I broke, I saw Murphy pull up after a FW 190 as it veered away from me, thwarted in its attack by his prompt action. My ammunition expended, I sought a means of retreat from a sky still generously sprinkled with hostile enemy fighters, but no Spitfires that I could see. In a series of turns and dives I made my way out until I was clear of the coast, and diving full throttle I headed for home.

About twenty miles from the English coast I overtook a lone Spitfire and was just about to pull out to one side to identify it when its hood flew off, followed a few seconds later by the pilot as he abandoned his aircraft. His parachute opened almost immediately. At that precise moment another aircraft dived into the sea over to my left, about three miles away. I could just see a parachute very near the water and in the vicinity of the spot where the aircraft hit the water. 'He must have got out just in time,' I muttered to myself as I climbed to gain height to transmit information on the position of the first pilot, now safely in his dinghy.

Having received an acknowledgement of transmission, I flew across to the spot where I judged the second pilot would be. I had lost sight of his parachute against the hazy background over the sea and had the greatest difficulty in finding the spot where his aircraft had hit the water; this I recognised by the large oily patch it had left on the surface.

Eventually I managed to locate the position of the dinghy and saw the pilot waving to attract my attention so I rocked my wings to let him know that he had been sighted. Again I gained height to broadcast his position and when this was acknowledged I flew low past the dinghy to indicate to the pilot that rescue was on the way. In the fleeting glimpse as I passed by I thought I recognised 'Mitzi', but it was impossible to be sure. By now my petrol was dangerously low and I was obliged to set course for the nearest airfield, Lympne. When I landed I had been airborne two hours and ten minutes; there was barely enough fuel left to taxi to the refuelling point.

While my aircraft was being refuelled I checked with Manston that my messages on the two pilots had been received and was informed that action had already been taken, and the rescue boats were on the way. Indeed, when I circled the airfield prior to my return to Rochford I could see two launches headed from the area; there seemed nothing further I could do, so I returned to base.

As I taxied towards the dispersal after landing I noticed nothing unusual at first, but when I got close I was amazed, and somewhat taken aback, to see how very few Spitfires there were in the parking area. I could see 'Brad' Walker waiting to greet me, and from the look on his face I knew something dreadful had happened.

'Relieved to see you back, sir, we thought you had bought it too,' was his depressing greeting.

'What do you mean, bought it too?' I queried anxiously.

'I'm afraid it's pretty bad; there's only myself and my number two back so far. The Controller thinks that there are two more at Manston—one crash-landed—but he is making a further check and will ring back as soon as he gets something definite.'

I knew we had lost at least three aircraft, and feared more, but this news appalled me.

Group Captain ALAN DEERE DSO OBE DFC

403 squadron had, in fact, lost exactly two-thirds of the aircraft and half the pilots sent on that mission.

As an antidote to the FW 190 the malleable Spitfire was

tossed back into the melting pot yet again to emerge as the Mark IX. But already a new fighter was coming, somewhat tentatively, off the British production lines. It was thrown into action hastily; among the first squadron commanders to take it into battle was one who had been a production test-pilot on the aircraft itself, Roland Beamont.

*

TYPHOON TROUBLES

For the Ministry of Aircraft Production it was a case of Hobson's choice. Neither the Spitfire nor the Hurricane was fast enough to match the new Focke-Wulfe 190 with which the enemy was launching a campaign of tip-and-run raids on coastal towns. Only the Typhoon had the speed.

Although the decision to use the Typhoon before it was ready was ultimately justified by the results, it meant in the beginning that the first Typhoon squadrons were virtually continuing the flight test development of the aircraft with one of the facilities for the job but every disadvantage. The price of the Typhoon's premature introduction to operational service was heavy. During the first nine months the casualty rate from teething troubles was greater by far than that from enemy action, and in the period July to September, 1942, the loss from engine or structural failure of at least one aircraft per sortie occurred on Typhoon wing practices and sweeps over the French coast. Without the tremendous pressure resulting from these accidents, however, it is unlikely that the Typoon would have developed and been available in adequate numbers to provide one of the finest ground-support aircraft for the invasion of Europe some eighteen months later.

The main consequence of the Typhoon's over-hasty appearance was recurring engine trouble. Emergency landings became an inevitable part of the routine of flying Typhoons; and the prospect particularly of engine trouble over the sea was not a happy one.

Patrols between Dungeness and Margate involved flying one-and-a-half sorties over the Channel at cruising speed to obtain maximum endurance, and at a height of under 200 feet to avoid radar detection. If engine trouble did occur, the aircraft's relatively low speed gave the pilot little chance of gaining sufficient height for baling out. All he could do was try to ditch, i.e. land the aircraft on its belly on the water and get out into his dinghy before it sank. But that meant really no chance at all. With its big scoop radiator under the nose, the Typhoon would not ditch safely, no matter how smooth the sea. Long before the aircraft could settle to a standstill the radiator had ploughed under the surface and turned the Typhoon over on to its nose, carrying it straight down to the bottom.

In the first month of patrols, 609 Squadron lost in this pattern, which was to become all too tragically familiar, two officers and one sergeant pilot in comparatively calm sea conditions: and another pilot, forced to attempt a ditching in a gale, was swallowed without a splash amidst the flying spray.

Only one man survived an engine failure in a Typhoon over the Channel during those early months. He had fought to get the cockpit hood off as he felt the radiator touch the water, but the release mechanism was stuck—another frequent difficulty with the Typhoon—and he was carried to the bottom of the Channel. When the whirl of his senses had subsided the Typhoon was resting on the sea bed and he was unharmed in the cockpit, which was providing a reasonably adequate air chamber. Still unable to release the cockpit canopy he escaped through the side windows, and surfaced in a boil of air bubbles to be picked up by a rescue launch.

But engine trouble was only part of the additional hazard that the pioneer Typhoon squadrons had to face. Tails began to break off the aircraft in power dives. In one instance, before the pilot had time to think of baling out, his aircraft disintegrated around him and he found himself dropping to earth in nothing but the seat. He managed to release the seat harness, pull his parachute and land safely. The majority were not so fortunate, and pilots understandably began to be affected by the depressing feeling that should they be lucky enough to escape engine failure, the aircraft's tail would probably fall off anyway.

Even in combat the constant threat that the unreliability

of engine or airframe would do the enemy's work for him was a more conscious menace than the guns of Messerschmitt or Focke-Wulfe. The day of the Commando raid on Dieppe saw the Duxford Wing bouncing a formation of FW 190s south of Le Treport. Diving out of the sun they took the FW 190s by surprise and damaged three of them; but the cost to the Typhoons was heavier. Two broke their tails and buried themselves in the soil of France.

EDWARD LANCHBERY

'. . . nowadays the safety of the production aircraft is very rarely, in fact almost never, in doubt.'

J. A. CROSBY WARREN

The Typhoon ultimately proved itself both as a low-level interceptor and as a tank/pillbox buster when armed with rockets.

*

For a pilot, most of the war was just flying—just as for a soldier it was marching. I make no apology for the length of this account by an Atlantic ferry pilot. It tells of a long flight

ACROSS THE WIDE ATLANTIC

My first aircraft was a Liberator. I met my crew in the briefing room before departure. Johnny Rayner, who also lived at the Pine Beach Hotel, was my first officer. The others I had never seen before. They had been allocated to my aircraft by Squadron Leader Coristine, the crew assignments officer. Ed Coristine was one of the world's great diplomats. He was responsible for the crew assignments which, to some types of aircraft, were not at all popular; but I don't think any of even the toughest Dorval characters ever questioned an assignment. One type of aircraft had too short a range of carburettor air temperature control and some of these were lost because the carburettors iced up and the engines stopped. Another had a defect in the exhaust manifold which sometimes cracked and allow-

223

ed the flame to come back on to the oil tank and set fire to the aircraft. Still another, a particularly notorious one, was lost in numbers without trace till one exploded in the hangar and a type of fault was found in the hydraulic accumulator.

The Liberator, however, was a popular aircraft which could fly over the weather, was fast, and could easily do Gander to Prestwick non-stop without going in to Greenland or Iceland for fuel. It was always outrageously overloaded, several tons above its designed gross weight. Furthermore, it had a very fine-sectioned wing which used to flex in alarming fashion in turbulent air. It frankly frightened me, and I could not ignore the thought that in very turbulent cloud a wing might fail: in fact several Liberators did disappear at night in bad weather on the South Atlantic crossings. In San Diego, California, I later met a man who had been intimately concerned with the design of the Liberator wing. Pinning him down, I explained that I had flown this aeroplane, very overloaded, and had not been happy to see the wing flex so much in turbulent air; so would he please explain to me just how it stayed on. He looked at me with a cynical smile and in a soft but significant drawl remarked, 'That's somethin' Ah've ben tryin' to figure out maself.'

I wished I had never met the man.

But I went out of Dorval that morning with Liberator BZ 873 on a new adventure. The weather was overcast with rain, the cloud base at above five hundred feet. The air was fine and sharp and the light wind had a strange whispering call from the icelands far to the north. Instead of warm, coloured islands beckoning from over the horizon of a blue sea there was something entirely new: a strange open clearness; white, untouched and infinitely pure with shimmering lights in the sky, calling from the overcast.

There was an urgent, eager note in the motors as I ran them up; a quiet confidence in the aircraft as she rolled into the runway to line up for take-off. But there was also a tenseness. Everything always seemed to be stressed to the limit in a screaming cataclysm of sound as this metal monster projected itself down the runway with its occupants committed very soon after it started to roll.

224

A voice from a world I had already left came over the radio from Dorval tower:

'873—cleared for take-off.'

Cowl flaps closed. All set to go, from the final check.

I eased the throttles forward and she started to move away; heavily started to roll her twenty-five tons of weight for speed to pass the load from wheels to wing. I touched her with an outboard motor to check the swing as she thrust blindly for movement in this early stage of the take-off and then gave her the full five thousand horsepower. She took it, blasting her way with all the thunder of the skies for speed to release her from the earth.

I rode with the Liberator through this terrific, screaming battle of forces. There was little for me to do but feel and watch and listen; and be ready for immediate action if she failed for an instant to give all the power she had in the battle with the forces of the earth. I felt the balance of the controls, just letting her go, straight down the centre of the runway, but ready—till she wanted the nose-wheel off the ground.

A quick glance at the power—2,700 and forty-eight inches. It was all there. The engineer's hand hard against the throttles, turbos set for full throttle take-off.

She tightened down, beginning to feel free. I glanced at the airspeed indicator. Eighty-five. Nearly ready for the nose-wheel. Now my right hand rested on the top of the tail-trim wheel. I felt her fore and aft balance with my left, on the control column, and stroked the tail-trim back a shade. There was something definite and satisfactory in the feel of the serrated metal of the trimming wheel. I knew it was going to bring balance and harmony to the whole machine as I eased it back to take all the load off the control column, and the nose-wheel came away.

Now the freedom of the air was coming. She roared with terrific rhythmic sound, lightly on the wheels as the wing took the load, and I saw the end of the runway coming in. Now it was all the air. There could no longer be any compromise with the earth if any of that tight-strung power should fail. She had to fly. I thought only of the air as she thrust for speed, and I knew it was coming. At 120 she was away, flying, finished with the earth. Only the blur of trees came in under the nose. We set her for the air. My right hand went up in signal for the engineer. He rammed forward the undercarriage lever and the wheels began to move up to bury themselves in the wing. Reduce power: to ease that all-out battle of the motors. I held her down, low over the earth to let her build up speed. Speed, again; to pass beyond that critical early dragging through the air. I drew back the throttles till the manifold pressure fell to 45 inches—felt the elevator trim till she was balanced fore and aft at 160, and let her start to climb.

The engineer signalled the undercarriage locked up. I pulled down the power to 42 inches and 2,450 rpm. At five hundred feet she was brushing the bottom of the cloud. 'Flaps up' to the engineer. She sank for a moment, and needed the tail-trim again. Then she began to fly. No undercarriage. No flaps to drag at the wing. She was running clean and free. I eased back the throttles to thirty-five inches and touched the flap of the propeller switches till the rev counters came to 2,300. That would do her. She was not so heavy out of Dorval for Gander. Johnny's hand went forward to snick off the booster pump switches. I watched out to the sweep of the propellers and touched the individual switches till they all spun true and the bleating went out of the engines. The last of the earth was swept away by cloud as I went on to instruments for the climb.

At eight thousand feet we broke out through the tops.

Above, it was bright and clear; clean blue sky without a cloud. I held on to 9,000 and levelled her off; eased the power to 2,000 and 31 inches, with two inches on the turbos to keep them running; let her cool for a couple of minutes, then cut the mixture to autolean. She held 165 on the ASI. I lined her up on the course and put her on the auto-pilot.

Everything was peaceful in this new world. Overhead the sky was blue. Away to the north it was faintly green, intensely clear on the cloud horizon. Johnny Rayner sat with a whimsical grin on his face, listening to the Presque Isle range. This was new to me. From far away under the cloud I heard the A signal coming in, with a touch of background; then Z Q Z, the double identification signal. It amused me only to find that the thing worked. Down in the Pacific there were no radio ranges at this time; no radio aid at all for some flights. Bred of necessity on the magnetic compass, the drift sight and the sextant, I had not yet completely discarded my suspicion of all radio aids to navigation. The course on the compass was for Gander airport, Newfoundland; and I expected my navigator to take the aircraft there direct without all this aural contact with earth. My interest in the Presque Isle range signals was academic at this stage, and I didn't want to listen to them. I was having a new experience; seeing new air. The sun was warm over the cloud top, striking into the cabin. Shafts of light moved slowly and regularly on the instrument panel as the aircraft swayed slightly on the auto-pilot. I looked over the oil temperatures and pressures, and across to the head temperature gauges. All were normal. The propellers were spinning with perfect rhythm. There was plenty of fuel. I was warm, comfortable, and at peace with the world.

Three hours out we passed over the edge of the cloud shelf and saw below the blue misted surface of the sea; away to the north the coastline of Anticosti Island under Labrador, and down by the starboard wing-tip the Magdalen Islands where Cabot Strait led out to the Atlantic. Away ahead in the distance the western hills of Newfoundland were hidden under formations of pink cumulus, built by the sun-warmed land. I held on at nine thousand. The island came in below, drifting in to the sweep of the starboard propellers: strange that here in the cold grey seas of kelp and granite it should have the form of an atoll: of the dream islands whose names are music in the blue seas of the South Pacific. Here it is Grindstone Island by Cabot Strait, a cold name; an island damp with mists of the Atlantic; strong with the smell of surging seas breaking on dark rocks close below cloud. Today there is sunlight and to the north the icelands and Nova Scotia out of sight behind the wing.

My eyes drifted over the engines. No sign of oil leaks. Numbers one and two head temperatures at 195°; three and four at 185°. I checked the cowl flap switches. All were fully closed. Well, they just ran on the cool side. Oil temperatures all at 72°; pressures seventy-nine to eighty-one. Fuel pressure constant at fifteen. Everything normal. I

227

touched the auto-pilot turn control to keep her on the compass course; called up the navigator for the estimated time of arrival at Gander. In a few minutes he passed up a slip, 'ETA Gander 1335'.

The cloud over Newfoundland thickened and lay flat upon the eastward land.

The radio operator handed me the latest Gander weather: 'Wind SE 10; overcast, ceiling 1,800; visibility 8 miles.' Improving. If it stayed like that we could break through for a comfortable approach. I put on the earphones, switched on the command receiver and tuned in to the range station at Stephenville, the US Army airport on the west coast of Newfoundland.

I heard the identification signal coming in: Dit da-da-da-Da. Dit da-da-da-Da. JT, JT. Equal signals—and then the continuous note of the 'on course' signal, a-r-r-r-r-r. Sounds from some hidden, unknown world. A name: Stephenville. We are smack on the centre of the range leg, still well away from the station. I switched off the radio, discarded the earphones, and watched ahead over the cloud top. A dark line approached and spread open below us, again revealing the sea. Good air below the cloud. Still plenty of time to break through for a contact approach before the land. I disengaged the auto-pilot, eased down the power and let her go, down for the sea.

At 2,500 feet she broke through the base. The ocean was calm and grey. Strange to me. I did not know this sea. Far in the distance a dark shadow hung under the cloud base; the western hills of Newfoundland. I picked her up with the throttles to cruising power and trimmed her again for level flight; touched the propeller switches again till the spinning shadows synchronised and a single note rang true from the engines. Down with Earth, she ate into the cold grey air towards the new land.

I was influenced by two thoughts in attempting this contact flight for Gander. By working the valleys and avoiding the hills in cloud it might be possible to get in with a lower ceiling than was permissible for a letdown on the radio range. If, en route, the cloud shut down to cut out safe visual contact, we could still pour on power and climb

228

into the cloud, to a safe height, coming in on the final range approach.

But I really wanted to skate low over Newfoundland: discover this new, dark land, holding the aeroplane in my hands, and feel the thunder of her engines in the hills, roar her over the uplands, and pour her down the valleys.

As we approached the land, mountain walls rose into the clouds, making an impassable barrier to low flight in sight of the ground. I turned her away to the north and we slid in where the land fell away, edging in towards the course for Gander base and holding deeper clear air on the port side as a ready way of escape. The wing spread over a wild land of rolling hills, hard, bare rocks, scrub, and black lakes like holes leading to darkness within the earth. The air was clean and invigorating and the large aircraft felt responsive in my hands; it was smooth, fast movement, flowing over my land.

I turned on the radio altimeter. It surprised me by rising and falling accurately with the contour of the land, coming down to meet the approaching hill-tops and rising as she flung back the rocks a few feet below the wing and sailed again serenely over a valley.

I was happy and exhilarated with the sure flight of this Liberator. Something was fulfilled. I worked her round towards Gander, checking occasionally from the map, and got within about twenty miles when the cloud shut down. I saw it in the distance merging in the hills; no crack of light; no possible outlet by a valley: a thick grey shroud, down before us.

I called to Johnny for 'auto-rich' on the mixture to the carburettor, snapped up the main propeller switch to bring up the revs and gave her the power with the throttles. The motors snarled and blasted the air with thunder as she raised her nose and bored up into the cloud. In a moment this strange new world was gone and I watched the little aeroplane on the gyro horizon in the instrument panel before me, and trimmed her for the climb.

I listened for the Gander range signals, checked the identification, and heard a clear N coming in. That checked our position, west of the airport from the map reading. The

229

radio compass was out; U/S. I turned her on to a bisector to cut the south-west leg and held her up in the climb.

At four thousand I levelled off for initial approach to the station, and called up Gander control to report our position and request the altimeter setting.

The signals changed as the started to cut into the range leg. Behind the da-dit of the N the continuous note of the 'on course' signal crept in. It built up, singing through the earphones as the N faded out. I let her go on, waiting for the A to come, to prove we had cut through the beam. A-r-r-r-r-r dit da-a-r-r-r dit da-a-r-r-r dit-da. Through the beam. We had crossed the invisible, audible road to Gander airport, down somewhere under the cloud. I turned her on the gyro ninety degrees to the left and listened for her to cut back out of the bush, into the road. Soon the on-course signal started to cover the A. I turned back to bracket the leg and get her running true towards the station. Eighty degrees on the compass held her, just on the right of the beam. I turned down the volume as it built up towards the station.

Palmer, the radio operator, handed me up the lastest Gander weather: 'Wind East, 5; overcast, raining; ceiling 400, with broken cloud at 200.' Bad. I double-checked the altimeter setting for the sea-level pressure so that it would correctly record our height during the descent; and held on to pass over the cone of the station.

The sound built up; shrieked, cut out, and it passed immediately into a clear A. Over the station. Invisible below us was the Gander Range station, three miles north-east of the airport. I signalled 'Gear down' to the engineer. 'Rich mixture' to cover later calls for higher power, and turned her away thirty degrees to starboard to pick up the east leg. Da-dit, da-dit, da-a-a-a-e-e-a-a-dit-da, and we crossed the leg, easing back the power for a rate of descent that would bring us out at the right height on our return over the station.

Everything was sound. Two thousand feet over the station; 1,256 minimum over the airport—the conditions laid down for instrument approach. I watched the falling height, the air-speed at 155; and listened. Twenty-two hundred feet. Two minutes to go. Ease the descent a bit. Dit-da-e-e-e-e-e-e-o-o-o-w-w-uh-h. The sound suddenly rose, wailed, cut out and a clear N came in.

Over the station, sixteen degrees to port for the airport leg. About a minute and a half to the beginning of the south-west runway. Seven hundred and fifty feet of height to give away to break through at the minimum. I called to Johnny for twenty degrees of flap to steepen the descent, touched up the propellers to 2,300, let the nose go down, and drew back the power. She sank on down through the cloud.

A minute to go. Round us must be the hills; straight ahead and close below, the invisible airport. With us there was nothing but the rumble of the motors, the flight instruments, and the sounds in the earphones. I glanced out an instant, searching down for the earth we knew was there. There was only the dark closeness of the cloud and rain streaming in, tearing harshly at the screen. There was tight suspense in the invisible closeness of the earth as I held the instruments with my eyes and felt their readings through my hands and feet on the controls. Forty seconds to go, eighteen hundred feet. No sign of the earth. I let her go down, brought up the rate of descent to go quickly to the minimum, then if there still were nothing I could ease her a shade below it approaching the runway.

Fourteen, thirteen. Twelve-fifty. Twenty seconds. Cloud; no sign of the earth.

'Stand by for the gear.'

Twelve hundred. Eleven-fifty. Eleven. Nothing. Blind rain and cloud smoking over the nose. A climax reached up, rushing in on us. No future in this.

'Gear up.' I pressed forward the throttles and lifted her out. Get clear of the earth. The motors hauled her away, up from the invisible hills. Wait—for the flaps, more height to cover the momentary letdown. Fifteen hundred. 'Flaps up.' For a moment she was light under me; sank, picked up, and moved away. I steadied the speed on 160. The little aeroplane flew just above the bar on the artificial horizon. Five hundred feet a minute on the rate of climb.

'Gander Tower from 879. Am proceeding to Stephen-ville.'

'879 from Gander Tower. Climb to seven thousand feet on the south-east leg and await instructions.'

'879: Roger.'

I followed the instructions from the Gander control and worked her up through the cloud. I didn't want to be delayed. Stephenville would be open for day approach, but uncertain for night. I wanted to get in as soon as possible. In a few minutes he came back.

'879 from Gander Tower. You are cleared to Stephenville. Weather: calm, overcast; ceiling two thousand; visibility eight miles.'

'879: thank you.'

I pulled her away and straightened up on the course for Stephenville. In forty minutes I turned in to the Stephenville range and brought her in over the station.

I got a signal through to Gander in the morning for Atlantic clearance out of Stephenville. Walking down to the aircraft I picked up a round, waterworn stone by the side of the road. It was very smooth and cold; hard with long endurance, like the hills and the rocks we had flown over. I could see in it the serene faces of the lakes and the still black ponds, the waters rushing down through hills of pine and birch trees to the strong grey sea. In the air on the way to Gander my fingers felt the deep texture of the stone in my pocket. I took it out and tossed it across the cockpit.

'Catch, Johnny. That's Newfoundland.'

We went out of Gander in the evening. She was tight and heavy, with full Atlantic load. I held full power as she plunged forward into the darkness off the end of the runway, and took all we had from the engines till she built up some speed. The weather was down again. In a few moments even the coal-black darkness of the land was gone and something close and faintly lighter than the night closed around her as she entered the cloud. There was an impression of a critical situation in the aircraft as she dealt with the heavy load in this blind struggle for the air above. The world was close before us in the luminous instruments that picked up a glow from the fluorescent lights and stared at us securely from the panel. I was relieved when the wheels were up in the wing, the flaps drawn back into

232

the trailing edge and the power was eased from that all-out blasting struggle that left no margin.

I gave her plenty of speed and power, and watched the flight instruments to keep her closely trimmed, trying to settle her to a steady climb as she hit the uneven air of the cloud. Outside there was nothing. Here in the pilot's cabin there was a strange security, a warmth of life in the instruments, the rhythmic roar of the motors, and the inhabitants of our world; but there was tension working for the height before we could feel the easy swinging stride of cruising flight, out with the stars above the cloud.

We broke through the surface at nine thousand feet and held on to eleven-three before again reducing power. I lined up the auto-pilot and snapped on the switch as each pair of lights flickered out. As she settled at eleven thousand on the altimeter the speed held steady at 175 on the ASI. I trimmed her there, let her go, and sat back to relax and enjoy the flight.

Now she was set in her own orbit, moving across the universe with the other stars, steady, above the grey mists of space faintly visible below.

Jack Hood, the engineer, handed up mugs of coffee. We needed it now, after the strain of taking the overloaded aircraft away from the earth and up through the turbulent weather. I didn't particularly want to know anything about our position for at least two hours. There was every kind of aid to navigation on the Atlantic. And we knew the weather to be good for this crossing. I wanted the navigator to conserve his energy so that he would be alert in the morning, and give me a reliable, exact position approaching Ireland.

Palmer, the radioman, handed me a note.

'We have a passenger. Sitting on my receiver.'

I looked back to the radio cabin. It was a large green grasshopper.

I called to Palmer. 'He looks a bit groggy. Try him with a shot of oxygen.'

We shot him a whiff from an oxygen line and he sat up, looking a good deal better. He scratched his head with his back leg and appeared very comical, like a horizontal

233

giraffe with front legs in its neck. Palmer got some lettuce for him out of a sandwich box, and we left him to it.

We ran through a light warm front about an hour out and then came out to night so clear and still and black that the aircraft seemed frozen motionless in the heavens. We got a star position when necessary, kept radio watch, kept the fuel up to her from the bombay tanks and continuous watch on the compass course, altitude, and engine temperatures and pressures. I didn't sleep. I seldom do in an aircraft, except when travelling in a resigned condition as a passenger. There is always something. Something to watch out of the corner of your eye, to think about and decide what you will do before it comes up; and always something new, however small, to take from the air. When a man reaches the stage when he feels he has learned all there is to know about the air, when he is simply bored, with nothing to do because everything is going well, it is time for him to stay on the ground.

About four o'clock in the morning I turned from an awed contemplation of the northern lights and relieved Johnny on the pilot's watch. The first signs of dawn were in the east. There was only a faint difference in the sky; just enough to give you that new sense of relief that day was coming over. We had been silent a long time.

'It's cracking, Johnny,' I called across.

The effect was electrical.

'What's cracking?'

'The dawn, Johnny.'

We both lay back convulsed with laughter, speculating on the things that could crack in the night over the Atlantic.

Palmer passed me a message. We stopped laughing. 'There's a Fortress in trouble. He's lost an engine and he thinks another is packing up.'

I pulled on the earphones and switched on the intercom. 'Get his position and course.'

What could we do? Drop him our rubber dinghy perhaps, if he got down and were able to show a light. We could stay with him for about three hours, till they got a Cat or a patrol vessel on the way.

'He's sending the SOS. I can't contact him.'

'Keep on trying.'

'Can't hear him now.'

We didn't hear him any more.

Five minutes later I saw a bright light far ahead on the sea. It looked like flames, burning up and dying; flaring again. But it was a ship. She passed right under us, brilliantly lit from end to end, presumably a hospital ship or a neutral. Nobody heard the Fortress again. She just didn't arrive at Prestwick.

Morning came with a sea of cloud below us. The stars had been good. It was still clear above and Craske, the navigator, had the position well fixed. Soon he would take a final distance out, from the sun. That would be all we could take from the sky. There was a big build-up over Ireland and the west of Scotland; with low cloud round the land; so the final approach would be a radio job, probably with a letdown on the Prestwick range. As a further check on our position Palmer had got a radio fix from Iceland and south-east England. It tallied with the star position. We were all set for our approach.

Visibility above the cloud was perfect. We were only two hundred miles out in the Atlantic now, in the region where it was wise to keep watch for the long-range intercepting Focke-Wulf Condors. I sent back instructions for a watch to be kept out the tail by the two passengers who had had the misfortune to travel with us amongst all the military equipment and draughts that whistled in through the gun turret. It would give them the dubious interest inspired by the possible anticlimax of being shot down while enjoying the morning.

About seven o'clock I tuned in to 255 MKC and listened for the Derrynacross Range. It was there all right; just a faint N in the 'on course' signal persisting through a lot of intermittent crackling, and the faraway squeak of the double identification. The sound of that range was like the lone cry of a world lost in the depths of the universe. It seemed infinitely far away; calling, in the failing hope that somebody would hear, and come.

As our reckoning told us that the coast of Ireland would be coming in soon, towers of cloud rose up before us and there were great gaps of smoke-blue darkness below.

Through one of these I saw a wandering white line and suddenly realised it was the Atlantic surf breaking on the rocky coast of Northern Ireland. Then there was a bright green field and a patch of red earth; the world; people would be living there. Immediately it was wiped away; gone, surely only a picture in my imagination, as we drove surging into the cloud and again there was nothing but ourselves, the roar of the motors, and the instruments in the panel before us. She began to bounce around, stabbing into the rough air and shaking the springy wing in a way that made her feel uncomfortable to me, too mechanical on the auto-pilot. I switched it off and flew her through the weather. I heard her cut through the north leg of the Derrynacross Range, the radio screaming and crackling through the great mountains of cloud and rain that lie over the hills of Northern Ireland. I made a quick mental estimate of time for Prestwick and called for an ETA from the navigator. We stabbed on through the cloud, the flexing wing shaking the whole structure of the aeroplane. Quite suddenly the whole sky opened up before us and we flew out into clear air. Coming in under the inboard motor I saw the Mull of Kintyre, and down over the starboard nose the great rock of Ailsa Craig showing through a wisp of low cloud. I eased down the power and descended to minimum height for safe approach. As we came in over the Prestwick station the cloud broke up completely. We let down the gear and straight away got clearance into the airport circuit. We set her up for the landing and, descending, she came around facing up for the runway. Flaps down. She sank in the last few hundred feet, dragged through on the engines. Everything off. The black surface of the runway rushed under her, the wheels took the load from the wing, and our metal monster came to rest.

SIR GORDON TAYLOR

*

What's that shining through the night?
Sweet Rathlin O'Birne;
What's that fourteen-second light?
Sweet Rathlin O'Birne.

236

Eff all your Astro, SE and DR,
When we see Rathlin we know where we are,
Sweet little light-house, we won't need that shite-house—
Sweet Rathlin O'Birne!

(Strictly a Coastal Command song from the training grounds—or waters—of Northern Ireland. Rathlin O'Birne still shines off the coast of County Donegal. Astro is star-sight navigation; SE the Coastal name for radar—Special Equipment; and DR is dead reckoning navigation.)

*

With its new aircraft, weapons and experience, Coastal Command was gradually switching to the offensive. The main German U-boat bases were now in the Bay of Biscay —which gave an opportunity to catch them on the surface (where their speed was over twice that when submerged) before they reached the Atlantic convoys.

'BLIP ON THE SCREEN!'

Let us take a representative attack. The contact is picked up by the Radar in the dark. A thin line of amber light is revolving continuously on a dark glass screen, and when this light is interrupted by a blip—by the presence of an object outside the aircraft—the first promise of a U-boat has come. A whale or a shoal of fish may cause this blip on the screen, or one of the numerous fishing-boats that have been such a nuisance during our patrols. When the blip has been received, the next task is divided into two periods. There is the brief interval of darkness while the aircraft is flying in, and the thirty seconds of the actual attack, after the Leigh light has been turned on or after the U-boat has been seen in the moon path. During that interval, the Radar operator must give the pilot accurate information as often as possible and the pilot must plan his approach accordingly. If the approach on the unseen target errs by only as much as three degrees, the attack will be abortive. The drift of the aircraft, the possible zig-zagging of the U-boat, and the fact that it may be submerging, must be taken into consideration. This is the problem in judgment for the pilot while he is flying in. From the movement of the blip on the Radar screen the pilot must assess the course and speed of the U-boat, by mental arithmetic and instinct. There is neither time nor light for formulae to be consulted. And the pilot must know exactly how much his Radar operator is likely to err in a crisis.

If the U-boat does not submerge, there is flak to contend with, directly the Leigh light has been turned on. It must be remembered that the pilot is not flying a fighter aircraft which responds delicately to control. A Liberator weighs about twenty-eight tons and it is stubborn to handle.

During the minutes of approach, the drill of the ten members of the crew must be as exquisitely concerted as ten separate instruments sounding one chord in an orchestra. It is here that years of training suddenly manifest themselves in one co-ordinated action.

The pilot is flying his heavy aircraft through the dark on a course calculated from the Radar operator's directions. The Radar operator is meanwhile watching the blip on the screen and operating his complicated set. The second pilot is looking after the engines, putting up the revs and boost as required, and at the same time setting up the automatic camera.

This is an important part of the exercise, for the photographs taken, automatically, during an attack, are not merely souvenirs for an album of victories. They must show the depth-charges entering the water in relation to the U-boat two or three seconds before they explode. It is from the position of entry, not the extent of the explosion, that the attack can be assessed.

During these same minutes, the navigator has to set up his bombing panel, check the selection of bombs, and see that the bomb doors have been opened. Then he must be ready to switch on the Leigh light. The wireless operator must flash signals back to base, so that they know of the possible target, and so that, if the aircraft is destroyed, it will not be a 'silent loss'. The engineer lies in the open bomb bay to watch the effect of the depth-charges when they enter the water: the front gunner and the two beam gunners must be prepared to give the U-boat hell the moment the Leigh light is turned on; and the rear gunner must prepare to give them a further burst when the aircraft has passed over.

A good captain expects his crew to perform all these tasks within a matter of seconds, so that, at the right distance, the engines may be set at the speed which will allow the aircraft to drop the depth-charges on target from a height of fifty feet. Then the orchestra pauses to watch for the conductor's baton. It falls, the light is turned on, and the target is revealed for this assemblage of preparation. Then the depth-charges are dropped, in a long stick, by the navigator. The aircraft flies through the flak and over the U-boat and, from his point of vantage, the rear gunner is able to substantiate the report of the engineer in the bomb bay. It has been a perfect straddle. The word straddle is important. A direct hit usually causes the depth-charge, which is not fused for contact, to break up. A close miss is therefore the perfect way of exploding the depth-charge, to do the maximum of harm.

Then comes the circuit before the aircraft can fly in and seek for evidence. Little wonder that the crew search the water hoping to see yellow dinghies, and white faces peering up, into the merciless beam of the Leigh light.

HECTOR BOLITHO

Not every flight resulted in an attack (the average was about one U-boat sighted every 400 hours flown).

*

We had been flying all day long at a hundred effing feet,
The weather effing awful, effing rain and effing sleat.
The compass it was swinging effing South and effing
    North
But we made an effing landfall in the Firth of effing
    Forth.

Chorus: Ain't the Air Force effing awful? (repeat twice)
            We made an effing landfall in the Firth of effing
            Forth.

239

We joined the effing Air Force 'cos we thought it effing
   right,
But don't care if we effing fly or if we effing fight.
But what we do object to are those effing Ops Room
   twats
Who sit there sewing stripes on at the rate of effing knots.

*

*In the Western desert, Rommel had been stopped on the
Alamein line—partly by the stranglehold Malta's aircraft
and submarines had on his supply route across the Mediterranean. Now both sides were fighting an economic war:
building up resources for the battle that would either push
Montgomery into the Suez Canal or Rommel back to
Tunisia. Behind the lines, in Cairo,*

THEY ALSO SERVED

Our Desert Air Force in 1941–2 were practically cut off
from the Mediterranean and equipment so urgently required had of necessity to be brought by the long sea route
of some 12,000 miles. It became necessary to make do with
our limited local resources and with a small nucleus of
RAF tradesmen work was set in motion to overcome our
deficiencies.

Advertisements in the local Cairo papers brought
astounding results. Each individual was vetted by the police
and doctor before being forwarded to the respective branch
of III MU that needed them. The MU had been fortunate in
the airmen posted from Aboukir Depot for they were the
'king-pins'. The local talent came from all walks of life, but
to find such different nationalities as Egyptians, Greeks,
Cypriots, Maltese, Arabs, Palestinians, Sudanese, Jews,
Copts, Armenians, plus a smattering of others, made one
wonder just how the work could ever run efficiently.

Fortunately the technical supervisor of local labour had
a working knowledge of seven languages, and owing to the
fact that many of the men understood two or more
tongues it was possible to get on a working basis.

The work of the engine-repair section was to receive all
the Rolls-Royce Merlin and Kestrel engines from the
Desert Air Forces, completely strip them to their last nut

and bolt, and after an overhaul and bench test get them back to the desert for further useful life.

These engines arrived from as far afield as Aleppo in Syria, Malta, Tobruk, in fact from all over the desert. In many cases they arrived completely covered with a coating of sand at least a quarter of an inch thick. Some had been dragged by tanks on to rocky ground before they could be loaded, and suffered considerably in doing so, yet those engines left No. I ER7 as jet-black gleaming power units with the guarantee of the RAF behind them.

The staff had received the guidance of a Rolls expert specially flown from England and this gentleman told them that if conditions were the same as at home the output per month should rise to ninety complete overhauls. Luckily he had not seen the effect of the Khamsin. This is a hot sand-laden wind blowing from the desert, and its effect on dissembled engines was substantial, transforming them from gleaming components, viewed and ready for assembly, to gritty, dull, inanimate shapes. The sand was forced into the shops through the wide spaces between roof and walls. In spite of this grave handicap the staff refused to be beaten and a record of some 106 engines were overhauled and sent back to the desert in the month of March 1942.

A general view of the ERS complications and trials can best be exemplified by an account of a typical day. It must be appreciated that the inhabitants surrounding No. 1 ERS objected very strongly to the shop being there at all. Threats had been made to burn the place and precautions were taken to safeguard life, limb and property. This necessitated an armed Egyptian policeman patrolling the place, a 'Gaffieh' or watchman to prevent pilfering, and an armed airman to check the passes of visitors and to use his discretion in case of trouble. These formed the day guard. At night six armed airmen stood by with an NCO with a telephone to use in emergency. In May 1942 this was changed to a guard of ten Indian troops under an NCO to relieve skilled airman from this duty.

Personnel arrived by truck via the Cairo main station, and carried out a number of intricate manœuvres to dodge the hordes of men, women, children, donkeys, camels, taxis, gharrys, all seemingly going to all points of the compass.

241

In time it was possible to judge reasonably accurately where to expect a shower of filth, garbage, chewed sugar-cane and spit, as the truck wended its way towards the shop. Craftily thrown stones and plenty of abuse announced the point of arrival, chiefly because the school inmates took a delight in throwing stones at a moving vehicle, and if one stopped to remonstrate the budding scholars performed works of art on the sides of the truck which were never taught at school.

Air Chief Marshal SIR PHILIP JOUBERT KCB CMG DSO

*

One major decision taken that summer was to try and improve Bomber Command's accuracy by creating a 'marker' force to pinpoint the target for the growing, but inexperienced, mass of the new squadrons. There were problems.

THE PATHFINDERS

At that time there were rumours that a Pathfinder Squadron was to be formed, composed of the best bombing crews from all squadrons.

Dim said: 'It seems a good idea to me, but I can see many snags.'

'What are they going to do?' someone asked.

'Go in low and light up the targets for us with flares. We stay high and safe and bomb accurately,' said Johnny.

'That's good.'

'That's fine.'

'Yes, but here are the snags,' said Dim. 'First it is hard to form a new squadron quickly, and if you form it quickly it is hard to form it well, and speed is what they want. I think it would be better to take the best squadron in the Command and call it the "First Pathfinder Squadron".'

'That means us,' said Taffy.

'No, we are about fifth now. I think 97 Squadron.'

A short argument followed in which it was generally agreed that 97 Squadron should be chosen.

'The second snag,' went on Dim, 'is losses. If they are going to go in low, their casualties are going to be high—

very high. How are they going to get away with it? New crews will take a long time to train.'

'Squadrons will have to give up their best crews,' suggested Wimpy, 'on a strictly volunteer basis.'

'Then the best squadrons will either be deprived of all their crack crews, or no one will volunteer and the Pathfinder will be starved.'

'That's right. Keen squadrons will cough up their best crews and lose their place on the photographic ladder, while a lousy squadron will do nothing about it and go up to the top.'

'C'est la guerre,' said Dim. 'It will be fair enough in the long run. But the third great snag, as far as I can see, is promotion in the squadron. If there are heavy losses, then it won't matter, but if there aren't, then good chaps who would become Flight-Commanders in an ordinary squadron would be kept down because they had volunteered to become Pathfinders. They would lose their promotion, and the old hands would stay on and keep their rank. It seems rather unfair.'

'That goes for all special squadrons,' I pointed out.

'I suppose so. Anyway, I wish they would hurry up and get cracking. Our bombing certainly needs a spot of accuracy.'

Wing Commander GUY GIBSON VC DSO DFC

*

The Pathfinders nevertheless came into being. Chosen to lead them was Donald Bennett, the pioneer of the Atlantic ferry, and since then a bomber squadron commander. He was given experienced crews, the latest radar and radio aids—and a new aircraft which nobody seemed to have ordered (the makers had designed and produced it on their own initiative) but which was to become one of the few immortals of the air:

MOSQUITO

We had a few of these bomber Mosquitoes which nobody wanted, but which had been ordered in a small test order by the Ministry of Aircraft Production. They had no armament of any sort, but were indeed very fast little craft. They had a bomb bay big enough to take four of our five-hundred-pound Target Indicators, and it seemed to me that if they could achieve the ceiling we required they would be perfectly suitable. I test-flew the Mosquito by day and by night, and we got on with the 'test installation' of the Oboe equipment. At a meeting at the Air Ministry on the subject, Bomber Command and the Air Ministry both very strongly opposed the adoption of the Mosquito. They argued that it was a frail wood machine totally unsuitable for Service conditions, that it would be shot down because of its absence of gun turrets, and that in any case it was far too small to carry the equipment and an adequate Pathfinder crew. I dealt with each one of these points in turn, but finally they played their ace. They declared that the Mosquito had been tested thoroughly by the appropriate establishments and found quite unsuitable, and indeed impossible to fly at night. At this I raised an eyebrow, and said that I was very sorry to hear that it was quite impossible to fly it by night, as I had been doing so regularly during the past week and had found nothing wrong. There was a deathly silence. I got my Mosquitoes.

Thus it was that the greatest little aircraft ever built came into the squadron service as a bomber in the Royal Air Force. From that decision grew many other things, not only for the Oboe squadrons but also for the general improvement of our bombing policy.

On the question of pyrotechnics, one might imagine that the situation was simple. I would therefore like to explain to those who had not had the pleasure of bombing Germany, that the enemy went to extreme lengths to divert the fall of bombs from the proper targets on to spots which were more attractive from his point of view. This was done in a number of different ways. Both before and after the advent of the Pathfinder Force, one of the most common customs was to create a target area adequately surrounded by defences and searchlights, and to let off dummy incendiaries, like our own, on the ground, so as to look as if there was a town being bombed and being defended. Many a crew would then drop their bombs into the middle of it all fondly believing that they were giving the real target a real pounding. Unfortunately, all too frequently this was simply a dummy town—in the open fields. The realistic nature of these dummies was quite staggering, and it is no reflection that many crews were caught by them. With the advent of Pathfinders we expected that the Hun would try to copy the markers which we used. Illumination, useful in opening attacks in good weather but useless once the smoke and dust of bombing had started, had certain advantages in the matter of identification of genuine surface landmarks. This, however, only applied to the early Pathfinder crews, and it was quite clear that the main force must aim at pyrotechnics of some sort. The intensity of the target indicators, which we subsequently referred to as TIs, was very great, and indeed right to the end of the war the enemy never really produced a very good copy. As we expected trouble, we arranged for all sorts of combinations and variations of colours changing, and colours throwing stars of different colours and the like. We were prepared to use different colours for different purposes, and indeed to change colours if necessary during a raid so as to ensure the correct aiming point even if the enemy were sufficiently alert to watch and copy. In addition, the bursting of the target indicators was carried out by barometric fuses, usually set to burst at relatively low levels between 200 and 500 feet. This meant that there was a slight cascade on to the ground, but that the main burning period was right on the ground itself. Each TI consisted of a large number of these pyrotechnic candles, ignited by the initial bursts, which meant that fire-fighters on the ground would take a very considerable time to get around to the job of putting them all out. Moreover, their burning period was relatively short anyway, and so there was no question of their being dealt with in that manner. Continuity of marking was achieved by replenishing from above.

In addition to these target indicators for ground use, we prepared something which was ridiculed and laughed at by a good many people. These were sky markers, and consisted of parachute flares of various colours throwing out stars (or not, as the case might be) so that we could mark a spot in the sky for a limited period, usually three to five minutes. I had done a few calculations on the use of such a method for blind bombing through thick cloud when it was impossible to see the glow of target indicators because of the density and/or depth of the cloud. These rough calculations seemed to me to indicate that the results to be achieved by such an apparently difficult method would probably prove just as effective as the slap-dash visual bombing that I had so often seen in the past. Roughly speaking, the idea was that the sky markers would be put down by a marker aircraft using Oboe or H2S, in a position so that after it had burned half its time it had drifted, in accordance with the wind found by the navigator, to the correct point through the line-of-sight of a bomber on to the aiming point, assuming that his bomb sights was set to his normal height and that he was approaching the target on the correct heading. This latter point was, of course, the most difficult one to achieve, but as we hoped that the relative accuracy of the fore and aft position would be greater than normal, the error in line was, we felt, acceptable. This proved to be the case in practice, and it was a method which we used frequently for the rest of the war.

It was in August 1942, that the squadrons of the Path finder Force assembled. Typical of the attitude of Bert Harris, our C.-in-C. to the Pathfinder Force, was the order which he issued to me that the squadrons were to operate the day they arrived, without missing a single night, and that no period would be allowed for preparation or for training. This was quite unreasonable, but the spirit behind it was so thoroughly 'press-on' that I made no attempt to argue. In accordance with the general principle of never wasting war effort or of ceasing to strike the enemy, I entirely agreed, and we were therefore prepared to operate the night the squadrons assembled. Actually they did not do so, as all operations were cancelled, but on the next night the Pathfinder squadrons went out, using visual methods only, to bomb Flensberg, a submarine base north of Kiel. We had no radar devices working, and the crews were not particularly trained for any special operations. The only thing special about the operation was therefore that we provided the most experienced crews with the means of illuminating the target by parachute flares. Giving them an excellent load of these devices, I sent them off to do their best.

Air Vice-Marshal DONALD BENNETT CB CBE DSO

The Pathfinders were even allowed to wear a special badge (once they had done ten operations and were regarded as fully trained). It was a 'small pair of gold wings worn under the medal ribbons'—in fact a small brass eagle already worn by NCOs over their arm stripes to show that they were aircrew. Wartime economy, you know. Their other concession was that they did twice the normal number of operations—from 30 up to 60—before being 'rested'.

*

M.H.D.O.I.F.

One of the best-known of flying awards, the Most Highly Derogatory Order of the Irremovable Finger, was awarded monthly from late 1942 onwards in Tee Emm— *the humorous (yet deadly serious) air safety magazine. One of the earliest recipients of the Order was a young Pilot Officer: his citation reads:*

This officer on returning at night from a bombing raid in very poor visibility discovered he had accidentally set red on black and so had for some hours been flying a reciprocal instead of the course for home. Realising his mistake he then set course for base (270°) expecting to get no further than Holland if lucky. When the fuel at last gave out—as he anticipated—he made a good forced landing and at once set fire to his aircraft to prevent it falling into enemy hands. He and his crew then made a quick escape across the countryside—only to find themselves almost immediately opposite the 'Rose and Crown', Little ——, England.

TEE EMM

*

The following rather blasphemous item was used, with adaptations, on many RAF stations throughout the Middle East and perhaps the world. The part of the Chaplain was NOT played by the station padre.

SERVICE OF THANKSGIVING FOR SAFE ARRIVAL IN IRAQ

Order of service.

1. Organ voluntary: the Dead March in Saul.
2. Chaplain: We will commence our service by singing hymn No 252 to the tune of 'There is a green hill far away'.

> There are some greenhorns far away,
>   All sitting in a boat,
> Just like the one that brought us here,
>   So let's sit back and gloat.—Airmen.

3. Chaplain: Dearly beloved brethren, I humbly pray and beseech you as many as are here present to accompany me with a glorious thirst and some ready cash unto the bar of the Service Institute, saying after me:

'Almighty and most merciful Records, we have heard and obeyed thy commands like lost sheep; we have followed too much the vices and desires of our own hearts, and there is no wealth in us. We have done those things we ought not to have done, and left undone those things we ought not to have left undone, and there is no hope in us. But then, O Records, have mercy upon us miserable first offenders, restore thou them that are penniless according to thy promise declared unto us in King's regulations and Air Council Instructions. And grant, O mosts merciful Records, that we may hereafter lead a goodly, riotous and inebriate life to the glory of thy most perfect filing system.'—Airmen.

4. Chaplain: Let us pray for our reliefs.

Congregation: Hear, hear.

Chaplain: O Captain of the *Somersetshire,* we pray thee to drop not thine anchor in the Shatt-el-Arab, nor to tarry overlong at Kasfret but to make all speed to relieve us from this torment which is ours. We pray thee to attend unceasingly to they cargo of souls that they may keep and maintain perfect health in body and mind and not be isolated. This we ask not for their sake but for ours.—Airmen.

5. Chaplain: Let us pray for the troopship.

'Almighty *Somersetshire*, queen of all troopships, we pray thee to spring no leak, neither to capsize, but to preserve thy good servants the Captain, the Crew, the Bo'sun, the Erks and All Other Persons Committed to Thy Charge. And more especially the Sweepers and Swabbers that they may faithfully discharge their duties to the Bibby Line and our immediate release.'—Airmen.

6. Chaplain: Bear up, for the boat is at hand.

Congregation: O boat roll on to save us.

Chaplain: O boat make speed to take us.

Congregation: And our mouths shall spew forth thy praise.

Chaplain: O Records make haste to post us.

Congregation: As all our trust is in thee.

Chaplain: Glory be to the Captain, the Crew and the Erks.

Congregation: As it was when we came, is now, and is ever likely to be. Will our tour never end?—Airmen.

7. Chaplain: We will now sing hymn number 664B

> O Boat, our curse in ages past,
>   Our hope for years to come,
> May we recline beneath thy mast,
>   And bear us to our home.
>
> These three long years within our sight
>   Are like a lifetime gone,
> Long as the guards we did at night,
>   So Boat do please roll on.
>
> O Boat, our curse in ages past,
>   Our hope for years to come,
> Let's hope the next will be our last,
>   And leave us safe at home.

8. Chaplain: I will now read the Church Notices:
There will be no Church Service next Sunday, as there

is a race meeting in Baghdad. My selections are given in the Parish Magazine, now on sale in the porch.

The collection today is on behalf of the Warrant Officers' Poor Children's Beer Fund, and you are asked to give generously.

Aircraftwoman Mary Jones is being baptised at the evening service and the gallery will be closed to onlookers. Members of the congregation are requested to refrain from singing 'O Salome' during the ceremony.

Quoted by C. H. WARD-JACKSON

There is a lot more. The hymn numbers are, of course, RAF forms: 252 being the charge sheet and 664B the one on which you pay for equipment you have lost.

*

Under two great air commanders, Tedder and Coningham, the Desert Air Force was becoming a flexible tactical force equivalent to anything the Luftwaffe had had before, and better than it had there now. One fighter leader flew

'PROPERLY DRESSED'

In the autumn of 1942, not long before the Battle of Alamein, Wing Commander Jackie Darwin took over command of 244 Wing, composed of two squadrons of Spitfires and two of Hurricanes. Darwin was a regular officer who before the war had served on the North-West Frontier of India and was also a keen follower to hounds. By a tragic misfortune he was dancing with his beautiful wife in the Café de Paris in London the night it was bombed, and she was killed in his arms. He never recovered fully from this shock, and developed a great hatred for the Germans and a complete disregard for his own safety. His pilots did not think much of flying next to him, for he always led them through the thickest of the flak, and whereas for some time he bore a charmed life, his wingmen were not always so lucky.

At this time the wing had a mascot, a seedy, mongrel dog called Rommel, and during periods of leisure Rommel was used to hunt the desert fox. The procedure was simple, though completely ineffective; every available Jeep was pressed into service and was driven at great speed over the desert until a fox was sighted, or one was suspected to have been sighted! At this moment Rommel would be launched from a moving Jeep, turn several somersaults and start off in the opposite direction to that desired, and the next few minutes would be taken up in catching Rommel. For some reason best known to himself, Darwin had with him his hunting kit complete—boots, breeches, and pink coat—and on the day of this particular story he was wearing it. Just as the hound was running well the wing was brought to immediate readiness and ordered to strafe enemy aeroplanes on the airfield at Daba.

The wing commander had no time to change and took off in his Hurricane in hunting garb. Later, when flying very low over the desert to escape the flak, he caught his propeller on the ground, the engine stopped and he came to rest, surprised but unhurt, in no-man's land. Luckily, a patrolling armoured car from the 11th Hussars was able to rescue him and took him back to their position near the front lines. He was taken into the dug-out mess, where he was met by the CO of the Hussars squadron with the words, 'This is the first time I've seen an Air Force officer properly dressed!'

Group Captain J. E. JOHNSON CBE DSO DFC

*

The aircraft ferry route to the desert war ran across the diagonal width of Africa. Flying single-engined aircraft over such country was always a risky business; not all made it. These notes were found with the pilot of one which had force-landed en route:

'I doubt if I shall live till the morning, I am getting weaker and weaker every minute. I have only three more gulps of water and I have such a terrible thirst, I should go somewhere, but where? I am completely lost. Good-bye, we shall meet where we all have to go one day. Please see that this little money which I have is handed to my parents. I am dying, thinking of them and of Poland. I give myself up to God. Time 2000 hrs., 9th May.

'Yesterday I walked for three hours towards the West, but I could go no farther. It took me five hours to return, I only just managed to do it. So long as it is cool I can still live, but when it gets hot I do not think I shall be able to stand it. Death is very near, I tried to take off. I have still 10 gallons but the accumulators are flat. I fixed down the key so that it buzzed all night. I looked for help but now help will not come. I feel that I shall not last long.

'Time 0900 hours, 10th May. I waited for ten o'clock in the morning. I had a feeling that at that time help would come. A dream of a man dying from starvation and thirst. Oh God, shorten my sufferings, there will be no help for me, let nobody land in the desert where there are no people, as there is no way out. Just like me, it is better to be killed. The sand storm was so thick that I could see nothing.

'Time 1200 hours, 10th May. It is terribly hot, I drink, or rather I lick my scanty sweat. I am suffering terribly.

'1345 hours—I hear an aircraft flying to the south, to my right, my last hope, I cannot get up to have a look. My last minutes. God have mercy on me.'

Sergeant Pilot MIKOLAJCZAK

*

Convoy losses came not only from U-boats and occasional surface raiders, but from long-range Luftwaffe aircraft in the Atlantic and whole squadrons of standard bombers along the route to Russia. To combat this, one of the strangest of RAF units was formed.

MERELY AN INSURANCE

Early last year the Merchant Ship Fighter Unit was born and nurtured on an aerodrome in the northwest country. Here met for the first time pilots from every type of job in Fighter Command, with one or two who had been instructors on fighter training stations. Upon first arrival we wandered about the Mess for an hour or two, trying to decide which chap appeared to be so intelligent that he would know something about this job for which we had volunteered. The Mess bar finally proved a common meeting ground, we found that not one of us knew anything at all—except that we were to go to sea with the Merchant Service. Having got that much satisfaction we all settled down for the evening and finally decided the MSFU was quite a jolly proposition. The next morning was spent in making the acquaintance of the admin blokes in our new HQ, and we were agreeably surprised to find them good types who, although they knew nothing either, would obviously have helped us if they'd known anything. It was tough on them that first day because they couldn't even find their own offices, whereas we could at least see a few Hurricanes standing around, and we did know where the Mess was.

In the afternoon we were called in by our CO, at the time Squadron Leader Louis Strange, DSO MC DFC and bar, who explained to us we would be attached to certain specially prepared merchant ships which, although doing normal cargo-carrying duties, would also be equipped with a fighter aircraft as protection against Hun bombers. Apart from being at readiness during daylight, we would have no other set duties since an aircraft crew of four were coming along and catapult maintenance would be done by naval ratings provided for that purpose. By this time we all had visions of palm trees, golden beaches and innumerable Dorothy Lamours, but were hauled back to reality by some unimaginative bloke asking the CO whether the many Naval lieutenants in the Mess had anything to do with our job. The CO said they had a whole lot to do with it, and explained that a Naval chappie would go alone with each pilot and, in the event of action, would guide the Hurricane by R/T, and would home it back to the ship should the pilot drive out of sight of the convoy. The fighter direction officer, or FDO, as he is called, would also be the administration officer for all the servicemen on board, and would thus have quite a lot of work to do.

Having received all the gen, we started our catapult practice before actually going to a ship. The catapult consists briefly of a steel runway eighty-five feet long, along which the trolley, carrying the aircraft, is forced by a bank of cordite rockets over a distance of sixty feet. Using 30-

degree flaps and six-and-a-quarter pounds' boost, a perfect take-off can be made without any loss of height at all, while in many cases the aircraft climbs directly off the trolley since the airspeed is often well over 80 mph.

When the catapult training is finished the pilot, FDO and aircraft crew are sent to the port of embarkation, where they organise the loading of the aircraft. This operation is usually accompanied by much amusing, though well meaning, advice from the merchant seamen who, while possibly competent to load a normal cargo, would soon bend a Hurricane if their methods were followed. I actually saw two foreigners, transporting a Hurricane on a lighter, use the overlapping port wing to prevent their barge from hitting the wharf wall. Naturally the aircraft suffered.

Apart from incidents such as this, which luckily are very infrequent, a voyage on a CAM ship can be very pleasant indeed, since on certain trips the ship soon passes out of the aircraft danger area and the pilot can sit back and anticipate the pleasures awaiting him at the port of arrival. The Captain, officers and even the crew are delighted to have us on board and do everything to help us, sometimes more than 'everything', since the Captain, if the pilot and FDO can cope, usually tries to spend about 24 hours out of every day in port entertaining us, ostensibly to celebrate a good trip out and a quiet one home, but really, I think, to make us feel happy on his ship.

When the ship arrives at its destination the pilot 'shoots off' and lands at a local aerodrome where his aircraft is serviced while the ship is loading, so that it can be placed back on the ship when the return convoy is ready to leave.

It all seems so simple, doesn't it? A pleasant sea voyage, lots of fun with the good types in the merchant service, and last, but by no means least, grand relations with the officers of the naval escort ships with whom we always work in close co-operation. In actual fact, however, the MSFU has not such as easy job as all that. Several of their ships have been lost by enemy submarine action, leaving a bewildered MSFU section sitting in a lifeboat while their Hurricane dropped down to Davy Jones. Many of our chaps have watched other ships in their convoy burning and exploding,

254

and have waited helplessly until the blitz has ended or until their own ship rends and shudders, and they have to lower and man their own ship's boats. For a long time both pilots and FDOs had to take everything while having no chance to attack. We were merely an insurance, an effective insurance too, since the air attacks on our convoys stopped as soon as the CAM ships began to operate. Yet, being an insurance, however good, is no consolation when no score is being marked up on the credit side, so it was with great delight that we learned in May of this year that Flying Officer Alastair Hay had catapulted from his ship while travelling in convoy to Russia and destroyed at least one He 111 and damaged other enemy planes.

In this encounter Flying Officer Hay was wounded in the thigh and his Hurricane was badly damaged, but he baled out and was picked up by an escort vessel within five minutes. He earned and received the DFC for such a good show, and is now quite fit again except perhaps for a slight taste of fluorescence which he said tasted horrible, and of which he scoffed quite a fair amount as he was waiting to be lifted out of the water.

TEE EMM

In fact, every operational flight ended in a bale-out: there was no way of landing a Hurricane back on an 80-foot catapult. The unit was not disbanded until September 1943, when the increase in long-range patrol aircraft and, particularly, small escort carriers made them superfluous.

255

1943

The tide had turned—at Alamein, Stalingrad, Midway, Guadalcanal. It was still a long way home, but now we were moving. The RAF was hitting its stride with new aircraft, equipment, techniques—and at last in reasonable strength.

But in one area at least the decisive battles were yet to come: the Atlantic. The U-boats were also reaching full strength, also adopting new equipment and tactics. The previous November had seen shipping losses of 814,000 tons—which proved the worst month of the war, although nobody could know that then. Coastal Command stepped up its Bay of Biscay campaign, trying to catch the U-boats close to the bases.

FIRST OP

By now you know the stage. It's the Bay of Biscay, where a lot happened and a lot didn't happen. When things were happening you forgot yourself as a person and got on with the job. When things were not happening everyone was a lot harder to get along with. Suspense was agony. After you got back home you wondered why in blazes you had thought yourself into such a state. You resolved to be cool, calm, and collected in the future. Next time you went out suspense began to work on you again.

A lot of squadrons were losing a lot of men. There were too many dinghies in the Bay. It wasn't pleasant to arrive on a unit, strike up an acquaintance with the fellow in the next bunk, then look round for him blankly a few days later to learn that he was dead. He was too young to die, and so were you.

When you started a tour you were a high-powered set tuned to the emotions of the people round you. Everything you heard was important. Everything you did and saw hit you with a nervous impact which took months to master. Every thump of your heart was the gathering beat of the drum of doom.

The first operational flight was the hurdle. It stood up in front of you in a black gown with a scythe in hand. It stood a mile high. You waited for it and sweated on it. It spoilt your sleep. It made you drop a steel mirror and a New Testament in one breast-pocket of your battledress, and heavy cigarette-case packed with cigarettes in the other. You put the New Testament on the side of your heart and you prayed and you searched your soul, and it wasn't funny because that empty bed next to you was a perpetual kick in the stomach.

Then your crew appeared on the ops list and you were to take off at 0100 hours.

You got into bed about seven o'clock and you lay there for three hours doing everything but sleep. You just thought and started gulping every now and then with your mouth open. That was the only way you could stop the thud of your heart.

A few minutes after ten you were struggling into your flying clothes. You had arranged them in painfully precise order on the empty bed next door; then it wasn't long before you were down in the air-crew mess eating the special rations, the bacon and the eggs, and drinking cups of tea. You actually ate greedily. You fairly stuffed it down. And at eleven o'clock you were in the ops room for briefing.

You hadn't been in the ops room before, and your eyes were like a movie camera, seeing all, recording all, missing nothing; the coal fire burning in the stove, the comfortable lazy warmth so strangely at odds with the winds outside, the chatter and the shuffling of feet, the senior officers, the rugged-up air-crew, the hard seats arranged one behind the other like the setting for a religious ceremony, the teacups, the Waafs, the continuing surge of the heart, the nerve-soothing balm of a good cigarette perhaps too deeply inhaled.

You sat down.

On the wall before you was a huge map of the patrol zone. There were ribbons all over it of different colours.

Each ribbon was a patrol. One of them was yours. There were numbers and arrows, and they were the positions of Allied and neutral shipping and their courses. There were bombing-restriction areas clearly marked. There were enemy aircraft motifs and U-boats motifs pinned here and there. And there were officers talking to you slowly and deliberately.

You listened in growing confusion and disquiet, to a recital of do's and don't's. You heard strange words without apparent meanings which were code expressions for secret procedures about which as yet you knew nothing. You were appalled by what you were expected to know and remember. You wondered whether it were possible for the captain to absorb it, or whether he sat there quietly nodding his head only to conceal the great gulf of his ignorance. You heard of radio frequencies, and studs—whatever they were—of Junkers 88s and Spanish warships and U-boats. You heard of merchant vessels scattered in a gale; of Allied and neutral and enemy fishing-vessels.

You heard the co saying 'Good luck.'

Then you were outside in the cold and the dark and the wind struggling down to the pier, clumping laboriously in your great boots, trailing the gang, laden with equipment and rations for thirteen hours in the air. Camera and binoculars, eggs and chops, charts and pigeons, bread and chewing gum.

For thirty minutes your pinnace purred down harbour towards Angle Bay, and you sat there and looked at the fellows who were your crew-mates and your heart kept pounding. You didn't say anything, just listened to the chatter which had nothing to do with ops. It was last night's picture-show, it was a car a fellow in Pembroke would sell for £20.

Suddenly the pinnace was bumping against the seaplane tender at the end of the flare-path and it was the scramble up into cold air again and an overpowering desperate yearning for bed.

You stood miserably in the middle of a heap of equipment on the deck in the cold wind. You heard the flare-path officer yell a few words at the captain. You heard the sea and you smelt it. You thought of your mother and of

258

the girl back home. You ached. You felt the slow rock of the pinnace and the constriction within you.

Then you were jumping down into the little dinghy and you saw the coxswain's upturned face in the light and you shuffled over to one side to make room for the rest of the crew; then the dinghy cast off.

Soon it was roaring northwards, bow high, stern low in the water, rolling like a fat horse, turbulent wake spreading luminously like a peacock's feathers; roaring into a great void of blackness; with the wind a raw ice against your cheeks; with the stars bright in the heavens.

Then the dinghy was losing speed and the rubber gun-wales were squealing against the Sunderland's hull.

The lights were on in the wardroom and that was the duty hand, one of the gunners, letting you know he was still alive although he felt half dead.

You scrambled into the wardroom, crushed amongst the many, into the smell of stale tobacco smoke, into the roar of voices and an immense feeling of uselessness.

The routine check of the aircraft began while the duty hand, still in his underwear, tried to drag on his trousers and rub the sleep out of his eyes. You wandered round watching everybody move through the orderly procession of duty; inspecting the bilges and the guns and the ammunition, adjusting the moorings for casting off, unlocking the flying controls, arranging the signal colours, checking the cockpit and the wireless and testing the engine controls, setting up the charts, blacking out the portholes, and clambering up top out onto the wing to examine the mainplane. They were working hard, all of them, and you were watching and thinking and listening and and you were sore in the pit of the stomach.

The captain and the first pilot settled down into the flying-seats in front of the blackout curtain, and the crew came up to the bridge and everyone checked their Mae Wests and secured the tapes that held them to the body.

An engine exploded into life and soon the two outers were running with a steady healthy beat. And that was the real beginning, the casting of the die, the jumping of the hurdle, when they slipped moorings and slowly taxied out into the harbour like a great bus, towards the lone line of swaying little ships blazing with lights which were the flare path.

IVAN SOUTHALL

*

Not only the big Coastal aircraft flew to the Bay. Now the Beaufighter, gradually being supplanted in its night-defence role by the speedier Mosquito, became a daytime aggressor.

REVENGE MISSION

The time required to bring the Squadron to a respectable standard of night-fighting turned out to be less than I had originally imagined, in spite of the influx of new crews. By the end of March, a month and a half after we arrived at Predannock, I felt that we were in pretty good shape, so I stepped up our offensive activities. The majority of crews were given a chance to visit the German over his own ground. We also flew a number of patrols into the Bay of Biscay. These we flew in daylight, usually sending two aircraft out in loose formation for mutual protection. We weren't lucky with them and suffered our first combat casualties. A relatively new Flight Commander and an experienced Sergeant Pilot took off with their navigators for a patrol off the Gironde estuary. They apparently ran into a large number of Ju 88 long-range fighters and both Beaus were shot down. The information came to us from our Intelligence Service, who had picked up the radio chatter of the German squadron involved. It left no doubt as to the result of the battle.

This was a serious blow to the Squadron. The crews we lost were popular so we thought in terms of revenge. Later information from Intelligence revealed a possibility that the Germans had been alerted to the presence of our aircraft by so-called neutral Spanish fishing boats. Those of us who had flown in the Bay had noticed these boats. The thought that my crews had been shot down because of the treachery of these people made my blood boil. Next morning I decided that regardless of the strict regulations concerning attacks on neutral shipping, these people would have to be taught a lesson. I again selected Black-burn as navigator and briefed another of my experienced crews for a mission of revenge. Group were told we were merely off on another routine patrol.

Just before lunch we set off, flying at wavetop height in line abreast about fifty yards apart. Our course took us to the Scillies then south-west, fifty miles off the coast of western Brittany, then due south, finally cutting in towards the French coast near the mouth of the Gironde. From here we would patrol some fifty miles out to sea. The southern extremity of our mission would take us to within sight of the north coast of Spain. We flew as low as possible to elude German-manned ground radar units along the coast of France. To ensure surprise I had briefed that unless we were in combat or some emergency arose, radio silence would be maintained between aircraft.

It was hot work in the Beau in these southern waters, with the sun turning our glass- and perspex-covered cockpits into greenhouses. Soon we were sweating freely. 'What was that?' I asked Blackburn over the intercom. to look towards the eastern horizon. Yes, masts of ships. I waggled my wings in our pre-arranged signal and banked sharply towards them, climbing to 1,500 feet. My number two followed. In a few seconds we were over several fishing boats. I confirmed they were Spanish from their flags. Right, you bastards, we'll teach you to help the enemy. Climbing again, I banked round with the other Beau following. I selected one vessel as my target and dived again. My gunsights were set and I flipped the switches to arm my guns. The range rapidly closed and then I noticed someone lying in the stern of the boat, arms behind his head, obviously sunning himself. I moved my thumb from the firing button. Whoever the figure was he or she was awfully small. In the fraction of a second while I was taking all this in, it dawned on me that it was a child—probably the son or daughter of the owner of the boat and quite oblivious of our evil intent. When I saw the child I knew I couldn't do it. I broke radio silence and called Davis. 'Hold your fire.' As we roared by at masthead height the child waved, quite unafraid. With that my anger against the treachery of these supposed neutrals left me. Even though some of them might have been responsible for the death of my two crews, I couldn't commit murder. Two hours later we landed back at Predannock. I started to explain to the pilot of the other Beau what had stayed my hand but it was unnecessary. I could see he understood.

Wing-Commander J. R. D. BRAHAM DSO DFC AFC CD

*

WHEN A BEAU GOES IN

When a Beau goes in,
Into the drink,
It makes you think,
Because, you see, they always sink
But nobody says 'Poor lad'
Or goes about looking sad
Because, you see, it's war,
It's the unalterable law.

Although it's perfectly certain
The pilot's gone for a Burton
And the observer too
It's nothing to do with you
And if they both should go
To a land where falls no rain nor hail
   nor driven snow—
Here, there or anywhere,
Do you suppose they care?

You shouldn't cry
Or say a prayer or sigh.
In the cold sea, in the dark,
It isn't a lark
But it isn't Original Sin—
It's just a Beau going in.

GAVIN EWART

The Beau eventually sprouted anti-shipping rockets, bombs, a few were even fitted with a special recoilless artillery piece (one such fought a duel with a German destroyer and crippled it). It became one of the best anti-shipping weapons. But, nose-heavy as it was, it remained a death-trap in a water landing.

*

Another mainstay of Coastal Command was the four-engined Sunderland flying-boat, derived from a pre-war civil airliner. Armed initially with seven .303 machine-guns, this gradually increased to twice that armament as crews added 'unofficial' gun positions to cope with Luftwaffe fighters which had less than half the weight and nearly twice the speed of the old boat. In such actions, the navigator stood up in the astrodome to get a view of the attackers and direct both gunners and pilot; he became 'Control'. He helped win

THE BATTLE OF THE BAY

Time 1835 hours—6.35 pm. The crew changed watch, which they did every hour. The pilots moved over, Amiss out of the flying-seat and Walker into it. Dowling into the right-hand seat. Another wireless operator sat down at the set and plugged in; the engineers changed and the relief gunners moved into the turrets. The reports, as always, came over the intercom. in correct sequence.

'Tail to Control. Goode in position.'

'Midships to Control. Fuller in position.'

'Nose to Control. Watson in position.'

'Control to all positions. Understood!' Simpson had left his charts and now stood in the astrodome. He looked out over the glaring sea and into the cloudless sky. 'Keep a sharp look-out,' he said deliberately. 'We're in the Tiger Country. We're approaching the position where the air-liner was shot down yesterday. It's on our course. Don't forget the dinghy.'

1845 hours. The boost-gauge and the rev. counter for the port-inner engine still fluctuated. The sea heaved gently, almost calm, but was marked by the long curving ripple lanes of the breezes. A suspicion of haze softened the tones of the water and the depths of the sky. Through the sky the great white Sunderland droned on and on.

1855 hours. The turrets moved slowly while eyes strained in the sunlight. This was indeed the Tiger Country, a slaughter-yard, a stage for a play of suspense and savagery, where all men at one time or another knew the meaning of fear. Here there were no parachutes and no patriots in the back country.

1900 hours. Goode, swinging his tail turret to the right, suddenly stopped. His eyes widened and his heart missed a beat.

'Tail to Control,' he barked. 'Eight aircraft. Thirty degrees on the port quarter. Six miles. Up one thousand feet.'

Pause. Electric silence. A moment or two of shock.

Simpson suddenly jumped to the astrodrome. Walker rammed his throttles wide and sounded the alarm. Dowling hauled on the pitch levers and the engines howled at twenty-six hundred revolutions a minute.

'Control to Tail. Can you identify those aircraft?'

'Twin-engined,' said Goode. 'Probably Junkers 88s.'

They were. They came sweeping in at high speed.

'Captain to Wireless Operator.' Walker's voice was sharp and urgent. 'Message to Group. O/A Priority. Attacked by eight Ju 88s . . . How's that inner engine, Engineer?'

'No worse, Captain. No better.'

'Captain to Galley. Have you got the bombracks out?'

'Ready, Captain.'

'Right. Bombs gone. You've got to work fast. Run in the racks, close the doors, and get cracking with the galley guns. Who's down there to man them?'

'Miles on the starboard, sir. Lane on the port.'

'Thanks.'

'Control to all positions'. That was Simpson again. 'They're spread all round us. Hold your fire until they're in range. Don't shoot before six hundred yards. Three are on the starboard beam; three port beam; one on each quarter. Range fifteen hundred yards; fifteen hundred feet up.'

Simpson paused and they all waited. Suddenly his voice was there again, precise, calm, yet underlaid with urgency. 'Okay. They're coming. One peeling off from each beam. Prepare to corkscrew. Twelve hundred yards. One thousand yards. They're firing. Prepare to corkscrew to star-board. Eight hundred yards. Corkscrew starboard. Go!'

Walker jammed over the wheel with a violent thrust of strength. The Sunderland screwed steeply down. Shell and tracer blasted right through it.

'Corkscrew port. Port. Now port. Go!'

Walker savagely reversed controls. The boat shuddered with shock and climbed giddily to the left.

The port-outer engine burst into flames. Smoke and fire scattered over the wing. Incendiary bullets ripped up the cockpit. Walker's compass blew up and sprayed him with blazing alcohol. Liquid fire splashed across the bridge and poured down the companionway into the bow compartment.

Through a confusion of sound and vibration and choking smoke Walker heard Simpson urging him to straighten up. But two more 88s were on the way in. They had blooded. They had scored in the first attack. They were screaming in for the kill. Walker yelled at Dowling, 'Take over! Fly it! We've got to get these fires out!'

Amiss wrenched the extinguisher from its bracket on the bulkhead and turned it full onto the captain, because Walker was burning.

Simpson's calm voice was still coming through the earphones.

'Eight hundred yards,' he was saying. 'Corkscrew port . . . Corkscrew port. . . .' And Walker was hearing it but seeing nothing, only smelling the smoke and the extinguishing fluid, and now the Sunderland was plunging down again and Dowling was fighting the controls. Amiss, hanging on his extinguisher and clinging for support to anything he could hold, was chasing the fires. Walker pressed the Graviner switch to extinguish the blazing engine. The fire snuffed out into clouds of white smoke which the aircraft left behind it as a billowing trail. The engine was finished. The airscrew windmilled and dragged and Dowling was up against it.

Walker swung on Amiss again. 'Give the wireless operator a message for Group, "On Fire".'

The 88s were still coming in, again and again. They pressed home their attacks with increasing fury and and reckless courage and Dowling could scarcely hold his aircraft. It was pulling like a mad thing to port into the dead engine. He wound the trimming-tabs over as fast as his hand could fly, but it still didn't take up the pressure; he still had full weight jammed against the rudder pedal to hold it in control.

Simpson's voice suddenly dropped in pitch. 'They're reforming. They've returned to the quarters and the beams.'

There was a pause, a breather for a few seconds. Amiss overcame the fires on the bridge and Walker again took the controls. There was a brief silence on the intercom. They were in terrible trouble, and there wasn't a man aboard who tried to deceive himself into believing that they weren't.

Suddenly a new voice came over the intercom. It was Fuller in the midships turret, up there on top in the weakening sunlight. He was singing:

'Praise the Lord and pass the ammunition,
Praise the Lord and pass the ammunition.'

'They're coming,' said Simpson. 'One from port and one from starboard. Firing from a thousand yards. We'll go starboard first. Eight hundred yards. Turn and dive starboard. Go!'

'Tighter, Captain! Now port. Port. Corkscrew port. He's coming right in. Tight as you can make it, Col.'

Shells and bullets crashed into the Sunderland. Tail had a go at the rapidly nearing fighter on the port but Midships didn't. Fuller's guns lay fully depressed with his turret turned starboard. He rested over his guns, eyes slitted. Little Fuller, no more than a boy—he even looked a boy—sat on his guns, barrels down, and watched the 88 on the starboard side hurtle at him, watched the bulletholes spatter all round him, yet didn't waver. He watched until that thundering 88 filled up the sky, head on, and was fifty yards off the wing-tip.

Fuller flashed his guns up, sighted and shot. Hundreds of rounds slaughtered the 88 as it broke away. Fuller poured them into it and suddenly it was a cloud of flame and black smoke and bits and pieces. It screamed vertically into the sea.

'Straighten up,' said Simpson, not unmoved. 'Straight and level. Get some height. They're coming again, two more of them in line astern on the port quarter. Twelve hundred yards. Prepare to turn and dive to port. One thousand yards and they're firing cannon. Eight hundred. Hold your fire. Turn and dive to port. Go!'

They went, over and down, a tight, giddy turn towards the sea.

The Sunderland didn't fire. No man fired except the 88. Nose and Tail and Midships sat over their sights and waited.

Shells and armour-piercing bullets crashed into the hull, shot away the elevator and rudder-trimming wires, severed the tail hydraulics, and slammed the turret violently against the stops. Goode collapsed over his guns.

Still the enemy came in. Still the Sunderland held it's fire. All it did was scream round its turn and didn't fire a shot. The first 88 broke away. The second came on and in to two hundred yards.

'Fire!' yelled Simpson.

They fired, Nose and Midships together, Fuller and Watson as one man. Tracers spun their lazy arc towards the Junkers. It pulled up sharply. It was almost a positive movement and broke away. Fuller and Watson followed him without pause or mercy. A thin stream of smoke came from the fighter's starboard engine; then a sudden burst of dark flame. . . .

It dropped towards the water and struck the surface in a smother of foam. It bounced vertically, hung for a split second, then plunged into the sea. A column of oily smoke shot up like a rocket.

'Praise the Lord and pass the ammunition,
Praise the Lord and pass the ammunition.'

'Superb,' said Simpson. 'Two destroyed. There's another coming in now on the starboard. Prepare to turn and dive to starboard. . . .'

267

Walker turned and yelled at Amiss, 'Get another message away, "Two shot down"!'

'Turn and dive to starboard,' said Simpson. 'Go!'

Amiss lurched back to the wireless operator and pencilled the three words on the signal pad.

'And now they're coming up from below. Watch them, Galley. One on each quarter. Fire as soon as you like. Tail, he's yours, too. Get into him. Good shooting, Galley. You've scared him off. 88 on the starboard is still coming in. Don't hold your fire, Tail, get into him! Control to Tail . . . Captain, Tail's bought it.'

A brief silence, then Walker's voice. 'Captain to Second Pilot. Get him out. Put in a galley gunner. Be slick.'

Then again it was Simpson's voice. 'An attack developing from the starboard. One thousand yards on the starboard bow. Two aircraft in line astern. Prepare to corkscrew starboard. Eight hundred. Corkscrew. Go!'

Suddenly the bridge was filled with smoke and flying shrapnel and broken glass. A cannon-shell burst inside the aircraft against the radio bulkhead, shattered the petrol gauges and every instrument in sight, wrecked the wireless during transmission, and wounded half the men on the the bridge. The wireless operator was injured, the first pilot and the navigator. Simpson came down from his dome in a heap with a lump of steel in his leg. Miles, down below on the starboard galley gun, clasped his stomach and collapsed.

Simpson pulled himself up into the dome again and sighted the 88s almost on top of him. He tried to speak into his mike but couldn't. The intercom was dead.

Walker dragged the Sunderland out of its turn and it took all his strength to straighten it up.

There was a long moment of dreadful confusion. It was chaos. The bridge was a maze of twisted metal and broken glass. It deeker of cordite. The intercom had been shot away. There was no wireless. The airspeed indicator had ceased to work. The flying controls were damaged. The airframe was warped. Walker looked out to port and actually saw the port-outer propellers and their reduction gear fall off the engine and tumble down into the sea. He also saw another 88 coming in on that side, already at short range, so he turned towards it, shouting at Dowling to help him. They turned and it took the strength of two men to control it.

Simpson still stood in the dome, his voice silenced. Now they had to fight without co-ordinated control. What the pilots saw they would be able to avoid. What they didn't see would shoot them down. Simpson dropped from his dome a second time and yelled desperately at Miller, the wireless operator, another man who had been silenced. 'Watch me,' he shouted, 'and tell the captain! Tell him what to do!'

Miller nodded, and so they continued. Simpson up in the dome again with his life-blood oozing over his boots, flying the evasive action with his hands and his screaming voice, and Miller mimicked him and passed it on to Walker.

Amiss was still trying to get to the tail turret to get Goode out and put another man in, but it took him a long while to get past the galley because it was there that he found Miles, convulsed over his gun, dying fast. With Lane's assistance Amiss lifted him clear and tried to get him through into the wardroom; but they couldn't open the door. They couldn't even smash it down. The airframe had twisted so far that the door was closed for ever. They'd never open it, that or any other door that was shut, neither could they shut the ones that were open.

They laid Miles down on the bomb-room floor and Turner came down from the engineer's bench and took Miles's place at the gun.

The battle continued. Walker and Dowling flew together, flew with masterful precision an aircraft which was scarcely an aircraft any longer, still turning and corkscrewing and diving into attack after attack with all the power the straining engines could find. The noise and the smell and the smoke and the vibration were indescribable.

Amiss was still struggling towards the tail. He was down on all fours like an animal, fighting his way an inch at a time along the catwalk up to the turret. The hull was like a colander and it was swimming in oil and de-icing fluid from punctured tanks and hydraulic lines. Amiss was flung from side to side with the violence of the evasive action. He was covered from head to foot in oil and muck.

He reached the turret. He couldn't stand up, just stayed on all fours shaken and half stunned. The rear of the aircraft was shot to ribbons. He could see out of it, out into the sky and the sea, through the great rents of cannon explosions and the multitude of small holes from machine-gun bullets. The turret itself was jammed over hard to port, and if Goode were alive it would be a miracle.

Amiss raised his fist and thumped against the turret door, and Goode looked down at Amiss and gave him a weak grin and turned his thumbs up. Amiss tried to get him out, but Goode wasn't interested, Despite shock, despite concussion, he mastered himself and began to move his turret with the pressure of his body alone. He elevated his guns, although he had only his fingers to fire them, and was back in the fight.

Up on the bridge the struggle went on in condtions of unbelievable disorder, yet in that material confusion they controlled their fate with an almost supernatural calm and discipline. Discipline wasn't imposed, it was a self-created force held firm by mutual example and a supreme spirit. Simpson stood in a pool of blood. Miller and Dowling ignored their injuries, Walker forgot his burns. Is there a man alive who would not care to be numbered amongst them?

Pause again. Another breather. The six 88s withdrew to the beams and the quarters to re-form for yet another time, for the final assault, for the ultimate kill.

Simpson began again to act his pantomine, Miller to mimic it, Walker and Dowling to put it into effect.

A single 88 opened the assault from the starboard quarter and Walker turned steeply into that attack—saw another coming from the port—and changed his turn into a violent corkscrew. The fighter on the starboard side broke off his attack surrounded by Fuller's long-range tracer, but the one on the port kept coming in with a fierce and sustained approach. Goode took up the challenge, fighting to hold his turret steady. He sighted it and depressed the sears of his guns with his fingers. He got it. Tracers ripped through the great jutting engines, and at point-bank range and not before, Fuller poured two hundred rounds into its belly.

The 88 screamed away like a winged bird in a crazy blazing arc, and smashed into the sea at three hundred miles an hour.

But the German airmen did not withdraw. They came again and again and again, driven by some peculiar desperation which we cannot even attempt to explain. Each attack was beaten back by a virtually impenetrable shield of tiny .303 bullets. Never in the history of German operations in the Bay of Biscay did fighters meet such phenomenal gunnery. Not one escaped undamaged.

Yet another aircraft closed in a suicidal onslaught across the starboard bow, and Watson in the nose emptied a pan of ammunition into its port wing. It vanished, engine ablaze, black smoke belching from the cockpit. They never sighted it again anywhere. Didn't see it go into the sea and didn't see it escape either.

Suddenly, so suddenly that the revelation came as a shock, only two 88s remained in the sky. Two only, and they sat off the port beam two thousand yards out, a shattered remnant of what had been a powerful fighting force; yet they came in again in line astern and the Sunderland prepared to meet the assault. But it didn't come. It petered out. They broke off at eight hundred yards without firing shot and, thrashed and humbled, turned into the east and headed for France.

At one thousand feet the triumphant N/461, alone in the sky, position unknown, throttled back its shuddering engines and slowly circled.

It was silence now, deep and breathless and pained, except for the engines' beat and the groaning of the tortured aircraft.

They relaxed, all of them, pale, trembling, lips black, tongues swollen fantastically in their mouths.

Walker weakly lifted himself from his seat, lit a cigarette, and thanked God.

And the silence continued. They weren't wholly conscious. They couldn't believe it had happened. They couldn't believe that this tattered shell remained in the air. They couldn't believe they had fired seven thousand rounds.

They couldn't believe that they had destroyed three Ju 88s, probably destroyed a fourth, possibly a fifth, and damaged three more. They couldn't believe they had dispatched the Bay Hunters almost into total oblivion. But the major revelation was yet to come. The British naval listening station which maintained a constant watch on German frequencies listened in wonder to the repeated calls which were directed to the enemy aircraft. Only two replied.

IVAN SOUTHALL

Walker and his crew—all Australians—reached Britain, crash-landed the riddled Sunderland near a beach and waded ashore, carrying the dead Sergeant Miles with them. Most of them died on a later operation.

*

And behind the scenes, groups of experienced and versatile pilots went on testing not just new aircraft but new equipment and new

BRIGHT IDEAS MARK III

One day we were delighted to have on the station a Whitley Bomber with rocket-assisted take-off. In this case, this consisted of a barrel under each wing containing some twenty-four rockets. We all tried it and the sensation was most impressive. Either one could climb at a fantastic gradient or accelerate to much more than the maximum cruising speed of the aeroplane. In either case, one fell back with a sickening finality to normal routine when the rockets were spent. As we put in a fair amount of practice on the Whitley, the RAE Farnborough thought they would like the Boscombe Down view of the much more formidable installation on a Short Stirling four-engined bomber. So this aircraft was duly flown over to us. Our chief engineer, Fred Rowarth, of Royal Aero Club handicapping fame, was suspicious of the installation from the start and made it quite clear that it was an RAE affair even though we were flying the aircraft. How right he was!

The system of rocket firing was more complicated than on the Whitley, but possibly more ingenious. As the throttles were opened for take-off, the rockets were fired progressively by means of a rheostat. Squadron-Leader Huxtable was the pilot selected for this job and he was a very fine sound man. Some months before he had survived a fantastic crash in an Albermarle which dived into the ground and blew up, hurling the crew all over the countryside. Luckily they had all survived.

When the Stirling was ready, an impressive gathering of important visitors arrived on the aerodrome, including a general, a cabinet minister, and several very senior RAF officers. Huxtable taxied the great aeroplane out and slowly turned into the wind. The brass-hats watched in silence. The Stirling advanced slowly. It approached the rocket-firing stage and then there was quite the loudest, longest and most satisfactory explosion yet heard on Salisbury Plain. The scene immediately around the Stirling was confused due to smoke, flames and spent pieces of rockets. When all cleared away, we saw the aeroplane. It had come to rest, one undercarriage partially collapsed, engines pointing in all directions, three propellers missing, and bits of blades here and there, but no one was hurt. At quarter throttle all the rockets had gone off at once, applying an acceleration which the Stirling's designer had never even dreamed about.

Wing-Commander H. P. POWELL AFC ARAeS

*

One of the strangest inventions of the war was the now-famous dam-busting bomb. Created by Dr Barnes Wallis, it was to breach the dams supplying the Ruhr with power, and flood part of the area into the bargain. To drop it, a special squadron, number 617, was formed from experienced crews; to lead them came Guy Gibson—who had collected two DSOs since the war started and had completed three tours. He was asked to do

JUST ONE MORE OPERATION

For the first week we started by having our dress rehearsals, and at the same time practising our attack on the ground in the radio room. All this time the water was getting higher on the dams that we were going to attack. Now it was only 5 feet from the top. When we had all got fully trained in our special form of attack we held a full-dress rehearsal which some few senior officers took an interest in. It was a complete failure. Aircraft went astray, some nearly collided, others went home browned off. The trouble was inter-communication. On attacks of this sort there must be no allowance for anything to go wrong, and things had gone wrong here. The radio-telephone sets which we were using were just not good enough. We would have to use fighter sets. When we got back I told the AOC that unless we were equipped with VHF the whole mission would be a failure. I told him that I had been asking for it for some time. He said, 'I'll fix it.' He was as good as his word. Within a few hours a party of men landed on the aerodrome and went to work. Next day the whole squadron was equipped with the very best and most efficient radio-telephonic sets in the whole of the Royal Air Force. And not only this, but my aircraft and the deputy-leader's had two sets on board, so that if one should go wrong we would have the other.

Next night we carried out another dress rehearsal, and it was a complete success. Everything ran smoothly and there was no hitch; that is, no hitch except that six out of the twelve aircraft were very seriously damaged by the great columns of water sent up when their mines splashed in. They had been flying slightly too low. Most of the damage was around the tails of the aircraft; elevators were smashed like plywood, turrets were knocked in, fins were bent. It was a miracle some of them got home. This was one of the many snags that the boys had to face while training. On the actual show it wouldn't matter so much because once the mines had dropped the job would be done and the next thing would be to get out of it, no matter how badly aircraft were damaged by water or anything else. But the main thing was to get the mines into the right spot.

By now it was obvious that we would have to carry out the raid within the next few days—perhaps only two days, because the water level had been reported just right for the attack. The training was now complete. The crews were

274

ready. In all we had done 2,000 hours of flying and had dropped 2,500 practice bombs, and all the boys were rather like a team of racehorses standing in the paddock, waiting for the big event. But the ground crews were working like slaves repairing the damage done to our aircraft.

We had been flying for about an hour and ten minutes in complete silence, each one busy with his thoughts, while the waves were slopping by a few feet below with monotonous regularity. And the moon dancing in those waves had become almost a hypnotising crystal. As Terry spoke he jerked us into action. He said, 'Five minutes to go to the Dutch coast, skip.'

I said, 'Good,' and looked ahead. Pulford turned on the spotlights and told me to go down much lower; we were about 100 feet off the water. Jim Deering, in the front turret, began to swing it from either way, ready to deal with any flak ships which might be watching for minelayers off the coast. Hutch sat in his wireless cabin ready to send a flak warning to the rest of the boys who might run into trouble behind us. Trevor took off his Mae West and squeezed himself back into the rear turret. One either side the boys tucked their blunt-nosed Lancs in even closer than they were before, while the crews inside them were probably doing the same sort of things as my own. Someone began whistling nervously over the intercom. Someone else said, 'Shut up.'

Then Spam said, 'There's the coast.'

I said, 'No, it's not; that's just low cloud and shadows on the sea from the moon.'

But he was right and I was wrong, and soon we could see the Dutch islands approaching. They looked low and flat and evil in the full moon, squirting flak in many directions because their Radar would now know we were coming. But we knew all about their defences, and as we drew near this squat and unfriendly expanse we began to look for the necessary landmarks which would indicate how to get through the barrage. We began to behave like a ship threading its way through a minefield, in danger of destruction on either side, but safe if we were lucky and on the right track. Terry came up beside me to check up on Spam.

275

He opened the side windows and looked out to scan the coast with his night glasses. 'Can't see much,' he said. 'We're too low, but I reckon we must be on track because there's so little wind.'

'Hope so.'

'Stand by, front gunner; we're going over.'

'O.K. All lights off. No talking. Here we go.'

With a roar we hurtled over the Western Wall, skirting the defences and turning this way and that to keep to our thin line of safety; for a moment we held our breath. Then I gave a sigh of relief; no one had fired a shot. We had taken them by surprise.

'Good effort, Terry. Next course.'

'105 degrees magnetic.'

We had not been on the new course for more than two minutes before we came to more sea again; we had obviously just passed over a small island, and this was wrong. Our proper track should have taken us between the two islands, as both were fairly heavily defended, but by the grace of God the gunners on the one we had just passed over were apparently asleep. We pulled up high to about 300 feet to have a look and find out where we were, then scrammed down on to the deck again as Terry said, 'O.K. —there's the windmill and those wireless masts. We must have drifted to starboard. Steer new course—095 degrees magnetic, and be careful of a little town that is coming up straight ahead.'

'O.K., Terry, I'll go around it.'

We were turning to the left now, and as we turned I noticed with satisfaction that Hoppy and Mickey were still flying there in perfect formation.

We were flying low. We were flying so low that more than once Spam yelled at me to pull up quickly to avoid high-tension wires and tall trees. Away on the right we could see the small town, its chimneys outlined against the night sky; we thought we saw someone flash us a 'V', but it may have been an innkeeper poking his head out of his bedroom window. The noise must have been terrific.

Our new course should have followed a very straight canal, which led to a T-shaped junction, and beyond that was the Dutch frontier and Germany. All eyes began looking out to see if we were right, because we could not afford to be wrong. Sure enough, the canal came up slowly from underneath the starboard wing and we began to follow it carefully, straight above it, for now we were mighty close to Eindhoven, which had the reputation of being very well defended. Then, after a few minutes, that too had passed behind and we saw a glint of silvery light straight ahead. This was the canal junction, the second turning point.

It did not take Spam long to see where we were; now we were right on track, and Terry again gave the new course for the River Rhine. A few minutes later we crossed the German frontier, and Terry said, in his matter-of-fact way: 'We'll be at the target in an hour and a half. The next thing to see is the Rhine.'

But we did not all get through. One aircraft, P/O Rice, had already hit the sea, bounced up, lost both its outboard engines and its weapon, and had flown back on the inboard two. Les Munro had been hit by light flak a little later on, and his aircraft was so badly damaged that he was forced to return to base. I imagined the feelings of the crews of these aircraft who, after many weeks of intense practice and expectation, at the last moment could only hobble home and land with nothing accomplished. I felt very sorry for them. This left sixteen aircraft going on; 112 men.

The journey into the Ruhr Valley was not without excitement. They did not like our coming. And they knew we were coming. We were the only aircraft operating that night; it was too bright for the main forces. And so, deep down in their underground plotting-rooms, the Hun controllers stayed awake to watch us as we moved steadily on. We had a rough idea how they worked these controllers, moving fighter squadrons to orbit points in front of us, sounding air-raid sirens here and there, tipping off the gun positions along our route and generally trying to make it pretty uncomfortable for the men who were bound for 'Happy Valley'. As yet they would not know where we were going, because our route was planned to make feint attacks and fox their control. Only the warning sirens would have sounded in all the cities from Bremen southwards. As yet, the fighters would be unable to get good plots on us because we were flying so low, but once we were there the job would have to take quite a time and they would have their chance.

We flew on. Germany seemed dead. Not a sign of movement, of light or a moving creature stirred the ground. There was no flak, there was nothing. Just us.

And so we came to the Rhine. This is virtually the entrance to the Ruhr Valley; the barrier our armies must cross before they march into the big towns of Essen and Dortmund. It looked white and calm and sinister in the moonlight. But it presented no difficulties for us. As it came up, Spam said, 'We are six miles south. Better turn right, skip. Duisburg is not far away.'

As soon as he mentioned Duisburg my hands acted before my brain, for they were more used to this sort of thing, and the Lanc banked steeply to follow the Rhine up to our crossing point. For Duisburg is not a healthy place to fly over at 100 feet. There are hundreds of guns there, both light and heavy, apart from all those searchlights, and the defences have had plenty of experience. . . .

As we flew up—'How did that happen?'

'Don't know, skip. Compass u/s?'

'Couldn't be.'

'Hold on, I will just check my figures.'

Later—'I'm afraid I mis-read my writing, skip. The course I gave you should have been another ten degrees to port.'

'O.K. Terry. That might have been an expensive mistake.'

During our steep turn the boys had lost contact, but now they were just beginning to form up again; it was my fault the turn had been too steep, but the name Duisburg or Essen, or any of the rest of them, always does that to me. As we flew along the Rhine there were barges on the river equipped with quick-firing guns and they shot at us as we flew over, but our gunners gave back as good as they got; then we found what we wanted, a sort of small inland harbour, and we turned slowly towards the east. Terry said monotonously, 'Thirty minutes to go and we are there.'

As we passed on into the Ruhr Valley we came to more and more trouble, for now we were in the outer light-flak defences, and these were very active, but by weaving and jinking we were able to escape most of them. Time and again searchlights would pick us up, but we were flying very low and, although it may sound foolish and untrue when I say so, we avoided a great number of them by dodging behind the trees. Once we went over a brand-new aerodrome which was very heavily defended and which had not been marked on our combat charts. Immediately all three of us in front were picked up by the searchlights and held. Suddenly Trevor, in the rear turret, began firing away trying to scare them enough to turn out their lights, then he shouted that they had gone behind some tall trees. At the same time Spam was yelling that he would soon be shaving himself by the tops of some corn in a field. Hutch immediately sent out a flak warning to all the boys behind so that they could avoid this unattractive area. On either side of me, Mickey and Hoppy, who were a little higher, were flying along brightly illuminated; I could see their letters quite clearly, 'TAJ' and 'MAJ', standing out like Broadway signs. Then a long string of tracer came from Hoppy's rear turret and I lost him in the momentary darkness as the searchlights popped out. One of the pilots, a grand Englishman from Derbyshire, was not so lucky. He was flying well out to the left. He got blinded in the searchlights and, for a second, lost control. His aircraft reared up like a stricken horse, plunged on to the deck and burst into flames; five seconds later his mine blew up with a tremendous explosion. Bill Astell had gone.

The minutes passed slowly as we all sweated on this summer's night, sweated at working the controls and sweated with fear as we flew on. Every railway train, every hamlet and every bridge we passed was a potential danger, for our Lancasters were sitting targets at that height and speed. We fought our way past Dortmund, pass Hamm—the well-known Hamm which had been bombed so many times; we could see it quite clearly now, its tall chimneys, factories and balloons capped by its umbrella of flak like a Christmas tree about five miles to our right; then we began turning to the right in between Hamm and the little town of Soest, where I nearly got shot down in 1940. Soest was sleepy now and did not open up, and out of the haze ahead appeared the Ruhr hills.

'We're there,' said Spam.

'Thank God,' said I, feelingly.

As we came over the hill, we saw the Mohne Lake. Then we saw the dam itself. In that light it looked squat and heavy and unconquerable; it looked grey and solid in the moonlight, as though it were part of the countryside itself and just as immovable. A structure like a battleship was showering out flak all along its length, but some came from the powerhouse below it and nearby. There were no searchlights. It was light flak, mostly green, yellow and red, and the colours of the tracer reflected upon the face of the water in the lake. The reflections on the dead calm of the black water made it seem there was twice as much as there really was.

'Did you say these gunners were out of practice?' asked Spam, sarcastically.

'They certainly seem awake now,' said Terry.

They were awake all right. No matter what people say, the Germans certainly have a good warning system. I scowled to myself as I remembered telling the boys an hour or so ago that they would probably only be the German equivalent of the Home Guard and in bed by the time we arrived.

It was hard to say exactly how many guns there were, but tracers seemed to be coming from about five positions, probably making twelve guns in all. It was hard at first to tell the calibre of the shells, but after one of the boys had been hit, we were informed over the RT that they were either 20-mm type of 37-mm, which, as everyone knows, are nasty little things.

We circled around stealthily, picking up the various landmarks upon which we had planned our method of attack, making use of some and avoiding others; every time we came within range of those bloody-minded flax gunners they let us have it.

'Bit aggressive, aren't they?' said Trevor.

'Too right they are.'

I said to Terry, 'God, this light flak gives me the creeps.'

'Me, too,' someone answered.

280

For a time there was a general bind on the subject of light flak, and the only man who didn't say anything was Hutch, because he could not see it and because he never said anything about flak, anyway. But this was not the time for talking. I called up each member of our formation and found, to my relief, that they had all arrived, except, of course, Bill Astell. Away to the south, Joe McCarthy had just begun his diversionary attack on the Sorpe. But not all of them had been able to get there; both Byers and Barlow had been shot down by light flak after crossing the coast; these had been replaced by other aircraft of the rear formation. Bad luck, this being shot down after crossing the coast, because it could have happened to anybody; they must have been a mile or so off track and had got the hammer. This is the way things are in flying; you are either lucky or you aren't. We, too, had crossed the coast at the wrong place and had got away with it. We were lucky.

Down below, the Moehne Lake was silent and black and deep, and I spoke to my crew.

'Well, boys, I suppose we had better start the ball rolling.' This with no enthusiasm whatsoever. 'Hello, all Cooler aircraft. I am going to attack. Stand by to come in to attack in your order when I tell you.'

Then to Hoppy: 'Hello "M Mother". Stand by to take over if anything happens.'

Hoppy's clear and casual voice came back. 'O.K. Leader. Good luck.'

Then the boys dispersed to the pre-arranged hiding-spots in the hills, so that they should not be seen either from the ground or from the air, and we began to get into position for our approach. We circled wide and came around down moon, over the high hills at the eastern end of the lake. On straightening up we began to dive towards the flat, ominous water two miles away. Over the front turret was the dam silhouetted against the haze of the Ruhr Valley. We could see the towers. We could see the sluices. We could see everything. Spam, the bomb-aimer, said, 'Good show. This is wizard.' He had been a bit worried, as all bomb-aimers are, in case they cannot see their aiming points, but as we came in over the tall fir trees his voice came up again

281

rather quickly. 'You're going to hit them. You're going to hit those trees.'

'That's all right, Spam. I'm just getting my height.'

To Terry: 'Check height, Terry.'

To Pulford: 'Speed control, Flight-Engineer.'

To Trevor: 'All guns ready, gunners.'

To Spam: 'Coming up, Spam.'

Terry turned on the spotlights and began giving directions—'Down—down—down. Steady—steady.' We were then exactly sixty feet.

Pulford began working the speed; first he put on a little flap to slow us down, then he opened the throttles to get the air-speed indicator exactly against the red mark. Spam began lining up his sights against the towers. He had turned the fusing switch to the 'ON' position. I began flying.

The gunners had seen us coming. They could see us coming with our spotlights on for over two miles away. Now they opened up and their tracers began swirling towards us; some were seen bouncing off the smooth surface of the lake. This was a horrible moment: we were being dragged along at four miles a minute, almost against our will, towards the things we were going to destroy. I think at that moment the boys did not want to go. I know I did not want to go. I thought to myself, 'In another minute we shall all be dead—so what?' I thought again, 'This is terrible—this feeling of fear—if it is fear.' By now we were a few hundred yards away, and I said quickly to Pulford, under my breath, 'Better leave the throttles open now and stand by to pull me out of the seat if I get hit.' As I glanced at him I thought he looked a little glum on hearing this.

The Lancaster was really moving and I began looking through the special sight on my windscreen. Spam had his eyes glued to the bomb-sight in front, his hand on his button; a special mechanism on board had already begun to work so that the mine would drop (we hoped) in the right spot. Terry was still checking the height. Joe and Trev. began to raise their guns. The flak could see us quite clearly now. It was not exactly inferno. I have been through far worse flak fire than that; but we were very low. There was something sinister and slightly unnerving about the whole operation. My aircraft was so small and the dam was so

282

large; it was thick and solid, and now it was angry. My aircraft was very small. We skimmed along the surface of the lake and as we went my gunner was firing into the defences, and the defences were firing back with vigour, their shells whistling past us. For some reason, we were not being hit.

Spam said, 'Left—little more left—steady—steady—steady—coming up.' Of the next few seconds I remember only a series of kaleidoscopic incidents.

The chatter from Joe's front guns pushing out tracers which bounced off the left-hand flak tower.

Pulford crouching beside me.

The smell of burnt cordite.

The cold sweat underneath my oxygen mask.

The tracers flashing past the windows—they all seemed the same colour now—and the inaccuracy of the gun positions near the power-station; they were firing in the wrong direction.

The closeness of the dam wall.

Spam's exultant, 'Mine gone.'

Hutch's red Very lights to blind the flak-gunners.

The speed of the whole thing.

Someone saying over the RT, 'Good show, leader. Nice work.'

Then it was all over, and at last we were out of range, and there came over us all, I think, an immense feeling of relief and confidence.

Wing Commander GUY GIBSON VC DSO DFC

It took four bombs to break that dam, two more to destroy the Eder one; the Sorpe, their third target, survived the one bomb that hit it. Post-war research has shown that only if all three had been destroyed would the raid have had a major effect on German industry. 617 Squadron lost eight aircraft and crews from the 17 that had crossed the enemy coast that night. Gibson was awarded the VC. There were 29 other medals awarded to surviving members. Gibson did yet one more operation, in a Mosquito, a year later. He did not return.

THE BOMB

It was almost twenty years after the war had ended, and more than twenty after its first use, that the RAF finally revealed the secrets of 'Upkeep', the dam-busting bomb. It was *not,* as has been suggested, a sphere. It was a cylinder like an oil drum, five foot long and almost that in diameter, hung crossways in the bomb-bay and given a backspin of about 500 revs per minute by an auxiliary motor inside the bay. This was started up ten minutes before dropping.

When it hit the water, the bomb skimmed like a stone, bouncing in shorter and shorter jumps until it hit the dam itself. Then, instead of rebounding away, the back-spin forced it against the wall and made it crawl downwards until it exploded, on a hydrostatic fuse set for 30 feet below surface, still clinging to the dam. It was a beautifully simple idea for positioning a bomb weighing almost 10,000 lbs to within a few feet.

Upkeep was never used again. But a smaller version, Highball (holding only one-tenth of the explosive), was developed for use, in pairs, by Mosquitoes against anchored shipping targets. There, the back-spin principle would place the bomb directly under the keel. But it took too long to iron out all the snags, and it was never used operationally.

THE EDITOR

Soon after the Dams raid, The Times *received the following letter:*

Sir,

In international bird-watching circles, the bombing of the Moehne Dam has caused grave concern. For three years previous to the outbreak of war a pair of ring-necked whooper swans nested regularly on the lake. They are almost the rarest of Europe's great birds. The only other pair known to have raised a brood during recent years were a pair of the Arctic sub-species which were photographed by the aunt of the late Professor Olssen, of Reykjavik, on their nest on the shore of Lake Thongvallavatn, Iceland, in 1927.

Has anything been heard of the fate of the Moehne pair,

284

probably the last in Europe? And, in view of the **rarity of** these beautiful birds, why was the bombing of their home permitted? Furthermore, assuming that this operation was necessary, could it not have been deferred until the cygnets (if any) were full grown?

Yours faithfully, etc.,
(quoted by PAUL BRICKHILL)

It turned out to have been written by two officers on 617's own station. The Times hadn't published it; maybe they were suspicious, or maybe Britain was finally, fully, at war.

*

Not every casualty came directly from enemy flak fighters, from simple collision or a navigation error that flew you into a 'stuffed cloud' that hid a mountain peak. Flying aircraft crammed with 100-octane fuel, there was always

THE PRICE OF FIRE

The ward is a long, cold room with bright-green curtains at the windows. There are yellow and mauve potted chrysanthemums on tables down the centre of the room, and a black iron coal stove at either end. Wicker chairs and a table covered with magazines stand in front of the far stove and this is where the patients, wearing Royal Air Force uniforms, gather. Five or six men are lying in the white-painted beds. The ward has the casual, cheerful, faintly bored feeling of any place where men are convalescing. But this ward is not like other wards, because no one here has a real face and many of them have hands that are not much good either. These men are the air crews who crashed in planes and were thrown or dragged clear of the burning wreckage, but they were not thrown or dragged clear quite soon enough. .

The men around the stove interrupted their conversation to talk to one of the patients in bed. The wagon that will carry him to the operating room is drawn up alongside the bed and a nurse is helping him onto it.

'What's it to be today, Bill?'

'Eyebrows.'

'Won't he be pretty?'

Then there is a chorus of cheerios, and the operating-room trolley rolls away. There was no special feeling about this because eyebrows aren't bad, the boy had been through so many operations and was so close to having a face again that this little extra pain did not worry him, and because men have been wheeled in and out of this ward all day long, and day after day, and each man alone has learned how to wait for and endure these trips.

In a bed farther down another boy is waiting; his turn will come after the eyebrows are made. He is going to get a nose. For weeks he has been growing the skin for his nose, in the form of a narrow sausage-shaped graft attached to the unharmed skin of his chest. His face is incredible and one hand is entirely gone. There is no expression in these burned and scarred faces; all the expression is in the eyes and in the voice. You cannot tell age either; fire takes that away too. The boy has light-brown tufty hair and good laughing eyes and a good voice, and a dreadful face that will soon at least have a nose. He is twenty-one, though you can know this only if you are told, and he was a chauffeur before the war, driving for the squire of his village. The welfare officer has arranged to get him an industrial job when he has enough of a face, but he does not want it. He wants to go back, with one hand and that face, and be a chauffeur again in his village. The village is home and what he loves, his people are there, the village is a recognisable world. And in fact they would all like to go back to what was before, before the war and the flames got them.

Around the stove there are now four young men gossiping together. One has just come from London and they are asking him about his trip. He is going to be operated on tomorrow and after that he will return to flying. He is an American from Columbus, Ohio, and he crashed in a Hurricane, and his face, they say, was simply pushed two inches back inside his head. His nose is flattened and the skin around his eyes is odd, but by contrast to the others he

286

looks fine. He feels fine too, because what he likes is to fly, and he will be doing that again. The others will not fly. They are talking easily and generously about his squadron and no one looks at the curled claws of hands of the nineteen-year-old Canadian, nor at the melted stump that the twenty-one-year-old English boy has, nor at the stiff reddish solidified fingers of a boy who always worked on a farm in Canada, and would like to again, and maybe some day his hands will bend just enough to let him do it.

The nineteen-year-old Canadian with the claw hands wants to be a boat builder. He is a darling, with a lively brain, and one half of his face is hardened twisted reddish meat and one half is fairly normal, so you can see what a nice-looking kid he was. He thought he'd lost his left eye, after he was pulled out of the wrecked plane, because he couldn't see from that eye. He was a gunner and his pal the navigator pulled him out and he said to his pal, 'Where's my eye? I've lost my eye somewhere here.' So his pal said, 'Well, we'll look for it, then.' They crawled around on the grass, dazed and burned, looking for the eye. This story, you may not instantly guess, produces roars of laughter from everyone because it just goes to show how dopey a chap can be.

MARTHA GELLHORN

*

But there were always new men coming in. However familiar the pattern of fighter sweeps over France might be, there was always somebody for whom it was all fresh and new. One such was a French pilot seeing France again for the first time in over two years on

MY FIRST BIG SHOW

1315 hours. I was already installed, firmly fixed to my Spitfire NL-B by the straps of my safety harness. I had tested the radio, the sight, and the camera gun. I had carefully adjusted the oxygen mask and verified the pressure in the bottles. I had armed the cannon and the machine guns and adjusted the rear-vision. Tommy was wandering round the aircraft with a screw-driver, getting the detachable panels firmly fastened. My stomach seemed curiously empty and I was beginning to regret my scanty lunch. People were busy all round the field. In the distance Deere's car stopped by his aircraft, under the control tower. He was wearing a white flying suit and he slipped quickly into his cockpit. The fire crew took up their positions on the running boards of the tender, and the medical orderlies in the ambulance. The hour was approaching.

1319 hours. Deep silence over the airfield. Not a movement anywhere. The pilots had their eyes glued on Mouchotte who was consulting his watch. By each aircraft a fitter stood motionless, his finger on the switch of the auxiliary starter batteries. Another stood guard by the fire extinguishers lying on the grass at the ready. My parachute buckle was badly placed and was torturing me, but it was too late to adjust it.

1320 hours. Mouchotte glanced round the twelve Spitfires, then began to manipulate his pumps. A rasping rattle from the starter, then his propeller began to turn. Feverishly I switched on.

'All clear?—switches ON!'

Kept in perfect trim, my Rolls-Royce engine started first shot. The fitters rushed round, removing chocks, dragging batteries away, hanging on to the wing-tips to help the aircraft pivot. Mouchotte's NL-L was already taxi-ing to the northern end of the field.

1322 hours. The engines of 611 were turning and the twelve Spitfires beginning to line up on either side of Deere's in a cloud of dust. We lined up behind them in combat formation. I took up my position, my wing-tip almost touching Martell's. I was sweating.

1324 hours. The twenty-six aircraft were all ready, engines ticking over, wings glinting in the sun. The pilots adjusted their goggles and tightened their harness.

1325 hours. A white rocket rose from the control tower. Deere raised his arm and the thirteen aircraft of 611 Squadron started forward. In his turn Mouchotte raised his gloved hand and slowly opened the throttle. Eyes fixed on Martell's wing-tip, and my hands moist, I followed. The tails went up, the Spitfires began to bounce clumsily on their

288

narrow under-carriages, the wheels left the ground—we were airborne.

I raised the undercart and locked it, throttled back and adjusted the airscrew pitch. We swept like a whirlwind over the road outside the airfield. A bus had stopped, its passengers crowding the windows. I switched over to the auxiliary tanks and shut the main tank cocks. Handling the controls clumsily and jerkily, I contrived to keep formation. The Spitfires slipped southward at tree- and roof-top level in a thunderous roar which halted people in the streets in their tracks. We jumped a wooded hill, then suddenly we were over the sea, its dirty waves edged with foam and dominated on the left by Beachy Head. A blue hazy line on the horizon must be France. We hurtled forward, a few feet above the water.

Some disconnected impressions remain vividly impressed on my memory—a British coastguard vessel with its crew waving to us; an Air Sea Rescue launch gently rocking with the swell and surrounded by a swarm of seagulls.

Out of the corner of my eye I watched the pressure and and temperature—normal. I switched on my reflector sight. One of the 611 aircraft waggled its wings, turned and came back towards England, gaining height. Engine trouble, probably.

1349 hours. Over the radio we could hear in the far distance shouts and calls coming from the close escort squadrons—and suddenly, very distinctly, a triumphant: 'I got him!' I realised with a tightening of the heart that over there they were already fighting.

1350 hours. As one, the twenty-four Spitfires rose and climbed towards the sky, hanging on their propellers, 3,300 feet a minute.

France! A row of white cliffs emerged from the mist and as we gained height the horizon gradually receded—the estuary of the Somme, the narrow strip of sand at the foot of the tree-crowned cliffs, the first meadows, and the first village nestling by a wood in a valley.

Fifteen thousand feet. My engine suddenly cut and the nose dropped violently. With my heart in my mouth and unable to draw breath I reacted instinctively and at once changed to my main petrol tanks. My auxiliary was empty.

Feeling weak about the knees I realised that through my lack of experience I had used too much power to keep my position and that my engine had used proportionately more fuel. A second's glide, a splutter, and the engine picked up again. At full throttle I closed up with my section.

'Brutus aircraft, drop your babies!' sounded Deere's clear voice in the earphones. Still considerably shaken, I pulled the handle, hoping to God that the thing would work . . . a jerk, a swishing sound, and all our twenty-four tanks fell, fluttering downwards.

'Hullo, Brutus, Zona calling, go over Channel C Charlie.'

'Hullo, Zona, Brutus answering. Channel C. Over!'

'Hullo, Brutus. Zona out!'

I pressed button C on the VHF panel. A crackling sound, then the voice of Squadron Leader Holmes, the famous controller of Grass Seed:

'Hullo, Brutus leader, Grass Seed calling. There is plenty going on over target. Steer 096°—zero, nine, six. There are forty plus bandits fifteen miles ahead, angels thirty-five, over to you!'

'Hullo, Grass Seed. Brutus answering. Steering 096°. Roger out.'

Mouchotte put us in combat formation:

'Hullo, Turban, combat formation, go!'

The three sections of four Spitfires drew apart. Below to my right the Gimlets did the same.

'Brutus aircraft, keep your eyes open!'

We were at 27,000 feet. Five minutes passed. The cloudless sky was so vast and limpid that you felt stunned. You knew that France was there, under the translucent layer of dry mist, which was slightly more opaque over the towns. The cold was painful and breathing difficult. You could feel the sun, but I could not make out whether I was being burnt or frozen by its rays. To rouse myself I turned the oxygen full on. The strident roar of the engine increased the curious sensation of being isolated that one gets in a single-seater fighter. It gradually become a sort of noisy but neutral background that ends up by merging into a queer kind of thick, heavy silence.

Still nothing new. I felt both disappointed and relieved. Time seemed to pass very slowly. I felt I was dreaming with my eyes open, lulled by the slow rhythmical rocking movement up and down of the Spitfires in echelon, by the gentle rotation of the propellers through the rarefied and numbing air. Everything seemed so unreal and remote. Was this war?

'Look out, Brutus leader, Grass Seed calling. Three gaggles of twenty plus converging towards you, above!'

Holmes's voice had made me jump. Martell now chimed in:

'Look out, Brutus, Yellow One calling, smoke trails coming three o'clock!'

I stared round and suddenly I spotted the tell-tale condensation trails of the Jerries beginning to converge on us from south and east. Christ, how fast they were coming! I released the safety catch of the guns.

'Brutus calling. Keep your eyes open, chaps. Climb like hell!'

I opened the throttle and changed to fine pitch, and instinctively edged closer to Martell's Spitfire. I felt very alone in a suddenly hostile sky.

'Brutus calling. Open your eyes and prepare to break port. The bastards are right above!'

Three thousand feet above our heads a filigree pattern began to form and you could already distinguish the glint of the slender cross-shaped silhouettes of the German fighters.

'Here they come!' I said to myself, hypnotised. My throat contracted, my toes curled in my boots. I felt as if I were stifling in a strait-jacket, swaddled in all those belts, braces and buckles.

'Turban, break starboard!' yelled Boudier. In a flash I saw the roundels of Martell's Spitfire surge up before me. I banked my aircraft with all my strength, opened the throttle wide, and there I was in his slipstream! Where were the Huns? I dared not look behind me, and I turned desperately, glued to my seat by the centrifugal force, eyes riveted on Martell turning a hundred yards in front of me.

'Gimlet, attack port!'

I felt lost in the mêlée.

'Turban Yellow Two, break!'

Yellow Two? Why, that was me! With a furious kick on

291

the rudder bar, I broke away, my gorge rising from sheer
fear. Red tracers danced past my windshield . . . and suddenly I saw my first Hun! I identified it at once—it was a
Focke-Wulf 190. I had not studied the photos and recognition charts so often for nothing.

After firing a burst of tracer at me he bore down on
Martell. Yes, it certainly was one—the short wings, the
radial engine, the long transparent hood: the square-cut
tail-plane all in one piece! But what had been missing from
the photos was the lively colouring—the pale yellow body,
the greyish green back, the big black crosses outlined in
white. The photos gave no hint of the quivering of the
wings, the outline elongated and fined down by the speed,
the curious nose-down flying attitude.

The sky, which had been filled with hurtling Spitfires,
seemed suddenly empty—my No. One had disappeared.
Never mind, I was not going to lose my Focke-Wulf. I was
no longer afraid.

Incoherent pictures are superimposed on my memory—
three Focke-Wulfs waggling their wings; tracers criss-
crossing; a parachute floating like a puff of smoke in the
blue sky.

I huddled up, with the stick hugged to my stomach in
both hands, thrown into an endless ascending spiral at full
throttle.

'Look out!   Attention! . . . Break!'—a medley of shouts
in the earphones. I would have liked to recognise a definite
order somewhere, or some advice.

Another Focke-Wulf, wings lit up by the blinding flashes
of its cannon firing—dirty grey trails from exhausts—white
trails from square wing-tips. I couldn't make out who or
what he was firing at. He flicked—yellow belly, black
crosses. He dived and fell like a bullet. Far below he merged
into the blurred landscape.

Another one, on a level with me. He turn towards me.
Careful now! I must face him!

A quick half-roll, and without quite knowing how, I
found myself on my back, finger on firing button, shaken
to the marrow of my bones by the roar of my flame-spitting
cannon. All my faculties, all my being, were focused on

one single thought: I MUST KEEP HIM IN MY SIGHTS.

What about deflection?—not enough. I must tighten my turn! More . . . more still . . . more still! No good. He had gone, but my finger was still convulsively pressed on the button. I was firing at emptiness.

Where was he? I began to panic. Beware, 'the Hun you haven't seen is the one who gets you!' I could feel the disordered thumping of my heart right down in my stomach, in my clammy temples, in my knees.

There he was again—but a long way away. He dived, I fired again—missed him! Out of range. Ranging, I persisted . . . one last burst . . . my Spitfire quivered, but the Focke-Wulf was faster and disappeared unscathed into the mist.

The sky had emptied as if by magic. Not one plane left. I was absolutely alone.

A glance at the petrol—thirty-five gallons. Time to get back. It was scarcely a quarter past two.

'Hullo, Turban, Yellow Two. Yellow One calling. Are you all right?'

It was Martell's voice from very far away.

'Hullo, Yellow One, Turban Yellow Two answering. Am O.K. and going home.'

I set course 320° for England, in a shallow dive. A quarter of an hour later I was flying over the yellow sands of Dungeness. I joined Biggin Hill circuit. Spitfires everywhere, with wheels down. I wormed my way in between two sections and landed.

As I taxied towards Dispersal I saw Tommy, with arms raised, signalling and showing me where to park.

I gave a burst of throttle to clear my engine and switched off. The sudden silence dazed me. How odd to hear voices again, undistorted by the radio.

Tommy helped me out of my harness. I jumped to the ground, my legs feeling weak and stiff.

Martell came striding towards me, and caught me round the neck.

'Good old Clo-Clo! We really thought you had had it!'

We went over to join the group by the door round Mouchotte.

'Hey, Clo-Clo, seen anything of Béraud?'

Béraud, it appeared, must have been shot down.

Bouguen's aircraft had been hit by two 20 mm shells. 485 Squadron had brought down two Focke-Wulfs. Mouchotte and Boudier had severely damaged one each.

I was now voluble and excited. I told my tale, I felt lighthearted, as if a great weight had been lifted from me. I had done my first big sweep over France and I had come back!

That evening, in the mess, I felt on top of the world.

PIERRE CLOSTERMANN DSO DFC

*

A big step towards the invasion of France came with the creation of 2nd TAF—Tactical Air Force. Based on the success of the Desert Air Force in close co-operation with the Army, the force would provide flying heavy artillery for the invasion. The first commander describes how it started for

SECOND TAF

One of my first actions after taking over command was to fly the Mitchell, Boston and Ventura so that I might assess their value as operational aircraft and try to understand from first-hand experience the operating problems of the crews. I came to the conclusion that both Mitchells and Bostons were excellent aircraft in every way, but that the Venturas were thoroughly bad, being slow, heavy, unmanœuvrable and lacking in good defensive armament.

I next called for an assessment of the average bombing error of the Group over the past nine months. I was told that to calculate this from the many photographs of bomb bursts would be a tremendous task, and did I really need it, because the bombing of the Group was excellent, as I could see by examining the photographs they held in the operations room. I replied that I was sure these photographs revealed some very good bombing, but I wanted to know what was the average error of all the other bombs not shown on the photographs on display. I explained to Dart, our operational research scientist, exactly what I wanted and after about a fortnight of long hours of work, with some outside assistance, he assessed the bombing error of the Group. I did not retain the exact figure in my records, but memory recalls that it was something like twelve hundred yards. I was appalled but not disheartened!

After visiting all the units in the group, meeting as many of the aircrew as possible, flying the operational aircraft, studying operational records and results, and knowing the bombing error, I now felt I had sufficient information on which to base a policy and prepare a plan to implement it.

Morale is the linch-pin of efficiency and fighting spirit, so first I thought out what were to be the fundamentals of my policy to obtain the standard at which I aimed. I decided to issue a clear statement on the immediate and future role of the Group, as I was convinced this would go a long way to clear up any doubts the aircrew might have had about the usefulness of their task, and give them a set purpose for trying to reach a higher standard of efficiency. By constant visits to units and talking to crews of the standard we must try to attain in the next few months, I tried to build up a real pride of achievement. I also increased the Group's operational activities, as I believe there is no better way of building morale in war than by active operations which are carefully thought out and properly conducted. Long periods of inactivity have the reverse effect, crews becoming bored and having too much time to think about the dangers lying ahead.

Lastly, I issued an instruction that station commanders were to take part in active operations with their squadrons, though I made it clear that I did not expect them to lead their formations unless they felt they were sufficiently in practice to do so, and that I did not wish them to carry out more than two or three operations a month. At the same time I started flying on operations with the squadrons, and David Atcherley, who had joined me as my Senior Air Staff Officer, also flew as a passenger. At that time he was unable to fly himself as he had a badly fractured arm in plaster. Sometimes he and I flew together in a

Mosquito on ground-level attacks on targets, and I am certain it helped to build up morale throughout the Group. As a tribute to his courage and high sense of duty, I would like to record that for over a year he flew on operations unable to use a parachute if need arose; and once when he slipped getting into my Mosquito and again broke his arm, which was still in plaster, he said nothing about it until our mission was over. Some might argue that it was a sign of a lack of balance on his part to fly and on mine to allow him to do so, but they did not witness the morale and spirit of 2 Group at that time. His example was an inspiration to us all. I personally thought it only prudent to hide my identity, as they Germans had circulated a description of me and put a substantial price on my head after my escape from France in 1940; so I became Wing Commander Smith, with the number of a genuine Smith of that rank, whenever I flew on operations. I had identification discs made and marked all the clothes in which I flew with his name, arranging so that my rank badges could be changed at will. Although these elementary precautions would probably not have borne overmuch investigation, I hoped they would give me the time I needed to make my escape break should I be unlucky enough to fall into enemy hands again.

Neither of us confined our activities to Mosquito operations but we also flew in the Mitchells, and David in particular flew as a passenger on many missions in these aircraft, observing and thinking out how efficiency might be improved. I am sure that by these methods we were able to bring up-to-date practical experience to bear on all our decisions affecting operational planning, training, policy and many other important matters. We were also able to watch the development of tactics and relate them directly to planning and the method of employment of our squadrons, and I feel convinced that this had a direct influence on improving the operational effectiveness of my Group and reducing our casualties. It is clear that if those who plan and control operations also take part in them, then no man is asked to do what his commander is not prepared to do himself, and surely that should be the basis of operational planning and leadership at the Group level of responsibility.

In addition to Atcherley and myself, a number of the Group Staff officers flew regularly on operations either as pilot or passenger, and it helped them a great deal to understand operational problems which were the daily worries of the squadrons. I also encouraged officers from the various Wing Headquarters to carry out a limited amount of operational flying, and these included chaplains, doctors, engineer officers, intelligence and operations-room officers. One army liaison officer flew as a gunner on over fifty missions.

When the Chaplain-in-Chief heard that Warner, a Church of England chaplain, had been on flying operations, he said to me:

'Basil, I am rather worried about our chaplains flying. Suppose anything happened to Warner. The regulations do not make allowances for the widow of a chaplain being paid aircrew rates of pension, and indeed the Treasury might query why a chaplain was flying on operations.'

'Padre,' I answered, 'don't worry about Warner or any other chaplain being killed—just trust in God.'

Air Chief Marshal Sir BASIL EMBRY
GCB KBE DSO DFC AFC

*

To illustrate Sir Basil's comments about the Ventura bomber, here is an air gunner's account of an operation in

THIS BLOODY CRATE

The target was Philips Radio Works, Eindhoven, Holland. Sunday had been chosen because a large number of the Dutch workers would be absent. The Group stressed that this was an important and valuable target. If it could be put out of commission, it would be a real body blow to the German war effort.

Nine-tenths of our load was incendiaries. We were to contribute four boxes of six, the Kiwis three, a third Ventura squadron three, making sixty Vents in all. Fighters were to go in ahead of us stirring up fighters. We were to be covered by some hundred Spitfires fitted with long-range tanks. This was an innovation that would cause consternation, surprise and loss to our enemies.

The attack was to be entirely low-level at zero feet, flak opposition was to be expected crossing the off-shore islands and at odd scattered points. It was expected to be heavy over the target areas.

As we drove to our kites Hally said, 'Well, it's something new, but I hope those bloody Spits keep close to us. I don't want to tangle with any Focke-Wulfs in this bloody crate.'

I looked at the faces of these young airmen who were about to be blooded. They were serious and generally quiet. As each crew got out the rest wished them luck.

It was a fine, windless day with a slight mist. As we streamed across the flat Norfolk countryside the field workers stopped to wave to the modern cavalcade that rode the sky so close above their heads. The North Sea was grey and unruffled. We crossed it at zero feet. Our box was tail-end of this bomber stream. A box consisted of six aircraft. No 1, the leader, had as his supports Nos 2 and 3 on either side. No 4 flew just below No 1 to miss his slipstream and was supported on either side by Nos 5 and 6. Thus, No 1 flew at approximately twenty feet so that No 4, which was ourselves, to dodge slipstreams, was down to ten feet. Despite the nervous qualms at the pit of my stomach, I found this new experience exciting.

The low-level approach was intended to spoof the enemy radar. The idea was that the island defences would be taken by surprise and we would be across them before they recovered.

What someone omitted to allow for was that the initial beating up by fighters and Mosquitos who had gone in ten minutes ahead would have the Jerry gunners right on their toes.

I heard Jack say, 'Enemy coast coming up' and then the sea beneath us began to churn white as the enemy gunners extended their welcome. Overhead, black smudges lined with red appeared as if by magic. Luckily, the heavies could not depress far enough to get our range, but the concentration of Bofors, 20 mm and light flak was terrific.

Two tremendous splashes that tossed water over our heads marked the passing of two crews, then we were over the defenders. A little to our right a plane plunged into the earth, skidded into a strongpoint and exploded in a burst of flame and debris. It suddenly struck me that in this sort of flying, parachutes were useless, if you went in, there were no survivors. I sweated across those islands that day and anyone who says they were never afraid on ops is a bloody liar.

Suddenly we were lying across the mainland. A few black smudges chased us but it looked as if we had passed the strongly defended coastal area. As we roared over the flat Dutch countryside the inhabitants out on their Sunday strolls waved frantically and jumped with joy. These Dutchies let it be known whose side they were on.

Bill had his head stuck out of the astrodome until the latter was blown away coming in over the coast, without giving him anything worse than a scare. He returned to the front of the kite.

Suddenly Jack said, 'That's an aerodrome' and the next moment we were skipping across an excellently laid out drome. This was a costly blue on someone's part, because two more planes ploughed in a smother of dust, flame and smoke. Probably this place had taken a beating earlier and was out for revenge. A cannon shell blew the perspex out on the starboard side of the cockpit, giving Bill his second fright but doing no damage.

The gunners poured a fusillade back without much apparent effect. A little further on we passed another Ventura burning fiercely. Four figures scrambling awkwardly in their flying boots away from it showed they at least had escaped. As we swept over them they turned and gave a forlorn wave.

In all this excitement I had completely forgotten about the target. Wilbur's voice 'Target coming up' brought me back to reality. It would be hard to give my impressions over the next minute for the area was a nightmare of burning buildings, smokestacks and high tension wires.

Jerry gunners still manned their weapons on rooftops even though the windows belched smoke and flame. We went through so fast that it was hard to pick a target so I

299

put my finger on the teat and sprayed the entire area. How we missed the stacks and wires I'll never know. I saw a Vent veer crazily and hit a smokestack plumb in the centre and plunge downwards in a welter of dust, bricks and flame.

Jack screamed 'Bombs away' and we swung violently to the left. The clusters of incendiaries flew off at a tangent, travelling almost horizontally to smash into the front of the building in such a welter of explosion and fire that it really shook me. I knew why the place was so thoroughly alight.

We straightened up and missed a set of high tension wires by inches. I saw a burning Ventura that had smashed into a row of tenement houses. This, I heard later, was the only instance during the entire raid where civilian property was destroyed.

The next moment we were doing a split-arse left turn as we went for home. It was only then that I noticed I still had my finger on the teat and that neither gun was firing. Around us in the air dog-fights were going on everywhere but enemy fighters appeared to have their hands full on that particular day.

We came out along a canal about three-quarters of a mile wide. Guns placed on either side turned in and churned the water white below us. Bill, who had gone to man the lower guns, had his third life when a shell hit both of them, curled them up in a 'V' but failed to explode.

Miraculously, no direct hits were scored on this fleeing target. A mile astern we saw a plane which turned out to be a Canadian Pete, limping home. The German gunners concentrated on this inviting target but again, despite a hail of shell, the crew came through.

We came out over a marshy flat area without a shot being fired which later prompted the thought, 'Why the hell didn't we go in that way?' It was a badly mauled squadron that limped home. Because of the absence of runways, planes all pleading various emergencies landed everywhere. The place was a shambles.

Our petrol indicators showed empty five miles from the station and we landed, like everyone else, straight into the wind, with another plane on our tail and, while taxi-ing back on the tarmac, ground to a stop completely out of petrol. At interrogation I found the six bomber gunners had come through, which was almost a miracle.

A check showed our losses as six, as well as five Kiwis and four of our co-squadron. A total of fifteen out of sixty.

A young gunner said, 'Well, that wasn't so bad.'

'Not bad,' said Hally dryly. 'Another three ops like that and we will have completed our tour.'

The young fellow looked at him open-mouthed and said, 'But it's thirty ops for a tour, isn't it'?

'That's right,' said Art, patting him paternally on the head, 'only we won't have to go that far.'

JOHN BEEDE

*

M.H.D.O.I.F.

After Beam Flying at night, the Instructor landed unwittingly at the wrong aerodrome. He then got out and sent the pupil solo.

The pupil then landed at base.

TEE EMM

*

As the North African campaign ended with the attempted escape of the remaining German troops from Cap Bon, the Desert Air Force found new and unfamiliar targets: troopships in retreat. Practising for such missions, they sometimes went too far.

1st May 1943

To the Mess President of No 244 Wing
Sir,

It has been observed by various individuals of unimpeachable character that Spitfires are making use of valuable dan buoys as targets.

These dans, which mark the way through a minefield, have been laid at enormous expense and with great skill and daring in order to safeguard the shipping bringing you your bully, biscuits, pickles and booze Repeat booze. Should the unlikely event occur of one of these buoys being sunk or damaged by your planes, no booze will be forthcoming. Calamity! ! ! !

For a fee we could lay a very large-sized beacon for you to practise on and perhaps hit.

Should this pernicious habit of buoy-strafing not cease, no further pennies will be contributed to buy you new Spitfires.

GEOFFREY R. PRICE LT RNVR
ROBIN BELL LT RNVR
C. W. PEARCE LT RNVR

*

With all Africa secure in Allied, or neutral, hands, the invasion of Sicily was promptly ordered. This was to be initiated by the first major Allied airborne operation, putting paratroops and gliders in behind the coastal defences to seize key bridges and generally unsettle the defenders—a move that worked so well on D-Day a year later. Over Sicily it worked less well. This is from a report by one of the pilots towing the gliders on

OPERATION LADBROOK

38. This was the main operation on the 9th. We were briefed at 1300 hours. We had no Operations Room on our aerodrome, and therefore had to go to No 296 Squadron for our briefing. This was disadvantageous, as it meant that we could not study the photographs and large-scale maps of the area at our leisure. We were briefed separately from No 296 Squadron, and were not told much about the main force. Our own force consisted of 8 Horsas towed by our 7 Halifaxes and one Albemarle, piloted by Wing Commander May of No 296 Squadron. Each Horsa was to carry 30 men of the South Staffordshire Regiment, with one Bren gun, a mortar and 20 bombs, and some Bangalore torpedoes (used for blowing up barbed wire). The total load was, I believe, 8,000 lb. The timing of the operation was done in an unusual way which did not prove effective. The time of our take-off was laid down and we were told to keep to it as strictly as possible. We were given no set time to re-

lease, but were told to fly at a certain air speed. The assumption was that in this way we would all release our gliders at the same time. The Halifaxes were told to fly level at 140 mph and climb at 130 mph. Unfortunately, because of the condition of our aircraft, none of us could manage these speeds. Wing Commander May in the Albemarle took off earlier than us and flew as arranged at 120 mph. As we could not keep to our air speed we released our gliders fifteen minutes after him.

39. We were briefed to fly to Malta at 500 feet. From here we were to climb to 3,500 feet (later changed to 4,000 feet). We were to fly along the south-east coast of Sicily until we came to a bay south of Syracuse. At a point in the bay, 3,000 yards from the shore, we were to release the gliders. The gliders were then to glide 7 miles towards their landing zone, which was a bridge over a canal south-west of Syracuse. We were given a night map of the area.

40. My glider pilots were Staff Sergeant Galpin and Sergeant Brown, who also had night maps of the area. I marked on both maps points along the coast A, B, C, D. Point D was the point of release. We also arranged a course for them to steer from that point to their landing zones. We were to keep in touch with the glider on the line intercom all the time. If that failed we were going to flash an Aldis lamp when we came to the point of release. Only if that failed were we going to use the TR9, and we evolved a little code of our own for release.

41. There was considerable discussion about the undercarriage of the Horsas. The tug pilots wanted the Horsas to jettison their undercarriages, as it made their tow easier. The glider pilots felt that it made their job much more difficult, as they could steer the glider on the ground after landing. These Horsas all had different brakes. I was in favour of the glider pilots. I felt that their job was so difficult already that nothing should be done to make it even worse. In the end the undercarriages of the Horsas towed by the Halifaxes were not jettisoned. They were, in fact, wired up, so that they could no be jettisoned. This was probably unwise, as in the event of engine trouble on the Halifax, the pilot might not be able to keep the Horsa airborne, whereas if the undercarriage could be jettisoned,

303

he would be able to carry on with the flight. The undercarriage of the Horsa towed by the Albemarle was jettisoned, as Wing Commander May said that he would not have enough fuel to return to base if the undercarriage was kept on.

42. We took off at 2005 hours. On take-off our standard inner boost regulator failed. We could only get +4 lb boost on this engine, and soon it dropped to +½ lb. As I could not maintain height I had to turn back to the aerodrome. Luckily when we were over the aerodrome it righted itself, and the boost went up to +9 lb. This circuit made us a little late. As we were still uncertain of our starboard inner, are decided to fly to Malta at 2,000 feet instead of 500 feet.

43. On the way to Malta my starboard outer radiator temperature gauge went unserviceable, so did the DR compass and the automatic pilot, on which I was relying to cover up my instrument flying. In spite of my instrument flying, my navigator managed to take several drifts on the way to Malta and after we had turned towards Sicily. He calculated that there would be a wind of 30 mph against the glider pilot after releasing. We decided to climb to 5,000 feet instead of 4,000 feet and to release the glider over land two miles nearer the target. As we were running along the coast of Sicily my navigator told me the wind was dropping considerably. We then decided to keep to our height of 5,000 feet and to release him in the pre-arranged position. We had a little flak from the coast—only two guns as far as I could see. I could see the coast and the harbur of Syracuse very clearly below, although it was not a clear night. The moon was still in the first quarter. It was low in the sky and behind us. As we ran along the coast we gave the glider pilot the points on the map as we passed them, and eventually D, the point to release. He released instantly. We flew back to base; nothing interesting happened on the way back, except that the boost regulator went unserviceable again. We were kept circling over the aerodrome for 45 minutes, and when we landed the moon was completely down and most of the flares had either been knocked out or had burnt out.

44. I met my glider pilot on his return to Africa, and he

told me his story. Evidently he was not able to see the coast when he released. However, he turned to the pre-arranged course and flew on that course without map reading for 1,500 feet. His air speed was 90 to 95 mph. At 3,000 feet he managed to pick up the Bay of Syracuse and flew along it. At 1,500 feet he saw the canal ahead and then he knew where the landing zone was. At 1,000 feet, as he was doing his circuit, he was caught in light machine gun fire. He made a dive approach, that is he came in low and fast at about 125 mph. He landed in the correct field quite intact, only breaking the nose wheel in a ditch at the end of his run. His thirty passengers disembarked and took the bridge without much opposition. They held it throughout the night.

Quoted by A. H. WHEELER CBE

Of some 130 gliders—most of them the smaller Waco Hadrians towed by C-47 Dakotas—nearly 60 came down in the sea, up to six miles off shore. So did many paratroops. Casualties were very heavy. Many tug pilots obviously failed to recognise the strong headwind; perhaps others, particularly in the unarmoured Dakotas, were slightly shy of the coastal flak.

*

Still others were going into the sea. This is an account by the second pilot of a Coastal Command Liberator based on Gibraltar which had less luck with the Junkers 88 hunters than the Sunderland earlier in the year.

IN THE DRINK

'We took off from Gibraltar on a September morning on an anti-submarine patrol. The weather was just the type that Coastal Command boys hope for; a steady wind, a warm and pleasant atmosphere, with enough cloud to protect us in case enemy fighters attacked us over the Bay of Biscay.

'Everyone was in high spirits. We wished to find and destroy a U-boat, which our crew hadn't done up to then. This, coupled with the ideal weather, was the reason for our feeling joyful and pleased.

'At one o'clock in the afternoon everything was going fine. We were travelling fairly close to the Spanish coast. It looked peaceful.

'Later, as we flew westwards, the wind gained in strength until there was no cloud to be seen. At ten minutes past three we had just levelled off at about 3,000 feet, everything shipshape, when we saw what was to prove a very fatal, solitary cumulus cloud. As we approached, one of our gunners shouted, "Aircraft dead ahead just entered cloud." The skipper immediately altered course to starboard: then, out of the corner of his eye, he sighted another aircraft attacking us in a dive from the port bow. He immediately shouted over the intercom, "Look out, boys! Junkers! Jettison bombs." While he shouted that, he was turning into the attack, hoping to get out of the enemy's sights. We both looked up and were just thanking God that we had foiled the attack when I saw flames spitting from the leading edges of the Junkers' wings. A second later the skipper turned to me and said, "They've got me," then seemed to go stiff.

'I took over the controls. A very upsetting feeling came over me because I could see the hole in his chest where the cannon shell had passed through. I shouted over the intercom that the skipper was hit but got no reply. It was several minutes later that I realised that the intercom was unserviceable. Then a horrifying dryness came into my throat. I couldn't swallow or part my tongue from the roof of my mouth because I realised that without fighter control from one of the gunners it was really a matter of time, unless clouds came along, before we were shot down.

'At twenty past three we knew beyond all doubt that there were four of them attacking us. And we knew that we would be very lucky indeed if we got away. The little cloud the Junkers had been dodging in and out of was far too small to conceal our Liberator.

'For the next two or three minutes the four Junkers circled around us while I was busy keeping the aircraft doing everything that they teach one not to at training school. Five minutes after, the second attack began, from the same Junkers as before.

'This time it was a starboard frontal attack. I immedi-

306

ately turned in, undulating fiercely. But this time he really had us fair and square in his sights. I had just pushed the aircraft over into an almost vertical bank when I looked up and saw flames coming from his wings again. My heart almost stopped beating, because this attack was identical to the first attack when the skipper had got his cannon shell. But I was lucky again as regards to myself, but poor Jimmy in the mid-upper was hit badly. He had bullets in his foot, leg and in his rear, and scratches all over his face and neck. He fell more than climbed out of the turret.

'I shouted for someone else to get in quickly as that turret has 0.5 guns, and Jerry doesn't like those. Jack was just about to get in when Jimmy called, "It's no use. The turret feeder block is busted." It was well and truly busted.

'While I had been throwing the aircraft about I noticed that the controls were getting difficult to move. I glanced around at the skipper's seat and found out why. His body had somehow got jammed in the controls. I would have got him out earlier had I been able to. I shouted to F/O Thornton behind me, who was a passenger, to get him out of the seat and sit there himself. After a bit of hard struggling he did. I was still throwing the aircraft about the sky as if it was a fighter: it is no easy job to keep one's balance when an aircraft is being flown like that.

'F/O Thornton had no sooner sat in the seat behind the armour plating when a hail of cannon shells came screaming through the aircraft, smashing every instrument on the panel except the air-speed indicator, and thudding into the armour-plating at our backs. It was a good job that he moved into that seat otherwise he would have been smashed to pieces later. It was in this third attack that our tail turret was smashed, and the tail gunner got a cannon shell through his backbone. He was fatally wounded, but he crawled out of the tail turret, just in time to get to one of the side guns. Then he got a good burst in, at one of them, just as he died. Although none of us saw, we believe that Junkers crashed into the sea, because from that moment there were only three attacking us.

'Suddenly the engineer came rushing out of the bomb bay. He knocked my hand off the throttles and shouted, as he was feathering the prop, that our No 2 engine was on fire. Luckily, the fire went out when the engine stopped turning. But by that time our No 3 engine was set on fire and throwing a 30-foot flame alongside the aircraft. It was in that attack that I think everyone in the aircraft got wounded as the bullets and cannon shells absolutely raked the aircraft from tip to tail. I got wounded in the arms and legs.

'I went to feather No 3 engine, but there were no levers there to pull. When I tried to get the engine fire extinguisher alongside me I found that it was covered with twisted bars of metal, done by cannon shells. From that time on they just did attack after attack. As I was getting weak I told F/O Thornton to push or pull the control column with me, so that I could keep the action fierce.

'The controls were getting fairly mushy and the aileron control was almost unserviceable. The flames were beginning to cook the petrol, the port wheel was hanging limply down, the flaps were unserviceable, two engines had gone and the outer two were beginning to seize up. So I decided to ditch. I shouted to the boys, "Emergency hatch open, ditching.' It wasn't easy for them to move because every one of them was wounded.

'When the boys were in their places, I started the aircraft into a shallow dive from a thousand feet and levelled out just above the tops of the waves. We had to go along the swells of the sea, until the aircraft was down near stalling speed. Then I sat her down before a wave could knock us down—more by good luck than judgment.

'The aircraft immediately sank and we went down with it—twenty feet under water—completely dark. The terrific impact with the water had broken its back and almost ours as well: like hitting a brick wall at a hundred miles an hour. It was far too dark to see anything. I just breathed in water and thought, "Here it is." We must have been under there nearly two minutes before any of us struggled free. No one can realise the horrible feeling it gives one, to be jammed in an aircraft under water and slowly drowning. But we did struggle free.

'When we finally got to the surface, all except the skipper and Pat, I suddenly saw daylight and took a deep breath of air. We were appalled to see only one dinghy: the rest had gone down with the aircraft. It wasn't easy getting seven of us into the two-man dinghy. Our Mae Wests had been riddled and didn't keep us up. Some could not swim and their wounds made it difficult to hoist them aboard. The sea was rough and we were sick over the side, from swallowing so much salt water.

'We hadn't been in the dinghy more than an hour when we sighted smoke on the horizon. Somebody said, "Surely we're not saved already," and started to wave the telescopic flag. The smoke came nearer and we saw the shape of a vessel altering course towards us. We all started talking and cheering like wildfire as we thought we were going to be picked up and saved. As the craft got nearer we saw it was a 517-ton U-boat with a modified conning-tower. It was dirty yellowish in colour. The navigator gave the order not to answer any questions; just to say "water".

'The U-boat came within twenty yards and we saw the Germans quite clearly. They were clean-shaven. One of them called, "You British? You Allies?"

'We did not answer: we just shouted "Water!"

'When the commander of the U-boat gathered that we didn't intend saying anything, he gave orders to his men to carry on, which they did, roughly in a westerly direction. Ben said, "Would you sooner be taken prisoner, rather than risk your chance of being picked up?" We all said, "No, we'd sooner take the chance."

'We were all highly thankful as none of us wished to be taken prisoner, especially on board a U-boat. We were thankful also because we were all expecting to be raked with machine-gun bullets at any moment so we were ready to dive into the water as soon as any of the Germans got behind a gun. Although some of us were badly wounded and dying, there still remained the thought that life is sweet, and we were determined to live as long as possible. Had they fired on us, I don't doubt that we would all have been killed, even if we had dived under the water. We couldn't have stayed there for ever and they would be certain to have got us when we came up.

'When the U-boat had passed on, we really gave vent to our feelings: a very lurid description of what we thought about U-boats and Germans in general. The description certainly isn't befitting to write on paper. There were some really choice words; among them, "The bastards have gone."

'Later on in the evening, we took stock of what we had and the results were not very encouraging. We only had two small cans of water, one small tin of orange juice, a green lemon and the usual Horlicks tablets and chocolate. As you can see, this was not going to last long between seven of us. And there was no knowing when we might be picked up—if ever. Ben said, "Well, boys, there isn't much chance of shipping being this far down the bay."

'Our morale was very low for a short while, but in true English fashion we soon got over our low feelings and started seeing how badly wounded each of us was. Ben had wounds everywhere; a lot of them being caused by the ditching and the rest by bullets and shrapnel. Jimmy had bullet wounds in his face and leg and also his rear. We had to lay him down in the bottom of the dinghy, as he was in so much pain. Then there was Jack: he had the front part of his leg blown off by a cannon shell. He said, "Even if we are saved I suppose I shall have to have my leg off when we get back." Dick had a bullet right between the shoulder blades. Mike, Jerry and myself were the most fortunate of all. Mike had only a cannon shell blow a piece out of the side of his knee. F/O Thornton had a scratch on one of his fingers, and myself a bullet in the wrist and shrapnel in the knees.

'When we had finished bandaging ourselves with odd bits of torn shirt and handkerchiefs, we settled down as best as possible along the walls of the dinghy, bracing ourselves so that we wouldn't fall back into the water. It was terribly cramped. Had any of us fallen out I doubt if the rest of us could have got him back again because we were beginning to feel the reaction from the attack and the ditching; also from the experience of being jammed in the aircraft under water.

'That night was hell to us. The biting wind went right through us, like a knife. We were soaked through and through again. There was no covering to protect us in any way whatsoever. Our wounds were paining us horribly, because our circulation was still fairly good. As the night went on each of us wanted to turn around or move our legs because of a cramped feeling we kept getting. This in the dead of night, with the sea throwing us around, was no easy matter. We didn't talk much. Just mumbled, "Bloody cold," or "For heaven's sake keep still," when someone moved. Never before were any of us so thankful as when the dawn came.

'All that day we kept a watchful eye out for aircraft or ships but we were all getting lower and lower in ourselves. We just looked at each other. We were chilled to the marrow of our bones. We had not even seen so much as a bird or a piece of driftwood. After we had had our meals of Horlicks tablets and a suck of the lemon all round, the lemon being finished after this, we began to settle down for another night. We were just about to give up hope when Mike sighted a Sunderland a few miles away. 'We said, "Good boy, Mike, nice work." Everyone cheered and began waving frantically. But it was to no avail as the Sunderland didn't see us at all. One could read the thoughts of everyone quite easily, as it was so plain to be seen.

'I thought of my wife and the little baby she is going to have. And of my people, who are not in very good health. I wondered how they would be now as they were sure to have been told I was missing. That thought was more horrible to me than anything I was suffering in the dinghy.

'That night was just one long nightmare. We had had no food or anything warm to drink that would help to keep out the bitter cold, and when dawn came we were so cold that the pain from our wounds had ceased. But another pain was coming, to our feet and legs, caused by the continual soaking from the sea. This meant that to bend or unbend our legs was sheer agony and torture. But we had to move every now and then because of cramp in our bodies. We had plenty of pain and agony.

'All that day we kept watch for aircraft until we felt our eyes would drop out from staring. About six o'clock in the evening we sighted an aircraft in the distance. But it was too far away for us to recognise what it was, let alone signal to it. So we just gave that one up as a bad job. We had our meal, which was the usual Horlicks tablets, and the tin of orange juice this time. Then we settled down as best we could to wait for the night of horror that was to come. That night the sea was very rough. The ones that could, took it in turns to keep the dinghy headed into the sea with an oar which we had found under the rubber seat. This was torture anew for us, because we had to sit upright in the dinghy and face the full blast of the weather. By the time the next one's turn cane, the one who had been guiding the dinghy was frozen stiff.

'The following morning, when it was light enough to see, we took stock of ourselves. Everyone was blue with cold and it was almost impossible for any of us to move our legs. Poor Jimmy and Jack. Their wounds were beginning to go gangrenous. They could see it and it turned them slightly hysterical. We managed to quieten them down though, with such things as, "We are bound to be seen today," and giving everyone a piece of chocolate, which is part of the small emergency pack.

'I can say, with the deepest sincerity, that a piece of chocolate to us in our condition was thought greater of and treasured more than a home-cooked dinner would be to people who had plenty. The mere thought of a home-cooked meal was nearly enough to send us mad. Our condition was so low by this time, and our nerves so frayed, that we began to be snappy towards one another. We barked, "Watch my foot," or "Look out for my arm." I think if it hadn't been for the fact that two aircraft passed nearby, four or five miles away, we would probably have started fighting. They missed us, of course, but they gave us hope. The slightest thing anyone did or said that didn't quite suit the other person near by, then an argument started straight away. All that day it was just one argument after another, and by the time nightfall came we each and every one of us were utterly exhausted.

'That night again was the same as the other nights, just one long torture. The wind was getting colder than ever, for we had been drifting in a northerly direction all the time. In one way this helped us, because of the greater possibility of seeing ships. But the water was getting colder. As I have said before the wind, coupled with the fact that our resistance was now very low, had rather drastic effects on our will to live. . . .

'Early next morning one of the boys started muttering to himself and flinging his arms about. Jack and I gave him some morphia. Then Jack cuddled into him to keep him warm, and I think that was one of the main reasons why he kept going that day, as he was able to get some warmth back into his body. But it also meant that Jack was getting worse, as he had nothing with which he could replace the heat.

'In the afternoon of that day we had luck at last. Dick sighted a Sunderland. We all waved our hands and the flag as best we could. When it saw us and altered course towards us, none of us could speak. We all had a lump in our throat as we were so happy to think at last that we were going to be saved, that we were almost crying. We signalled frantically for the aircraft to land as the sea was smooth. The captain realised what we needed for he dived over us and dropped Horlicks tablets and water in some Mae Wests to which we frantically paddled. When we got the water in the dinghy we all went crazy for a while, because instead of trying to save it for as long as possible, we just drank tin after tin until the whole dozen tins had gone.

'Soon after dropping the water the Sunderland made off for base, as his fuel was probably getting low by this time. That night Catalinas came over with searchlights to keep in touch with us. But we had nothing to signal back. One of the flame floats they dropped fell near to us. The flame was five or six feet high and we had to paddle away or it would set us on fire. Although the searchlights swept across us several times, they didn't seem somehow to see us, and just before midnight they gave it up and went away.

'The next day never seemed to be coming as we were all so eager to have another aircraft around us to show that they were still in touch with us. Though we strained our eyes continually that day, we never saw an aircraft anywhere. It wasn't until late in the afternoon that we gave up hope and resigned ourselves to our fate. Late that evening we decided to try fishing with bent hairpins and a piece of string. We brought the hairpins in Gib., for our wives. We used chewing gum for bait. We tried for over two hours but we had no luck and gave it up as a bad job. We tried a piece of rag as bait and fish came up to the surface. But they would not bite. If we had caught any fish, it wouldn't have been fried either, as by this time we were hungry enough to eat it raw and really enjoy it. In any case, there wasn't likely to be any frying-pan in the dinghy with which to fry the fish, so fried fish and raw fish were to us just a thought.

'After we had given up fishing, we tried knocking down seagulls which were flying around us, fully determined to eat them raw and suck their blood. There were about twelve of them, crying and swooping.

'We beckoned them with our fingers and said, "Come near, my beauty." But they were far too quick for us to hit with the oar and so we had to go hungry again, having only one Horlicks tablet each that day.

'As the night came we began to get very thirsty and, try as we could to resist it, in the end we were drinking sea water like ordinary water. When the first one drank it, we said, "Stop, you'll go mad." But he did not stop. We all drank it in the end. I think that was one of the main things that hastened his death, because just around midnight he died. We stripped him and took his personal effects, and then buried him at sea. Jack said a little prayer for him, the rest of us closing our eyes and placing our hands together. Early the following morning Dick died, and we did the same again, and I think those two prayers were the sincerest I have ever heard, as every word was meant, and it came from the bottom of all our hearts.

'Early the following morning two Sunderlands arrived, but we were far too gloomy to shout or cheer. We just acknowledged them, and when they dropped their supplies we picked some of it up, being far too weak to get it all. They dropped a first-aid kit on a parachute, but although we tried hard, the remaining five of us, we just could not get it aboard. We were too weak. So we cut the parachute away and used it to break the wind. In one of the packs we picked up there were some distress signals, and our eyes glistened when we saw these, as it meant we could keep in touch with the aircraft that night.

'The dinghy by this time was leaking badly at the valve,

and we had to pump it up about every hour. This was using up all our remaining strength, but we managed to keep going somehow. That night Catalinas came over again with searchlights. This time we were prepared and we let off distress signals every now and then and kept in touch with them until they left for their base.

'Early the following morning one of us went delirious and, after trying to bite everyone for about half an hour, he collapsed in the bottom of the dinghy. He tried to bite at Bill's jugular vein, to suck his blood.

'After this little bit of trouble we settled down in a more or less dopey condition. About an hour later two Sunderlands came along, one of them circling us, and the other going off in one direction and returning again. We knew what this meant, but by this time we were too far gone to even trouble about being saved. We agreed to pump the dinghy up once more and if we weren't picked up by the time it deflated, we would go down with it, as our will to live had long been extinguished.

'Luckily, about twelve minutes after we had made this decision, HMS *Wildgoose* appeared on the horizon. Instead of cheering or shouting with joy, we all just sat there with tears in our eyes, for at last we were saved. They picked us up at about a quarter to ten that morning. They took us below into the marvellous warmth and gave us boiling coffee, which we drank as if it were only lukewarm. All our feelings had gone out of our bodies. The doctor took charge of us then, and as there wasn't room for all of us in his ward, I was taken aft to a cabin.

'Later that night another died, and sometime later Bill died as well. The doctor did not tell me until about a week later, as he wanted me strong enough to be able to take it, in case it had a fatal effect on me. All that day I lay in bed, thinking of them, what they had gone through, how they had suffered, and when they were safe aboard ship to suddenly pass away and to have suffered in vain.'

JACK FOSS quoted by HECTOR BOLITHO

In all, only three of the crew of nine survived.

*

We are the Air-Sea Rescue, no effing use are we;
The only times you'll find us are breakfast, dinner and tea.
And when we sight a dinghy, we cry with all our might:
'Per Ardua ad Astra—up you, Jack, we're all right.'

*

LINCOLNSHIRE BOMBER STATION

Across the road the homesick Romans made
The ground-mist thickens to a milky shroud;
Through flat, damp fields call sheep, mourning their dead
In cracked and timeless voices, unutterably sad,
Suffering for all the world, in Lincolnshire.

And I wonder how the Romans liked it here;
Flat fields, no sun, the muddy misty dawn,
And always, above all, the mad rain dripping down,
Rusting sword and helmet, wetting the feet
And soaking to the bone, down to the very heart. . . .

HENRY TREECE

*

*Now expert at their nightly trade, Bomber Command
crews were directed to the first of the intensive 'fire-storm'
raids—*

GOMORRAH

Never before had an aerial offensive against a single city
been so carefully planned and perhaps this preparation was
the greatest example of the fullest possible attention being
paid to scientific RDF aids to ensure that the most effective
strategy might be derived from their proper use. The C.-
in-C. and Air Vice Marshal Saundby were once more to
display their advanced and progressive thinking by basing
their entire plan of attack on the RDF that was available to
the forces which were to be despatched on four successive
nights to destroy, on each occasion, one quarter of the
city of Hamburg. Around the new Gee and H2S the form
of the offensive was prepared in detail. For the defence of

his forces, the C.-in-C. decided to utilise for the first time the highly secret strips of foil paper known as Window, which had been so cut that, when scattered in large quantities over defended areas, it would destroy completely the ability of the enemy locators to detect approaching aircraft.

By 24th July the stage was set. By nine-thirty on that morning Hamburg was doomed, and the operation, which went by the ominous code name of 'Gomorrah', was about to begin. As the last hours of that day were running out, a force of seven hundred and forty Lancasters and Halifaxes were nosing their way through the darkness across the North Sea in an easterly direction. Navigators were busily checking their position at regular intervals with Gee, maintaining with absolute accuracy their exact and predetermined route to the target. Pilots were implicitly following the instructions of their navigators in the full knowledge that these emanated from accurate scientific devices which were fundamentally incapable of giving anything but the correct answer.

With complete confidence they turned in towards the coast from their predetermined turning point which was a position exactly fifteen miles north-east of Heligoland. The Gee set could not be wrong. They turned. Then, knowing that they would soon cross the coast in the neighbourhood of Cuxhaven, the navigators and bomb-aimers suddenly focused their attention on the H2S indicator. Slowly the clock-like finger of the time-base rotated round and round as they gazed into the cathode ray tube, waiting for the appearance of the coastline which they knew must inevitably display its presence in exact replica by a shimmering green trace, accurately distorted to bear a precise resemblance to the shape of the coast over which they were about to pass. Then at the bottom of the cathode ray tube the coastline appeared. Deliberately it slid up the tube until it passed the centre and slowly the tube became filled with a series of bright patches of light closely related to the shapes of the surrounding towns. To the right was a black-snake-like ribbon of clear and easily identifiable definition. The River Elbe was deliberately unfolding itself as far as Hamburg, displaying with vagueness at first, but later with detailed clarity, the bright fingers of the dock area. As the city of Hamburg approached the centre of the tube it became more and more doomed.

Group Captain DUDLEY SAWARD OBE

*

A German night-fighter pilot takes up the story:

WINDOW ON HAMBURG

The early warnings from the Freya apparatus on the Channel coast indicated a large-scale British raid. In the late afternoon various flak units, night-fighter wing and civilian air-raid posts had been given orders to have their full complement at action stations. What were the British up to? What city that night would be the victim of these well-prepared raids? Every ominous presentiment was to be fulfilled that night. In all ignorance, the night-fighter squadrons took off against the British bombers, whose leaders were reported over Northern Holland.

I was on ops and flew in the direction of Amsterdam. On board everything was in good order and the crew was in a cheerful mood. Radio operator Facius made a final check and reported that he was all set. The ground stations kept calling the night fighters, giving them the positions of the bombers. That night, however, I felt that the reports were being given hastily and nervously. It was obvious no one knew exactly where the enemy was or what his object would be. An early recognition of the direction was essential so that the night fighters could be introduced as early as possible into the bomber stream. But the radio reports kept contradicting themselves. Now the enemy was over Amsterdam and then suddenly west of Brussels, and a moment later they were reported far out to sea in Map Square 25. What was to be done? The uncertainty of the ground stations was communicated to the crews. Since this game of hide-and-seek went on for some time I thought: To hell with them all, and flew straight to Amsterdam. By the time I arrived over the capital the air position was still in a complete muddle. No one knew where the British were, but all

318

the pilots were reporting pictures on their screens. I was no exception. At 15,000 feet my sparker announced the first enemy machine in his Li. I was delighted. I swung round on to the bearing in the direction of the Ruhr, for in this way I was bound to approach the stream. Facius proceeded to report three or four pictures on his screens, I hoped that I should have enough ammunition to deal with them!

Then Facius suddenly shouted: 'Tommy flying towards us at a great speed. Distance decreasing . . . 2,000 yards, 1,500 . . . 1,000 . . . 500 . . .'

I was speechless. Facius already had a new target. 'Perhaps it was a German night fighter on a westerly course,' I said to myself and made for the next bomber.

It was not long before Facius shouted again: 'Bomber coming for us at a hell of a speed. 2,000 . . . 1,000 . . . 500 . . . He's gone.'

'You're crackers, Facius,' I said jestingly.

But I soon lost my sense of humour for this crazy performance was repeated a score of times and finally I gave Facius such a rocket that he was deeply offended.

This tense atmosphere on board was suddenly interrupted by a ground station calling: 'Hamburg, Hamburg. A thousand enemy bombers over Hamburg. Calling all night fighters, calling all night fighters. Full speed for Hamburg.'

I was speechless with rage. For half an hour I had been weaving about in a presumed bomber stream and the bombs were already falling on Germany's great port. It was a long way to Hamburg. The Zuider Zee, the Ems and the Weser disappeared below us and Hamburg appeared in the distance. The city was blazing like a furnace. I was a horrifying sight. On my arrival over the city the ground station was already reporting the homeward flight of the enemy in the direction of Heligoland. Too late! The flak gunners had already ceased to fire and the gruesome work of destruction had been accomplished. In low spirits we flew back to our airfield.

How could the German defences have been rendered so impotent? We know today. The British had procured an example of our successful Li apparatus and had found the counter-measure. With ridiculous strips of tinfoil they could now lure the entire German night-fighter arm on to

319

false trails and reach their own target unmolested. It was a simple yet brilliant idea. As is well known, radar works on a determined ultra-short-wave frequency. By dropping these strips of tinfoil the British jammed this frequency. In this way the air goal was achieved and for the night fighter the bomber had once more become as invisible as it had been before the invention of the Lichtenstein apparatus.

While the main bomber stream far out to sea was flying towards Hamburg, smaller formations had flown over Holland and Belgium to Western Germany, dropping millions of tinfoil strips. These 'Laminetta' appeared on the German screens as enemy bombers and put various ground stations out of action. The smaller formations, according to schedule, next dropped enormous quantities of flares—the famous Christmas trees—over various cities in the Ruhr. A few bombs were also dropped. The night fighters streaked towards these signs of attack from all directions, looking in vain for the bomber stream.

In the meantime the leaders of the British main raiding force reached Heligoland unhindered and dropped more strips, putting the ground detectors out of action. At one blow both ground and air defence had been paralysed. In daylight on the following morning whole areas of Holland, Belgium and Northern Germany were strewn with these strips of foil. Certain people maintained they they were poisonous and that they would kill all the cattle. The innocuousness of these small pieces of tinfoil on the ground was soon apparent, but in the air they were deadly—fatal for the life of a whole city.

A few days later we heard further details of the agony of this badly hit city. The raging fires in a high wind caused terrific damage and the grievous loss of human life outstripped any previous raids. All attempts to extinguish them proved fruitless and technically impossible. The fires spread unhindered, causing fiery storms which reached heats of 1,000°, and speeds approaching gale force. The narrow streets of Hamburg with their countless backyards were favourable to the flames and there was no escape. As the result of a dense carpet bombing, large areas of the city had been transformed into a single sea of flame within half

Bomber boy: Guy Gibson (in the hatchway) and his crew embarking for the historic dam-busting raid on 17th May 1943

Short take-off, no landing: a Hurricane of the Merchant Ship Fighter Unit does its sixty-foot rocket-propelled run

The pilot of the Sunderland which took this picture had flown 500 hours without sighting a U-boat – until two minutes before. The depth-charge sank it. Note the smaller splashes contributed by the aircraft gunners, who killed most of the group on the conning-tower

Shipping strike: a wild melee of Beaufighters over a German convoy in 1944, and the splash of cannon shells and rockets hiding (and blinding) a flak ship. An attack like this was supposed to last no more than two minutes

By night: a Lancaster over the fires of Berlin in January 1945. This may also give some idea of the bomber's vulnerability to night-fighters

By day: a Lancaster over the wasteland of Cologne, after three years' steady bombing

This Halifax of 51 Squadron lost ten feet of its nose to a direct flak hit; the navigator, bomb-aimer and pilot died. The flight engineer flew it home

All the comforts of home: a Spitfire's overload tank is filled with beer for a flight to a captured airfield in Normandy, a few weeks after D-Day. (Later a system was invented for hooking the barrels directly on to the Spitfire's bomb shackles)

They also served who only stood and pushed – a Spitfire on a French airfield in 1944

Typhoon conditions: on a flooded Dutch airfield in 1945 a Typhoon, two 100lb bombs hidden by spray, taxies out for a ground-attack operation

A unique snapshot photograph, from the ground, of a Spitfire repeating Wing Commander Beaumont's trick of tipping of a V-I flying bomb into a dive. The size of a V-I as a target may be estimated, too

And why such tricks were tried: a V-I seen from a camera-gun. You were shooting at a ton of explosive at about 250 yards and nearly 400 mph an hour. Thousands of small fires joined up to become a giant conflagration. The fiery wind tore the roofs from the houses, uprooted large trees and flung them into the air like blazing torches. The inhabitants took refuge in the air-raid shelters, in which later they were burned to death or suffocated. In the early morning, thousands of blackened corpses could be seen in the burned-out streets. In Hamburg now one thought was uppermost in every mind—to leave the city and abandon the battlefield. During the following nights, until 3rd August 1943, the British returned and dropped on the almost defenceless city about 3,000 block-busters, 1,200 land-mines, 25,000 H.E., 3,000,000 incendiaries, 80,000 phosphorus bombs and 500 phosphorus drums; 40,000 men were killed, a further 40,000 wounded and 900,000 were homeless or missing. This devastating raid on Hamburg had the effect of a red light on all the big German cities and on the whole German people. Everyone felt it was now high time to capitulate before any further damage was done. But the High Command insisted that the 'total war' should proceed. Hamburg was merely the first link in a long chain of pitiless air attacks made by the Allies on the German civilian population.

WILHELM JOHNEN

Post-war research shows that the Hamburg attack (taking 'attack' to cover four major night raids spread over ten days, with daylight raids by American Fortresses in between) caused more casualties than any other. Bomber Command's losses were 86 aircraft—or 2.8 per cent of the total sorties flown, a relatively light loss.

*

'Window' went on being used but with declining effectiveness as the Luftwaffe improvised new night-interception techniques. This was always the story with any new aid. And by now the German night fighters were as expert as the British; their opportunities for acquiring experience were that much greater. A former RAF night-fighter pilot was sent to help the bombers in their task:

Visits to Group headquarters and bomber stations conveyed more the size of the Command than did the order of battle in the operations-room at the Command headquarters, and I began to understand now why it was that the frequent losses of thirty or more bombers, when spread over the many squadrons that made up the Command, were not crippling. Considerate staff officers explained to me the more detailed Group plan for an attack on Berlin, and at a station of that Group I attended a briefing on the plan. A whistle, half in protest and half in jest, went up as the curtain was drawn aside, revealing to the crews the night's target and their route. I looked at those intent faces. They were ordinary-looking men. They must have come from all sorts of families and homes and have been to all sorts of schools, a group typical, I thought, of the Service. In these highly trained crews brain was more important than muscle, and they were as expendable as the infantry of the first war; these men, too, had to 'go over the top', and it happened several times a week. Was this, I have since wondered, the end of a phase in warfare, the high-water mark in wastage restricted to experts?

Did they realise how small were their chances if once seen by a fighter? I guessed that none knew that the exhausts of their Lancasters could be spotted from a mile and a half, and that they could be seen as silhouettes against the stars from nearly a mile away, while the fighter could be seen against the ground at only about a hundred yards. There were grim thoughts, and knowing full well the theoretical bias against the big bomber, I hoped that the facts would never be known by the crews, but would become more and more dominant in the moulding of tactics and the trend of planning. My feelings towards these men were of simple admiration, and later, when I heard stories of the occasional superstitions which gave to some of them comfort and a feeling of greater security—a pilot's lucky pair of boots, the whip which another cracked before and after each operation, and the suicidal speciality of a third of flying well away from the bomber stream in which all the fighters were believed to be—my admiration was tinged with a mixture of sadness, pity and sentiment which is hard to describe.

322

Standing near the marshalling point I watched the departure one night of a station's force of thirty Lancasters. Each machine took up its position on the runway; each engine was run up with a thunder that shook the ground and, while final checks were made, Waafs standing near waved to friends among the crews who, helmeted, masked and confined in perspex cages, responded with a supremely confident thumbs-up fist. Throttles were opened wide, brakes were released and, in a great commotion, the first machine rolled off, the gunner perhaps dipping his guns in salutation. Gathering speed rapidly, it receded into the gloom and left the earth, disappearing momentarily, to reappear, as it climbed, against the last light of day. As one bomber was airborne another was there, ready to go. The departure of this force took little more than forty minutes, and then I was taken to the station-commander's house for a drink and dinner in comfort. That particular night—the target was not Berlin—thirty came back to that station, and all but two were down within forty-five minutes without trouble. This was no stunt, but a miracle of organisation and drill which happened regularly; it was, one felt, an ultimate performance like the highest high jump. It might be bettered, but the margins would be fractional only.

To add to the staff officer's picture of the Berlin raid, I visited the station where German radio was intercepted, and there I was able to listen to some of the enemy fighter-controller's orders and to get an idea of the reaction to the raid. Very early on all fighters were sent to Berlin, and I knew that some of those men I had seen at the briefing would soon be up against it. The German controller sounded calm and unhurried as he repeated mechanically with much guttural rolling of the Rs, 'Alle Dromedar-r-re nach Bar-r-e'—Dromedare being the call sign of a certain group of squadrons and Bare being their code name for Berlin. My blood ran cold; this was gruesome and depressing. The enemy would be waiting there in hordes, and I believed there would be disastrous losses.

The broadcasting from this station of bogus instructions to enemy fighters, of reports of deterioration of weather and orders to land, had started some little time before and had been an immediate success. Confirmation of the success of this subterfuge came from the enemy controllers themselves, who became angry and as abusive as fishwives; they were answered back and, had it been possible to feel sorry for Nazis, one would have felt sorry for those fighter crews who had to listen.

That night our 'spoof' was moderately successful. A bogus order from us was countered by the German controller telling his crews not to listen to the Englishman; the latter then countered by an almost word-perfect repetition of those instructions. Identities became confused after a few such exchanges and, to annoy and upset the crews and further to add to the confusion, our broadcaster began an impassioned impersonation of Hitler. The tension broke and we laughed heartily.

Air Commodore RODERICK CHISHOLM CBE DSO DSC

*

Yet another new move in the night war was sending RAF night fighters, by now starved of custom over Britain, along with the bombers to intercept the interceptors. The Air Council, perhaps over-conscious that British AI radar was better than its German counterpart, had long resisted pleas to loose AI fighters over enemy territory. It finally relented, although the AI sets were rather elderly models, and the aircraft were Beaufighters rather than Mosquitoes. But they had an extra card up their sleeves: a device to locate and home on German AI sets, known as

SERRATE

The moon was high and the night beautifully clear, when at about 1115 we heard the rumbling of many aero engines passing over. We could faintly make out ten Lancasters or Halifaxes a few thousand feet up and still climbing on their easterly course towards Germany's arsenal, the Ruhr. Hundreds more of these huge machines loaded with destruction would meet them over the North Sea and the stream of aircraft would stretch in a seemingly endless line for about 100 miles. Those who straggled off to one side because of faulty navigation would be easy targets for enemy fighters.

I checked my watch. 'O.K. let's go.' Sticks and I climbed aboard our Beau. Once cleared by the control tower we were to maintain radio silence until our return to England. As we climbed, Sticks watched his AI for signs of the masses of bombers that must be in our vicinity. Soon he told me over the intercom that he had many contacts all around us. The bombers were scattered between 10,000 and 18,000 feet. We decided to level off at 12,000 feet because the information we had from Bomber Command Headquarters was that the enemy tended to hit the lower-flying bombers hardest. We droned slowly over the North Sea and below us I could see the moon shimmering on the unfriendly waters. Thirty minutes later the faint outline of the Dutch islands at the mouth of the Scheldt hove into view. We were bang on course. As usual Stick's navigation was perfect.

The countryside below us was completely blacked out, although on a night like this it was easy for us to find our way. Rivers, canals and even rail lines stood out clearly. Up ahead I could see the beams of a few wavering searchlights, but nothing else that looked hostile. Yet we knew that on the ground Luftwaffe defence centres were issuing orders to night-fighter airfields to scramble squadrons of night-fighters. At this moment Me 110s and Ju 88s would be roaring off the landing fields throughout Holland, Belgium and western Germany to meet their hated adversaries, the bombers. Only this time, unknown to them, six Beaufighters were lurking in the stream.

Sticks was now continuously scanning the Serrate and AI scopes. 'I've got a number of indications of night-fighters, Bob. I'm taking the strongest-looking signal. Turn starboard 10 degrees and let's see if we can get this one.' We were now flying towards the signals emitted by a German night-fighter's AI. The technical limitations of Serrate gave us no idea how close or far the aircraft was until we picked up contact on our own AI, but we could tell his relative position to us in space. Flak appeared in the distance and bombers ahead of us were now under attack. 'Sorry, Bob, that signal has disappeared. But I have another. Port 20 degrees.' I banked the Beau round to our course and the aircraft rocked suddenly as we hit the prop-wash of another aircraft in front of us. I couldn't see anything but it was probably one of our own bombers. Again after a short chase, no luck. The Serrate signal disappeared, but always there were others indicating the presence of large numbers of enemy fighters. It seemed that the enemy left his AI on only for short periods.

By now we were approaching the Ruhr and the flak ahead was becoming intense as the bombers started to unload. Fires and explosions could be seen for many miles away as Oberhausen received mortal blows. But this wasn't a one-sided battle. Off to the right there was a vivid flash in the sky, then a flaming comet streaked earthwards. I noted the position and cursed. It was probably one of our bombers. 'Keep a good check on the equipments, Sticks. There are plenty of Huns about.' Up ahead was another fire in the sky, gradually sinking lower and lower to crash in a sheet of flame, marking the grave of another aircraft. Things were getting hot.

We were close to the flaming ruins of Oberhausen and the sky above us was filled with bursting anti-aircraft shells and the flares released by the Pathfinders to show the main force where the bombs should be dropped. There were so many bombers over the city that the German gunners couldn't hope to aim at individual aircraft. They threw up a curtain of steel in the hope of driving off their tormentors. It was in vain. The attack continued.

By now the leading bombers were turning away from the target and setting course for home. So skirting the flaming city, we headed back among their tracks. So far, I had only seen fleeting glimpses of dark shadows as we passed close to one or two of our bombers, although we flew through the prop-wash of many as we criss-crossed the stream in what seemed a fruitless search for the many German fighters.

Then there was excitement in Sticks's voice, as he called, 'Bob, I've got another signal, turn gently port.' As I manœuvred the Beau I counted three other aircraft on fire in the air within my range of vision. I knew our bombers rarely shot down a German night-fighter so I could only assume the enemy was exacting vengeance for the raid.

326

'Bob, I think this one is behind us. The signal is strong.'

'Have you anything on the AI yet?'

'No, but keep turning.'

It was an eerie feeling, knowing that we were playing a deadly game of hide-and seek with an unseen foe.

'Bob, I've AI contact 2,000 yards behind. Hard as possible port.'

'Are you sure it isn't one of our bombers?'

'Yes. It isn't. The Serrate and AI signals match up. Keep turning, he's only about 1,000 yards and 20 degrees on your port and a little above. Now ease the turn a little, and watch it. You're closing fast, you should see him in a second. He's only 600 yards and still well over to port.'

'I've got him, I've got him,' I yelled excitedly.

In the moonlight I caught a glimpse of an aircraft on my port beam. At that moment he straightened out, heading south at 10,000 feet. An Me 110. Perhaps he had lost me on his AI. At 400 yards' range I opened fire, gradually easing off the deflection so that as I rolled in astern of him the dot on my electric gunsight was centred on his fuselage. Explosions appeared all over the Me. Burning brightly he dived steeply towards the earth. By now Sticks had his head out of the 'office' and was shouting encouragement as he watched our enemy crash in a mighty flash of flame. This was no time to relax. 'Keep a look-out on your set, Sticks. There are lots of the blighters about.' Checking the position of our fight, I noted that the Me 110 had crashed on the north-east shore of the Zuider Zee.

Wing Commander J. R. D. BRAHAM DSO DFC AFC CD

*

A small loss rate is one thing to a commander—it is his job to count the cost without sentiment. To one who is a per cent of the percentage, it feels like this:

ABRACADABRA, JUMP, JUMP

Like a stab in the back, the starboard inner engine suddenly screams and spews flame. Don reaches for the feathering and fire buttons. He might just as well have sat back and sung the Lord's Prayer. Faithfully he plays out the little game he was taught but, in the language of the times, you have had it.

Aching with the sheer muscular effort of holding up the plunging port wing, you feel the elevators tighten as the nose goes down with a lurch.

Too tired to think you hear your voice giving the queer little order they taught you one drowsy summer day at the operational training unit in pastoral Oxfordshire; the absurd jingle you had never really thought you would ever use:

'Abracadabra, Jump, Jump. Abracadabra, Jump, Jump.'

Repeating it, you think how damn silly it sounds.

As was its intention though, it leaves no room for doubt or confusion.

Over the intercom you hear Bill shouting to Mac.

Don, after several fumbling tries in the dark, has clipped the parachute pack to your chest harness. Then he is gone, sliding down under the instrument panel into the nose, where Smith has already followed the jettisoned hatch out into the slipstream. Even at a time like this, Smithy's reaction to my final order had been jestingly phlegmatic.

'You mean I can stop shoving this goddam Window out the slot?' he rumbled.

Mac calls up from somewhere in the dark shambles of the fuselage, his voice tense over the intercom. He can't find his parachute pack. You feel like telling him to jump without it. Instead you urge him, 'For Christ's sake hurry, Mac. She's going.' Somehow he finds it where it was hurled from the storage rack during our evasive action and then he, too, is gone. You check if anyone is left in the aircraft. You are quite alone. The intercom is silent except for the slipstream roaring through a microphone where someone has left their helmet plugged into a turret.

Suddenly, you are conscious of feeling tired.

The main responsibility of the whole night, the crew, is off your shoulders. You can't do any more for them, right now.

The end must be so near for you that it hardly seems worth the sweat of trying to get out of the aircraft.

Then you think, how would the boys feel if they knew

you just sat there and waited for it? Surely to God something will go right tonight, even if it's only baling-out.

Suddenly frantic to live, you rip off your helmet, slide out of the seat with the stick held hard over until the last possible second and then hurl yourself headlong down into the nose. There's a jerk as your parachute harness fouls something. God Almighty. Mentally stunned, hanging head-down over the open escape hatch, there's nothing left in the world but the slipstream howling past.

The aircraft winds up a G-Force that drags your face across the metal ribs of the fuselage.

The inevitable fact that in, maybe, less than sixty seconds you are going to be killed relaxes you into a mental torpor of fatalism. It's all so inevitable and so quick that it's a waste of time worrying now. It's just not your night. It's too dark to see much anyway, but you close your eyes and hope it won't hurt. Then the thought of being face-down in the nose when 'Z-Zebra' hits the ground revolts you into frenzied action.

'I will get out!' you shout. 'I will get out!' Over and over again. God knows why. There's nobody to hear you.

Wrenching and tugging at your fouled harness, you feel something cold and hard hit you. It punches the air out of your lungs, lashes your eyes with your tie and pins your eyelids closed. You can't even think straight but it's air. Lovely night air and somehow you've hurtled out right into the middle of it at Lord only knows what speed.

Then, as you feel yourself slowing up and your numbed, breathless senses record the fact that you are tumbled over and over, you reach for the shiny metal handle of the parachut rip-cord.

It's not there.

Where the packed parachute should be, the steepening trajectory of your fall chills the sweat of your chest. The pack must have been ripped off when you tugged the harness free from the aircraft. Whatever did happen just doesn't matter now.

Once again you accept the fact that in a few seconds, maybe before you can finish thinking the thought, you will be dead. This time, too, you are no longer frightened. It's not courage; it's just that there's no point in being scared. There's no point in anything, now.

Not all the pious prayers in the world nor all the riches in the palaces of nations could delay by so much as one infinitesimal second the downward plunge of your body to earth. You are alone with your destiny.

Mainly, you only feel rather sorry for yourself, in a quite impersonal sort of way. It seems a lonely way to end what has been, so far, a good life. Just a bag of blood and bones and flesh falling unseen out of the sky, not even a dog barking.

If only someone were watching; someone, even a German, to cry in delight, 'There he goes; he's had it!'

It's an anticlimax; a train leaving a deserted station without farewells; a ringing-down of the curtain on the last act with every seat in the theatre empty.

Thinking these thoughts you realise that your body is fighting for life again; its hands are clutching at the air, trying to grasp at the parachute pack which may be falling through the darkness near it; its legs kicking spasmodically. It could be anyone's body but your own.

Something wraps itself around your neck with a not unpleasant jerk and, simultaneously, from up above you comes the inexplicable sound of an invisible sail flapping in the dark.

It's your parachute canopy. It has opened and you are hanging from it. You don't know how or why; you don't remember grabbing anything. Maybe it was streaming behind you on torn harness and you fell on it and tore at the rip-cord. What the hell, anyway! You don't care. It could be the wings of the angel of death himself flapping for all that it matters.

Life, with all its unhappened sorrow and laughter, stretches beautifully before you.

Choking for air as the loose harness wrapped around your neck begins to tighten, you get both hands between your throat and the stiff webbing bands.

The parachute spins slowly, you with it.

Relaxing in the safe anonymity of the night you seem almost to sleep with the relaxation of strain.

Fantastic in the darkness, the fires of Hanover rotate

330

slowly past your line of vision. Temporarily, you are deaf and can see but not hear the restless jittery sparkle of flak and the bomb and photoflash explosions flickering across the sky like summer lightnings.

The stricken city, and its lurid reapings of the harvest of total war, disappears behind your back as the parachute spins you round facing the dark side of the sky.

Your right flying boot fell off when the parachute opened (the can of orange juice is somewhere down below, damn it) and your feet feel stiff and cold.

Below, in the greater darkness that is Germany, a glowing cancer of fire festers, its proportions swelling magically as you fall towards it. It's Z-Zebra', cremated in a funeral pyre of savage beauty. Grimly, you reflect that the Luftwaffe won't be getting much out of that; then fear grips you lest you land sprawling in the blaze.

Then the flaming, spewed-out wreck rotates behind you.

The parachute is swinging you back and forth and you can see something dark underneath.

Even while you're wondering whether it's a lake or a wood a thousand feet below you, your left leg suddenly doubles up agonisingly under your body and you yell involuntarily as something hits you right on the back of the neck, slugging you so hard you feel sick and dizzy.

It's the solid ploughed earth of Germany.

You are completely, utterly and finally shot down.

You are also thankfully and undeniably alive.

You know you are, because behind the looming hills of the Harz Mountains you can see the serene glow of the rising moon.

It's rising over burning smoking Hanover.

A piece of cake.

GEOFF TAYLOR

*

This is my story, this is my song;
I've been in this Air Force just too flaming long.
So roll on the *Nelson,* the *Rodney, Renown*—
And they can't sink the *Hood* 'cos the bastard's gone down.

*

During a night flying exercise the pilot turned round and round a red light which he saw on the ground and had lost 2,000 feet before he realised the light was not on the ground after all, but was the port navigation light on his own wing-tip.

TEE EMM

*

THE CRUEL TREES

I once stood on a road in northern Burma in the midst of a high tumbling wilderness of hills whose jungle-clad sides seemed to hush the valleys into an awed quiet. There were no birds, no sounds.

I had reconnoitred this country before, but only from the air, so that my knowledge of it was superficial. But had not yet begun to realise that this morning I was seeing and learning the meaning of it the better by climbing from the plains on a motor cycle.

The road had led me above ragged scuds of monsoon cloud between which parts of the Imphal Valley were to be seen in the distance, bright in the sun. Up here the weather was showery and uncertain, but beyond, over the hills in which the battle was still going on, I could see rain clouds, mountainous and black.

This was the country and this the weather which pilots had learned to respect as much as the Japanese fighters or flak. Sometimes those who had been forced down in it had walked back, but seldom. They would be exhausted, feverish, and bitten by leeches. Yet I had seen in the face of more than one man that such things were not all that lingered to make convalescence slow.

It was the nightmare of trees, trees, trees. Trees whose roots were tangled in their very minds. I remembered the pilot of a Spitfire who had been forced to bale out in a thunder-cloud, the mad whirl of whose up-currents had tumbled his aircraft about as though it had been no more than a leaf in the wind. He had wandered in the jungle for three days and four night before being found by friendly hillmen. He had been severely bitten by leeches, one of which had penetrated not only a thick woollen sock, but his flying overalls and his trousers. He had, in that short time, lost nearly a stone in weight. His feet were raw and swollen from walking most of the first day and all of the following night along a river-bed, knee-deep in water. This had been his only clear path out of the bamboo thicket into which he had landed. He had emerged, but only into a jungle of trees through which he had had to shoulder and hack his way throughout all of the second day.

Now that he was safe he was haunted by those trees and the yet imagined sounds of water. For every one of those four nights it had rained, and by day there had been no sun to dry his saturated clothes. He had not slept then. He felt he would never sleep again.

Again, I remembered that it had been less than fifty miles from where I now stood that a Hurribomber pilot had been forced down. For twelve long days he had wandered without food other than his emergency rations, which are sufficient only as a diet for three days. By the time he had been found by friendly Burmese villagers on the thirteenth day, he had become half-crazed with hunger and had begun to eat leaves, roots, and something which he has since believed to be the dried manure of an animal.

He returned to his squadron in the Imphal Valley, escorted by an Army patrol which had been contacted by the Burmese. This was on the twenty-eighth day.

I looked again at the small hill, shaped like the crown of a witch's hat, which overlooked the road. It must have been a Japanese position, since the bunkers around its perimeter, and the gun emplacements which honeycombed its summit, all commanded the northern aspect. I was later to see that it was typical of thousands which had been blasted by the 250-pound bombs of Vengeance dive-bombers or Hurribombers, before being stormed and taken by the bayonets of our troops or the kukris of the Gurkhas.

Evidently the bombs had been accurately placed among the closest concentration of bunkers near the top of the hill. The jungle had been ripped aside so that the blackened trunks of trees hung out drunkenly towards the road. I saw bits of khaki webbing, remnants of ammunition boxes, cocoa tins. Half buried in the landslide from one of the bomb-bursts lay a bone, bleached grey, and already shot through with maggot holes.

It was then that I realised that war to us who fly must always be more spectacular, remote, and less bloody than to those on the ground; and it was a sobering thought to any pilot (lest he deceive himself) that we lived only a fraction of our time amid the sordid surroundings of our battles. I thought of the rough but comfortable little mess I had left behind in the valley that morning, the soullessly efficient surgery of an aircraft's cockpit; and now, this hillside, already half buried in weeds and the silence of the hills.

Did we, who fought this hectic, piecemeal war of the airman, understand this other war in which men fought not only the corporeal enemy, but fought also this jungle, too dense even for the sun; this rain, this heat, and worst of all, fought believing themselves forgotten?

Even those of us in the RAF who could not forget, since we ourselves were part of this forgotten army, did not comprehend it all.

Wing Commander BARRY SUTTON DFC

*

M.H.D.O.I.F.

This officer's squadron, flying Hurricanes, took off—somewhere out East—to intercept some Jap fighters. There also took off on the same job a squadron of Mohawks. . . .

A grand dog-fight ensued, and recognition was evidently a trifle difficult in the mix up; for F/Lt. —— was heard to say afterwards, on explaining a Certain Incident: 'I *thought* he was a Mohawk; that was why I only gave him a short burst.'

TEE EMM

*

Now, in Arakan on the border of Burma, the 'forgotten'
14th Army was starting its long counter-attack. Ahead and
overhead they had, for the first time, Spitfires.

ALADDIN'S TREASURE

There was more now in the air than a sense of urgency and
cheerful optimism. Spitfire V's were in flight, to the joy of
the squadrons which were equippped with them and the
envy of those which were not, and they had a brief immediate triumph. The fast Japanese Dinah's, which in appearance were not unlike our own Mosquitoes, had been
flying with arrogance even over Hurricane airfields to
photograph anything they desired. When by nearly bursting its engine a Hurricane did succeed in shooting one
down, the Japanese treated it as a rare phenomenon unlikely to recur, and they continued to fly with impunity
above the Hurricane ceiling. And then Spitfires, based
around Chittagong for protection of the port, shot down
three Dinahs in turn and the effect throughout the command was electric.

But victories did not at first come in the quick succession for which the destruction of the fast Dinahs led men
to hope. One occasion at this time which the enemy could
claim as a success was a new stroke aimed at Calcutta, with
the dual object of damaging the port and demoralising the
city. Divining that over our broad front fighter defence in
depth could not be so uniform, and that Calcutta would
still rely on Hurricanes, the enemy sent sixty bombers and
fighters out over the Bay of Bengal to smash the great
Indian port. The Arakan Spitfires were scrambled and
guided out to sea.

Ground operators in Arakan watched the green fluorescent 'blips' on the radar scope grow brilliant against the
fainter green caused by the permanent radio-echo from
the hills, and they were able to guide the Spitfires close to
the attacking waves flying north. Then, when it seemed
that the fighters were almost at point of contact with the
enemy, radar plots showed our fighters returning over the
sea to base. The enemy had flown beyond Spitefire range.

The Japanese had put a maximum effort into this attack,

but the long route which they chose in order to avoid interception precluded a respectable weight of bombs being dropped. In a raid that could be little more than a successful publicity stunt they caused some civilian casualties but no important damage to ships or docks. One soldier was killed. Next day a few Spitfires moved back across the sea to the defence of Calcutta and the raid was not repeated.

Unfortunately for the Japanese their success at Calcutta gave them a surfeit of confidence which was soon to be costly.

Many of our fighter pilots inevitably knew that they were likely to be killed in the offensives of the New Year, yet because they believed in the absolute superiority of their aircraft, as yet untried in major conflict with the Japanese, morale was never higher. Christmas at the Arakan airfields was not the less gay because of the hazards of coming encounters. One Spitfire squadron staged a pantomime to which the others came. It was given in a jungle glade on Christmas night, with a clear sky. Between the audience and the airfield men could see in the dusk the paddy ripening into golden shades; behind them lay the forest, in which elephants were trumpeting. The show was 'Aladdin' and the humour of course was local, with Aladdin's mother a 'dhobi-wallah' or washerwoman who made her profits by tearing off shirt buttons and selling them back to the owners. Two navigation lights, red and green, flickered as jewels in the djinn's turban, while Aladdin's cave was strewn carelessly with what then were the rarest things in India —Spitfire tyres. Great applause was that night given to the stars in the show, almost every one of whom was destined to be killed in the coming weeks.

AIR MINISTRY

1944

It had to be this year. It just might have been in 1942, just could have been in 1943—but in 1944 it had to happen. The Allies had to go back into France. From the beginning of the year, the British-based RAF effort was carefully—and subtly—angled to this end. Bomber Command shifted to oil and communications targets; 2nd TAF attacked key points in France; Fighter Command escorted them and American 8th Air Force daylight missions.

LIBERATOR

Here and there in the Fortress formations there were gaps. From close to you could see machines with one, sometimes two, stationary engines and feathered propellers. Others had lacerated tail-planes, gaping holes in the fuselages, wings tarnished by fire or glistening with black oil oozing from gutted engines.

Behind the formation were the stragglers, making for the coast, for the haven of refuge of an advanced air base on the other side of the Channel, flying only by a sublime effort of the will. You could imagine the blood pouring over the heaps of empty cartridges, the pilot nursing his remaining engines and anxiously eyeing the long white trail of petrol escaping from his riddled tanks. These isolated Fortresses were the Focke-Wulf's favourite prey. Therefore the squadrons detached two or three pairs of Spitfires, charged with bringing each one back safe: an exhausting task as these damaged Fortresses often dragged along on a third of their total power, stretching the endurance of their escort to the limit.

On this occasion Ken sent Carpenter and me to escort a

Liberator which was only in the air by a miracle. Its No Three engine had completely come out of its housing and hung on the leading edge, a mass of lifeless ironmongery. His No One engine was on fire, the flames slowly eating into the wing and the smoke escaping through the aluminium plates of the upper surface, buckled by the heat. Through the tears in the fuselage the survivors were throwing overboard all their superfluous equipment—machine guns, ammunition belts, radio, armour plates—to lighten their machine, which was slowly losing height.

To crown all, there was a burst in the hydraulic system, freeing one of the wheels of the undercart which hung down and increased the drag still further.

At 1,800 revs., minus two boost and 200 mph we had to zig-zag to keep level with him. We had been hunched up in our uncomfortable cockpits for two hours already, and we were still over France, twelve miles behind the main formation. Ten Focke-Wulfs began to prowl round us, at a respectful distance, as if suspecting a trap. Anxiously Carp and I kept an eye on them.

Suddenly they attacked, in pairs. Short of juice as we were, all we could do was to face each attack by a very tight 180° turn, fire a short burst in the approximate direction of the Hun, and immediately resume our position by another quick 180° turn. This performance was repeated a dozen times but we succeeded in making the Focke-Wulfs keep their distance. They eventually tired of it—or so we thought.

Over Dieppe the fighters gave way to the flak. We were flying at about 10,000 feet. The German light flak opened fire with unbelievable ferocity. An absolute pyramid of black puffs charged with lightning appeared in a fraction of a second. Violently shaken by several well-aimed shells, Carp and I separated and gained height as fast as we could with our meagre reserves of petrol. The poor Liberator, incapable of taking any sort of violent evasive action, was quickly bracketed. Just as, after a few agonising seconds, we thought it was out of range there was an explosion and the big bomber, cut in half, suddenly disappeared in a sheet of flame. Only three parachutes opened out. The blazing aluminium coffin crashed a few hundred yards from the cliffs in a shower of spray, dragging down the remaining members of the crew.

With heavy hearts we landed at Lympne, our tanks empty.

PIERRE CLOSTERMANN DSO DFC

*

The RAF had a well-deserved reputation for escaping captivity. This is the story of the biggest escape of all, led by perhaps the most famous escaper, Squadron-Leader Roger Bushell. He had been shot down during the Dunkirk evacuation and captured by the German army.

BIG X

The first place to which they took him was Dulag Luft, a transit camp for aircrew prisoners near Frankfurt. After a period of solitary confinement, Bushell made a survey of the camp. In the playing field, and just outside the compound wiring, there was a goat in a kennel. If a hole were dug in the floor of the kennel and a trapdoor fitted to support the goat, a man could remain concealed from the sentries and stay outside the compound as the prisoners returned from the playing field after exercise. The hole was dug by relays of prisoners hiding in the kennel one by one, the sand being taken away in vessels used for feeding the goat. If the guards had counted the number of times the goat was fed their suspicions would have been aroused, but they did not. Bushell planned to hide in the kennel on the evening before a separate tunnel escape involving a number of prisoners; to climb the single wire surrounding the sports field as soon as it was dark, and thus to confuse his pursuers with the twenty-four hours' start over the tunnellers.

On the prospect of staying in the kennel until dark, someone asked him, 'What about the smell?' and Bushell replied, 'Oh, the goat won't mind that.'

It was an easy matter to falsify the roll call, and he got away smoothly. With his fluency in German and experience of the winter sports areas he set course for Switzerland, travelling by day in a civilian suit bought from one of the guards at Dulag Luft. He was able to engage safely in brief conversations, and navigating with the aid of guide books purchased from shops along the way he went to Tuttlingen by express train, and from there to Bonndorf by suburban line. His plan to throw the Germans at Dulag Luft off the scent was entirely successful, for none of the eighteen men who escaped by tunnel got farther than Hanover before being arrested, by which time he had outdistanced the radius of search.

From Bonndorf Bushell reached on foot the point he was making for, a few kilometres from the Swiss border. Things had gone almost too well and, being aware of his habitual over-confidence, he sat down for two hours and made himself generate caution for the last decisive stage. He had the alternatives of waiting for nightfall, with all its problems, or of bluffing it out by daylight. He chose the letter.

In the border village of Stühlingen he was halted by a guard. Pretending to be a drunken but amiable ski-ing instructor, Bushell was being conducted towards a checkpoint for an examination of his papers when he broke loose and bolted, dodging bullets, into a side street. The side street proved to be a cul-de-sac and he was run to earth within a minute. The officer to whom he was taken turned out to be a German he had known in his ski-ing days, and Bushell ventured to suggest that for old time's sake he be set free with a ten minutes' start. For once his persuasive charm had no effect, meeting only with a stony, Teutonic refusal.

Bushell served a punitive sentence in a Frankfurt gaol, intended to soften his morale; but he was made of firmer stuff and on being moved to Barth, near the Baltic coast, he escaped again with a Polish officer.

The two men separated, and Bushell was stumbling along a road near the concentration camp at Auschwitz on a dark night when he blundered into a sentry he had not seen, knocking him to the ground. With an instinctive courtesy he helped the soldier to his feet, handed him his rifle and said, 'Sorry!' The game was up once again.

It was decided to move this troublesome officer to a new

camp, and he was herded into a cattle truck with several other prisoners and taken from Lübeck to Warburg. What pleasures awaited him there Bushell did not stay to see, and with five others prised open the truck's floorboards and dropped on to the track as the train was moving. One of the prisoners dropped on to the rail and lost both legs as a truck rolled over him.

With a Czech named Zafouk, Bushell reached Czechoslovakia where the Resistance boarded them with a courageous family in Prague. Bushell appreciated this limited freedom and would dress in civilian clothes and take daily walks around the city while waiting for the Resistance to complete arrangements for his transfer to Yugoslavia. But the assassination of the tyrant Heydrich activated a house-to-house search for students suspected of the crime. At the time, Bushell happened to be in a cinema with the daughter of the household where he was staying, and the audience was ordered to file out for a check on identity cards. As Bushell could not speak the language, his girl companion did the talking, but he was suspected and sent to a Gestapo prison in Berlin.

Bushell's cell was one of a number on either side of a corridor, and when they had locked his door and withdrawn he put his face to the grill and asked softly: 'Is anyone here British?' A voice four cells away in the direction of the latrines replied, 'Yes, Flight-Lieutenant Marshall, RAF.'

Marshall, who had known Bushell before the war, was also an escaper and had been captured in the same cinema and at the same time. Conversation between the two was restricted to furtive whisperings of a few seconds' duration whenever Bushell passed Marshall's cell. It took several days for Bushell to explain that he was refusing to admit his identity for fear of repercussions on the Prague family, which would be telling the same story as his. He was tormented by the thought of what would happen to them. One evening he whispered that he had left a note in the lavatory. When Marshall found it tucked behind the cistern it contained Bushell's service number, rank and full name. 'They are going to shoot me,' it stated; 'Please pass full particulars to the Red Cross.'

341

But Bushell learned that the Prague family had been executed and he admitted his identity. Until he did so he had consciously forfeited his right to protection by the Geneva Convention. Again a bona fide prisoner-of-war, he was sent to Stalag Luft III at the end of 1942, and it was here that he received his ultimatum: if he ever escaped again he would be shot.

Stalag Luft III, the large prison camp at Sagan, eighty miles east of Berlin, was a good camp and had only been opened the previous spring. The north compound to which Bushell was committed could almost have been a luxury camp; it held a thousand prisoners, was spacious and boasted private kitchens and washrooms with every barrack. There were excellent facilities for entertainment, and the commandant, Baron Von Lindeiner, hoped the British prisoners would enjoy their stay and even wish to remain in Germany after the war. His prisoners regretted that they had no desire to stay in Germany, war or no war, and bent their entire energies—diverted every useful item of food or material, subverted every sport or educational group, directed every imaginative talent—towards the predominant objective of escape.

The commandant and the senior British officer at Sagan both advised Bushell to take no further chances. 'I can't possibly stay here for long,' he replied; 'the winters are terrible.' But first he had a spell in 'The Cooler', the camp goal, to undergo.

'The Cooler' was so overcrowded with delinquent prisoners that those assigned to it had to wait their turn until a cell was available. When Bushell was called he again found himself a few cells away from Marshall, and while the guards were not paying much attention they resumed their discussion. Bushel was obsessed by the prospect of being mysteriously liquidated, or of the circumstances surrounding his death being mis-represented. He was less afraid of dying, though he cherished life, than of being shot in cold blood on a false pretext such as resisting arrest, a thing he was far too sensible to do. 'If anything goes wrong,' he told Marshall, 'you'll know what to think.' He gave Marshall names and addresses of people to be informed in such an event.

Upon his release from 'The Cooler' Bushell flung him-self with such intensity into the theory and practice of escape that, after playing minor roles in several escape bids, he rose rapidly through posts of ascending seniority in the Escape Organisation to Intelligence Officer, and finally to its top position—Chief Executive or 'Big X' of the North Compound. He studied case histories and learned from past mistakes; organised departments to take care of cloth-ing, forged documents, rations, logistics, engineering and security, presiding over his cabinet like a prime minister. His nimble brain cut through to essentials quickly. Three tunnels were to be constructed, and they were to be of such refinement that discovery of any one would lead to the belief that it must be the only one. To avoid danger of a security leak the word 'tunnel' was banned from all dis-cussion. They were to be called 'Tom', 'Dick' and 'Harry'.

As 'Big X' Bushell introduced a new and important con-cept—that of collectivism, the abandonment of unco-ordinated private enterprise and concentration on a highly efficient and centralised organisation. As a corollary, there were to be no more inflexible timetables, and if for any reason the guards' (or 'ferrets') suspicions were aroused, all work was to cease immediately and not to be resumed until the security department gave the all-clear.

New arrivals at the compound were always impressed by their first encounter with Bushell, when he grilled them on what they had seen of the local area. His rather sinister appearance, with the gash over one eye, his forceful per-sonality and well-developed powers of interrogation lent an awe-inspiring quality to the grim and clandestine sur-roundings of an improvised headquarters.

His intensity of purpose partially concealed a gentle-ness that was very real. 'Goon baiting'—playing practical jokes on the guards and undermining their morale—was an understood responsibility of the prisoner, not just a game. Despite his mastery of the art, Bushel sometimes expres-sed a compulsive remorse. 'It's not really fair,' he would say, 'some of these poor bastards are so simple they haven't a chance.'

343

'Tom' was discovered by sentries, and 'Dick' was then used solely as a repository for sand as work proceeded with 'Harry', now the only chance. Food and escape equipment was provided by the organisation for over two hundred escapers, considered the most optimistic estimate of the number which would get through the tunnel before it was discovered. If everything worked perfectly it would be possible for one man to go through every two minutes, making a total of two hundred and fifty during the eight hours of darkness. Long experience had taught, however, that there would always be hitches beyond the planners' control.

'Harry' was a miracle of planning and improvisation. With a length of 336 feet, 28 feet deep at the entrance in the north compound and 20 feet high at the exit among trees outside the double electrified wiring, it was furnished with electric lighting, manually operated air conditioning and relays of trolleys connecting three 'half-way houses' to carry prone escapers singly to the far end. 'Harry' had taken two hundred and fifty men working full time a year to dispose of the sand it displaced. A highly co-ordinated teamwork was devised to despatch the maximum number of men in the minimum time. Except for about forty priorities who were thought to have the best chance of reaching England, each man on the escape list got there by drawing from a hat. He had his belongings checked by the inspection committee to obviate jamming in the tunnel through the carrying of excessively bulky packages, was given an allotted time to arrive at Hut 104, which housed the entrance, and was thoroughly indoctrinated in his drill.

The organisation fixed the night of 24th March 1944 as the one for the break-out, twelve months after the commencement of work on 'Tom', 'Dick' and 'Harry'. Every known factor had been weighed: the weather would be suitable for travellers on foot ('walkers'); there would be no moon; a strong wind would disturb the adjacent pine forest and drown any sounds made by leaving the tunnel.

From mid-day the engineers finished off final details, connecting wiring and installing extra lights, while the forgery department filled in dates on the forged papers. A little after nine o'clock two engineers went to open the exit. Every man was in his place, and zero hour was nine-thirty. Then there occurred a train of mishaps: there was a delay in opening the shaft, and not until ten o'clock did those waiting down the shaft feel the gust of cool air which told them the surface had been broken. Word was then passed back that the exit, contrary to plan, was several yards short of the trees. As the papers were all date-stamped Bushell decided that the escape must continue, and hurriedly conferred with his colleagues on the escape commitee to work out a revised method of control at the exit, necessary to avoid detection by the guards in their look-out posts. As the escapers moved forward on their trollies, further delays were caused by those who had broken the baggage regulations and got stuck in the tunnel with the bulkiness of their suitcases. The rate of departure dropped from two to twelve minutes per man. To add to these complications, an unexpected air raid on Berlin caused the camp electricity to be switched off, and with it the tunnel lighting. Over half an hour was lost as margarine lamps were substituted.

Bushell was noticed to be calm but more thoughtful than usual. Dressed as a businessman he had teamed up with Lieutenant Scheidhauer of the Free French Air Force, with whom he planned to travel by train to Alsace. Both were on the priority list and were among the first to leave. As the delays multiplied Bushell, in smart civilian suit and con-verted service overcoat, with astrakhan collar and felt hat, an efficient-looking briefcase in his hand, glanced at his watch and called down the shaft: 'Tell those devils to get a move on; I've got a train to catch.'

Bushell and Scheidhauer caught their train at Sagan sta-tion. Two days later, during the most extensive search the Reich had ever been forced to mount for escaped prison-ers of war, they were recaptured at Saarbruecken railway station by security policemen and taken to Lerchesflur gaol. There they were interrogated by the Kriminal-polizei and admitted being escapers from Stalag Luft III.

When he learned of the escape, Hitler was incensed; he was angered at the tying-up of German resources in a time of great national stress and particularly afraid of an upris-

ing among the foreign workers. At a stormy meeting with
Goering, Himmler and Keitel, he gave instructions for the
prisoners to be shot.

On orders received by teleprinter from Gestapo headquarters in Berlin, Bushell and Scheidhauer were hand-
cuffed behind their backs and driven in a car along the
autobahn leading to Kaiserslauten. The car was stopped
after a few miles, the handcuffs removed, and the prisoners
allowed to get out and relieve themselves. They must have
known what was coming. Both were shot in the back,
Scheidhauer dying instantly, Bushell after a few minutes.
It was 28th March 1944.

TOM MOULSON

*Seventy-six prisoners got out through 'Harry': three reached
Britain. Of the remainder, all recaptured, fifty were executed. It is only fair to say that the Luftwaffe had nothing
to do with this.*

*

DER TAG

As D-day approached the tension increased. There was a
day of panic when a member of the Air Ministry staff—
having received the final list of times, dates and places of
landing—decided that he had better keep it on his person
rather than lock it in his office. Somehow or other he managed to drop the precious document, labelled in large letters 'Top Secret', in the road as he was on his way to his
quarters. A young airman, walking with his mum, spotted
the paper, picked it up and, immediately seized with its importance, hailed a passing taxi, bundled Mum inside and
shouted to the driver, 'The Air Ministry.' Here he demanded to see the Chief of the Air Staff. Rather naturally,
the doorkeeper refused him admittance. Frantic with im-
patience, he was about to commit assault on the doorman
when an officer, hearing the row and given a short outline
of the affair, passed the boy on to the 'Holy of Holies'. The
CAS wasted no time. The airman and his mum were whipped off into confinement, where they were held incommuni-

cado until the landing had taken place. Mum was very angry, particularly over the matter of Dad's meals and general welfare. The boy was shocked, but understood the reason. The Air Ministry official received very severe punishment.

Air Chief Marshal Sir PHILIP JOUBERT KCB CMG DSO

*

Preparations for the Big Day took many forms. For the dam-busting 617 Squadron, now commanded by Leonard Cheshire, it was an odd build-up to an odd task:

THE HOAXERS

Cochrane sent for Cheshire and took him walking in the grounds of headquarters away from listening ears.

'You'll be doing no more operations for a month,' he said, 'and then you'll be doing a very special one. You'll spend the next month training for it. I warn you now it's going to be dull training, but it may be the most important job you've done. You will have to fly more accurately and carefully than you've ever imagined.'

He would say no more, but next day a scientist, Dr. Cockburn, arrived at Woodhall from London and also took Cheshire walking. They lay alone on the grass by the airfield, obviously for privacy, and the imaginative Cheshire was highly intrigued by the 'cloak and dagger' atmosphere. Cockburn said: 'I understand you can be trusted to keep your mouth shut, so I'm going to tell you something a lot of Cabinet Ministers and generals don't know yet. You know by now an invasion is coming off very soon. If the weather is right it will be in about a month, and landings will be made west of Le Havre. We want to fool the Germans we're going in somewhere else.'

Cheshire waited.

'On that night,' Cockburn went on, 'there's going to be a big convoy fourteen miles wide passing across the Channel at seven knots.'

'Sounds a pretty big invasion,' Cheshire said.

'That isn't the invasion. They'll be heading towards Cap d'Antifer, on the other side of Le Havre.'

'A diversion!'

'Yes.'

'I must say,' Cheshire said, 'it sounds a pretty big diversion. Have they got all those ships to spare?'

'No. They won't be ships. They'll be you and your boys.'

Cheshire rolled over and looked at him. 'Us!' he said blankly and then got the glimmerings of an idea. 'Dropping window?'

'That's it,' said Cockburn. 'It's going to need the most precise flying you've ever done. Can you do this . . . can you all fly in a very wide formation, invisible to each other, and do a lot of intricate manœuvring, keeping within three seconds of all your e.t.a.'s and within twenty feet of your height?'

'My God! I don't know. Doesn't sound very possible.'

'It'll have to go on for hours and hours,' Cockburn said, 'so you'll do it in two waves. Eight aircraft for a few hours and then the second eight taking over from them.' He went on to explain the technique: lines of aircraft a set distance apart, flying precise courses at precise speeds and height, throwing out window at intervals of a precise number of seconds. The planes would fly thirty-five seconds on course, turn evenly, fly a reverse course for thirty-two seconds, a slow turn again back to the first course and start throwing out more window. They would thus start the original course again at a point slightly ahead of where the previous one started and the first of the new lot of window would drop from the aircraft at the moment that the first bundle dropped on the previous leg hit the water, so there would be no interruption of the steady blips on German radar. It would go on like that for eight hours, timed to give an effect of a large convoy several rows of ships deep moving at seven knots towards the French coast.

'We've got the theory worked out,' Cockburn said at the end. 'Are you good enough to do it?'

Cheshire said, 'I think my crews are good enough for anything, but I don't think they're going to be happy doing a stooge job on invasion night.'

'It so happens,' Cockburn said, 'that there'll be no flying

job more important than this on that night. You might tell them that. The fact that they may not be fired at is beside the point.'

The training never let up except for one day when the weather closed in. Otherwise there was no moment, night or day, in the next month when some 617 aircraft were not flying, particularly by night, cruising at a steady 200 mph on a steady course and height, curving in even turns to reverse courses, turning back on the stop watch, unspectacular, tedious and demanding meticulous car and skill. Understandably the crews, with the uninhibited sap of youth running in them, became restless, and Cheshire, bubbling as ever with ideas, evolved schemes to occupy them. The first was a route march that left them limp and protesting.

Next, from the Commandos, he got the idea of an escape exercise so that, if they were ever shot down and got away with their lives, they would have a few clues about getting back through hostile territory. It was a Sunday afternoon when he lined up all the crews who were not flying, took away their hats and all their money, packed them in covered vans so they could not see outside and drove them to different spots twenty miles from the airfield. He warned them that the Home Guard and police had turned out with orders to nab any airmen without hats, and promised every one who got back safely a bottle of beer. So the game started.

Some cut across the fields to walk, some stole bikes to pedal, some hitched lifts in lorries. The police and Home Guard nailed at least half of them and there were some thrilling chases across country. One man, running from the Home Guard, fell into a canal; another, caught by a policeman, entered a little too warmly into the spirit of the thing and laid the constable out with a sizzling punch. After that the police entered more warmly into the spirit of things too, and locked six of them up for the night.

Only Nicky Knilans and his team had the best idea; they hitched a lift to the White Horse pub, where they were known to the point of affectionate notoriety, borrowed money from the publican and drank ale till closing time, whereupon they borrowed their bus fare home. Police stopped the bus, so they jumped off the back, took to the woods and straggled home hours later to demand their prize beer.

With only monotonous training instead of ops at night the tension had relaxed and the mess became almost a home from home. Cheshire's ex-film-star wife, Constance Binney, was a cheerful influence; she played the piano beautifully, and after dinner the crews clustered round and sang.

Several dogs haunted the mess, and one Scottie used to jump out from dark doorways and snap at passing ankles. It became a favourite trick among the boys to imitate the Scottie. Nicky Knilans saw McCarthy coming up the stairs one day, so he got down on his knees in a dark doorway and waited. He heard the footsteps clumping along the hall and as the legs appeared leapt out with a growl and grabbed the nearest ankle in his teeth, looked up with a grin . . . and the grin faded. McCarthy had turned off into a room and Knilans saw a strange wing commander looking down at him blankly. The wing commander shook his head and walked on, all his views on Americans fully confirmed.

They all sensed the invasion was drawing near; Cheshire had the idea that the Germans might drop paratroops on British airfields on D-Day, so he persuaded Doc Watson's armament section to issue as many aircrew as they could with either a revolver, Sten gun, rifle or hand grenade. It was one of his few sad mistakes. For three days life was a precarious possession at Woodhall. First they set dinner plates up on the lawn near the mess and loosed off at them with Sten guns from the second-floor windows. That palled after a while, so they started lobbing hand grenades in the general direction of the sergeants' mess. At night time Buckley became a terrible menace, keeping a vigil by his bedroom window and loosing off clips from his Sten gun over the heads of late home-comers so that they had to crawl to bed over the back lawn on their bellies.

Even Witherick, who was known to be too durable for death by any of the known methods of war, commented uncomfortably, 'Hell, the only time you're safe on this damn squadron is when you've in the air! It became obvious that German paratroops were less of a menace than the local aircrew army, so Cheshire collected all the weapons and returned them to the armoury. Peace descended once more on the mess, to the regret of Shannon and McCarthy. Shannon and McCarthy were rarely seen apart; they drank together and dined together and it was logical, therefore, that they should act together to revive the reign of terror, climbing to the roof of squadron headquarters to drop a Very cartridge down the adjutant's chimney. They knew the innocent Humphries had a fire in the grate.

A Very cartridge in artful hands is like a semi-lethal firework; exploding in a confined space it resembles a small but concentrated bombing raid, providing a monstrous crash, sheets of coloured flame and clouds of choking smoke. Half the beauty of the thing is that it goes on for about fifteen seconds. They dropped it down the chimney and started laughing as the waves of sound came rocking up from below.

Unfortunately it was not Humphries' chimney, but the commanding officer's. Cheshire scuttled out, pursued by flashes and rolling fumes, ran on to the tarmac and spotted his two flight commanders hiding behind a chimney. With aristocratic dignity he said nothing, but for several nights Shannon and McCarthy found themselves doing duty officer together, an irksome task which kept them out of their beds and abstentiously patrolling the station buildings.

Throwing Very cartridges into the mess fire had long been a favourite sport, so Cheshire thought it time to issue a stern order that no firearms, cartridges or pyrotechnics of any kind be brought into the mess building.

He was woken that night by a scuttling outside his window, threw it wide open and saw a rat running across the roof. Quick as lightning he grabbed his own .38 revolver from his dressing-table and took a pot-shot that bowled the rat over and echoed through the quiet night like a small cannon. Cheshire was still leaning out of his window, revolver in hand, when the next window shot open and the head of Danny Walker poked out. 'Got the dirty rat that time,' Cheshire said triumphantly and became conscious of

Walker's eyes staring coldly, focusing on the hand that held the gun. He felt his face going red and ducked inside, laying the pistol down, and heard Walker's voice next door, talking loudly to a mythical room-mate, 'But I tell you, old boy, I distinctly heard the man say that no one under any circumstances was to have a firearm inside the mess.'

PAUL BRICKHILL

617 carried out the task, which was as dull as they had expected and as accurate as their commanders had demanded. The 'convoy' they—together with Stirlings from 218 Squadron—represented was attacked by German E-boats and coastal-defence artillery. And a lot of German soldiers stayed east of the Seine until it was too late.

*

D-Day in fact turned out to be almost equally dull for the rest of the RAF. The Luftwaffe had few fighters left in France; Allied air supremacy was almost total. But the invasion made little difference to the pattern of operations —except that the flak gunners of Royal and American Navies contributed an additional hazard. A theoretically tour-expired air gunner in 2nd TAF describes his last operation:

PUBLICITY TRIP

That night I got so full I didn't remember going to bed. Strangely enough I wasn't elated over the completion of my flying term. I puzzled this one out till I realised it was the sixty-four ops that was the focal point; sixty-five ops was the norm for three tours. It was like scoring ninety-nine runs in a Test and retiring, or getting to match point in a tennis match and giving up. I felt I would never be able to say truthfully I had completed three tours.

His crew were to take three journalists—two English and one Dutch—on a special night flight, the intention being that they would give the public an article on TAF's doings. Would I fly with them as tail gunner? Bill was highly ex-

352

cited over this chance for some free publicity. However, they wanted a properly trained tail-end Charley and I was the only one on the station who fitted the bill.

I said I'd think it over. At mid-day I hit myself with a few sherbets. They were enough to tilt the scales; when he and his pilot came across I said 'Yes'.

Special intercom connections were to be put in for our visitors so they could listen in to our discussions. At briefing, I found we were to carry an extra navigator as the standard one was to be fully engrossed with OBOE. Four extra bods was a helluva lot. I sincerely hoped we didn't have to get out in a hurry or someone was sure to be killed in the rush.

Five planes were briefed for a bash on a railway junction. In addition to OBOE, two Mosquitoes were to drop markers on the target five minutes before we went in, thus ensuring 100 per cent success—and good publicity!

The journalists didn't seem over happy with their assignment. One, a sombre-looking character, asked me had I had much experience. I told him this would be my sixty-fifth op. 'I suppose,' he said with a nervous laugh, 'we can expect some flak and fighter opposition.'

'You can certainly expect fighters,' I replied. 'The place is lousy with them. Flak's generally of minor consequence.' I asked, 'Have you done much flying?'

'Oh, yes, I did a couple of trips to Paris before the war.'

'How about your cobbers?'

'The Dutchman has flown quite a bit but Tom,' indicating a fair-haired, stoutish character, 'has never been up in a plane before.'

'Have they shown you how to hook on a parachute?' I asked.

'We've got the harness and all that. You don't think we'll be needing it, do you?'

Our pilot was like a cat with two tails. He sprouted false heartiness. He was already reading the headlines in the newspapers. I recalled my first impression of him as a gong hunter and hoped he wasn't going to put on any special acts for his passengers. I found before we took off that our extra navigator was a complete sprog on his first op but thought that OBOE plus the Mossie markers would offset him.

Because twilight held till close on 11.30 pm we took off at 11 pm, the idea being that by the time we hit the enemy coast it would be dark. A solid bank of cloud extended from 1,200 feet to 21,000 feet so we flew just below it. As we progressed, the wonderful panorama of sea might the Allies had gathered for this greatest sea invasion of all time unfolded itself. Under cover of darkness this great concourse of ships was ferrying reinforcement, ammunition and supplies to extend the slender foothold they had gained. They sailed in groups of approximately fifty vessels and stretched as far as the eye could see in almost every direction.

We were about one-third of the way across and were passing over one of these convoys when the first tracer spiralled up towards us. I reported, 'Flak from ships dead below.'

The pilot said, 'Fire the colours of the day smartly, second navigator.'

The skipper said, 'We're coming up on to another group. who, even though we were out of range, continued to reach for us with their fiery fingers.

The skipper said, 'We're coming up on to another group Be ready with the colours, navigator.'

As we passed, this mob, taking their cue from the other, let us have it. It was bloody hot.

The pilot said savagely, 'Have you fired those colours, navigator?' Over the intercom a timid voice said, 'I forgot to bring them, sir.'

There was a silence while the pilot threw the plane into some smart evasive action. As we passed out of range he said sarcastically, 'I suppose you forgot your parachute, too.'

There was momentary silence and the timid voice replied, 'Yes, sir.'

I reckon this was one of the smartest crossings of the Channel on record for a Mitchell, every time we got anywhere near one of these groups we copped the lot. Sometimes, in trying to miss one we would end up between two fires. There were some unprintable things said about navy escorts that night.

As a result of these upsets we hit the enemy coast ten minutes earlier than we should have, not a pleasant thought. It meant we'd be stooging around in dangerous skies for that extra period.

We skirted the narrow perimeter of the battlefield. It was alight with the eerie glow of battle as two mighty armies tried to grind each other into the ground. Out at sea great flashes showed the presence of battleships pouring in their contribution to this upheaval of fire and steel.

It had been decided should anything go wrong with the Mosquito arrangements we would bomb on OBOE. The navigator soon reported a sustained and effective jamming and that he was unable to get anything.

Simultaneously, at 5 o'clock at about 400 yards I saw a Ju 88. It was banking gracefully. The pale moonlight glinted on its wings. I reported immediately and said, 'I don't think he's seen us.' Bill said, 'I can see him, Johnny.'

The pilot said, 'Give him the works, gunners.'

I thought I was hearing things and said, 'Don't fire at him, Bill, he's moving off.' It was a commonsense rule that you didn't reveal your presence to a fighter. If he didn't want to have a go you left him severely alone.

A few minutes later we had our hands full. A single-engined fighter flashed by us and came around in a neatly executed curve of pursuit. I'll say this for our pilot, he could fly. He beat two smart passes then skipped into the clouds. When we came out a few minutes later for a look-see he was gone, but in the confusion of pursuit we were flying west, into the incoming aircraft stream. I heard a startled squeak from someone and a great black four-engined bomber flashed past feet above us. We rocked in its wash as it disappeared into the night. It couldn't have been closer.

The pilot asked the No 1 navigator if he had picked up anything. He reported continued jamming. He asked the second nav for a course, but, because of our gyrations, he was completely lost and admitted it. The pilot had a few uncomplimentary things to say, but it wasn't the sprog's fault. Better and more experienced observers than he would have lost themselves in these circumstances.

After a period the OBOE operator said he had a signal and considered we should be in the target area. The time was right for the markers, but where the hell were the Mossies? We stooged around waiting for the markers to give as an indication. It later turned out they didn't show up. I could feel the note of frustration in the pilot's voice. Here he had everything lined up for a perfect line-shoot, and everything seemed to be going wrong.

We had come down to 500 feet in an endeavour to locate our target. Then Bill announced a line of twelve vehicles at 3 o'clock. In the dim light it was impossible to see what they were, but even at a distance of 600 yards they looked big enough. We did a circuit and the pilot said, 'Let's beat them up.'

It didn't make sense to me. We hadn't reached our objective, still had a full bomb-load, and here he was talking about attacking another target. Besides, this was my last op. I put my spoke in and said, 'I wouldn't advise it, sir. We haven't bombed yet.'

He said, 'Are you afraid, Beede?'

I replied, 'No sir, but commonsense dictates we bomb and get back by the shortest and quickest route.'

He said, 'Prepare plane for action, we're going to attack line of vehicles at 9 o'clock.' We came down to 200 feet. He said, 'Let them have it.'

I'll never know what those things were, but for every shot we threw at them they threw fifty back at us. We seemed to be completely enveloped in tracer. Boy, was it a surprise packet. We broke that engagement smartly and I felt like saying, 'Serves you right, you know-all bastard.'

Time was running out. Our bombing time had passed. The pilot said, 'We'll have to find a secondary target.' We stooged around and finally laid our eggs on a road junction.

OBOE was still on the blink so he asked the second nav for a course home. He gave one with a complete lack of confidence. The pilot said, 'We'll fly under the clouds, let's hope we don't strike too many fighters.' Bill spotted the Ju 88 as it whirled around us and came in from 7 o'clock. He was a persistent cuss. He made four attacks before we lost him by seeking cloud cover.

The pilot said, 'I'll stick in here for a while. Give me a course, navigator.' He gave one by guess or by God. After a while the pilot said, 'I'm coming out. See if you can get me a pin-point.'

We got it all right, a forest of searchlights and a hail of flak. We were bang over Dunkirk, an unhealthy spot at the best of times, but doubly so at this moment. The skipper showed commendable tactical sense and put the plane into an almost vertical dive and we crossed the sea front at less than 100 feet. Luckily it was mostly heavy stuff, which, unable to range, burst above us. The cones of searchlights could not hold the swift-moving target. A flak ship anchored off shore gave us a pasting in the short time we were in its vicinity and I felt the plane shudder as 20 mm cannon shells struck.

As soon as we were clear of this pest the pilot called for a report from all crew members. The only one that didn't answer was Bill. He called him twice and then said, 'You had better check the mid-upper turret, rear gunner, and if the gunner is incapacitated, take over.' I felt like questioning the wisdom of this move. If Bill had had it, it meant the plane would be defenceless while I made the transfer from rear to mid-upper. On the other hand, I realised he could be hit, bleeding to death. The journalists, if they were alive, could come in handy here.

I came out of my rat hole backwards. My feeling was one of urgency. The transfer was made more difficult by the pilot, once he had cleared the flak ship, climbing steeply to cloud base. This, in view of our reception coming across, was a wise move.

What I did not know was that the mid-upper in the wild dive to sea level had pulled out his intercom plug. Just after I started my retreat along the pitch-black tail he rectified this and reported himself as being right. It was just as well he was because I had almost reached the turret when a fighter, either attracted by the Dunkirk Commotion or called by the defence, attacked viciously from 7 o'clock. The pilot, in answer to the mid-upper's evasive order, threw the plane into a sharp diving turn to left. The first intimation I had was that the plane seemed to fall away from beneath me. I had a momentary feeling I was

357

falling and then collided with a bone-shattering bang against something very solid.

The journalists told me afterwards I had collided with a flare chute and was knocked cold for twenty minutes. In that period we shook off the attacker, and, free of Nazi jamming, the navigator had set a course for home. I came to with my head propped on a parachute.

Not being plugged in, I still didn't know the score. All I could remember was the urgency of my mission. I could dimly discern the bulk of the turret above, so climbed up and tentatively pulled at a leg that was hanging down, and nearly had my teeth knocked down my throat for my pains. Bill was obviously not only alive but kicking. Although I wasn't feeling like it, I climbed back to my hole and reported in.

The pilot said, 'Where have you been, rear gunner?' even though one of the passengers had reported my accident.

I said 'I'd like to ruddy well know myself.'

We landed without incident. The kite had half a dozen whopping holes in it and innumerable small ones. How the hell someone wasn't killed or seriously wounded I'll never know. This, I knew, was the end of my flying.

The journalists' reaction to the pilot's efforts was the opposite to what he expected. By unanimous consent they declared he was bloody well mad. The article eulogising our flight was never published.

JOHN BEEDE

*

Allied fighters had been landing in Normandy from less than three days after the invasion. On 11th June, the first French pilots in the RAF returned to

A NIGHT OUT IN FRANCE

11th June 1944

We were on 'readiness' after tea when suddenly we were informed that we were going to spend the night in France.

The 'Met' forecasted fog over the south coast for the next morning, which would immobilise the fighters. On the other hand the weather over France would be reasonable and clearly, if the Spits did not patrol the beach-head, the Luftwaffe would come out in strength over Normandy and make a nuisance of itself.

To avoid this, half a dozen squadrons were to take off that very evening, land as best they could on half-finished emergency fields, spend the night there, and be ready at dawn for any eventuality. Each pilot must take two blankets and a box of K rations.

Jacques and I were distinctly excited at the idea of being the first French pilots to land in France. We decided to don our full regalia and Jacques took his flask of brandy to celebrate the occasion suitably.

A dash for the billets on our motor-cycles. We took off at 1830 hours and, after a normal patrol—nothing out of he ordinary to report—we met over Brazenville.

'Hallo, Yellow Three and Four; Hallo, Blue Three, you pancake first. Good luck!'

Sutherland was telling us the Captain, Jacques, and me, to land first. Very decent of him.

Jacques and I, in close formation, landed just behind the Captain in an impenetrable cloud of dust. Christ, what dust! It was white and as fine as flour. Stirred up by the slipstream of the propellers it infiltrated everywhere, darkened the sky, suffocated us, found its way into our eyes and ears. We sank in up to our ankles. For 500 yards round the landing strip all traces of green had disappeared—every growing thing was covered by a thick layer, stirred by the slightest breeze.

Two commandos whose eyes only were visible under a crust of dust and sweat. with Tommy-guns slung on their backs, helped me to jump down from my plane and laughed when they recognised my uniform.

'Well, Frenchie, you're welcome to your blasted country!'

Jacques emerged out of a cloud, a handkerchief over his face, and we shook hands—a moving moment all the same. We were treading French soil after four years' absence.

If the truth must be told, instead of the deep emotion I was expecting, what I felt most was profound regret at having brought my smart new 'best blue' uniform to such

359

a dump. Already I looked much more like a powdered circus clown than an officer of the Armée de l'Air!

A Captain from the Canadian division stopped in his jeep on his way past to warn us:

'No straying from the airfield. No crossing from one side of the track to the other. Don't touch anything. Avoid areas marked by cloth strips, they are still mined. The Huns have left mines everywhere and only half an hour ago a man was killed and two others wounded by a German sniper hiding in a wood half a mile away who has got telescopic sights.'

We all met again behind a hedge where a mobile canteen gave us tea, biscuits, and marmalade (all liberally sprinkled with that blasted dust).

Our strip was absolutely stiff with ack-ack—at least a dozen Bofors on the alert with the crews in position. When we expressed astonishment at the enormous quantity of empties round the guns a sergeant told us that if we waited until eleven o'clock that night, we would soon understand.

We spent the next two hours dispersing our planes and refuelling them with two-gallon cans; we puffed, we sweated, we coughed. I spent my time bemoaning my uniform's fate. When night began to fall we opened our rations, had a slice of ham and a few biscuits, then set off in search of a hole to spend the night in. Cautiously ferreting round in the orchard next door Jacques and I discovered a tent full of chairs, tables, coco-nut matting, and large boards covered with maps. After a bit of re-arranging we succeeded in dossing down with our blankets in reasonable comfort.

2230 hours. It was now quite dark. Jacques and I went off to have a smoke and a chat with two Canadian officers. A few stars were shining. To the south-east we could see the glow of Caen burning. All was quiet. Suddenly we heard the hum of an aircraft in the sky.

'Hallo,' I said, 'That's odd. It sounds like a twin-engine, but it certainly isn't a Mosquito.'

We looked up, trying to locate the sound. It seemed almost immediately above us.

'Don't worry, Pierre,' said Jacques after a moment's

360

thought, 'if it was a Hun the ack-ack would already have opened fire.'

He had scarcely finished when a characteristic swishing sound disclosed the fact that a large bomb was coming straight down on us. In a fraction of a second the two officers evaporated. I dived under a lorry and Jacques, trying to follow me, tripped over an apple-tree root and fell flat on his face. There was a terrific crash. The earth quivered, a burning gust of air slapped our faces and glowing splinters bespattered the tent, the trees, and the lorry and bounced back sizzling on the dew-covered grass.

At that moment the ack-ack opened fire. The sky above us turned into a moving mass of 40 mm tracer shells rising in thick snaky clusters. It was as light as day. Our heads buzzed from the continuous roar. Shell fragments fell as thick as hail, bringing down branches and leaves from the trees, riddling the tents, and clanging on the lorries and empty drums. Somewhere on the field a Spit caught fire and the flames brought the Junkers 88s clustering round like moths.

The bombs began to fall thick and fast. You could tell them apart by the sound—the big thousand-pounders went 'Frrrooommm' as they fell, while the medium ones whistled 'Phweephweephweeeee—Bang!' One fell so close that the impact threw me in the air and I gave myself a large bump against the lorry's differential. A Bofors, less than ten yards away, was blazing away all the time in bursts of five shells. The barking noise pierced our ear-drums. Deafened, battered, we crouched under our lorry, shivering with funk.

Round about 1 am there seemed to be a lull. I sprinted across to our tent to fetch our blankets. I managed to find them under a pile of big boxes and boards, which had collapsed when the first bomb had gone off. If we had been there, we should have had all that down on our heads.

When I got back Jacques had crawled out and was dusting himself and swearing.

Suddenly a pyramid of tracer rose from Arromanches, where the convoys were concentrated, and, like a gas ring with jets lighting up in succession, the whole sky again flared up. The searchlights leaped out of the shadows and started probing the clouds.

Within a radius of twelve miles from our strip there must have been a good three thousand ack-ack guns. As the radar equipment was primitive and control non-existent, all those guns—Bofors, 3-inch, 7-inch etc.—fired away more or less haphazard, all at once. The ammunition seemed inexhaustible and the crews just kept their feet on the pedal.

The Junkers 88s and Dornier 217s came over in groups of about a dozen every five minutes or so and stooged around in the middle of this inferno, letting go their bombs more or less anywhere. It didn't really matter where, as the beach-head was so full of troops, ammunition dumps, convoys of lorries, concentration of tanks and planes that they could scarcely fail to score a bull practically every time.

The nightmare went on until 3 am. Worn out, petrified with cold, we ended up by going to sleep, only to be awakened an hour later by the stand-to siren. We emerged from our lorry haggard, grimy, dusty, hirsute, with rings round our eyes and coated tongues and—we nearly passed out from the shock—we had spent the night under a lorry-load of 20 mm shells!

Scarcely able to breathe, we staggered off to join our comrades (who were in no better shape) round the field kitchen where we queued up for a drop of tea. It took a long time as there were only five mugs, the tea was scalding, and there were twenty-four of us. Our two Canadian friends from the evening before were there—we thought they had been pulverised by the explosion.

'Oh, you know,' said one of them modestly, 'we are now pretty hot at sprinting. We've been here a week and we're unbeatable!'

Just at that moment we heard the noise of several engines approaching. Everyone climbed the bank round the perimeter to get a better view. Bang! bang! bang! bang! Three Focke-Wulfs jumped the hedge at the other end of the field and opened fire.

I remembered hearing a few bullets whistling past, a few shells explode in front of us on the field, raising spurts of dust, and suddenly we found ourselves in the shelter, a good length ahead of the Canadians, in an avalanche of pilots, mugs, tea, biscuits, and flying boots, after all that we didn't even have our cup of tea!

We went back to Ford in time for lunch—minus four aircraft destroyed or damaged during the bombing. We spent two hours sitting under a nice hot shower.

PIERRE CLOSTERMANN DSO DFC

*

Already established 'over there' was 'Johnnie' Johnson's wing of Canadian-piloted Spitfires. They set up their own

SUPPLY ROUTE

Our mess was located in a large tent on one side of the orchard. We lived exclusively on the tinned compo rations, and soon became bored with this monotonous but adequate diet. The Canadians deplored the absence of fresh meat, milk and fruit juices, and wanted good fresh bread instead of the hard biscuits. Each day a twin-engined Anson landed at St Croix from Tangmere carrying mail, newspapers and urgently required small spares. I sat down in my caravan to write a note to Arthur King back at the 'Unicorn' in Chichester. I told him of the dreariness of our food and asked him if he could arrange to deliver to Tangmere a supply of fresh vegetables together with bread and perhaps some meat. If he could get this stuff to Tangmere, the pilot of the Anson would do the rest and we should be very grateful.

The following day the Anson turned up with a crate of tomatoes, loaves of new bread, fresh succulent lobsters together with a reasonable supply of stout. Arthur maintained this private supply organisation until we moved out of the narrow confines of the beach-head area and we were able to purchase what we considered to be the necessities of life from local sources. One day a small party of press correspondents came to see the wing and I invited them to stay for lunch. They were somewhat reluctant to accept my offer as they had considered driving to Bayeux, where a reasonable meal could be obtained. However, they took a keen interest in the proceedings when the lobsters and local wine were set before them. Naturally, they enquired as to our arrangements for the supply of such essentials and I told them of our base organisation in Sussex which centred upon Arthur King.

Some few days later, the story was published in one of the national newspapers. It had an amusing sequel, since Arthur was invited by a representative of His Majesty's Customs and Excise, who solemnly told him that an export licence would be necessary if he persisted in this sort of thing!

Since its introduction to the Service in 1939, the versatile Spitfire had participated in many diverse roles and had fought over a variety of battle-grounds. It had appeared as a fighter, a fighter-bomber and as a tactical reconnaissance and photographic reconnaissance aircraft. Now it fulfilled yet another role, perhaps not so vital as some of the tasks it had undertaken in the past, but to us of supreme importance. Back in England, some ingenious mind had modified the bomb racks slung under each wing so that a small barrel of beer could be carried instead of a 500-pound bomb. Daily, this modern version of the brewers' dray flew across the Channel and alighted at St Croix. The beer suffered no ill effects from its unorthodox journey and was more than welcome in our mess.

Group Captain J. E. JOHNSON DSO DFC

*

But barely a week after D-Day, the Germans struck back with

VERGELTUNGSWAFFE EINS

For in the early hours of the morning of the 13th a newcomer appeared on the scene. It was a quarter past four and the clouded sky was turning from black to grey when the commander of a Mosquito Wing stood talking to his Chief Operations Officer on the aerodrome at Gravesend. They were very weary. All night their aircraft had ranged over Normandy, among the silent villages and above the roads littered with wreckage. As they walked towards their tents they heard an odd noise in the eastern sky, like a motor-cycle running under water. Almost before they had picked out the crude cruciform shape and the bright light at its tail they knew what it was, for they had hunted its lairs for months past. They watched it as it flew straight over their heads and bustled on towards London. It had hardly passed when there was a sudden silence, then a pause followed by a reverberating explosion. They stood and looked at the billowing cloud of smoke that showed faintly in the sky towards the river.

At last the Operations Officer spoke. 'From now on,' he said thoughtfully, 'nations will have to learn to be very polite to one another.'

Air Marshal PETER WYKEHAM KCB DSO DFC AFC

Alas, an optimistic view.

*

BRIGHT IDEAS MARK IV

'Night after night we are robbed of our sleep,' began a correspondent from Kent. 'It is in your power to destroy these fiendish machines!!!' 'Re Flying Bombs,' wrote another from Tunbridge Wells: 'It is a mystery to many of us that the authorities, *with all their resources,* cannot keep us from this *continual attack.* It is a pity that *many of our men, shot down abroad,* are not here to protect lives and *property.'*

Ideas put forward included tethered Zeppelins firing harpoons, bolas launched from aeroplanes, huge butterfly nets, 'weapons' filled with carbolic acid, clouds of gas, and a variety of airborne hooks and grapples. One letter offered to put a curse on the launching crews, and in another (forwarded by Sir Hugh Dowding) a lady medium suggested that she detect the sites by means of an 'out-of-body experience'. Various reprisals were suggested.

This correspondence grew to a size where Hill was obliged to employ a wholetime staff officer to deal with it.

But he saw and acknowledged every serious letter; a formal reply being sent to the merely crazy, a conciliatory answer to the anxious, and an appreciation to any letter that seemed helpful, or that carried a suggestion, as some did, that was well worth following up. In the latter category was a correspondent who carefully analysed the behaviour of the bombs in a series of tabulated stages of reasoning, each step being logical and leading to the next. He concluded that the gun belt should be removed and that greater scope should be given to the fighters. Those members of the Command staff who thought the same were heartened by the reinforcement of this well-reasoned study, but they were cast down again when it was pointed out to them that the writing paper was headed 'Kent County Mental Hospital' and surcharged by a rubber stamp with the words 'The Medical Superintendent accepts no responsibility for the contents of this letter'.

Air Marshal PETER WYKEHAM KCB DSO OBE DFC AFC

*

In the end, it was a careful re-arrangement—though not quite on these lines—of fighter and gun 'zones' that brought flying-bomb interceptions to above 80 per cent. The only day fighter that could comfortably outpace a V1 was the new Hawker Tempest, a high-speed derivative of the Typhoon. It was rushed into service—again, before all the development work had been completed. Part of the rushing was done by women pilots of the Air Transport Auxiliary.

STORM IN A TEMPEST

Diana had taken off in her Tempest and was cruising along happily at the desired speed of 300 mph. She sang as she went because she had struck a patch of better visibility than she'd expected, and it was all very pleasant streaking along through the air in that light, sensitive machine. Suddenly there was a bang that shook and rocked the plane and when she had recovered she found herself covered with a shower of metal. 'Engine blown up' registered in her mind and instantly, almost without knowing that she did it, she throttled back and put her nose down to sustain her flying speed. 'Somewhere to land' was the next flash and she began to look this way and that for a large field. She knew she must land pretty quickly because an engine that had seized could, because of the repercussion inside it, explode and blaze at any moment. All this took in reality only a second or two and as she saw a field that she thought she could get down in, wheels of up of course, she registered again that the engine seemed to be ticking over quite happily, and then suddenly she was conscious of a draught round her feet, and looking down saw that the floor was no longer there and instead were the exposed wire of the various instruments, and below that a jagged gap through which she could just see the chequered, distant earth. Her map had been torn from her hand with the blast and was now spread-eagled above her head on the glass hood, kept there by the rush of air. She wasn't at all sure that she was very much better pleased with the gaping hole than she would have been with a seized engine, because she knew it would alter the flying attributes of the aircraft considerably. She decided to fly up to a safer height and try a stall or two and see how the stalling speed differed from the normal. When she did she found that she stalled at 180 mph instead of the normal 110 and she realised that she'd never be able to land at that speed, nor put her flaps down to aid her.

She was very near Kenley now and she did a dummy run low over the aerodrome. They probably thought she was just beating it up as she went over so fast and so they gave her a red light and she went away again, up, up high into the air once more to practise and see what she could do at this high speed. Eventually, after more manœuvres, she decided to try to land the thing. She did a few circuits round the airfield, then flew over it again to give them an indication that all might not be well and as she began her approach she realised she had got their interest and that a group had collected and the fire-tender was standing by. She still seemed to be coming in at a roaring speed, and then as her wheels touched the earth she began instantly to apply a touch of brake, not much or she'd whip over on to her nose, then more, and eventually she knew she was running smoothly across the airfield at a more or less normal speed. She applied full brake and came to a sudden standstill and then turned towards dispersal, as if nothing had happened. 'Coo, miss,' said the airman on duty as she taxied up, 'what 'ave you done with it, left 'alf at 'ome?'

ALISON KING

*

One of the first operational Tempest pilots was the man who had done the same job for the Typhoon: 'Rollo' Beamont, whose two squadrons eventually destroyed 638 V1s. At least two went down by

TIP AND RUN

He was following a radar track over cloud. From the reports over his radio-telephone, he knew that he must be getting close to the V1, and when he found a hole in the cloud three miles inland from Hastings, he decided to get underneath the layer to look for his target. He put the nose of the Tempest down, and immediately caught his breath. Emerging from the misty wisps of cloud and headed straight in his path was the shadowy shape of a flying bomb. In that glimpse he knew that he had no time to pull out of the dive or turn away from the bomb. His only hope lay in getting across the track of the V1 first. Instinctively he jammed the throttle wide open and leant against the control column, thrusting it as far forward as it would go and pushing the Tempest into a full-power dive. For a horrifying moment he had a plan view of the small mid-wing monoplane with its single fin above the jet of orange flame, and the fuselage filled with a ton of explosive; and then the nose of the V1 leaped vertically past his cockpit and was gone. With the wings trembling and vibrating under the strain he pulled out of the dive into a climbing turn and tore round to attack.

His eyes blinked in disbelief. The target had disappeared. He searched the sky intently and at last spotted below him an orange ball sprouting wings, which disappeared in a flash and a mushroom of smoke in the soil of the Sussex Downs. The Tempest's slipstream had upset the robot plane's gyro-control and sent it plunging to earth.

Soon afterwards Beamont remembered the incident. The Germans seldom sent over the V1s singly but launched them usually in waves of half a dozen or more. Beamont shot down one at the coast and chased after a second. He caught it near West Malling, and opened fire from 220 yards. The guns gave one short burst and stopped. He was out of ammunition.

Beamont cursed. There was no other fighter in the vicinity to take over the target. He drew in closer until he was flying alongside, formating on the V1. He eyed it calculatingly. If he could tilt up one wing, that should send the robot over in a dive to earth. It was not an operation he relished. A touch of the wings was liable to swing the Tempest and flying bomb straight into one another and blow them both to fragments. But was it really necessary to hit the wing? His slipstream had done the trick before, although there could not be much future in making a habit of diving so closely past a flying bomb's nose.

He thought quickly. Surely the V1 could be upset by the airflow over the top of his wing without the need for any dangerous direct contact. Carefully he edged closer, dropping slightly and sliding the wing tip of the Tempest underneath that of the V1. The wings rose and fell, wavered and then rushed alarmingly towards one another. He kicked the rudder and skidded sharply away out of danger. Recovering he saw unhappily that the V1 was still on its course for London. He swung back into position and once again began to crab carefully towards the flying bomb.

His nerves were tense, willing the wing to stay steady, as slowly converging they raced towards London at 380 mph. Once he dipped his wing and slithered in until the tip was below that of the V1. Checking and holding off, and alert for the feel of the slightest suggestion of turbulence in the airflow, he cautiously raised his wing. The gap between the machines narrowed to six inches. Anticipating every movement he steadied the Tempest and held her rigid, watching breathlessly. Then painfully slowly it seemed, the

airflow over the Tempest's wing took effect. The wing of
the flying bomb lifted and the V1 heeled over in a dive to
earth.

EDWARD LANCHBERY

*Not long afterwards, Beamont took his Tempests to France,
where he was shot down by flak and captured.*

*

*In France the break-out from the Normandy beach-head
was achieved with a British straight left and an American
right hook, squeezing the retreating Wehrmacht into the
'Falaise Pocket'. For the Allied fighter and ground-attack
pilots, this became*

THE KILLING-GROUND

Broadhurst's twenty-two squadrons of Spitfires and
Typhoons, armed-up with bombs and rockets, were at
readiness on their airfields. The pilots were anxious to be
let off the leash. Every second that elapsed before we
struck meant that more of the enemy would get across the
Seine. But a confused ground situation held us back.

Elements of the Polish Armoured Division, which
formed part of the Second Canadian Corps, reported their
position at Chambois when they were, in fact, some distance away at a place with a very similar name. The
identity of the east-bound columns at Chambois had to be
established beyond all doubt. Our group commander gave
this vital task to his most able and experienced ground-
attack leader, and Charles Green roared off in his Typhoon
and flew low over the suspect transports. Soon afterwards
he was talking to his group commanders.

'What are they, Charles?' said Harry Broadhurst.

'Huns, sir,' replied the wing commander.

'How low were you?' said the air vice-marshal.

'Fifty feet, sir,' answered Green.

'Are you absolutely sure they're Germans?' persisted the
senior officer.

'I saw their black crosses—and the square heads of the drivers!' was the classic reply.

When the Spitfires arrived over the small triangle of Normandy, bounded by Falaise, Trum and Chambois, the Typhoons were already hard at work. One of their favourite tactics against long streams of enemy vehicles was to seal off the front and rear of the column by accurately dropping a few bombs. This technique imprisoned the desperate enemy on a narrow stretch of dusty lane, and since the transports were sometimes jammed together four abreast, it made the subsequent rocket and cannon attacks a comparatively easy business against the stationary targets. Some of the armoured cars and tanks attempted to escape their fate by making detours across the fields and wooded country, but these were soon spotted by the Typhoon pilots and were accorded the same treatment as their comrades on the highways and lanes.

Immediately the Typhoons withdrew from the killing-ground the Spitfires raced into the attack. The tactics of the day were low-level strafing attacks with cannon shells and machine guns against soft-skinned transports, including all types of trucks, staff cars and lightly armoured vehicles. Here and there amongst the shambles on the ground were a few of the deadly Tiger tanks, and although the cannon shells would have little effect against their tough armour plate, a few rounds were blasted against them for good measure. As soon as the Spitfires had fired all their ammunition, they flew back at high speed to their airfields, where the ground crews worked flat out in the hot sunshine to re-arm and refuel the aircraft in the shortest possible time.

Throughout this day and on all subsequent operations in the Falaise gap the Luftwaffe failed to provide any degree of assistance to their sorely pressed ground forces. Faced with the threat of losing their forward airfields to our advance, they were busily occupied in withdrawing to suitable bases in the Paris area, so our fighter-bombers enjoyed complete air supremacy over the battle area. Quick to exploit such a great tactical advantage Broadhurst issued instructions that until such time as the Luftwaffe reappeared to contest our domination of the Normandy sky all his aircraft would operate in pairs. This was a wise decision, for it meant that pairs of Spitfires and Typhoons could return to the fray immediately they were turned round on the ground. Detailed briefings were unnecessary since all pilots knew the area and the position of our own ground troops. Valuable time was saved and it was possible to put the maximum number of missions into the air. Before Falaise an individual fighter pilot had rarely flown on more than three or four missions on any one day, but now it was not uncommon for a pilot to fly six times between dawn and dusk.

The trees and tall hedgerows, in full foliage, afforded some cover to the Germans, who tied large green branches and shrubs on to their trucks in an effort to conceal them from the eyes of our pilots. A gleam of reflected sunshine on metal here, a swirl or eddy of the dust there, or fresh tracks leading across the fields were sufficient evidence to bring down the fighter-bombers with their assorted armoury of weapons. When darkness fell and brought some relief to the battered Germans there was time to take stock of the situation and to add up the score. My own pilots had amassed a total of slightly more than 200 destroyed or damaged vehicles, plus a few tanks attacked with doubtful results. For once the weather was in our favour, and the forecast for the morrow was fine and sunny. The pilots turned in immediately after dinner, for they would require all their energy for the new day. As they settled down to sleep, they heard the continuous drone of our light bombers making their flight across the beach-head to harry the enemy columns throughout the short night.

The Canadians were up well before the dawn, and the first pair of Spitfires retracted their wheels as the first hint of a lighter sky flushed the eastern horizon. The Germans were making strenuous efforts to salvage what equipment they could from the débâcle and get it across the Seine. Such enemy action had been anticipated: some of the Typhoon effort was diverted to attacking barges and small craft as they ferried to and fro across the river. Once more the Spitfire pilots turned their attention to the killing-ground and attacked all manner of enemy transports wherever they were to be found. They were located on the highways and lanes, in the woods and copses, in small villages and hamlets, beneath the long shadows of tall hedges, in farm-yards and even camouflaged with newly mown grass to resemble haystacks. During the previous night many of the enemy had decided to abandon a great proportion of their transports: they could be seen continuing the retreat on foot and in hastily commandeered farm-carts. Sometimes the despairing enemy waved white sheets at the Spitfires as they hurtled down to attack; but these signs were ignored; our own ground troops were still some distance away and there was no organisation available to round up large numbers of prisoners.

On this day, 19th August, my Canadians claimed a total of almost 500 enemy transports destroyed or damaged, of which many were left burning. Even so, this score was not outstanding since Dal Russel's wing easily outstripped us with a score of more than 700. Afterwards our efforts in the Falaise gap gradually petered out, for the transports and personnel of the German Seventh Army had either been eliminated or had withdrawn across the Seine. The Falaise gap ranks as one of the greatest killing-grounds of the war, and is a classic example of the devastating effects of tactical air power when applied in concentrated form against targets of this nature. During these few days, pilots of the Second Tactical Air Force flew more than 1,000 missions and practically wiped out no less then eight infantry divisions and two armoured Panzer divisions. The Second Tactical Air Force had in fact turned an enemy retreat into a complete rout.

After the fighting had ebbed away from Falaise, we decided to drive there and see the results of our attacks at first hand. We thought that we were prepared for the dreadful scenes, which Eisenhower later said could only be described by Dante. On the last flights the stench from the decaying bodies below had even penetrated through the cockpit canopies of the Spitfires. Another, and perhaps the most important, object of our visit was to bring back a suitable German staff car, since it was obvious that we should soon be on the move across France, and a comfortable Mercedes would provide a welcome change from our hard-riding jeeps. After we left Falaise behind, all the roads were so choked with burnt-out German equipment that it was quite impossible to continue the journey. The bloated corpses of unfortunate domestic animals also lay in our path, so we took to the fields and tried to make some progress across country. Each spinny and copse contained its dreadful quota of dead Germans lying beside their wrecked vehicles, and once we came across the body of what had been a beautiful woman lying sprawled across the back seat of a staff car. We found our limousines, which consisted of Renaults, Citroëns, Mercedes and strangely enough a smooth Chevrolet. We had brought ropes, jacks and a few jerrycans of petrol, but it was impossible to extricate any of the cars. Soon we abandoned our search and left the fields and lanes, heavy with their rotting burden in the warm sunshine.

Group Captain J. E. JOHNSON DSO DFC

*

M.H.D.O.I.F.

An excuse for taxiing too fast:

'The brake pressure was very low and the brakes not working efficiently, so I was taxiing fast to get to the hangar before an accident occurred.'

TEE EMM

*

The RAF's reputation for escaping was based not only on the indomitable spirit of men like Bushell and Bader, but on the peculiar circumstance of their trade that could land them in enemy territory as unexpectedly to the enemy as it might be to themselves. A soldier or sailor could hardly achieve this. One such who escaped without having been captured was a Spitfire pilot.

IT ISN'T LIKE THE MOVIES

On 29th September, Robert Carson was shot down at an awkward moment. He had made two runs over the convoy on the Dutch road, seen his shells slamming into the truckloads of panicky German soldiers and was running in for the third time when the engine banged frighteningly, something shot out of the flat, mullet-head cowling in front and the Spitfire shuddered violently as the engine seized.

An axiom among fighter pilots says that troops are always eager to meet the man who has been strafing them. Carson swept about a hundred feet over their heads, speed dropping as he used it to claim a little height, trying to stretch his glide as far as he could, though any high-performance fighter glides dead-stick like a brick. He swung left towards a field, snapped his flaps down and held her off till she squashed and slid noisily to a stop. Unclipping, he swung out of the cockpit and, looking back, saw the soldiers fanning fast off the road towards him half a mile back. Cursing his clumsy flying boots, he ran like hell the other way. At that time Carson was just twenty-one, compact and nimble, with large, capable hands.

He tore through a hedge, across two fields and dead ahead saw a canal about twenty-five feet wide barring his path. Without breaking step or faltering he took off in full run on wings of fear and landed in the middle, going right under because it was deep. The shock of the cold water brought him out of the panic and he half swam, half floundered to the far side, pulled himself on to the bank and was running again. The country was dead flat, like so much of Holland; no cover anywhere.

Ten minutes later he stumbled almost to his knees, feeling he could run no more. The breath sawed hard in his throat and his heart was pounding in his ears. Looking back fearfully he did not see a single German soldier and understood why when a Spitfire rose steeply over the fields, pulling round in a climbing turn at the same moment as the crackle of its distant cannon fire reached him. He wondered which of his friends it was and because he had once been strafed himself, felt almost sympathy for the vengeful pursuers caught in the open fields and cringing into the grass as they waited for it.

Half walking, half jogging, he passed some farm workers, who stared open-mouthed, and later saw three farmhouses ahead. They all looked the same; making a quick decision he walked cautiously round the back of the middle

one, and a florid, middle-aged man came out in farm
clothes, looking startled at the battledress and flying boots.
Quick-witted, the farmer grasped the situation instantly,
grabbed Carson by the arm and hustled him into a barn
by the house. In stumbling English and with gestures he
made the boy understand that he was to burrow under
the hay if he heard Germans, and then turned and ran out
of the barn. In a minute he slipped quietly back through
the door carrying over his arm a good brown tweed suit,
and as he helped Carson off with his battledress and into
the suit he managed to make him understand that he
would like the suit back after the war. Carson, who knew a
few German words, gathered that it was his Sunday best.
The farmer pulled some of the hay aside then and underneath Carson saw a sten gun and a couple of automatics.
The farmer handed him a 7mm automatic. 'Allies', the
farmer said, grinning, making signs to indicate that the guns
had been dropped from the air. Suddenly solemn again he
told Carson he was lucky to have chosen this farm. The
ones on either side belonged to Dutch Nazis. On a map he
pointed with a thick forefinger to show that the spot was
about a hundred kilometres from the Canadian troops.

After dusk he led Carson over fields to a house in a
nearby village called Krimpen, on the banks of the Lek
River, and outside the back door Carson met Dirk, the
hearty, burly ship repairer. Dirk took him down to the
river where he had his ships and on a barge moored there
Carson relaxed in a bunk with some bread and cheese
and passed a peaceful night.

Dirk told him in the morning that he would arrange to
get him a Dutch identity card. In the evening he came back
a little flustered and said the Germans were searching the
village. Taking the boy by the arm and talking to him in
incomprehensible Dutch, he led him out into the main
street, past a disciplined little troop of the searching German soldiers (Carson blushing like a schoolgirl and feeling
very guilty) to a schoolteacher's house which the Germans
had already searched. Chris, the schoolteacher, was a smiling obliging, blond man who sheltered Carson for four
days till a man came one evening, spoke briefly to Chris,

and after he went Chris handed Carson a neat piece of folded green cardboard.

'Rub this in your hands till it looks worn,' he said. 'It is your new identity card. You are Piet Smit, land worker, and I will call you Piet. Get used to it.'

Carson looked at it and said in wonder: 'It really looks real.'

'It is real,' Chris said, 'Except for the signature. We get the cards from the official stocks. Now . . . we will arrange for you to go north where you will find more food and fewer Germans.'

'Away from the front?'

'Yes. You will shelter in a house. It will not be exciting. There is a curfew at seven, the Germans start shooting after it, so your nights will be dull for a young man, but you must wait till the armies catch up with you.'

Carson said: 'Sorry. Not me. I'm no good at that. I want to have a go at getting through the lines.'

'Do not be foolish,' Chris said severely, the schoolmaster coming out in him. 'You will be caught. Or killed in the battle. Or both. You should do as we say.'

'Look, Chris,' Carson said, 'I do appreciate all you've done but I'd go silly sitting on my bottom all day. Other people have got through the lines. Why shouldn't I?'

'You hear only of the lucky ones who get through,' Chris explained. 'Not the unlucky ones. There are more of them.'

'I was always lucky,' Carson insisted.

After half an hour's argument Carson was still stubborn so Chris, slightly ruffled, brought out of a downstairs closet a battered old bicycle without tyres. 'It is the best I can do for you,' he said, and added tersely, I hope it brings you luck because that is what you are going to need.'

In the morning Chris went out and came back in about half an hour with a sinewy, extremely competent-looking girl of about twenty. She was pushing a bicycle and Chris introduced her as Griselda. 'She will guide you south to a house,' he said.

Griselda smiled briefly. She was apparently ready to go and five minutes later Carson rode off about a hundred yards behind her, the battered rims of his bicycle wheels clattering over the cobbles so that he thought everyone must be staring at him.

Coming up to the ferry over the Lek he saw a German soldier on board collecting fares and felt his heartbeats quicken with fear. Chris had briefed him well: Carson handed the German the correct money (it was the first German he had dealt with) and the soldier muttered something at him, but Carson was pretending to look at his front wheel and the German moved off. Two more Germans searched some of the passengers as they got off on the far side but Carson, sweating, landed unmolested. He saw a line of Red-Cross lorries waiting on the road; at least they were white, with red crosses painted on the sides. All of them were packed with obviously healthy and well-armed German soldiers.

For nearly six hours that day he rode a hundred yards behind Griselda, who seemed to be tireless. About six-thirty they went through a winding village called Blesk-graaf, and when Carson came out on the other side he could not see the girl. He rode back through the village but there was no sign of her and he started worrying about the curfew. It was so close to curfew time that he guessed this was the village where he was supposed to spend the night. But where?

He rode back through the village again; still no sign of Griselda, but a doctor's plate caught his eye outside a house and the name on it was Englese. It seemed an unmistakable omen; walking round to the back of the house he knocked.

The doctor himself came to the door, a bony, stooped, elderly man. Carson said in stumbling German 'Ich bin Englische Flieger-offizier,' and the doctor said quickly in thick English, 'Come inside at once.' It never even crossed his mind that Carson might be a disguised German trying to trap Dutch Resistance people. Dutchmen were usually wary of them (with plenty of reason), but the doctor said later he did not think a German could ever have an accent like Carson's.

Shortly after curfew time Carson was sitting down to dinner with the doctor; five minutes later the maid rushed in trembling and said there were two German soldiers at the door. Carson dived out of the French windows into the back garden and hid among some rhubarb. The doctor called him in half an hour later and said the Germans were only making a routine check and now he had been searched it was safer than ever.

Next day the doctor brought an eager youth and a girl in and told Carson they would guide him to an address in the town of Dordrecht. It was the system as before, Carson riding his rattletrap old bike behind the two guides. A German check post gave him a bad fright on the way, stopping him and asking for his papers. He pulled out his identity card, the German looked casually at it, handed it back, and Carson rode on.

In Dordrecht they took him into a grey-stone house in a garden back from the road, showed him into a room, smiled and walked out. Across the room, watching him closely, sat a silent young man; short and thick-set with fair, close-cropped hair. The man merely gazed, tight-lipped, saying nothing and Carson sat in another chair. A quarter of hour passed; the man had not opened his mouth and Carson felt the silent tension getting unbearable. He was fidgety wondering what sort of test this was and then he heard the other man say something explosively under his breath. It sounded like 'God-dam,' and Carson said:

'I say, do you speak English?'

'I sure as hell do,' said Lieutenant Grover P. Parker, of California, who had been shot down two days before, been captured, escaped that morning from the Dordrech lock-up and been picked up by the Dutch.

The tension broke and they each burst into a torrent of words. A few minutes later an English-speaking Dutchman came into the room and apologised for being so long. (They realised later he had probably been listening, waiting for them to talk naturally to each other so he would know whether either was a German 'plant'.) He said he was going to send them to a place called the Biesbosch, an area of thickly overgrown marsh in the fork where the Waal flowed into the Maas River. There was a well-armed Organisation there, he added, and the Germans were usually frightened to go into it.

379

Another fair young Dutchman came in the morning and led them for several miles across quiet country till they came out on the Maas River at a spot where a skiff was moored. Across on the far shore they saw a tangle of thick reeds about seven feet high, and here and there a tree. 'Biesbosch,' the Dutchman said briefly. He rowed them across to a rotted landing stage and led the way along a narrow, beaten path that was almost a funnel where the thick, dry-green reeds crowded in on both sides, curving over their heads. Stagnant canals choked with weeds and reeds kept cutting through the path and they crossed them on narrow planks.

The path sharply spread out into a small clearing and in a canal running along one side of it a man sat in a canoe. 'Ach, der Kommandant,' the guide said half to himself, half to Carson.

He gave a hail and the man paddled to the bank and climbed out. The guide spoke in Dutch and the Kommandant solemnly shook their hands and said in English with a stiff accent, 'How do you do?' He was about forty, fair and sharp-featured with sunken cheeks, wore a thick crewneck sweater and had a big automatic pistol stuck in the waistband of his pants. It was a keen face, Carson thought, but 'hooded', curiously empty of active expression. He found in the times that followed that the Kommandant seldom let a flicker of emotion show. The main thing for the moment was that he spoke English. He said, 'If you will always do as I say you can stay with us. I am afraid it is not comfortable.'

The guide turned back and they followed the Kommandant along more winding paths for a quarter of an hour till Carson became aware of the long low shape of a barge lying surprisingly in the reeds. The Kommandant led them on to the deck over a plank and Carson saw that it was moored in another choked canal. She was an old and dirty barge with only a little faded, peeling paint on her.

Looking curiously around they followed the Kommandant along the rusty deck to a cabin at the rear, and as he put his head in the door Carson caught the sweaty smell of bodies. A dozen or so men were lounging inside, some on bunks, a couple at a table, dressed mostly in singlets and pants, and all of them looking unshaven and dirty. With a shock he saw a young woman lying on a bunk; she looked heavy and sluttish.

The Kommandant called one of the men and a big broad-shouldered young man of about twenty-four swung off a bunk and came over. 'This is Jan,' the Kommandant said. 'He will take care of you.' Jan put out his hand and said in a deep voice and very good English, 'I do hope you do not mind sharing a bunk.'

They found he had been quite a cultured student until the Germans had interrupted his studies; since then he had become a ruthless young man, though to Carson and Parker he was always friendly and cheerful. Like most of the Dutch they had encountered, he was fair-haired.

Jan introduced the others, but they seemed a graceless lot and all Carson and Parker got were a few grunts. Even the girl was unfriendly. They dined that evening on bread and potatoes, and most of the potatoes were pitted and bad. Carson was oppressed by the smell, the surly carelessness and the general foetid atmosphere of the Biesbosch. He asked Jan how soon they could move on towards the Allied lines, but Jan said that the country farther on was thick with Germans and check points and that the Germans were taking savage measures with anyone they caught.

Stay here and wait until they reach us,' he said. 'It will not be long now.' He added wryly, 'We have been waiting a long time and it is worth waiting a little more.'

He found them a top bunk and Carson and Parker crammed into it together, though they had little sleep because the girl and another man were in the bunk below, behaving with absolutely no inhibitions whatsoever.

In the morning Jan took them off the barge for a walk and led them deep into the middle of the Biesbosch, where they came out of the narrow paths to a peaceful clearing with a canal running through it and a pretty stone bridge arching over the canal. It was warm and sunny and they stopped to rest on the bridge. Jan was saying, 'You know we are doing more than just waiting here. There is another barge . . .' He stopped as Carson let out an alarmed little cry. He was looking past Jan's shoulder, and Parker and Jan swung round and saw two German soldiers walking out of the reeds into the clearing. One had a rifle slung over his shoulder, the other wore a pistol holster on his belt. They headed straight for the bridge.

Jan mumbled, hardly moving his lips, 'Do not look aggressive. I will do the talking.' Carson put his hand in his coat pocket, gripped the butt of his pistol and thumbed the safety catch to 'Fire'. Parker, he thought, would undoubtedly be doing the same.

He saw that the soldier with the holster wore the skull and cross-bones of a Panzer division on his collar. Under it was a thin face and sharp eyes. The other German was younger and looked rather seedy. They walked on the bridge and stopped in front of Jan, looking wary but not truculent. The man with the skull and crossbones badge spoke. Carson got the bare gist of some question about a nearby farm. Jan answered him in German, and while they talked the two Germans kept watching the three of them.

The older man must have become aware of the atmosphere. He stuck his thumbs in his belt; his fingers lay over the holster flap and Carson saw him surreptitiously pulling the flap loose from the brass stud. Parker apparently saw it too, because he suddenly drew his own pistol and yelled, 'Hände hoch!' The younger German gave a little cry of shock, jerked his rifle off his shoulder and it went off point-blank, the bullet passing between Carson and Parker. Then he was running and it all happened very fast.

Carson had his pistol out; he fired and the running German fell on his face and started screaming. Parker was shooting jerkily, his face expressionless. His first bullet hit the other German in the stomach, the second one went through the side of the neck as the German spun round and the third one went through his left hand; then the German went down.

The man Carson had shot was moving on the ground like a weak crab, and Carson thought vaguely, 'This isn't like the movies at all. He should be dead.'

PAUL BRICKHILL

Carter and Parker stayed with the Dutch Resistance until the area was liberated by British troops some weeks later. There were then seventy German soldiers held captive in the barge's holds. They were as glad to see their 'liberators' as were the two pilots.

*

The Mosquito bomber, flying fast and low, offered the RAF a chance for a private war against the Gestapo, who usually set up a headquarters-cum-prison in a large building in the centre of occupied towns. The object was to kill as many Gestapo agents as possible, destroy their records of Resistance work, and—if feasible—release their prisoners. By late 1944, the main targets were in Denmark.

The second raid was against the Gestapo headquarters in Copenhagen. The Gestapo had occupied the offices of the Shell Oil Company in the centre of the town, and the building was known as the Shell House. As usual we had the target and the approaches to it modelled, and planned the operation with the greatest care because the slightest error in navigation or bombing would cause heavy casualties among the Danes.

Shortly before the operation took place, I was worried to learn that a large number of the Resistance Movement were imprisoned in one wing of the building and it seemed certain they would perish in the attack. I discussed this with Major Truelson, temporarily attached to my headquarters while we were planning the operation, and he assured me that they would sooner die from our bombing than at the hands of the Germans, adding:

'Who knows—some might not be killed and succeed in escaping, as happened at Aarhus, and anyhow their death will save many more Danish lives, so don't worry.'

I asked him about a house near the target which I thought was almost certain to be damaged, and he replied with a grin:

'The Germans use it for immoral purposes and so if one bomb hits it by accident, it would be excellent!'

About this time we were experiencing a spell of bad weather and for over a fortnight waited to get the right conditions over Denmark and the route from England. Meanwhile the Danish Resistance members were anxiously awaiting the attack. Many of their leaders had been arrested and we were told that unless we could destroy the Gestapo records soon, the work of the patriots in Denmark would be suppressed and most of the leaders put to death. In spite of the urgency I refused to attempt the raid until I was satisfied that the weather would be favourable, otherwise failure was certain and the patriots would be worse off than before.

We had to move Mosquitoes from the Continent to England for this operation, so we needed a favourable forecast over a fairly wide area for forty-eight hours ahead. As I could not afford to take eighteen Mosquitoes off night interdiction for too long a period, I was anxious not to move them to England more than one day in advance of the operation. I was in constant touch with the Central Meteorological Forecasting Establishment and at last got the news for which we had been waiting.

Shortly before the operation took place we learned that several units of the German Fleet had anchored in Copenhagen harbour. This meant a very considerable increase in the anti-aircraft defences, but we worked out by the help of our target model that if we succeeded in gaining initial surprise in our approach to the Shell House and withdrew by following a main thoroughfare through the town, flying below the roof-tops, the flak from the ships could not hit us. And this was to be our plan.

As at Aarhus, we used eighteen Mosquitoes with a Mustang escort. The first section of fighters was detailed to silence some light anti-aircraft guns sited on the roof of a building near the Shell House which would have been very deadly if allowed to fire on the Mosquitoes unchallenged. In actual fact we surprised the defences and these particular guns were not manned when our attack went in.

Bateson, who had led the raid on The Hague, led the attack, and Peter Clapham and I flew as No 3 in his formation. We had a rough and boisterous flight across the North Sea, and flying at fifty feet above the waves called for great concentration and physical endurance under the conditions. Our windscreens were soon covered with an oily salt spray, making flying even more difficult. Near the Danish coast I opened a side window and managed with difficulty to clear a small portion of the windscreen through which I could get a limited view ahead.

As we streaked across the beautifully green Danish countryside we noticed that many Danes waved, some saluting us, and we also saw that many of the houses were flying the Danish flag.

I have rarely flown behind a better leader than Bob Bateson, who had with him that very able navigator, Sismore, to help him steer a perfect course to the target. We had now worked up to our maximum cruising speed and were flying just above the ground in perfect formation, preparing for our final run up to the target. At times we had to pull up to avoid high-tension cables, trees and other obstructions, but our mean height was below tree-top level. It was an invigorating and satisfying sensation, especially as we were on our way to strike another blow at the evil Gestapo.

First one check point and then another flashed past us, and I knew we were steering an absolutely true course for the target. Peter, in his usual imperturbable and entertaining manner, was giving me a running commentary on what was going on outside, warning me of our approach to high-tension cables, chimneys and so on, an invaluable help to the pilot on such occasions. We had flown together on so many operations and understood each other's temperament so well that it was like dancing with the perfect partner.

Copenhagen was in view and buildings began to flash past. Peter said:

'That's the target. Straight ahead of us over those small lakes.'

We were now tensed for the moment of bomb release. Suddenly a bridge appeared ahead of us and I saw some poles, possibly light standards, sticking up. I eased the aeroplane up a little and then down again a few feet. By this time Peter had the bomb doors open, and the target seemed to be approaching us very fast. I pressed the bomb release and pulled up just over the top of the Shell House, and then down again almost to street level. Glancing up, I could see flak bursting just above the roof-tops. Next instant a Mosquito passed over us, certainly not more than ten feet above. Below us I saw people in the street throwing themselves flat and others dashing for doorways. Soon these hectic moments were over, and we were clear of Copenhagen and on our way back to Norfolk.

Unhappily Kleboe, who was flying just behind me, hit one of the uprights on the bridge to which I referred, and crashed into a convent school. The second wave of aircraft, thinking this was the target, bombed the wreckage, causing loss of life to many innocent children. Naturally this unfortunate incident caused great sorrow and distress in the Group, but the Danes accepted it with brave and stoic hearts, and acclaimed the attack as a blow for freedom.

We lost three Mosquitoes and one Mustang on this occasion, but succeeded in completely demolishing the Shell House, destroying all Gestapo records, liberating all the prisoners without the loss of a single life, and killing twenty-six Gestapo. It will always remain a miracle to me that anyone inside the building survived to tell the tale.

Air Chief Marshal Sir BASIL EMBRY
GCB KBE DSO DFC AFC

*

In the Far East the far-flying Catalina was used for anti-sub patrols and, on this occasion, mine-laying.

JETTISON!

For some hours we have been flying north-westward away from our homeland, flying so low on the water that we appear to be skimming the surface.

As the sun sinks lower, sky and sea merge into one bright screen of many colours, the varied hues of tropical sundown—cerulean blue, vermilion, lemon yellow, with the cumulus clouds a powdery white, dusted here and there with brick-dust, and the dull blue of night.

The setting sun marks the direction of our goal, Java. The last daylight is fading, and from the haze and cloud-shadows land appears.

As darkness descends, lines of bright lights appear in the hills, where a large bushfire has been raging, adding its smoke to the clouds and haze. We pass close to an island

and in a few minutes we are off into the inky blackness of the night.

We pass over other islands, rising to a sufficient height to clear the tops of trees and hills. Here and there flickering lights tell of native activity and, as we get closer, hour by hour, to our target, we see pinpricks of light which come from enemy rifles. To them we are a black shadow zooming close over their heads. We show no light, fire no gun, for our nefarious mission requires stealth. We hope to achieve surprise, and can imagine the jabbering and angry profanity we cause.

This night is specially chosen; no tropic moon will rise to stare at us and light up the clouds to snowy white, to silhouette us for target practice. We bypass beautiful Bali, slumbering in the murk out of respect to the large air base at Den Paser.

Time begins to drag. All the days of flying and preparation since leaving our home base, and now we have already been in the air for many hours on this flight. Once we had left on our mission long-range fighters patrolled the initial and final stretches of the trip, protecting us in the dangerous daylight hours. In enemy waters the night protects us, as the Japanese have strangely neglected the use of night fighters.

Our aircraft has a good captain, Flight-Lieutenant Len Froud, referred to as 'Young Hero' because of his small boyish figure. Our mission is to drop mines into the enemy harbour. My job is second pilot, and I have the satisfying task of actually releasing the mines when the navigator gives the word. He is in the bow, to locate the target and then to carry out the precision navigation required. All the crew have been shown the plan of attack and the target maps and photos of the harbour, so that they understand the other men's duties as well as their own. The other second pilot is aft in the blister compartment with the gunners, and has a good view of the whole proceedings.

With only ten minutes to go we suddenly arrive at the east coast of Java, and turn north along it, close over trees, beaches and rivers, the clumps of bush showing black against the silver filigree of the paddy fields on the low coastal areas.

387

More flickering lights, like fireflies, reminding one strongly of the Java of peacetime; the strong sweet smell of this densely populated and fertile island is heavy in the air. To us, speeding the last few miles to our target, the massive land appears to be slumbering. Hardly a sign of the great city of the Kali River, where the harbour is formed by the strait between Java and the adjacent island of Madura, only two miles distant.

At last we are coming up to our datum point, which has to be well identified—we cannot afford a mistake. We turn over it on our first run, the navigator with his stop watch counting the seconds aloud. The pilot is concentrating on flying a perfectly steady course, airspeed, and altitude. Then the signal is given, I pull the release, and the blister reports, 'Port mine gone,' as the wing is relieved of its heavy load. Counting the seconds again, for the second minedrop, when a clattering series of explosions and sparks comes from the port engine—'We've been hit!'—and as the engine continues to backfire violently its power is lost and the wing droops. The engineer puts the mixture into full rich, the pilot jettisons the starboard mine, and opens up the starboard engine to maintain height. By now we are very close to the water, and still closer to the trees on shore as we circle slowly around.

The port engine at last begins to run smoothly, at intervals. We increase power and climb away. We have just got over the initial confusion and begin to realise our danger, when bang goes the starboard engine—just one little backfire, but how shattering to our remaining ten per cent of confidence!

As we turn away to sea, other Catalinas are arriving over distant parts of the harbour; we can see searchlights and gun-flashes where the local committee of welcome is hard at work. We have all recurrent visions of being captured if we are forced down.

We are now flying east, climbing steadily, and the engines are both running well, but the port oil tank is leaking badly and will only last another hour. On reaching 8,000 feet we trrn between the mountain peaks of eastern Java. Being close above the cloud-blanket the volcanic craters and lava flows are hidden. Then we come to the edge of the clouds and see the green slopes of the southern coast. Here we set course for home, still over 800 miles distant.

While the port engine lasted, our ears were attuned and our hearts synchronised with it, dropping a few revs every time it backfired. At last the oil runs out, and the engine has to be stopped before it seizes up. The screw is then fully feathered to reduce drag. From then on our ears and hearts transfer their interest to the starboard engine, and we live by its steady hum for the remainder of our journey. We soon find that the aircraft will not maintain height on one engine, and we lighten it by jettisoning all extraneous weight. The engineers begin to tear the auxiliary machinery out, using spanners, hammers, hacksaw and, above all, the axe! The gunners throw out all the guns and ammunition, sea-markers, flame floats, and still the aircraft continues to lose height although the speed is now down to 70 knots, fluttering along like a wounded bird and not much above stalling speed. The altimeter gets many a quick glance—no more encouragement is needed to jettison all parachutes and harness, Mae Wests, heavy personal gear, nearly all the radio equipment, spare tool-kits, all but two charts, chart-drawer, sextant case, catwalks, engine mounts, all canvas screens, covers, stretchers, seats, and finally all small personal gear not attached to a body. I become the most hated member of the crew as I induce them to part with their revolvers, bags containing expensive shaving kits, and, when the radioman comes to me with a receiver in his arms and tears in his voice, I take it from him and hurl it overboard to save him having the sacrilege on his conscience.

We keep the rubber dinghies, with water, concentrated food, a first-aid kit, and some distress flares, in case we sink into the sea and have to abandon the aircraft. By this time our rate of descent has slowed right up and is imperceptible by normal standards. We had been tempted early in the piece to jettison some fuel, thinking that there was far too much for one engine, but at the high power at which we are driving it, the fuel consumption is double its normal cruising rate and it is using the same as two engines. Of course using up the fuel slowly lightens the aircraft as we go along. After two hours there is nothing left to throw out, and the remaining hours become very boring.

There are eleven of us on board, including a US Navy officer, who becomes a constant source of cigarettes. Eventually the furious smoking to soothe the nerves makes the cabin atmosphere so dense that I retreat to the bow. As we near home our speed slowly increases, and we are fortunate in having only a slight head-wind.

Finally the shore of Australia comes in sight and we make a good landfall, with little fuel left. After over twenty hours of flying it is a very good landing—may all your landings be as happy!

(The failure of the port engine and the oil-leak were later found to be caused not by enemy action but by the breaking of a rocker-arm.)

Wing Commander BRET HILDER

*

As the year closed in, it became apparent nobody was going to be 'home by Christmas'. But one priority target remained for Bomber Command: the last of Germany's battleships, the Tirpitz. Moored in a Norwegian fiord, it had already been attacked once (and damaged, although the RAF did not know this) by 617 squadron—now under the command of Wing Commander J. B. 'Willie' Tait. In November they had a second try, carrying 72,000 lb. 'Tallboy' bombs.

TALLBOY V. *TIRPITZ*

Next day the weather was improving. Tait was playing football with his crews on the airfield, surrounded by the circle of silent cloaked Lancasters, when he was summoned to the operations room, and there, still in striped jersey and studded boots, he got his orders. In a few hours they were flying up to Northern Scotland.

That was about the afternoon a paper was dumped in an 'In' tray in Whitehall, and a senior officer with a lot of braid round his sleeve picked it out and frowned when he read the rather peremptory suggestion from High Circles that instead of 'tallboys' on the *Tirpitz* raid they should drop 2,000-lb armour-piercing bombs. In the room at the time was an airman who had done a lot of work in developing the 'tallboy'. 'Oh God,' he said, 'the two-thousand-pounders'll never do it! What do we do now?' The high officer pondered, his fingers relaxed and the slip of paper floated back into the 'In' tray. 'Have lunch,' he said, and added a moment later, piously, 'I'll look into this tomorrow. I do hope I'm in time.'

Some time afer midnight the weather Mosquito, sliding through darkness on the way back from Tromso, reported fog in the fiords and cloud half-way up Norway. There was a possibility Tromso might be clear by dawn, but there were distinct icing conditions (a real bogy for heavy-laden aircraft). It was not encouraging. Tait discussed it with the Met. men, and at the end he said, 'All right. We'll give it a go.'

Over Lossiemouth stars were glinting in a clear sky and the air was frosty. Tait drove out to his aeroplane and found the dangerous rime ice already forming on his wings in spite of the glycol the ground crew had poured on the leading edge. One by one round the field the engines were whining and coughing explosively, bringing the big bombers to quivering life. When Tait started his starboard inner it let out a high-pitched scream as the started motor stuck in engagement. He hoped it would clear before the engine seized—in much the same way as he hoped the rime ice would clear. With 7 tons of fuel and 6 tons of bomb, each plane was grossly overweight at 32 tons. No margin for any trouble on take-off.

At 3 am the straining engines dragged them into the air, the great wheels slowly retracted and locked, the engines relaxed and they turned slowly on course at 1,000 feet. (Tait's engine chewed the gears off the starter motor and was all right. He was flying his own aircraft again, 'D Dog', for the first time since she was crippled over the Kembs Dam. He always had luck in her.)

They flew slowly to save petrol, flame floats bobbing on the water in their wake as they checked for drift. Tait had slipped in the automatic pilot and tried to doze, as he always did on outward trips over water; he believed in taking sleep when he could get it, but seldom got it.

The sky was paling in the east as they reached the Norwegian coast, turned right, climbed over the mountains and dipped into the inland valleys. The sun lifted over the horizon and the valleys lay soft under snow, flecked with bare rocks. Snow crests surrounded them, tops laced with pink like vast wedding cakes, except to the south, where the sun splintered on the ice-peaks and sparkled with the colours of the spectrum like a diamond necklace, radiantly lovely. Fog-filled lakes passed slowly below but there was no cloud. Rendezvous was a narrow lake cradled between steep hills a hundred miles south-east of Tromso, and Tait flew slowly towards it, saw no water but recognised it as a long pool of fog in the trough and over it saw aircraft circling like black flies.

He flew across it firing Very lights to draw them, and they turned in behind and started to climb towards Tromso. That was the moment the radar picked them up, and within a minute the fighter operations room at Bardufoss knew that enemy bombers were closing on the *Tirpitz*. At 14,000 feet the bombers were all at battle stations. One last mountain shouldered up, and as they lifted over the peak it lowered like a screen and there again, folded in the cliffs, lay Tromso Fiord and the black ship, squat in the distance, like a spider in her web of torpedo nets. It was like looking down from the 'gods' on a Wagnerian stage, a beetle in green water cupped in the snowy hills, all coral and flame. There was no cloud. And no smoke screen. *Tirpitz* lay naked to the bomb sights.

Even the air was still. On the flanks of the gaggle Tait saw the front rank riding steadily. They seemed suspended; motionless but for the sublime hills falling slowly behind, immaculate and glowing with the beauty of sunrise and the indifference of a million years to the ugliness of the intrusion. So must many an Arctic coast burn unseen.

Far below the basin seemed to sleep in the shadow, but *Tirpitz* broke the spell with a salvo, sparkling from stem to stern with flashes as billows of smoke from the guns wreathed her and drifted up. Her captain had just radioed urgently to Bardufoss to hurry the fighters.

Tait opened the bomb doors and slid the pitch levers up

to high revs.; the engines bellowed and the exhausts glowed even in that cold light. Black puffs stained the sky among the gaggle as the flak reached them, and then the guns round the fiord opened fire. Tait watched anxiously for the smoke pots, but the smoke never came (the pots were there all right, just brought down from Alten, but the Germans had not yet primed them). The bomb sight was on and the ship drawing nearer while the gunners in the rear turrets watched the ridges anxiously for the first fighters. It was all up to the rear gunners when the fighters came; there were no mid-upper gunners.

Now it was water, far below, sliding under the nose. Tait felt his hands on the wheel were clammy, and Daniel's breathing rasped over the intercom. The bomber was unswerving, shaking in the engines' thunder, and out of the cockpit Tait could see the bomb doors quivering as the airflow battered at them. The red light came on—ten seconds to go . . . seconds that dragged till 'D Dog' leapt as the grips snapped back and the bomb lurched away. Tait hauled hard over to the left and on either side saw others of the front rank doing likewise.

One by one the gaggle wheeled as the bombs went. They watched, wordless, through the perspex for thirty seconds till a great yellow flash burst on the battleship's foredeck. From 14,000 feet they saw her tremble. Another bomb hit the shore; two more in close succession hit the ship, one on the starboard side, by the bridge, and another abaft the funnel (one of them was Astbury's). Another one split the sea five feet from her bows, and then the smoke pall covered her and only dimly through it they saw the other bursts all inside the crinoline of nets.

One constant glare shone through the smoke. She was burning. There came another flash and a plume of steam jetted 500 feet into the air through the smoke as a magazine went up.

Three minutes later 9 Squadron bombed the dark shroud over her, and then the black flies crawling in the sky turned south-west and curved down towards the sea, picking up speed for the run home. They never saw a fighter. The last thing they saw as the smoke lifted was the *Tirpitz* starting to list.

The cloud they had feared closed in on the long slog home, and Tait was driving blindly through it when his artificial horizon collapsed in a mess of ball bearings and mechanism. After eleven hours in the air his eyes felt like hot coals as he focused rigidly on the other instruments; then the aerial iced up and they could not get a homing for a long time, and when they did it was a diversion. Lossiemouth was cloaked in rain, and Tait turned east and found a small Coastal Command field, where he touched down smoothly.

At the control tower a young pilot officer asked if they had been on a cross-country, and Tait primly pursed his mouth, looked in aloof shyness at the ground and said, 'Yes.' A torpedo-bomber squadron lived on the field, and later he told the co where they had been.

'Did you get her?' the co asked.

'I think so. Gave her a hell of a nudge anyway.'

'Thanks,' the co said. 'We might have had to do it. Low level. I shouldn't have like it.'

PAUL BRICKHILL

The 'nudge' was enough: back at base, Tait found reconnaissance photos showing the Tirpitz had capsized. A thousand of her crew were trapped and drowned.

*

For the last three months Pierre Clostermann, whom we last met returning to France, had 'flown a desk' as a rest from operations. After a battle with the French Ministere de l'Air—who wanted him to live through the war to help re-create the French Air Force afterwards—he got back into the firing line. But not on his beloved Spitfires. Posted to Tempest, the first step was to learn about its predecessor, the Typhoon.

THE BRUTE

At last a ray of sunshine. In the afternoon I would therefore be able to have my first crack at a Typhoon.

I arrived at my flight with all my kit, and reported to my

instructor, MacFar, an Australian, called 'Immaculate Mac' because of his scruffy appearance.

With my parachute on my back it took three people to help me up to the Typhoon's cockpit, which is nine feet off the ground. As the plane is very streamlined there is nothing to hang on to. You have to get your fingers in hollows which are covered by metal plates on spring hinges. They close up again when you removed your hand or your foot, just like a rat trap. In the end they hoisted me up, settled me in, slapped me on the back, shouted 'good luck', and I found myself all alone inside the bowels of the monster.

I rapidly called back to mind all the gen my instructors had given me. As the exhaust gases had a high carbon dioxide content, and seeped into the cockpit, you had to breathe oxygen all the time. I therefore hurriedly put on my mask and opened the intake valve. On take-off Typhoons swing hard right and I therefore adjusted the rudder trim very carefully. I opened the radiator wide. I checked the locking of the undercart—the lever looked uncomfortably like the one for the flaps. I lowered the flaps control to open up the pneumatic circuit in order to avoid ram effect just as I started up.

I switched on the instrument panel light. I regulated the throttle lever—open five-eighths of an inch (not one fraction more, otherwise the carburettor would flood and there might be a blow-back). I pushed the pitch control lever right forward, and then back an inch or so, to avoid run-away in the constant speed unit.

I verified that my tanks were full and selected the centre fuselage tanks for the take-off (gravity feed in case the pump packed up). I unscrewed the Wobble pumps; one sent a mixture of alcohol and ether into the carburrettor, the other a mixture of petrol and oil to the cylinders.

I inserted a cartridge into the starter. (The Koffman system, which uses the violent expansion of explosive gases to get the engine turning. If the engine doesn't start first time it will almost certainly catch fire, being bung full of juice.)

With one finger on the coil booster and another on the starter button, I fired the cartridge. The mechanic, hanging on to the wing, helped to 'catch' the engine and it started up with a deafening roar. The amount of noise is about five times as great as in a Spitfire. After missing a few times, the engine settled down to a reasonably steady rhythm, though not without exuding oil at every pore. The sound of the engine and the way it vibrated struck me as suspicious. My nerves were very much on edge and I didn't feel at all easy in my mind. What on earth had ever induced me to return on ops?

These reflections probably lasted some little time because, when I looked up, there were the mechanics looking slightly surprised and waiting for a sign from me to remove the chocks.

I began to taxi—a bit too fast. I must be careful not to overwork the brakes. They over-heated very quickly, and hot brakes don't function.

That engine! You moved forward quite blindly, picking out the way like a crab, with a bit of rudder now left, now right, so as to be able to see in front. Once I was on the edge of the runway, before venturing further I cleared the plugs, as per instructions, by opening up to 3,000 revs, and a film of oil immediately spread over my windshield.

Two Typhoons who were in the circuit landed clumsily, but the controller seemed disinclined to give me the green light. I stuck my head out to make a sign, even though I would probably get a dollop of boiling oil in the eye. Still a red light. Christ, I must have forgotten something—and my confounded engine was beginning to heat. My radiator had already got up to 95°. A glance round—my flaps were at 15° all right, my radiator was open. . . . Hell, the radio! I quickly switched it on and called:

'Hullo, Skydoor, Skydoor, Tiffe twenty-eight calling. May I scramble?'

The controller replied by at last giving me a green light. Here goes! I tightened my straps, released the brakes, carefully aligned myself on the white line down the middle of the concrete and slowly opened the throttle, with my left foot hard down on the rudder bar.

I had been warned that Typhoons swung, but surely not as much as this! And the brute gathered speed like a rocket! I corrected as much as I could with the brakes, but even then I found myself drifting dangerously to the right.

Half-way down the runway my right wheel was practically on the grass. If I came off the concrete I would gracefully flip on my back!

To hell with it! I tore her off the ground.

This plane just had no lateral stability at all. I still went on drifting to starboard and, with those miserable ailerons that only 'bit' at speeds higher then 100 mph I daren't lower my port wing too much.

Luckily they had hauled F. hangar down, after a series of accidents all due to the same cause, but even then I passed uncomfortably close to E hangar.

I retracted my undercart but forgot to put the brakes on. A terrific vibration which shook the whole plane from stem to stern reminded me that my wheels had gone into the cavities in the wings still revolving at full speed. I only hoped the tyres hadn't been ruined.

Really, it had been very pleasant behind that office desk. . . .

In the end I got my hand in a bit and felt better. There was a tendency to skid in the turns, but it wasn't too bad.

Just a wee dive to see what happened. Phew! With its seven tons, the thing's acceleration down hill was simply fantastic. I realised with satisfaction that as far as speed was concerned this was much better than a Spitfire. What would it be like in a Tempest!

Half an hour quickly passed and I began to summon up courage for the landing. First a circuit at full throttle at 420 mph, to clear those bloody plugs all over again. But after that I couldn't seem to reduce speed enough to lower my undercart with safety, even though I throttled back, swish-tailed violently, and lowered my radiator. One circuit, engine ticking over, at 300 mph. Another circuit, at 250. In desperation I did a vertical climb, without the engine. This took me up about 3,000 feet but it reduced my speed to about 200 mph. At this low speed the machine was horribly unstable, and letting down the undercart had an unexpected effect on the centre of gravity. Once again, though I had been warned, I was taken by surprise, this time by terrific swings, more like incipient spins than anything else.

I asked for permission to land. Cautiously, nice and

straight, and with a good reserve of speed. I made my approach, lowered the flaps, and everything went off fine until I tried to level out—those thick wings seemed to have plenty of 'lift', but they were treacherous. I had just begun to ease the stick back when the whole contraption stalled and dropped like a stone. Then it bounced back a good thirty feet with its nose in the air, amidst an appalling din.

I opened up like mad to break the fall, wrestling at the same time with the ailerons so as not to land on my back.

Eventually, after bucking two or three times like a mustang, my Typhoon finally calmed down and rolled drunkenly down the runway, which now looked distinctly short. However, I managed to stop before ramming the scenery, in a cloud of smoke and oil. A strong smell of burnt rubber rose from my poor tyres, which had stood up valiantly to seven tons landing on them at 120 mph.

Luckily my poor landing didn't seem to have attracted much attention—there had been such rotten ones that afternoon, including two involving serious damage, that, as long as the kite was still in one piece, it was considered as a good 'arrival'. My face was moist, but my morale was better.

PIERRE CLOSTERMANN DSO DFC

1945

Everybody knew the war in Europe would be won this year —but it still had to be won. The Luftwaffe was far from finished; the year was barely six hours old when mass formations of fighters and fighter-bombers, flying low under the Allied radar, pounced on airfields in France, Holland and Belguim and destroyed some 300 Allied aircraft on the ground. It was one of the RAF's biggest defeats, softened only by the fact that few pilots were lost since so few even got airborne. But Luftwaffe losses had also been heavy; the result was that the tactical air war came to a virtual halt for a week.

*

But Bomber Command was still marching almost nightly against Germany, although now it was the secondary cities which suffered under the most experienced strategic air force in the world—aided by roving Mosquito night fighters. German night-fighter pilots made a wry joke about the low levels they had to fly to live long enough to earn the Knight's Cross. A Luftwaffe pilot describes one such night at

RITTERKREUZ HEIGHT

On this night which was to prove fatal for the city of Würzburg I had been in readiness with my wing from 1900 hours. We still did not know which German city was to be rotted out within the next few hours. Division merely said that two large formations had started from the London area. I got ready with my crew for a tough op. The Naxos apparatus—our talisman against the Mosquitoes—was checked once more, for our lives depended upon it. Half an hour later the fighter-directing officer fired a green flare. Orders to take off. . . . Both my engines started well, but then the props stopped. I pressed once more on the starter and revved up. I had injected a highly explosive mixture into the pistons but the engines would not fire. My fellow pilots were already on the runway. I tried once more but in vain. The mechanics rushed up. Feldwebel Schoppke and Obergefreiter Quandt knew my machine backwards. It could only be some trifling hitch, for these two trusty mechanics had kept my machines in perfect order since my first ops in 1941. I had never had any engine trouble.

'Come on, Schoppke, get in the crate and try your luck,' I shouted above the din.

At that moment a young NCO came rushing over from the ops room. 'Latest enemy position, Herr Hauptmann. The bomber stream is just short of Ulm. In a few minutes it will be overhead. Probable target Nuremberg.'

Hell, I thought. I must get in the air or else I shall be a laggard. Schoppke went on trying to get the engine to run. The last warning came from the ops rooms over the loudspeaker.

'Achtung, achtung! Enemy bombers will be overhead in a few minutes. All lights out. Immediate action stations. Mosquito attacks are to be expected. Careful on taking off.'

With or without care I had to get in the air. At last the engine started and long white flames poured from the exhaust pipes. Schoppke pushed the throttle forward and the machine bucked. No sparking plugs failure and no jerks in the engine. I jumped on the wing and slapped my leading mechanic on the shoulder. He helped me to fasten the parachute and I taxied to the start.

Grasshoff called up the Headquarters which answered immediately: 'Lobster from Thrust—I'm taxi-ing to the flarepath. Please light up when I give full throttle. Switch off as soon as I'm airborne.'

'Victor, victor,' replied Lobster. 'Look out for Mosquitoes. Good luck.'

I taxied in the dark and took up my place on the runway. After a brief glance at the instruments and the engines I gave her full throttle. The flarepath lights went on and were switched off as soon as I was airborne.

I had hardly levelled out the machine when Mahle shouted: 'Look out, Mosquito!'

I thought as much. The Tommies had waited until the fish was on the line. But I did not intend to make things easy for them. I hedge-hopped over the fields and shook off my pursuer. The British were very tough but they did not propose to indulge in any near the ground aerobatics. My crew breathed with relief. We'd made it. We all felt rather uncomfortable after this display of stunting. I zoomed and forced the engine to take me up to 12,000 feet. On the tactical waves we heard new enemy reports. Suddenly there was decisive news.

'Achtung, achtung! Bombers are flying in the direction of Nuremberg. A moderate-sized formation reported over Ulm making for Würzburg. Probable objectives. Nuremberg and Würzburg.'

'They're not even going to respect the hospital city of Würzburg,' growled Mahle. 'There really aren't any armament factories there.'

I thought for a moment. Würzburg or Nuremberg. I decided for the former and changed on to a northerly course. The night was reasonably clear apart from a few 'regulation clouds' at 9,000 feet. 'We might be able to use them if a Mosquito gets on our tail,' said Mahle. The air seemed empty. In the distance we saw the ribbon of the Main. The moon treacherously lit up the great river. Grasshoff reported contacts on his radar. Then the storm broke. We were approaching the bombers. Before we had got to the enemy, the Master of Ceremonies had dropped his marker flares over the city. Parachute flares drifted slowly down, making the night look ghostly.

'Courier 800 yards ahead,' reported Grasshoff.

At that moment a slight ticking began in my headphones. Long-range night fighters! Despite this warning I remained on my course and gave my Me full throttle. The ticking grew louder.

'Mosquitoes,' shouted Mahle.

I took avoiding action. The British pilot's tracers went wide below my right wing. The hunt started again. Now we

401

were flying directly over the city among the bomber stream.

Then the appalling destruction began. On the orders of the Master of Ceremonies the four-engined bomber crews opened their bays and rained incendiaries on to the city below. The phosporus ignited as soon as it hit the air and joined into a huge burning cloud which slowly settled on the city. It was a Dantesque and terrible sight. Those unfortunate people who were still in the city! This fiery cloud knew no pity. It sank on churches and houses, palaces and citadels, broad avenues and narrow streets. At the outset burning drops spurted from the cloud causing isolated fires. Then the burning veil enveloped Würzburg. In a few moments a gigantic patch of flame lit up the dark night and turned the clouds to scarlet. Würzburg was burning. By the glow of the doomed city the bombers found their direction. The small wings and slender bodies gleamed brightly. I could have shot time and again, but as soon as I was in position Mahle shouted: 'Achtung! Mosquito!' I had instructed him only to warn me in case of great danger. Thus I dared not reflect when his words rang out. The delay of a second and we should fall like a blazing torch out of the sky. Then a four-engined Lancaster crossed my path. Without a thought I poured a long burst into its fuselage and wings. The crate exploded in the air and spun down with its crew. That was my only kill over Würzburg and incidentally my last kill of the war. It attracted the entire enemy night-fighter pack on my heels. We could hardly watch the bomber crash on the ground before they set upon us. The Naxos apparatus lit up constantly. Mahle no longer shouted 'Achtung!' but sat and fired his tracers at the Mosquitoes. No avoiding action—no banking—no hide and seek in the clouds was of any avail. The British pilot remained on my tail. Fortunately he always began from long range and his aim was inacurrate.

And then suddenly Mahle shouted in terror, 'Mosquito close behind us.'

His voice made me shudder. Even as I banked the burst hit my machine. There was a reek of smoke and fire. Terrifying seconds ahead, but I let my machine dive to be rid of my pursuer. The altimeter fell rapidly—2,500 . . . 2,000 . . . 1,500 . . . 1,000. Now I had to pull out unless I wanted to go

402

straight into the ground. I pulled with all my might on the joystick and got the diving machine under control. Luckily the controls answered. There was still an acrid smell of smoke in the cabin. Perhaps a cable was smouldering, but the engines were running smoothly.

We hedge-hopped over Swabia towards our airfield in Leipheim. Mahle lit up the cockpit with his torch. Everything was in order. Then he focused it on the engine. There was a white trickle on the starboard wing. Petrol! One of the pipes had been shot through and the fuel was leaking out. The needle on the fuel indicator slowly sank to empty. This was a fatal situation. But misfortunes never come singly. Mahle reported reactions in the Naxos, and the sinister tick-ticking started again in the headphones. The British never give up. This one pursued us even to our airfield. We had to land and avoiding action was impossible. It was pointless coming down anywhere except in Leipheim. Grasshoff called the airfield which replied faintly. A few terrifying minutes . . . I pumped the petrol from the port into the starboard tank with the electric pump. Would we have enough? If the right engine conked it would be the end. I now spoke to the ground station myself. Everything depended upon a skilful landing or else the Mosquito would shoot me down as I approached the runway.

'Lobster from Thrush 1. Come in, please.'

'Thrush 1 from Lobster. Victor, victor. Loud and clear. Take care—night fighters circling the airfield.'

That was to have been expected. The Britisher did not want to miss me.

I replied, 'Victor, victor. I must land. Little fuel left. Don't light up. I'll land blind. Put a white lamp on the landing across and one red lamp at the end of the flare-path. Don't switch on.'

The ground station had understood my plan to fool the Mosquito. Mahle sat at his guns in the rear cockpit. I lowered the wing flaps to 20' and circled at low speed over the airfield. The British were searching. The ticking in my headphones was continuous, but the fellows did not dare to come down. I was more than 100 feet above the ground. Tensely I watched the proceedings on the runway. At any moment the two ground lights would go on. The perspira-

403

tion was pouring from my forehead. I only hoped that the two lights would be sufficient to bring my machine down in safety. I must rely entirely upon my instruments, for the two petrol lamps would neither give me my height nor the direction of the machine. Should I not let them turn on the lights just as I landed? But this seemed too risky. The Mosquitoes were looking with Argus eyes at this field, and if it lit up they would immediately see the machines parked and the sheds. During these reflections I gained height. The red control lamps of the petrol tanks lit up. That meant fuel for not more than five minutes. I must land. . . .

I had tuned in my radio to the ground station in order to give the Tommies no hint. But now I was in great danger. I pressed the button.

'Lobster from Thrush 1. Hurry please, hurry please. Fuel for another five minutes.'

Oberfeldwebel Kramer replied at once. 'Thrush 1 from Lobster. Lamps in position. You can land.' We looked for them and Mahle was the first to discover them. They gave a very faint light. Directly above the white lamp I started the stopwatch and set my machine on its course. The white light disappeared behind the tail unit. If I flew correctly as I came in over the field it would bob up ahead of me.

Mahle suddenly shouted: 'There's one ahead to starboard. A bit higher.'

I only caught a glimpse of exhaust pipes disappearing in the darkness.

'For God's sake don't shout so loud, Mahle,' I replied.

The seconds passed. If only my fuel would last out. A short pressure on the hydraulic gear. Undercarriage lowered. . . . At any moment now the white lamp would appear in the darkness. My eyes peered into the night. There it was. Throttle back. Float . . . The wheels touched down. I put on the brakes and the machine gradually came to a standstill. We'd made it. Grasshoff opened the cockpit roof.

'Herr Hauptmann, the Tommies are droning right overhead. Something's up.'

I cautiously gave a little throttle to prevent the flames darting from the engine. Any reflection would betray us.

In the darkness we taxied to our dispersal pen. Then the accident happened. An over-eager mechanic, trying to be helpful, flashed his green torch. The Mosquitoes were on the watch.

I turned the machine into the wind and cut off the engine.

WILHELM JOHNEN

*

On 13th February, the full weight of Bomber Command was thrown against a hitherto untouched city:

DRESDEN

Normally, when a squadron was briefed for what they regarded as a worthwhile target, they raised a cheer when the station commander came to the rostrum to speak, even when the target was tough like Hamburg or Berlin. With Dresden the cheers were absent. With Dresden there seemed to be a definite, perhaps a studied, lack of information on the city and the nature of the defences. Encouraged though they were by talk of Gestapo Headquarters and poison-gas plants, many of the crews were distinctly unhappy when they heard about the refugees. One of the squadrons of No 100 (Radio Counter Measures) Group was briefed in full about the nature of the target; the intelligence officer even suggested, probably not seriously, that the very object of the raid was to kill as many as possible of the refugees known to be sheltering in the city, and to spread panic and chaos behind the Eastern front. This remark, however, did not meet with a jocular reception and to the last man the whole squadron decided to co-operate, but only to the letter of their orders: it was still the practice of a few bomber crews to take along bits of concrete and old bottles to drop on enemy villages and towns they passed over. Unanimously they voted to show their disapproval for this mission by omitting this practice for the night. This kind of reception was, however, by no means general in Bomber Command for the night's operation; especially in stations where the real nature of the city had been obscured, the reaction 'was the usual light-hearted chaff, probably covering their concern at the distance of the target', as a bomb-aimer described it.

Three of the Lancasters of the two pathfinder squadrons had been equipped as special Link aircraft; their task was to communicate the instructions of the Master Bomber in Morse to the bomber force if the speech transmitter equipment installed in the bombers should fail or be jammed. Sometimes one of the bomber wireless operators would switch on his VHF set by accident, jamming communications between the bombers and the Master Bomber; at other times the Germans themselves were responsible. The Links also acted as means of communication between the Master Bomber and the Group's base in England. Corrected weather forecasts and wind estimations were exchanged between the Master Bomber and the base; on such operations the Master Bomber was required to make a snap judgment of the success of the raid and pass it back to England even as he was still over the target.

On the Dresden raid, the three Link Lancasters were all provided by 97 Squadron. In Link 1, piloted by a Flight Lieutenant, a special wire-recorder had been installed to make a permanent record of the progress of the attack; the record would be produced at the raid assessment inquiry into the execution of the raids on Dresden during the following days: RAF Bomber Command was still eager to learn from its mistakes, and to develop and extend its procedure and techniques.

As the Master Bomber's Mosquito was still approaching the target area, he switched on one of his two VHF speech transmitters; now for the first time radio silence was broken over Germany: 'Controller to Marker Leader: How do you hear me? Over.' The Marker Leader replied that he could hear the Master Bomber clearly 'at strength five.' A similar inquiry of the first Link aircraft recorded that communications between Link 1 and Master Bomber were 'loud and clear'. The whole operation would be directed in plain speech, code-words were used only for prime orders like 'Recall', or 'Mission Cancelled'. No acknowledgement was required by the Master Bomber except for the order 'Go home'. The cloud was still quite apparent over the target area; the Master Bomber called up the Marker Leader once more: 'Are you below cloud yet?' 'Not yet,' replied the Marker Leader. He too had just lost nineteen thousand feet in less than five minutes; the navigator in the Master Bomber's aircraft had in fact suffered agonies from ear trouble during the descent. The Master Bomber waited, then asked the Marker Leader whether he could see the Primary Green dropped by 83 Squadron. 'Okay, I can see it. The cloud is not very thick.' 'No,' confirmed the Master Bomber. 'What do you make the base of it?' After a moment the Marker Leader replied, 'The base is about 2,500 feet.' It was time for the marking to begin. The flares were burning very brilliantly over the city now; the whole town looked serene and peaceful. The Marker Leader in his Mosquito inspected the target carefully: to his surprise he could not see one searchlight, not one light flak piece firing. Cautiously he circled the town, picking up his bearings.

'As I flew across the city it was very obvious to me that there was a large number of black-and-white half-timbered buildings; it reminded me of Shropshire and Hereford and Ludlow. They seemed to be lining the river which had a number of rather gracefully-spanned bridges over it; the buildings were a very striking feature of the city's architecture.'

In the marshalling yards of Dresden-Friedrichstadt he could see a single locomotive puffing industriously away with a short length of goods wagon. Outside a large building which he identified as the Central Station—he had spent the afternoon at Woodhall Spa studying the mosaic aerial picture of Dresden—there was another plume of smoke where a locomotive was struggling to pull a passenger train with some white coaches out into the open air.

Then it was time to begin his first run up on the marking point. Over the Central Station he was two thousand feet up. Now he began to dive sharply; he kept a wary eye on the altimeter: the target indicator bombs were set to burst barometrically at seven hundred feet. If released below that altitude, they would either set the little wooden plane on fire, or not cascade properly.

His eyes tracked the railway lines out of the Central Station, round in a right-hand curve to the river. Just to the left of the railway bridges lay his marking point; now that he was in the position to commence his run, he called out, 'Marker Leader: Tally-ho!' to warn off other markers who might otherwise be commencing marking runs; from two thousand feet the Mosquito dived to less than eight hundred feet, opening its bomb-doors as it entered upon the straight run-in to the aiming point. The first flash cartridge fired as the camera was pointing at the Dresden–Friedrichstadt Krankenhaus, the biggest hospital-complex in Central Germany. In its lens the camera trapped the picture of the 1,000-pound target indicator bomb slipping out of the bomb bay, the finned canister silhouetted menacingly on top of a small oblong building in the hospital's grounds.

The Marker Leader levelled out briskly, maintaining a high speed, as he still did not know whether there was any flak to come up, and as the flare illumination of both Dresden and his aircraft was particularly good. The camera flashed a second time: the bomb was a dark fleck above the brightly lit stadium. One of the Mosquito pilots who had not been warned of the new camera technique shouted an involuntary, 'My God, the Marker Leader's been hit,' to his navigator. But at the same moment the first red marker bomb cascaded perfectly into a blaze of light.

The Mosquito swooped across the stadium towards the river at 300 miles per hour. Its camera was still flashing regularly once per second. The third flash was over the hospital's railway siding; a hospital train from the Eastern front was unloading there: now it was recorded for all time on a strip of film before the bombers arrived to blast the sidings from the map. The fourth flash showed the Marker Leader that he was across the River Elbe; a cotton-wool plume of steam coiled up from a single saddle-tank locomotive puffing along the railway running beside the Japanese Palace Gardens. 'Marker Two: Tally-ho!' The second Marker Mosquito was already following the railway lines round, ready to estimate the overshoot of the Marker Leader that he was across the River Elbe; a cot-

At the same time, the Master Bomber checked the three Dresden stadiums on his District Target Map, checked the stadium that had been marked, and announced grimly:

'You've marked the wrong one.' For a moment the VHF radio recorded only uncomfortable breathing. Then there was a relieved: 'Oh no, that's all right, carry on.' The Master Bomber could clearly see the red marker flare burning in a brilliant crimson pool not far from the stadium. 'Hello, Marker Leader,' he called, 'that indicator is about 100 yards east of the marking point.' This initial marking shot was extraordinarily accurate. When one remembers that during the first night of the Battle of Hamburg in 1943, the markers of the official Pathfinder Group were anything from half a mile to seven miles wide of the aiming point, also using a visual technique, the fundamental difference between the standards achieved by the two Bomber Groups can be judged. 'Controller to Marker Leader: Good shot! Back up, then; back up.' 'Marker Leader to all Markers: Back up, back up.' 'Marker Five to Marker Leader: Clear?' 'Marker Two to Marker Leader: Tally-ho!'

The time was six and a half minutes past ten. Zero hour was still nearly nine minutes away, but the target marking point was clearly and unambiguously marked. There remained only for the other Mosquitoes to unload their red marker bombs onto the one already burning, to reinforce the glow. The only thing which was concerning the Master Bomber was the visibility of the marker bombs through the thin layers of cloud, especially for the Lancaster bombers who had been stacked in the top height band at some eighteen thousand feet; the Lancaster squadrons had been briefed to approach the marking point at different altitudes to avoid collisions as they fanned out over the city. A specially equipped Lancaster of 97 Squadron had been positioned at eighteen thousand feet over Dresden. This was Lancaster Check 3. 'Controller to Check 3: Tell me if you can see the glow.' 'I can see three TIs through cloud,' replied the Check Lancaster. The Master Bomber, thinking that the Check had reported seeing only 'green TIs', queried this. 'Good work. Can you see the reds yet?' 'Check 3 to Controller: I can just see reds.'

One after another two more Marker Mosquitoes tally-ho'd and dropped their reds on the stadium. The Master Bomber remembered that the Mosquitoes only carried one marker each, and warned them to 'take it easy'; they might be needed later on. The time was seven minutes past ten, Zero minus eight. The marking had proceeded much better than expected. 'Controller to Flare Force: No more flares, no more flares.' One more Mosquito called out its intention of marking the stadium. A trifle impatiently the Master Bomber called out to all the markers: 'Hurry up and complete your marking and then clear the area.' A brilliant concentration of red markers was now burning around the stadium, each marker a pool of burning candles, scattered over a radius of several hundred square feet, too numerous to be extinguished even if there were any Germans brave enough to venture into what must seem to them the very heart of the target area.

In Dresden the Horizont flak-transmitter was warning: 'The formation of nuisance raiders is orbiting from Martha-Heinrich 1 to Martha-Heinrich 8; the first waves of the heavy bomber formations are at Nordpol-Friedrich, now Otto-Friedrich 3; their heading is East-North-East.' MH1, MH8, OF3—these were all the appropriate squares of the grid overprinted on the flak commanders' plotting charts; in their excitement, however, the speaker had confused the nuisance raiders—in fact the nine Mosquitoes of the marker force—with the heavy bombers, and vice versa. Moments later, it dawned on the flak commander of the area that these were in fact the pathfinder Mosquitoes arriving from the Chemnitz area, and the heavy bomber formations were approaching over Riesa from the northwest; at once a signal was passed to the local ARP Control Room in the basement of the Albertinum building. The last broadcast report from this Control was a shrill: 'Bombs falling on the City area! Comrades, keep sand and water handy!' But still the citizens had not been warned to take cover.

The Master Bomber made one final check with the Lancaster in the top height band: 'Can you see the red target indicators?' The reply was satisfactory. 'I can see the green and the red TIs'. It was nine minutes past ten, zero minus six. The marking was complete, and the Master Bomber wanted the attack to begin at the earliest possible moment; his tanks would only allow him to stay over the target for another twelve minutes. He wanted to witness the commencement of the attack and ensure that all went well.

It was at this moment that the Dresden people, by now cleared from the open spaces and listening apprehensively in their basements and cellars to the sound of the light Mosquitoes racing backwards and forwards across the rooftops of the Saxon capital, were informed for the first time of the nature of the real threat to their city. At 1009 the ticking clock which replaced wireless broadcasts during alerts in Germany was sharply interrupted. The unmistakably Saxon voice of a very agitated announcer broke out of the loudspeakers: 'Achtung, Achtung, Achtung! The first waves of the large enemy bomber formation have changed course, and are now approaching the city boundaries. There is going to be an attack. The population is instructed to proceed at once to the basements and cellars. The police have instructions to arrest all those who remain in the open. . .'

In his Mosquito three thousand feet above the silent city, the Master Bomber was repeating over and over into his VHF transmitter: 'Controller to Plate-rack Force: Come in and bomb glow of red TIs as planned. Bomb glow of red TIs as planned.'

It was exactly 10.10½ pm.

The Marker Leader called up the Master Bomber, asking: 'Can I send the Marker Force home now?'

It occurred to the Master Bomber that the Germans might well have a decoy site in the neighbourhood; without a target-map in his possession showing such sites it would not be wise to discount the possibility. 'Controller to Marker Leader: If you stick around for a moment, and keep one lad with yellow, the rest can go home.' 'Okay, Controller. Marker Leader to all markers: Go home, go home. Acknowledge.' One after another Markers Three, Four, Five, Six, Seven and Eight acknowledged: 'Going home.'

The Marker Leader spotted a circling aircraft with its green and red navigation lights on. This was asking for trouble over enemy territory. 'You have your navigation lights on,' he warned the aircraft. The lights did not go out. It must, in fact, have been one of the German Me 110s still

411

circling to gain height; but the Mosquitoes were completely unarmed, and short of ramming the fighter, there was nothing that anybody could do about it.

The Master Bomber was still broadcasting to the main force bombers: 'Controller to Plate-rack Force: bomb concentration of red TIS. As planned as soon as you like.'

The guns defending Dresden were still silent. Not even a muzzle flash was to be seen. It began to dawn on the Master Bomber that in fact Dresden was undefended. He could safely order the heavy four-engined Lancasters down to bomb from lower altitudes, thereby ensuring a more even distribution of bombs over the sector marked for attack. He called up the Link 1 Lancaster which was in constant Morse contact with the bombers: 'Tell the aircraft in top height band to come down below the medium cloud.' 'Roger.' By 1013 the bombs had started falling on Dresden. The Marker Leader called the Master Bomber's attention to the characteristic heaving explosions of the huge 4,000 pound and 8,000 pound high-explosive bombs, designed to smash the windows and rip off the roofs of the highly combustible Dresden Old City buildings, some of them dating back over a thousand years. A vivid blue flash split the darkness as a stick of bombs, falling wide of the target sector, detonated; the crews decided later that an electricity installation must have been hit.

'Marker Leader to Controller: The bombs seem to be falling okay now. Over.' 'Yes, Marker Leader. They look pretty good.' 'Hello, Plate-rack Force. That's good bombing. Come in and aim for the red TIS as planned. Careful overshoot, somebody! Somebody has dropped very wide.' 'Controller to Marker Leader: Go home now, if you like. Thank you.' 'Hello, Controller: Thank you, going home.' 'Good work, Plate-rack Force. That's nice bombing,' commented the Master Bomber.

The Lancasters ran up to the marking point on the stadium squadron by squadron, each aircraft approaching the stadium and the brilliant glow of red marker bombs on a different heading, some heading due south, others almost due east, fanning out across the blazing Old City. The whole of the cheese-shaped sector was a mass of twinkling fires and, here and there, the brilliant flash of the big explosive

412

bombs, churning up the debris and splintering the buildings, lit up the city's roof-tops.

By eighteen minutes past ten the patterns of bombs were covering the whole sector, and one or two tell-tale splashes of lights were visible in the dark areas outside. The Master Bomber had seen these bomb loads go down wide too, and now he warned the rest of the force of Lancasters: 'Hello, Plate-rack Force: Try to pick out the red glow. The bombing is getting wild now. Pick out the red glow if you can, then bomb as planned.'

He had another three minutes in which he could stay over the city. In the near distance he spotted something else beginning to glow. The red and yellow glow of a German decoy site being vainly ignited. The thing the Germans never realised when they designed decoy sites was that a burning city from the air was an untidy, turbulent mass of billowing smoke, bursting high-explosive charges, and irregular patches of myriads of incendiaries; the German decoy sites were built in neat rectangles, the burning 'incendiaries' tidily scattered at regular intervals across the ground. Nevertheless, it was the Master Bomber's duty to ensure that no bomb loads were needlessly drawn astray by decoys. On this occasion he did not consider that the decoy was worth wasting a yellow cancellation-marked bomber on; he merely broadcast to all crews of the remaining Plate-Rack Force bombers: 'Decoys at twelve to fifteen miles on a bearing 300 degrees true from town centre.' A minute later he repeated the warning: 'Complete bombing quickly and go home. Ignore the decoy fires.'

At twenty-one minutes past ten on the night of 13th February 1945, the Master Bomber called up the Link Lancaster aircraft for the last time, as he turned his Mosquito on to the new bearing which would take him home. 'Controller to Link 1: Send home:

' "TARGET ATTACKED SUCCESSFULLY STOP PRIMARY PLAN STOP THROUGH CLOUD STOP." '

DAVID IRVING

Nobody has admitted responsibility for ordering the Dresden raid, but it now seems clear that it originated at a level higher than the Command itself. It may well have been a

413

political gesture to impress the advancing Russians (who occupied the city soon after) with Western air power. Civilian death figures are very uncertain, but the author of the above account recently revised his estimate of over 100,000 down to about 25,000. It would have been higher had not some bomber crews, who were no fools and had to be something of individualists, deliberately pitched their loads wide. But it remained a black mark on the Command's record and was probably why bomber crews never received a special campaign star at the end of the war (as did the relatively few Battle of Britain fighter pilots). A small point, perhaps—but the Command lost twice as many dead as did Dresden; forty times as many as Fighter Command in The Battle.

*

Step by step, the RAF fighters moved forward. Leading a wing into Holland went 'Johnnie' Johnson, by now the RAF's leading 'ace'.

We struck camp and pressed on to Twente. The airfield had been used by the Luftwaffe, but the brick runway had been bombed many times, and although it had been patched up, odd bricks lay all over the place and the surface looked uneven and dangerous. A fine-looking strip of grass lay alongside a wood on the east side of the airfield. The surface seemed reasonably dry and I thought it would make a far better runway than the crumbling bricks.

I circled Twente in my Spitfire that afternoon. I had a careful look round to clear my tail before making the final approach to our grass strip, for we were very near to the front and I didn't want to get bounced with wheels and flaps down. I landed safely, and an airman waved me to a dispersal point near the central building. I switched off and heard the usual tinkling of the engine as it cooled. The airman bent over the cockpit to lend a hand with the straps.

'Well, how do you like . . .' I began, and looked up as a lean, grey Messerschmitt roared a few feet over our heads.

The Hun had seen us, and over the far side of the field began to turn for his strafing run. I tore a finger-nail on the Sutton harness. Then I scrambled out of the cockpit with the parachute still strapped on, tumbled down the easy slope of the wing root, fell to the ground and grovelled under the belly of the Spitfire. We could hear the Messerschmitt boring in. What a bloody way to buy it, I thought. After five years and just made a group captain!

We heard two crumps in quick succession above the noise of the engine, then a large explosion when the Messerschmitt hit the deck. The two of us scrambled to our feet: on the far side of the field a column of dark, oily smoke rose into the calm spring air. The boy and I slapped dirt from our uniforms and laughed together. I said:

'Fill her up, son. I want to take off in half an hour.

Someone produced a jeep and I drove across the Twente airfield to thank the crew of the Bofors gun who had undoubtedly saved us from a nasty smack. They belonged to the RAF Regiment, and now, in their shirtsleeves, busied themselves about their gun. I shook hands with each one and congratulated them:

'A magnificent piece of shooting,' I said. 'Absolutely first class! I'll send you a crate of beer over as soon as I can get my hands on one.'

'Excuse me, sir,' said the young corporal, 'but would you confirm the 109 for us?'

I looked puzzled and pointed to the smouldering wreck about a hundred yards away.

'Surely that's all the confirmation you want,' I replied.

'Well, sir,' explained the corporal, 'they'll never believe the Regiment has shot down an enemy kite with only a couple of rounds.'

I led the wing on the Berlin show at the first opportunity. For this epic occasion our first team took to the air. George led a squadron and Tony Gaze flew with me again—the first time since we flew together in Bader's wing. We swept to Berlin at a couple of thousand feet above the ground, over a changing sunlit countryside of desolate heathland, small lakes and large forests, with the empty, double ribbon of the autobahn lying close on our starboard side.

We shall not easily forget our first sight of Berlin. Thick cloud covered the capital and forced us down to a lower level. The roads to the west were filled with a mass of refugees fleeing the city. We pressed over the wooded suburbs, and Berlin sprawled below us with gaping holes here and there. It was burning in a dozen different places and the Falaise smell suddenly hit us, the corrupting stench of death. The Russian artillery was hard at it: as we flew towards the east, we saw the flashes of their guns and the debris thrown up from the shells. Russian tanks and armour rumbled into the city from the east. Tony said:

'Fifty-plus at two o'clock, Greycap! Same level. More behind.'

'Are they Huns, Tony?' I asked, as I focused my eyes on the gaggle.

'Don't look like Huns to me, Greycap,' replied Tony. 'Probably Russians.'

'All right, chaps,' I said. 'Stick together. Don't make a move.' And to myself I thought: I'm for it if this mix-up gets out of hand!

The Yaks began a slow turn which would bring them behind our Spitfires. I could not allow this and I swung the wings to starboard and turned over the top of the Yaks. They numbered about a hundred all told.

'More above us,' calmly reported Tony.

'Tighten it up,' I ordered. 'Don't break formation.'

We circled each other for a couple of turns. Both sides were cautious and suspicious. I narrowed the gap between us as much as I dared. When I was opposite the Russian leader I rocked my wings, and watched for him to do the same. He paid no regard, but soon after he straightened out of his turn and led his ragged collection back to the east.

We watched them fly away. There seemed to be no pattern or discipline to their flying. The leader was in front and the pack followed behind. Rising and falling with the gaggle continually changing shape, they reminded me of a great, wheeling, tumbling pack of starlings which one sometimes sees on a winter day in England. They quartered the ground like buzzards, and every few moments a handful broke away from the pack, circled leisurely and than attacked something in the desert of brick and rubble. In this fashion they worked over the dying city.

Group Captain J. E. JOHNSON DSO DFC

*
416

For everybody, there was the

LAST OP

Just as I was about to return to our Dispersal, a formation of torpedo-carrying Beaufighters passed immediately overhead in a roar like thunder, coming from the north. There were swarms of them, about three Wings. They were on their way back from the monster shipping-strike organised against the notorious convoy at Kiel.

One of them had an engine on fire—there was the telltale trail of black smoke—and tried to land on our field. He went into a spin about 500 yards off and crashed with a terrific explosion near the bathing pool. The fire tender and the ambulance tore off.

'Christ, what's all the hurry?' murmured Peter West. 'There can't be much left.' How right he was. Ten minutes later the ambulance came slowly back, bearing the pitiful remains of the pilot and the observer.

We were still talking about it at dinner, an hour later in the mess, when Spy rushed up:

'Phone for you, Pierre.'

Who on earth could be wanting me at this ungodly hour? I leapt into the jeep and tore off to the Intelligence Room.

Ops on the phone:

'Take down the following, for immediate action: Grossenbrode air-naval base, reference N.54.22 E.11.05. Over 100 large transport aircraft loaded on beach and at anchor. Strong enemy fighter cover probable. Turn all available effectives on the designated objective. Strafe if possible. Actual method of execution left to your discretion. Inform Kenway of your plans at least ten minutes in advance. I will try to give you anti-flak Typhoons. Do not rely on them too much. Good luck.'

I said thank you and hung up. This sounded exciting, but I was furious. How delightful, after such a day, to be sent off again, at 8 pm on an objective like that!

I studied the wall map. Grossenbrode was about ninety miles as the crow flies, but the 'Met' reports said that Lübeck Bay and the Hamburg area were completely blocked. There was thundery cloud, with showers, up to 20,000 feet. We would have to make a detour to the north.

Tyres screeched on the concrete. The jeeps were beginning to arrive, carrying bunches of pilots. What with their interrupted dinner and the heavy day they had had, they were not in the best of tempers. A few were munching improvised sandwiches.

Everybody there? O.K. I quickly outlined the situation. We hadn't enough available aircraft to fly as a Wing, in formation by flights. So we would fly in twice three flights, each of four planes echeloned to starboard. As Bruce Cole was on leave I would lead the first formation of twelve Tempests and MacDonald, from 486, the second. Like that I hoped my twenty-four planes would be under control.

I couldn't then and there give precise details as to how the strike would be carried out; I would give the necessary orders on the spot over the radio. It would be more a question of what turned out to be advisable than a premeditated plan. In any case I had neither the necessary data nor the time to elaborate a plan of attack.

'Synchronise your watches . . . It's 2007 hours. Engine startup at 2015 hours. I shall take off as No 1, will do a wide circuit over the airfield to let the twenty-four planes get into proper formation, and I shall set course on the target at 2025 hours. Any questions? O.K. then, get weaving.'

For the other three in my section I chose F/Lt Bone, F/O Dug Worley and young Sgt Crow, whose third operational trip this would be. Not a particularly experienced trio, but I had no choice. I couldn't decently ask pilots who had already had three trips that day and who were completely creased, to do a fourth and certainly pretty tough one.

2015 hours. 'Grand Charles' was ready. The engine was already ticking over and Gray, lying on the wing, did a thumbs-up to show that everything was in order. The vast concrete expanse, framed by the great dark hangars, was alive with movement. As I strapped myself in I looked around. Engines ticked over, starter cartridges went off with a bang, mechanics rushed with maps or parachutes forgotten at the last minute. Pilots climbed awkwardly into their cockpits, festooned with Mae Wests and parachute harnesses.

2016 hours. 'Chocks away.' At 2025 hours, with the sun already low on the horizon and heavy cloudbanks rolling eastwards, I set course north, slowly gaining height. The formation this evening was lousy—difficult to fashion a homogenous team out of personnel from three different units.

'Come on, Filmstar, pull your bloody fingers out!'

Blue Section, which ought to have been on my left, was wandering about to my right, 1,500 feet above me. Yellow Two, Three, and Four were trailing along more than half a mile to the rear. I was on edge and called them to order without mincing my words.

We flew round Hamburg to avoid the clouds of dirty smoke rising from the burning buildings. My aircraft at last decided to fly in formation.

We flew over Neümunster at 10,000 feet and got shot at, very sloppily, by an 88 mm battery. We veered to starboard and set course 052°. The weather was deteriorating and I had to zigzag to avoid the blocks of cumulus which rose high in the sky like white towers.

'Hallo, Kenway, any gen?'

'Hallo, Filmstar Leader, Kenway answering, nothing at all.'

No signs of the recall I was secretly hoping for.

We were scarcely twenty miles from our objective when an impenetrable barrier of cloud blocked our way. I dived, followed by my formation, to try and find a way through underneath, but all we met was heavy rain and visibility zero. We quickly turned 180°, climbing and then 180° again, bringing us back to our original course.

What was to be done? One plane by itself, or at a pinch a couple, might succeed in getting through, but for a compact formation of twenty-four to try it was not only a ticklish business, it was damned risky. I insinuated as much to Kenway.

'Hallo, Kenway, Filmstar Leader here. The weather stinks.'

Kenway's answer was straight to the point and his tone of voice left no room for doubt.

'Filmstar Leader, press on regardless.'

All right then; 'Cloud formation, go!'

I divided up my planes into independent sections of four, each one taking up box formation. We would have to try to get through the clouds on a set course and hope to join up again the other side.

We plunged into the storm and immediately lost sight of each other. Christ, it was pretty bumpy in there and I concentrated hard on my instruments, with an occasional eye open for my three unfortunate companions, who were keeping as close as they dared. The layer of cloud was luckily not very thick. After a very few moments we emerged over the Straits of Fehmarn, near Heiligenhafen. The sky was clear before us, all the way. My cockpit had got fogged up but now it cleared and I prepared to pin-point our position.

'Look out, Filmstar Leader!'

In a fraction of a second the sky had filled with a whirling mass of aircraft . . . an unforgettable sight!

Below, to the right, the big airfield of Grossenbrode, with its seaplane base and its runways crawling with multi-engine aircraft. Beyond, a calm sea with a few ships at anchor. Behind us, a solid wall of clouds from which my Tempest sections were just emerging haphazard and at various heights. All round us were massive groups of thirty or forty German fighters on patrol. One of them had already seen us and was swooping down on Yellow Section.

In front of us, either on the ground or just taking off, were more than 100 enormous transport planes—theoretically my primary objective. In the air, about 100 enemy fighters. One group at 1,500 feet, another at 3,000, a third at 4,500, and two others on a level with us, i.e. about 10,000 feet. Above us there were certainly one more, perhaps two. And I only had twenty-four Tempests!

My mind was quickly made up. Filmstar Yellow and Blue Sections would attack the fighters above us, and Pink,

Black, and White Sections, commanded by MacDonald, would engage the Focke-Wulfs below us. In the meantime, I would try to slip through with my Red Section and shoot-up the airfield. I passed this on over the radio and then, closely followed by the rest of the section, I released my auxiliary tanks and went into a vertical dive, passing like a thunderbolt at 600 mph through a formation of Focke-Wulfs which scattered about the sky like a flock of swallows. I straightened out gradually, closing the throttle and following a trajectory designed to bring me over the airfield at ground level, from south-west to north-east.

All hell was let loose as we arrived. I was doing more than 500 mph by the clock when I reached the edge of the field. I was sixty feet from the ground and I opened fire at once. The mottled surface of the anchorage was covered with moored Dornier 24s and 18s. Three lines of white foam marked the wake of three planes which had just taken off. A row of Blohm und Voss's in wheeled cradles was lined up on the launching ramps. I concentrated my fire on a Bv 138. The moorings of the cradle snapped and I passed over the enormous smoking mass as it tipped up on the slope, fell into the sea, and began to sink.

The flak redoubled in fury. A flash on my right, and a disabled Tempest crashed into the sea in a shower of spray.

Jesus! The boats anchored off shore were armed, and one of them, a large torpedo boat, was blazing away with all it had. I instinctively withdrew my head into my shoulders and, still flying very low, veered slightly to the left, so fast that I couldn't fire at the Dorniers, then quickly swung to the right behind an enormous Ju 252 which had just taken off and was already getting alarmingly big in my gunsight. I fired one long continuous burst at him and broke away just before we collided. I turned round to see the Ju 252, with two engines ablaze and the tailplane sheared off by my shells, bounce on the sea and explode.

My speed had swept me far on—straight on to the torpedo boat which was spitting away with all her guns. I passed within ten yards of her narrow bows, just above the water and the thousand spouts raised by the flak. I caught a glimpse of white shapes rushing about on deck and of tongues of fire from her guns. The entire camouflaged superstructure seemed to be alive with them. Tracer shells ricocheted on the water and exploded all round over a radius of 500 yards. Some shrapnel mowed down a flock of seagulls which fell in the sea on all sides, panic-stricken and bleeding. Phew! Out of range at last!

I was sweating all over and my throat was so constricted that I couldn't articulate one word over the radio. Without realising it I had held my breath through the whole attack and my heart was thumping fit to burst. I regained height by a wide climbing turn to port. What was happening? The situation looked pretty grim. A terrific dog-fight was going on above the airfield. Three planes were coming down in flames—I was too far to see whether they were friend or foe. Another, pulverised, had left a trail of flaming fragments in the sky and a fifth was coming down in a spin, followed by a white trail of smoke. Yet others were burning on the ground.

The radio was transmitting an incomprehensible chaos of shouts, screams and curses, mingled with the vibrations of cannon firing. Near the torpedo boat, in the middle of a patch of foam, the remains of a plane were burning and heavy black smoke curled up from the sheet of burning petrol.

What had happened to the rest of my section? Not a sign of them in the sky. I had seen a Tempest crash on my right when the attack began, presumably Bone's. The machine which had been shot down by one of the German ships was Crow's, I was sure. As for Worley, he was invisible.

I thought for a moment. Ought I to try to join in the fight against the German fighters ranging above Heiligenhafen, or ought I to try a second run over the German base, taking advantage of the flap that was probably going on there?

Rather unwillingly I decided on the second course. I went down to sea level again and began to fly round Fehmarn Island at full speed. Suddenly I found myself face to face with three Dornier 24s, probably the three which had taken off from Grossenbrode a few seconds before our attack and whose wake I had seen. Do 24s are big three-engined flying boats of about nineteen tons, fairly slow but well provided with defensive weapons.

When I had recovered from my surprise I sheered off to keep outside their crossed fires, opened the throttle wide and zigzagged back towards them, taking photos. Then, keeping out of range of their machine-guns, I drew a deliberate bead on the first one. After two bursts one of his engines was on fire and another was coughing. He tried a forced landing, but as on this side of the promontory the sea was rough he capsized and did himself considerable damage.

Immediately I made for the two others, who were skimming the water and attempting to get away. Long black trails escaped from their overworked engines. I felt almost sorry for them. With my 250 mph margin of speed and my four cannon, it was almost like potting two sitting birds. I chose the left-hand one, which was heavily laden and had lagged slightly behind the other. But this time, the bastard turned very cleverly at the last moment. Carried forward by my speed I found myself, like a fool, having to turn within point-blank range of his rear gunner who hit me with three bullets. Luckily they were only popguns of 7.7 mm. A side-slip brought me back into firing position and my shells ravaged his fuselage at less than 100-yard range. His wing tanks caught fire. The rear gunner shut up. Within a few seconds the machine was enveloped in flames. The pilot tried to gain height to allow his crew to bale out, but he was too low. Three men did jump, all the same. Only one parachute opened and that closed again at once, swallowed up by a wave. The big machine was nothing but a ball of fire rolling a few feet above the crests of the waves in a thick trail of black smoke. A few seconds later it exploded.

I looked for the third one. It had miraculously vanished into the landscape, probably behind one of the little islands in the strait. This business had brought me right round Fehmarn and I climbed to 10,000 feet. There was Grossenbrode behind the hill. I swallowed the lump in my throat, instinctively tightened my safety straps and once again dived for the airfield for another strafe.

This time I took them by surprise. The flak was otherwise engaged, firing rather haphazardly in the general direction of the swarm of German fighters and Tempests. I swept between two hangars and emerged over the airfield at full throttle. There were so many aircraft piled up there that I didn't know which to choose. Right in my sight there was a row of enormous transport Arado 232s. Before my shells exploded on the first two I had time to take in the curious fuselages, the big doubledecker cabins, and the twenty-four-wheeled undercarts needed to support these gigantic machines.

A flak shell exploded within a few yards of my plane and shook it violently. Once out of range I broke away in a climbing spiral and found myself plumb in the middle of the scrap, which by this time was beginning to slacken.

I tried to rally my aircraft, but in that confusion it was difficult. The first thing I saw was a Tempest in a dive. It was spinning, increasingly fast. Then both the wings broke off . . . a few seconds later a bright flame leapt up between two hedges . . . no parachute.

Two FWs tried to engage me in a dog-fight, but I quickly got rid of them by breaking away under them. JF-H piloted by Bay the Australian, was in difficulties, its engine smoking. He was engaged with a Messerschmitt which was defending itself very cleverly, gradually reducing speed and beginning to get the upper hand. I roared towards the '109' and caught him by surprise, hitting him with at least two shells in the wing-root. The pilot, taken aback, instinctively reversed his turn and Bay, now in position, fired in his turn, hitting him again. Panic-stricken the Hun again reversed— I fired—he broke away—Bay fired—the Hun seemed to hang in the air for a moment, then one of his wings folded up in flames. The pilot managed to bale out all right, but his parachute screwed up.

At last my Tempests began to reform and, two at a time, cautiously withdrew from the scrap. The Huns gave ground and turned back one by one. They dived towards Grossenbrode, from which a column of smoke rose up in the sky —probably the two Arados burning.

A belated Focke-Wulf had slipped in amongst us and was desperately waggling his wings. Followed by Bay, I immediately went for him. A long burst—then suddenly my guns rattled noisily—no ammunition left. However, the Focke-Wulf had slowed down and was beginning to smoke, so I must have hit him after all. Bay fired in turn, point-blank, and pulverised him. He burst like a ripe tomato. This time the parachute did open.

The sun had now slid down, over there, behind the Danish islands. My patrol reformed in the luminous twilight. I counted the planes; two, four, eight, ten, eleven—and then two others, lower down, laboriously catching up, probably damaged.

With navigation lights on we flew back towards Fassberg in the deepening night. Already the outlines of the landscape were becoming blurred. The warm evening air gently rocked my 'Grand Charles'. As we approached the airfield, undercarts and flaps down, I wondered what Mitchell, our engineer officer, would have to say when I brought him back thirteen planes out of the twenty-four.

PIERRE CLOSTERMANN DSO DFC

*

Then came the end in Europe. For some it was sudden: the nights suddenly quiet because no engines had to be tested for the dawn; the days suddenly long because they knew there would be a tomorrow. But for others, in the prisoner-of-war camps, it was a more drawn-out affair.

THE LONG LIBERATION

10th April. After weeks of better and better news, and of resigning ourselves to waiting for a few more weeks until final liberation, morale took a jolt last night with the information that the camp is to be moved to Munich on the 11th by cattle-truck at sixty to a truck. This means travelling through the area of armed reconnaissance in front of the spearheads of Leipzig and Nuremberg areas. That the Germans can be capable of such an intention at a time like this is typical of their mentality. If the train reaches Munich without being strafed by our fighters, it will be an amazing stroke of fortune (and I know well enough what 20-mm can do to trains). However, should this move come off, my policy will be to try and stay behind with the sick. This is the allied target area—not Munich.

Two days ago we saw a Mosquito release a cloud of

leaflets overhead at about 20,000 feet. Intelligence reports that the contents are telling Russian prisoners-of-war that they will be liberated within ten to fifteen days.

The Russians have been literally starved by the goons and are dying in dozens of TB. The hospital is crammed with them. We had collections of food which we can hardly spare for them. Meanwhile great preparation of emergency food. Am fairly well off this time. One lives and learns. Over and above the Red Cross parcel I have acquired six chocolate bars, a tin of fish and three pounds of chocolate pemmican by judicious trading during the past weeks. So even without food from the Germans I should have nearly two weeks' food at a bare living rate. In addition I have just traded a blue sweater and a pair of Jack Sharkies for two boxes of prunes, value 2s. 6d. but two days' food.

Midday. Germans announce officially that we move tomorrow. Have sent name in as unfit to travel—this is only partially true. But one risk is as good as another and I prefer this one as a far better chance of liberation.

11th April. We have informed the Germans that this move is being carried out entirely without our co-operation. The only possible reason must be that we are intended to be held as hostages in the last stronghold in the mountainous area of Munich.

3 pm, Thursday, 12th April. After another night of tension, the camp was marched out to entrain for the incredible journey through the battle area to Munich this morning. As a notable change from the normal practice the move took place to the endless accompaniment of '*bitte,*' absolutely no '*Raus! Raus!*' at all.

Even more amazing, my scheme has come off. I have been left behind with the sick bods against all the advice of the well-meaning older kriegies who were, I think, suffering from a surfeit of sour grapes. This was the best chance, and now, not three hours after the main party had gone, comes the news that the Allies have cut the Magdeburg–Berlin autobahn. They could be here tomorrow.

The suspense is something of which I have never experienced the like. Waiting for a big low-attack show is a tea party in comparison! Atmosphere is electric.

The German officer on *appel* said, when I asked permission to remove a partition in a block for a new camp office: 'One does not start a new building at five to twelve.' At least they know the form.

The main party was still reported at the station, having spent the night in the trucks waiting for an engine which the Reichbahn people think is unlikely to materialise.

At 9.30 pm we received word that the boys were coming back as transport is impossible. Tank spearheads are reported at Brandenburg, Wittenberg—thirty miles from here—north of Halle and Leipzig. We are directly in front of the three-pronged thrust, and nothing short of fantastic ill-fortune can prevent our freedom in the next few days.

Saturday, 14th April. We worked late into last night trying to repair the damage in the blocks, caused by the departed kriegies themselves. In seven barracks there was hardly a serviceable bed. After appeals we received about fifteen per cent assistance in the big job of making sure that the returning boys would have at least a place to sleep. It is galling, the number of men who are not in the least concerned about the welfare of their friends and think only about themselves.

Still, somehow we arranged things, and this morning the first party came in at 10 am, to the accompaniment of clapping and cheering from the Poles, and a loud chorus of 'Hey, hey, the gang's all here!' from the Americans, accompanied by a trumpet, a violin and a mouth organ.

During yesterday's *appel* we held a two minutes' silence at attention in memory of Roosevelt who died yesterday. Particularly effective as the Americans were not on *appel* at the time, and remarkable because the company of German guards, who had paraded and were about to march off, remained at attention with us.

Reminder that the Germans are still in control came last night when two RAF NCOs attempted to climb the wire at the eleventh hour. One attacked a sentry with a bottle and was shot and killed. The other wounded. Bloody fools.

15th April. Terrific raid on Berlin suburb about twelve miles north of here last night. Made London show seem quite insignificant. Incredible din and display. Patton has a security blackout on the drive across the Elbe at Magdeburg. It is fifty miles away and is heading for us. Groups of kriegies stand in the compound all day staring south-west.

The atmosphere has more than expectancy, however, as the *abort,* always unsavoury, has sprung a leak.

Today's big tragedy—I sat on my pipe and broke it.

Monday, 16th April. Tantalising news that the camp at Magdeburg to which the remainder of Luft 3 were sent from Sagen, has been liberated intact! When will our turn come?

Tuesday, 17th April. Another great Fortress raid passed over this morning. Mustangs and Thunderbolts are constantly in sight. Every thud and explosion, every flash of light in the sky is taken to be an indication of the advancing Americans.

Stalag 11A consisting of some 4,000 Allied soldiers was evacuated into this area last week and, having arrived, had nowhere to go. They are living in the open, with no food supplies and no medical attention, and are in a tragic condition. The SBO sent our last reserve of Red Cross parcels to them yesterday together with two doctors and drugs.

Four hundred Russian sick were suddenly taken from our camp yesterday for destination unknown.

Wednesday, 18th April. Day after day, rumours add to the tension. The Russians are advancing fifty miles to the east, the Allies form miles to the west and south, but we are still here! The new optimisty has not borne fruit and now there is a new situation: no more Red Cross food.

Thursday, 19th April, night. The strain of boredom of the last few days was relieved at midnight when the Wing Commanders were routed out for a meeting with the SBO. His office was crammed with a circle of figures crouched round the table upon which lay a map of the area and two guttering lamps. He told us that the Russians had broken through south-east of us, were less than thirty miles away, and that the Germans proposed to march the whole camp unit of 4,000 prisoners-of-war in hostile country with no destination and no supplies of food or drugs, and most probably no shelter. The whole district is a battle area and such an action on the part of the goons cannot but have tragic results.

Friday, 20th April, morning. Still no further action by the Germans. We have our remaining food stocks packed and ready. Whether we go or stay, there will be no more food in a week's time. With the possibility of freedom nearer than it has ever been, the chance of getting the chop is rather great. But to hell with the war! The only course is to relapse into one's normal state of mental rigidity and sunbathe.

Saturday, 21st April. The most amazing day of my life. All night fires raged, guns thundered, and cannon shattered and at dawn a violent tank battle took place at Luckenwalde. Jüterbog, twelve miles to the south, is in flames. FW 190s are ground-strafing within sight at all times. In short we are in the front line.

(By now most of the German guards had deserted, leaving the prisoners in charge of their own camp).

We are in the most critical of all stages now. Nearly free but without news of relieving forces, and in this country of brutality and horror anything might happen yet.

We know that the Russians are all round us. Perhaps they will be here tomorrow. I win £30 if they are. It is grand to have a job again. Quite a strange thing using a telephone!

Hell! An FW 190 has just strafed the whole length of the camp. I must go and see if there have been casualties.

Midnight, and no casualties. The organisation is almost complete. Amazingly enough the telephone network is operating and I have a set in my temporary office-cum-bed-room now. Very tired, have checked and arranged pickets on the wire of the NCO's compound.

Sunday, 22nd April, midday. Russians are here in force. Fighting all round. Local tank commander's attitude is very brusque and dogmatic. I don't think they like us very much. Tanks charging up and down have torn up our communications and in places the wire. The French are hysterical, the British a little less so, and the Norwegians are calm. The Americans are reported only a few miles away. I hope they get here before this comedy becomes a tragedy.

At long last the Red Air Force's close support Aira-Cobras, Yaks, and Stormoviks fly above us. So do the Luftwaffe, putting up a brave show to the last. It was fascinating to watch a silver dart of a Messerschmitt delta jet dive straight down on to a formation of forty Fortresses, then bang! bang! and a Fortress fell away while the Me 163 shot straight up into cloud.

In another scrap two Me 109's shot down three out of twelve Aira-Cobras without loss. The Aira-Cobras were flying in formation under cloud. I caught a glimpse of the 109s as they dived straight astern, shot down two of the Cobras, and whipped up into cloud leaving the rest of the formation running round in circles wondering what had happened. Farther on the Me 109s came down again through another hole in the cloud and destroyed the third Aira-Cobra. They suffered no loss themselves.

1 pm. The Russians depart leaving us in temporary control. They have brought up a quantity of flak already, so it seems as if the area is nearly stabilised. However there are still plenty of bangs, and plenty of great unneighbourliness in this area.

The news announces tanks penetrating deep into Berlin.

Evening. Violent fighting in the woods to north. Shells whistling and screaming overhead, and 109s dive-bombing the autobahn. The Russians have added heavy flak to their set-up here. The din is fantastic. More fierce fighting on the boundaries and cannon-strafing by Junkers 88s. Two Serbs and a number of Russians killed in the fighting round the camp. Violent action between a Russian tank and Germans as it left the main gate. The Russians seemed to win. They have taken General Ruge with them to fly him to Moscow. This leaves the SBO as the senior Allied CO.

(Undated.) Told officers and pickets to dissuade the men from going through the wire if possible, but if told to 'b—— off', to 'b—— off' promptly and avoid incident. Then talked to the chaps in the blocks and reported to the SBO. Suggested that all compounds should be open, giving free circulation throughout the whole camp but within the wire. Bed at 2.30 am. Strafed by a Ju 88 at 4 am. Cannon shells all over the shop but fortunately no casualties.

8 am. Another direct threat to officers. Three sections of the wire cut away and Army NCOs loose. The RAF hanging-fire though pretending to follow Army lead. Walked into each barrack and addressed the men. Think I put the position over and am more certain than ever the trouble is due to just one or two bad characters. At one point nearly used

430

the SBO's authority to throw the worst types into the cooler, but steered clear. Am sure freedom of circulation within the whole camp would ease the situation.

This is the worst couple of days in my experience without exception. The feeling of the possibility that we might lose control of a mass of desperate men, under conditions of front-line war and artillery shells, machine-guns, rifles, aircraft cannon and bombs going off all round, is inclined to be unpleasant. I think we can hold our own, but it is not a comfortable position.

Russians killed off four German wounded hiding in the woods. Nice people!

Stormoviks and Yaks in great numbers today. They seem to operate well on their side of the front! Dog-fights between four Aira-Cobras and one Me 109 overhead this afternoon. The Russians seem to weave violently at all times. The Yak is a good little fighter in the Spitfire class.

Our pet Junkers 88 low-strafed us with front guns again in the moonlight. Plenty return 20-mm fire from the town. Very interesting to be at the other end for a change. I admire these Luftwaffe boys for carrying on to the grim end.

A Russian patrol found four French POWs in a house outside the camp with some women. Russians shot and killed the Frenchmen for refusing to obey an order. They probably wanted the women for themselves.

Our own trouble has died down for the moment. We have averted a riot I suppose, but in actual practise discipline as such is gone.

Wednesday. Still no Americans. This waiting is tricky. Plenty of food now when at odd moments I can find time to eat. Yesterday I had my first hot drink and a meal of bread and rhubarb at 3.30 pm. The Russians are giving us all they can. Very friendly now and much back slapping, but no respect.

Thursday. Situation tense again in my compound. NCOS are not the slightest bit prepared to meet the officers halfway, and are quite certain that we are there to make life unpleasant.

In all this turmoil the thought that we are no longer in fact prisoners-of-war and should be home soon is difficult to grasp and is not in the least exciting.

431

Saturday. So ends this demoralising week of passing on and handing out orders that one knows perfectly well will not be carried out. Held a roll parade to check ration strength this morning. The men took a lot of persuasion and diplmacy to turn out for that. Last night the news of a link-up between the Americans and Russians at Torgau cheered everyone immensely. The later report that a jeep bearing three American war correspondents had been seen on the way to Berlin should do much to settle the present unrest.

Watched a Mig shoot down a 190 in four short bursts. Very pretty.

Wednesday. Ten days since the Germans left. One of the biggest battles we have seen is now raging on the north-east and northern borders of the camp. Rifle and tommy-gun fire is incessant and mortar duel is in progress with us in no-man's land. The radio has announced the release of all camps taken by the Americans and British, but has said nothing of us. Our people must be worried. So are we.

Thursday, 1800 hours. The first Yanks in the camp. Two war correspondents in a jeep from the lines at Magdeburg. They are taking Beatty, our press correspondent, back with them tomorrow and he will fly to Eisenhower's head-quarters with our records. Maybe things will start moving. All the boys want to push off west and are doing so in increasing numbers. I would be right with them if I hadn't this damned responsibility. Wrote a brief note home and put it in the jeep. It might get through.

Friday. Sunshine. Many more peole walking west. Two hundred of the men from this compound alone walked out yesterday. The position is intolerable. We can and should march the camp west to the Elbe with of course the Russians' approval. The Americans are at Wittenberg. Only thirty miles away—one day or so on a bicycle.

1600 hours. American colonel from Davescourt head-quarters here, said our evacuation starts at once! Trucks arriving tonight and we shall be flown home. Can it be true! Shall we, shall I be out of this country of death and home in England? It is almost too much to expect.

Wing Commander ROLAND BEAMONT'S diary,
quoted by EDWARD LANCHBERY

It was too much to expect. The Americans sent the trucks, the Russians sent them back. It was another two weeks before they got home.

*

M.H.D.O.I.F.

The last award of the war:

As Duty Flying Control Officer at a forward airfield in Germany, not only did he fail to recognise a Focke-Wulf 190 in the circuit, but nonchalantly gave it a red Very light for approaching to land downwind. The German pilot, ignoring the pyrotechnic, made a perfect landing, and gave himself up.

A Joint to the Order is awarded for his subsequent telephone message to Duty Flight: 'Please look after that Mustang which has just landed downwind.'

TEE EMM

*

CURTAIN LINE

'Take off your tunic and greatcoat,' they said, 'and leave them here.'

'And don't leave anything in the pockets,' they warned us. 'Because you won't see your uniform again.'

So we emptied our pockets of cigarette-ends, the double-headed penny we use for tossing for duties, the odd three-halfpence left over from pay-day, and the half of a Naafi wad which we were saving because it still had one of our teeth in it. Then we took a last guess at which stains on our jacket were made by Naafi tea and which were hop-produced, and handed it in.

We were led to the brightly lit showcase which stands just inside the Civilian Clothing Centre and they left us to brood lovingly over a line of nattily dressed models.

'There,' they told us, 'have a good look. Take your time. Choose exactly what you want. And we'll send you out looking just like that.'

433

We needed a good look, too. It was so long since we'd worn civvies that we'd even forgotten that you don't wear a belt around the jacket of a lounge suit.

So we took quite a time to choose a suit. Back through the long years our memory ranged to the time when we were the well-dressed man-about-town. There were blues, browns, and greys, herring-bones, pin-stripes, chalk-stripes, tweeds, flannels. They came in the single-breasted (button one, show three—as the jargon used to go), double-breasted, and sports style.

Finally we settled on a chaste grey with a dashing chalk-stripe in it. Then we went to be measured.

Now, they don't make a suit to measure for every man who calls at the Civilian Clothing Centre, but they have such a wide range of fittings, and they take such care, that if they can't fit you from stock you must be the type that qualifies for marker in the awkward squad.

And we mean fit. There's none of that legendary business of holding out an arm while an assortment of clothing is flung across it to the chorus of ' 'Urry along there—they're all made the same, so they all fit.'

For, besides having a tremendous assortment of suits in many sizes, they classify your figure in one swift glance as short, regular, or long, or (gently and diplomatically) as portly short, portly regular, or portly long. So, whether you have a front like a bay window, or whether you have, like the bathing-beauty, a perfect profile all the way down, they can still fit you perfectly.

So the Civilian Expert (and he was precisely that) juggled his tape around selected parts of our anatomy, did a little swift logarithmic calculation, and came back with a suit in the design we'd chosen.

We put it on. We looked in the glass.

And there was a catch in our throat.

Was this us? This immaculately suited young and eager heart, this glass of fashion, mould of form—was it really us?

It was. Clothes make the man, and we were made. True, little could be done about the face, but people might view even that with some tolerance when they saw us in this wonder suit.

434

The Civilian Expert came back. There was a nice reverence in his manner.

'Not bad,' he said.

He brushed a calculating hand over the shoulders, gave a tug here, a smoothing there, expertly eyed the bracing of the trousers.

'Ye-es,' he murmured. 'Quite nice. No alteration, d'you think?'

We nodded mutely, terrified that he might find some excuse to take this beautiful suit away from us.

But it was all right. The suit was out for keeps. And then with the same loving care we were fitted with a raincoat. We could have had this in a variety of shades and it was cut very generously with no skimping or tightness.

Next a shirt. This was easy. There were sizes ranging from $13\frac{1}{2}$ to 18, and we were able to get a shade that might have been made with our suit in mind. We got two collars and finished off this part of the business by being given neat little mother-of-pearl cuff-links and studs.

A tie, now. There really was something for everybody here. Whether you were the type that wears a tie to cause jeeps to rear up on their hind wheels, or whether you preferred a tie that showed nice and proper restraint and a consideration for your fellow creatures, you just couldn't miss.

Any civilian would have envied us our choice of shoes. There were half-sizes, and, moreover, three separate fittings to each size. So, whatever Service boots have done to your feet (and what they've done to ours is nobody's business) you can have shoes that make your feet look grand and feel grateful. Black or brown, and several styles—the choice is yours.

And finally, a hat. There were no bowlers, so this disposed of the rumour that we were all to be issued with perspex bowlers with the RAF roundel on the side. But we were offered a soft felt in brown, grey or blue. We could have had, alternatively, a 'pork-pie' or a cap. The only fly in the ointment at this stage was the fact that we found that our Service cap had given our starboard ear a permanent list, but maybe it won't notice.

Heart a-flutter, we then collected all the new gear we'd

chosen and dived into a little private cubicle to change.

Ever see a butterfly emerge from a chrysalis? That was us when we came out of that cubicle. Cinderella, before the Tannoy announced 2400 hours, had absolutely nothing on us. You'd have bought a gold brick from us without stopping to think.

So we were ready for Civvy Street. And all we had to do now, we felt sure, was to knock on the door of any big business establishment and they'd offer us a managing-directorship right away. Maybe they'd give us a cigar, too. Frankly, when they saw us in this outfit, we couldn't see how they could help themselves.

Corporal E. H. DODIMEAD

Sources Quoted

Armstrong, Anthony, 'Flies' (from *Punch* 1942), 147–50

Barker, Ralph, 'From fifty feet', from *The Ship Busters* (Chatto & Windus 1957), 161–7; 'Takeover Bid', from *Down in the Drink* (Chatto & Windus), 196–201; and 'The New Boy', from *The Thousand Plan* (Chatto & Windus), 207–12.

Bates, H. E., as 'Flying Officer X', 'It's Never in the Papers', from *The Greatest People in the World* (Jonathan Cape 1942), 167–70

Beaumont, Wing Commander Roland, 'By Eye Alone', 78–80, 'Tip and Run', 368–70, and 'The Long Liberation', 425–32, all from *Against the Sun* (by Edward Lanchbery, Cassell 1955).

Beede, John, '. . . Will Report by 0001 Hours . . .', 109–12, 'Lack of Moral Fibre', 117–19, 'This Bloody Crate', 297–301, and 'Publicity Trip', 352–8, all from *They Hosed Them Out* (Australian Book Society 1965).

Bennett, A. V. M. Donald, 'Mosquito' from *Pathfinder* (Frederick Muller), 243–7; captain on first Atlantic delivery flight, 92–4.

Bolitho, Hector, 'The Yanks are Coming', 68–70, on anti-bomber ideas, 116–17, on Sergeant Ward vc, 165–7, 'Blip on the Screen!', 237–9, 'In the Drink,' 305–15, all from *A Penguin in the Eyrie* (Hutchinson 1955).

Braham, Wing Commander J. R. D., 'Such Things Happen', 105–6 'Revenge Mission', 260–2, 'Serrate', 324–7, all from *Scramble* (Frederick Muller 1961).

Brickhill, Paul, 'The Hoaxers', 347–52, 'Tallboy v. *Tirpitz*', 390–4, from *The Dam-Busters* (Evans Bros. 1951); 'It isn't like the Movies', 374–82, from *Escape or Die* (Evans Bros. 1952).

Chisholm, Air Commodore Roderick, on a Beaufighter crash, 96–7, his first aerial victories, 101–5, shoots down

friendly aircraft, 105–9, 'Roger Charlie Mike', 128–31,'. . . .
Also Attacked Targets in Northern Italy . . .', 212–13, on
offensive radio counter-measures, 321–4, all from *Cover
of Darkness* (Chatto & Windus).

Churchill, Sir Winston, speeches quoted 65–165; 'Battle of
Britain Day', from *The Second World War* (Cassell), 73–8;
letter declaring war on Japan, 175.

Clostermann, Pierre, 'Screwball Beurling', from *Flames in
the Sky* (Chatto & Windus), 190–5; 'My First Big Show',
287–94, 'Liberator', 337–9, 'A Night out in France', 358–63,
'The Brute', 394–8, 'Last Op', 417–25, all from *The Big
Show* (Chatto & Windus).

Corby, Herbert, poem 'Missing', 170.

Crook, Flight Lieutenant D. M., fired at any bomber, from
Spitfire Pilot (Faber & Faber), 69.

Cunningham, Group Captain John, combat report on night
engagement, 100–1, mentioned 108, described in night
engagement, 124–8.

Deere, Group Captain Alan, 'A Private Dunkirk,' 47–51,
'Focke-Wulf 190', 217–20, all from *Nine Lives* (Hodder
& Stoughton); mentioned as wing leader, 287–92.

Dodimead, Corporal E. H., 'Curtain Line', from *Slipstream*
(ed. by Squadron Leaders R. Raymond and David Langdon,
Eyre & Spottiswoode 1946), 433–6

Donahue, Flight-Lieutenant Arthur, 'The Gremlins', 131–2,
'The Last Days of Singapore', 176–82, all from *Last Flight
From Singapore* (Macmillan 1944).

Douglas, Sir Sholto (Lord Douglas of Kirtleside), describes
schemes for defeating night bombers, 81–3, 'In Single Combat'
151–3, from *Years of Command* (written with Robert Wright,
Collins 1967); mentioned as staff officer, 70

Dowding, Lord Hugh, letter to War Cabinet 1940, 45–7,
from *Leader of the Few* (by Basil Collier, Jarrolds).

Drinkwater, Colin, description of the blitz, 95–6 (previously
unpublished).

Embry, Air Chief Marshal Sir Basil, 'Second Taf,' 294–7,
low-level attack on Gestapo HQ at Copenhagen, 383–6, all
from *Mission Completed* (Landsborough Publications).

Ewart, Gavin, poem, 'When a Beau Goes In', 262

Fergusson, Bernard, air defence of Crete, from *The Black
Watch and the King's Enemies* (Collins 1950), 123–4

439

'The Balloon goes up', 38–40, from *Fighter Pilot* (Hutchinson 1955).

Robinson, Leading Aircraftsman L., 'Last Flight From Menidi', quoted by Sir Philip Joubert from *The Forgotten Ones* (Hutchinson), 122–3.

Saward, Group Captain Dudley, 'Operation Millenium', 207–8, 'Gomorrah', 316–18, from *The Bomber's Eye* (Cassell 1959).

Shirer, William, 'The First Bombs on Berlin', from *Berlin Diary* (Hamish Hamilton), 66–8.

Slessor, Marshal of the RAF Sir John, 'Bright Ideas Mark II', from *The Central Blue* (Cassell), 115–16.

Smith, Constance Babington, 'The Camera Never Lies', 113–15, 'A Yard of U-boats', 156–8, from *Evidence in Camera* (Chatto & Windus).

Southall, Ivan, 'First Op', 256–60, 'The Battle of the Bay', 236–72, from *They Shall Not Pass Unseen* (Angus & Robertson 1956).

Sutton, Wing Commander Barry, 'The Cruel Trees', from *Jungle Pilot* (Macmillan 1946), 332–4.

Taylor, Geoffrey, 'Abracadabra, Jump, Jump,' from *Piece of Cake* (Peter Davies 1956), 327–31.

Taylor, Sir Gordon, 'Across the Wide Atlantic', from *The Sky Beyond* (Penguin), 223–36.

Treece, Henry, poem 'Lincolnshire Bomber Station', 316.

Tuck, Wing Commander Stanford, quoted and mentioned in 'Stanford Tuck's Two Baths', from *Fly For Your Life* (by Larry Forrester, Frederick Muller 1956), 60–4.

Verity, Wing Commander H. S., notes for pilots' on secret agent missions, from *S.O.E. in France* (Michael Foot, H.M. S.O.), 213–17.

Wallace, Graham, quoting Squadron Leader J. Kent, from *Biggin Hill* (Putnam), 77–8.

Ward-Jackson, C. H., quoting 'Service of Thanksgiving for Safe Arrival in Iraq', from *The Airman's Song-Book* (Sylvan Press 1945), 284–50.

Warren, J. A. Crosby, on aircraft safety, from *The Flight Testing of Production Aircraft* (Pitman 1943), 223.

West, Air Commodore F., quoted on laundry problems in 'phoney war', from *Winged Diplomat* (by P. R. Reid, Chatto & Windus 1962), 26–8.

Wheeler, A. H., 'Operation Ladbrook', from *That Nothing Failed Them* (G. T. Foulis 1963), 302–5.

Wykeham, Peter, 'Back Every Friday', 31–5, 'Vergeltungswaffe Eins', 364–5, 'Bright Ideas Mark IV,' 365–6, from *Fighter Command* (Putnam 1960).

Index

Notes: names of authors quoted are italicised; the rank given is that at the time of the original publication. For those referred to in the text, the rank is normally that of the latest reference. Names of specific aircraft types are only indexed where the extract referred to gives serious information about their performance, handling qualities, etc.

Individual raids, campaigns, etc., are only indexed where the action was sufficiently brief to be covered in a few pages and it is felt that the pages referred to do give a reasonable historical coverage.

444

445

On the following page are details of the
companion volume to
THE WAR IN THE AIR:

FREEDOM'S BATTLE VOLUME 1:

THE WAR AT SEA

edited by John Winton
foreword by Admiral of the Fleet the
Earl Mountbatten of Burma

THE WAR AT SEA

Well-known and lesser-known actions are here: the Battle of the River Plate, the sinking of the *Bismarck*, the Malta convoys, as well as the end of the *Rawalpindi*, the gallant sortie of 825 Squadron against the *Scharnhorst* and the *Gneisenau*, the landing-craft actions at Anzio, in Sicily and Normandy.

Far better than any single narrative, the extracts build up a complete picture of the War at Sea as it was experienced by the men who fought it.

'The great majority of the items in this collection are eye-witness accounts, written by a variety of people—survivors, seamen, captains of ships, Wrens, pilots, poets, admirals, war correspondents. Comparatively few of them are professional writers, but their accounts of their experiences have a vitality and an impact upon the reader's imagination which most of the carefully and painstakingly researched post-war histories lack.'

If you would like a complete list of Arrow books please send a postcard to P.O. Box 29, Douglas, Isle of Man, Great Britain.